IMMORTAL RAIN

VOLUME 6

BY
KAORI OZAKI

HAMBURG // LONDON // LOS ANGELES // TOKYO

Immortal Rain Vol. 6
Created by Kaori Ozaki

Translation - Michael Wert
English Adaptation - Sam Stormcrow Hayes
Copy Editor - Aaron Sparrow
Associate Editor - Alexis Kirsch
Retouch and Lettering - Benchcomix
Production Artist - James Dashiell
Cover Design - Ann-Marie Horne

Editor - Bryce P. Coleman
Digital Imaging Manager - Chris Buford
Pre-Press Manager - Antonio DePietro
Production Managers - Jennifer Miller and Mutsumi Miyazaki
Art Director - Matt Alford
Managing Editor - Jill Freshney
VP of Production - Ron Klamert
Editor-in-Chief - Mike Kiley
President and C.O.O. - John Parker
Publisher and C.E.O. - Stuart Levy

A  Manga

TOKYOPOP Inc.
5900 Wilshire Blvd. Suite 2000
Los Angeles, CA 90036

E-mail: info@TOKYOPOP.com
Come visit us online at www.TOKYOPOP.com

ISBN: 1-59532-799-1

First TOKYOPOP printing: July 2005
10 9 8 7 6 5 4 3 2 1
Printed in Canada

OUR STORY SO FAR...

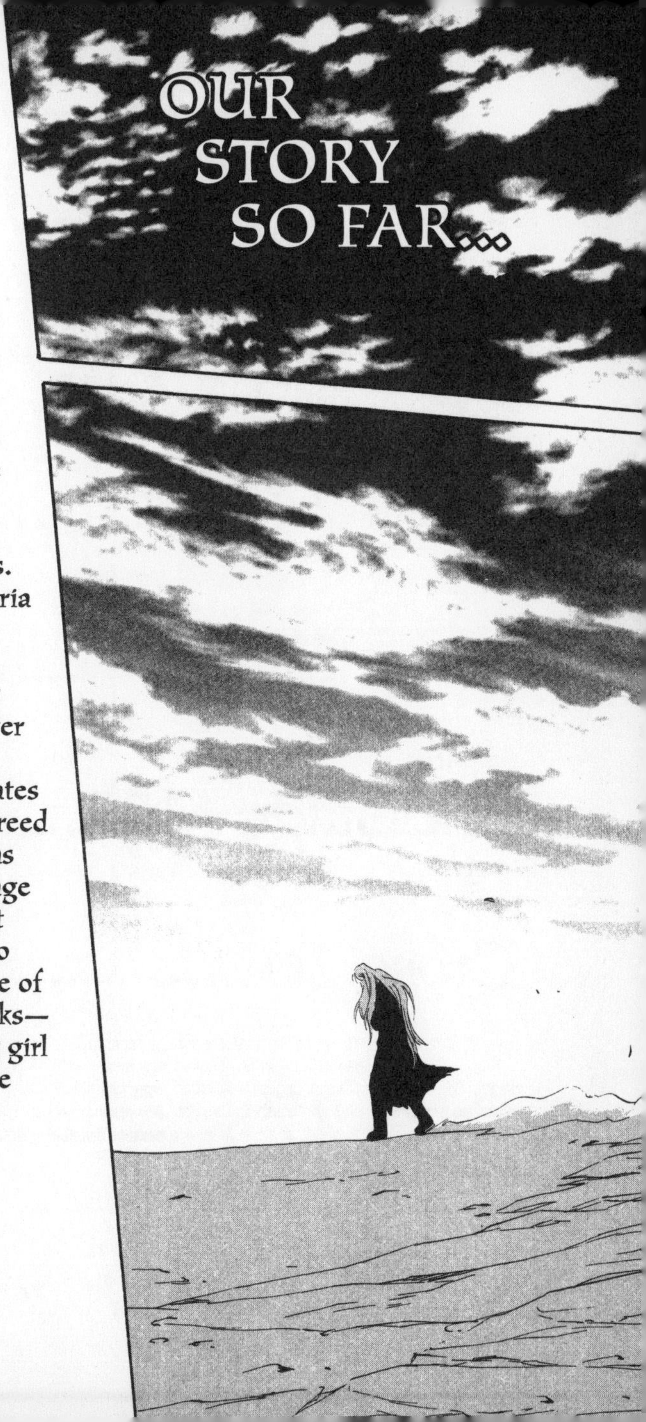

For months Machika has searched for Rain, finally stowing away on a plane bound for the capital, Raimei. Along the way she is aided by the most unlikely of allies—Eury Evans. Later, at the Calvaria headquarters, Machika meets Ys, who is secretly unfolding his master scheme. While Ys sinisterly manipulates Machika, Rain is freed by Eury, who seems to have had a change of heart. Then, just as Rain is racing to Machika's side, one of Ys' creatures attacks—sending the young girl plummeting out the window!

IMMORTAL RAIN

CONTENTS

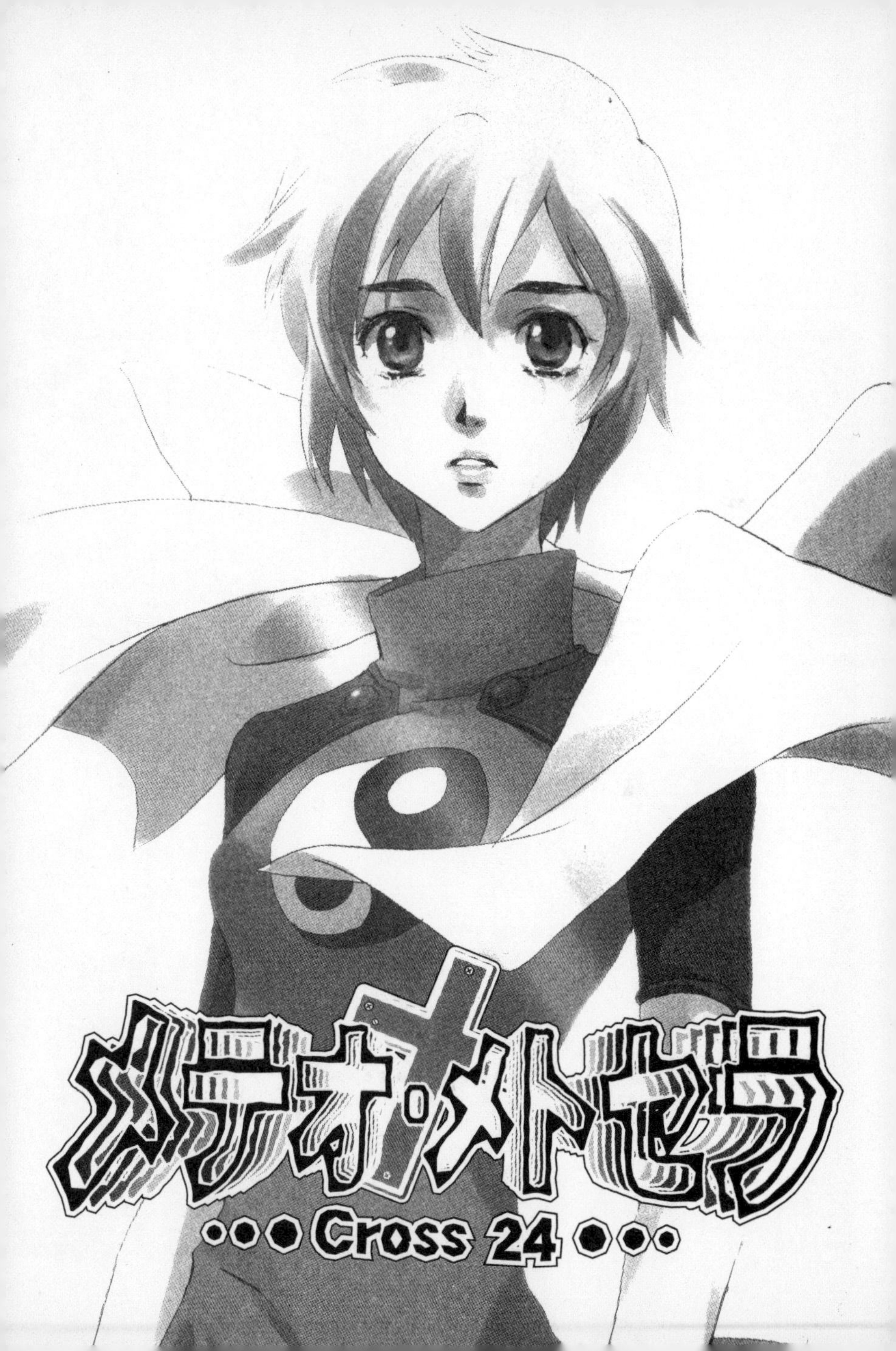
クラデオ・メトセラ
Cross 24

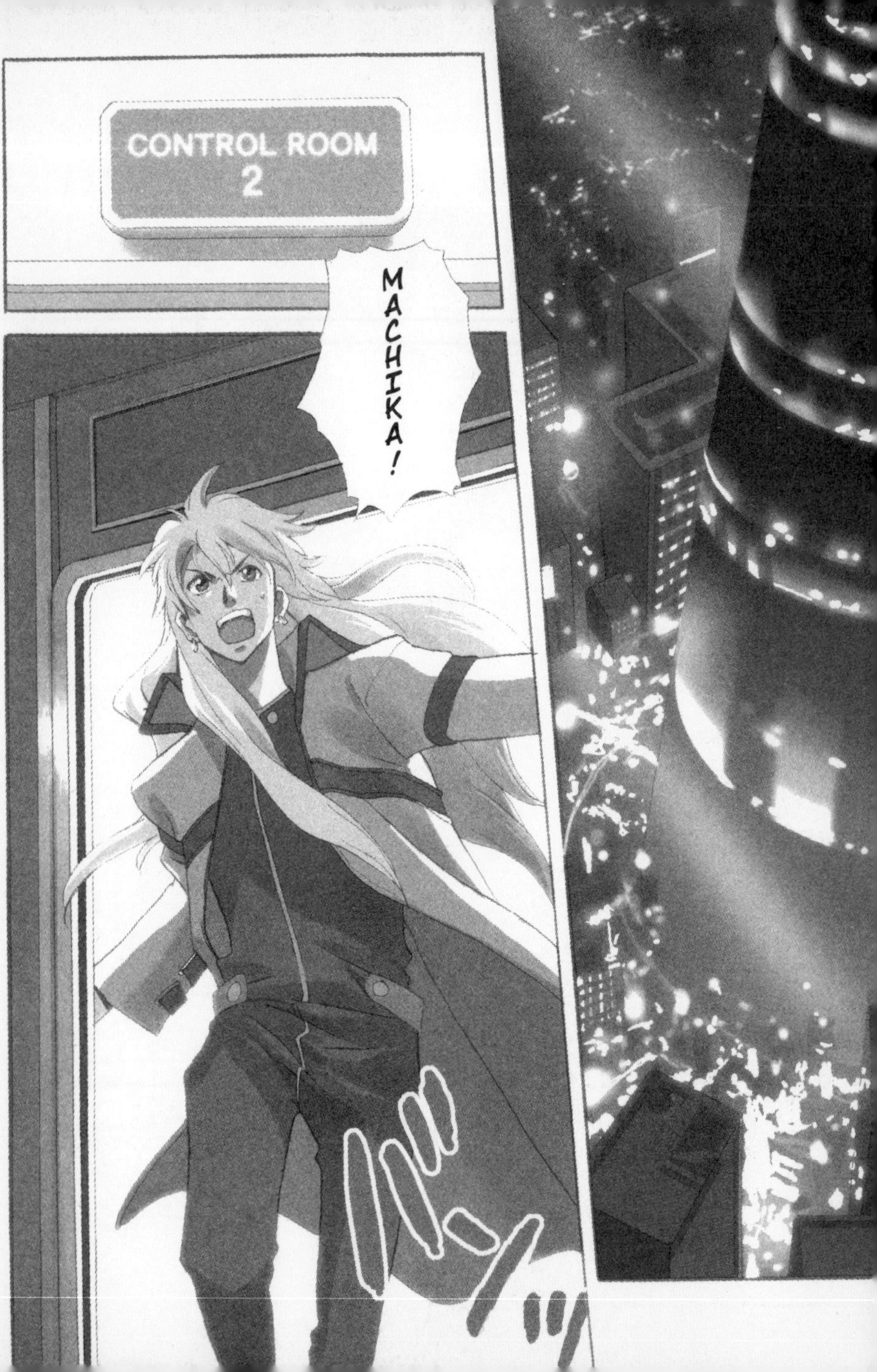
CONTROL ROOM
2
MACHIKA!

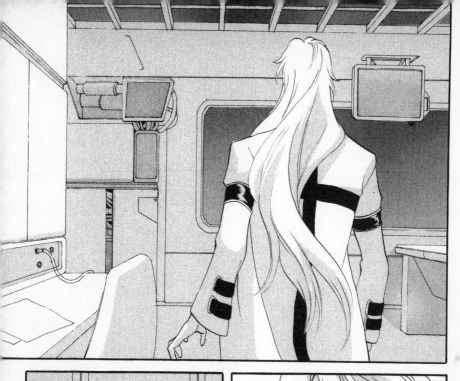

SHE'S NOT HERE.

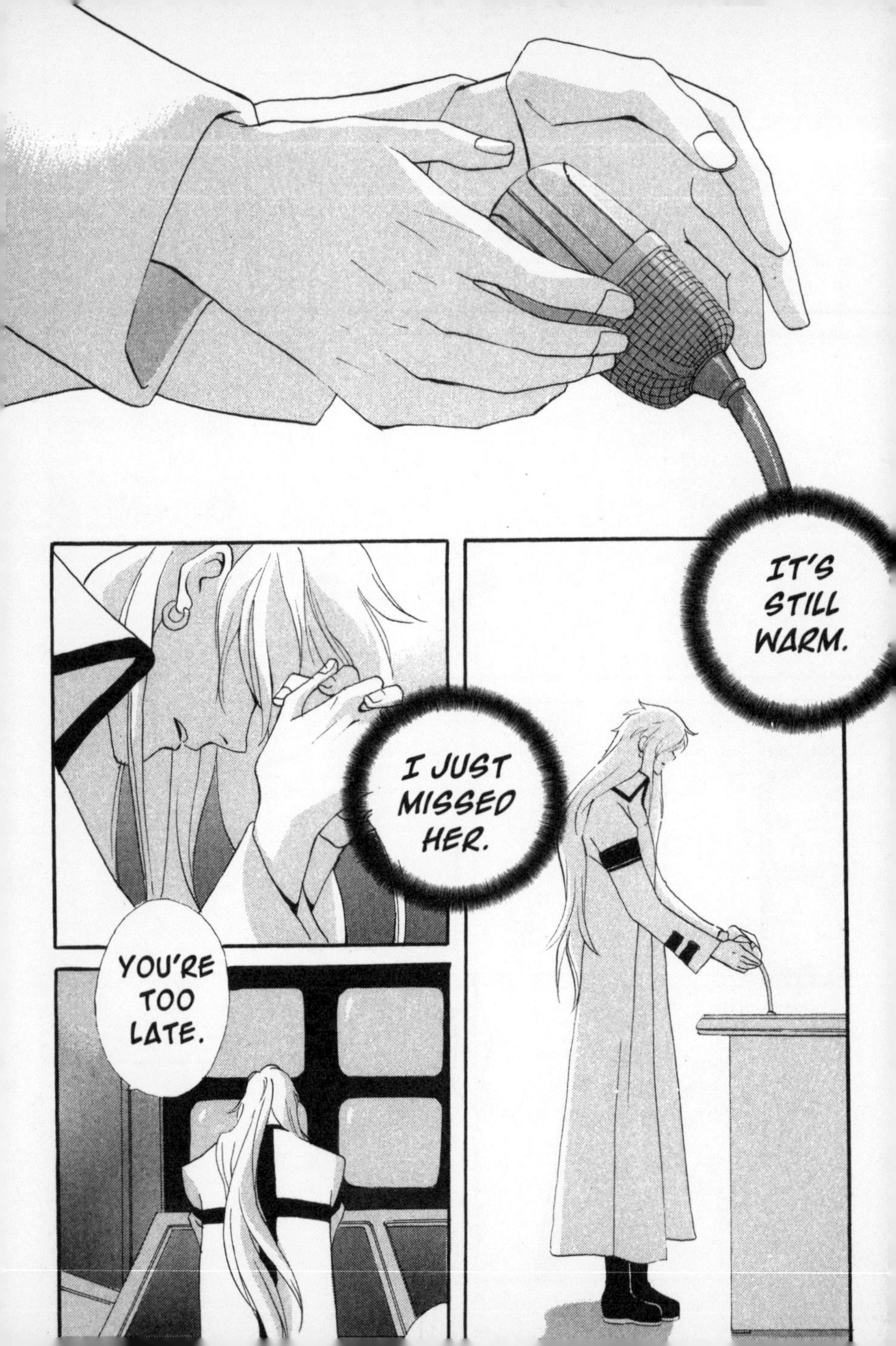
IT'S STILL WARM.
I JUST MISSED HER.
YOU'RE TOO LATE.

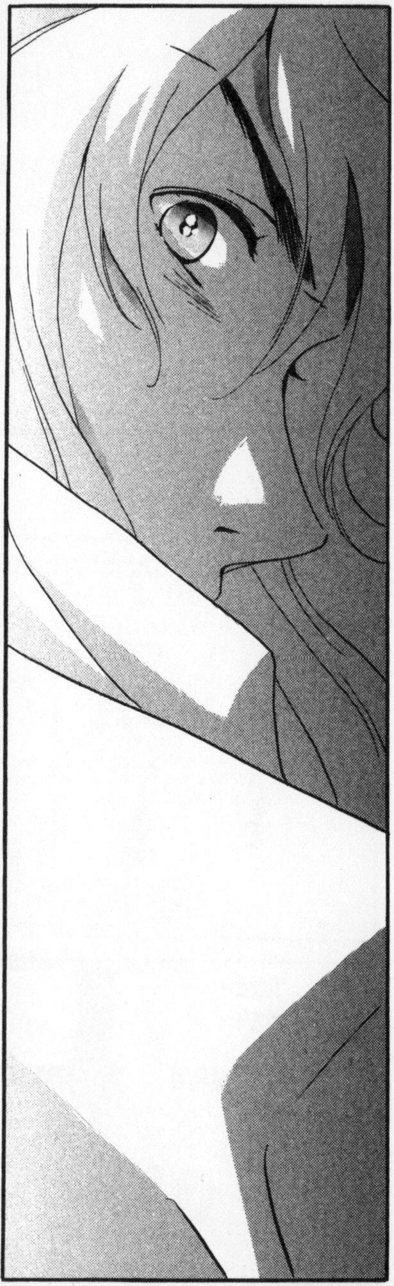
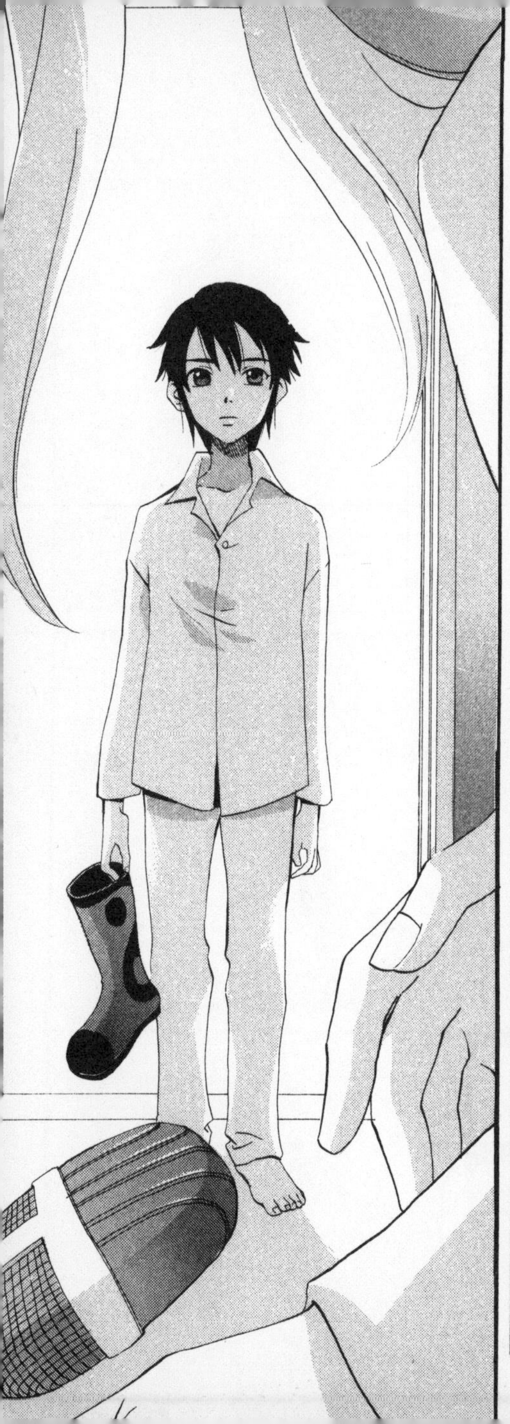

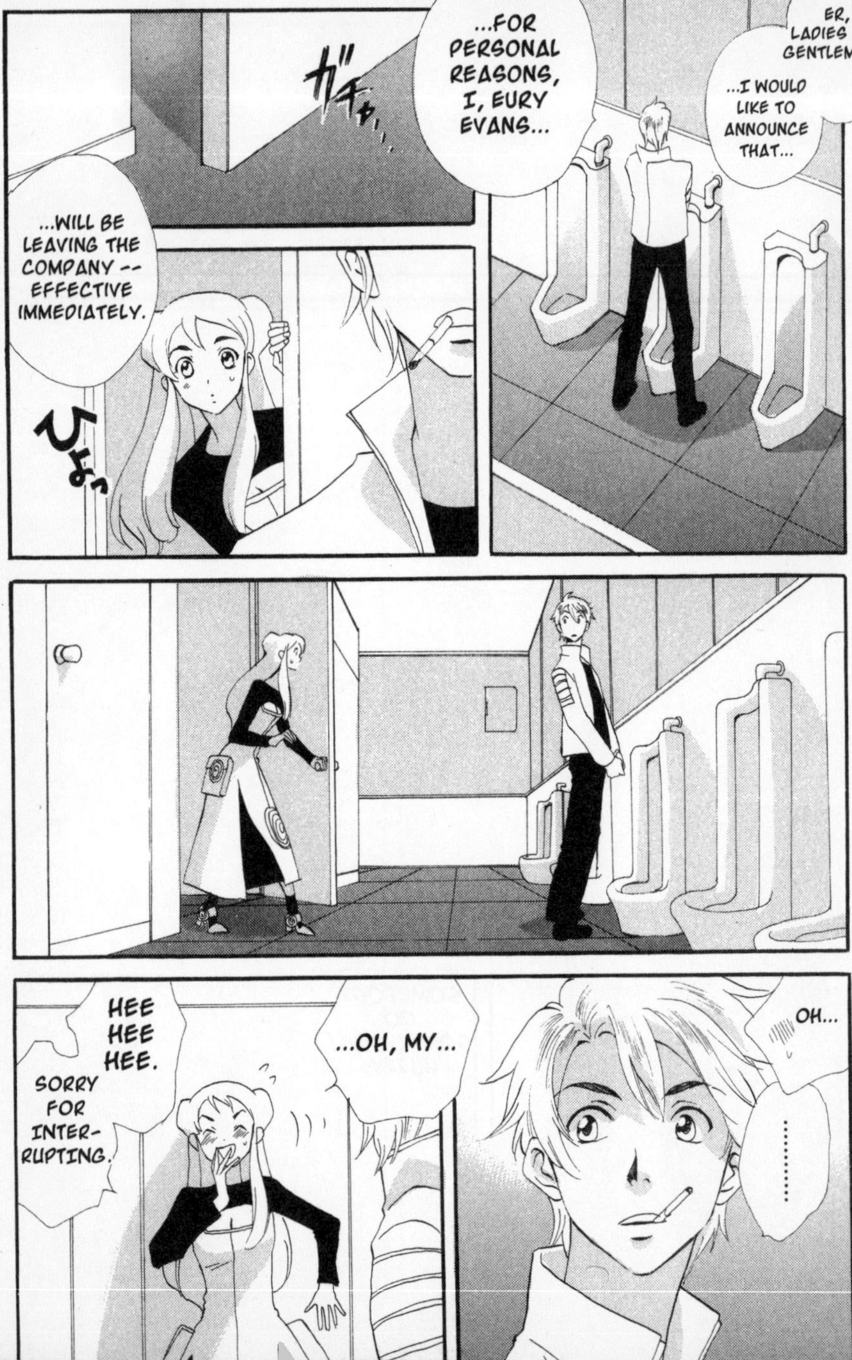
ER, LADIES AND GENTLEMEN...
...I WOULD LIKE TO ANNOUNCE THAT...
...FOR PERSONAL REASONS, I, EURY EVANS...
ガチャ...
...WILL BE LEAVING THE COMPANY -- EFFECTIVE IMMEDIATELY.
ひょっ
OH...
......
...OH, MY...
HEE HEE HEE.
SORRY FOR INTER-RUPTING.

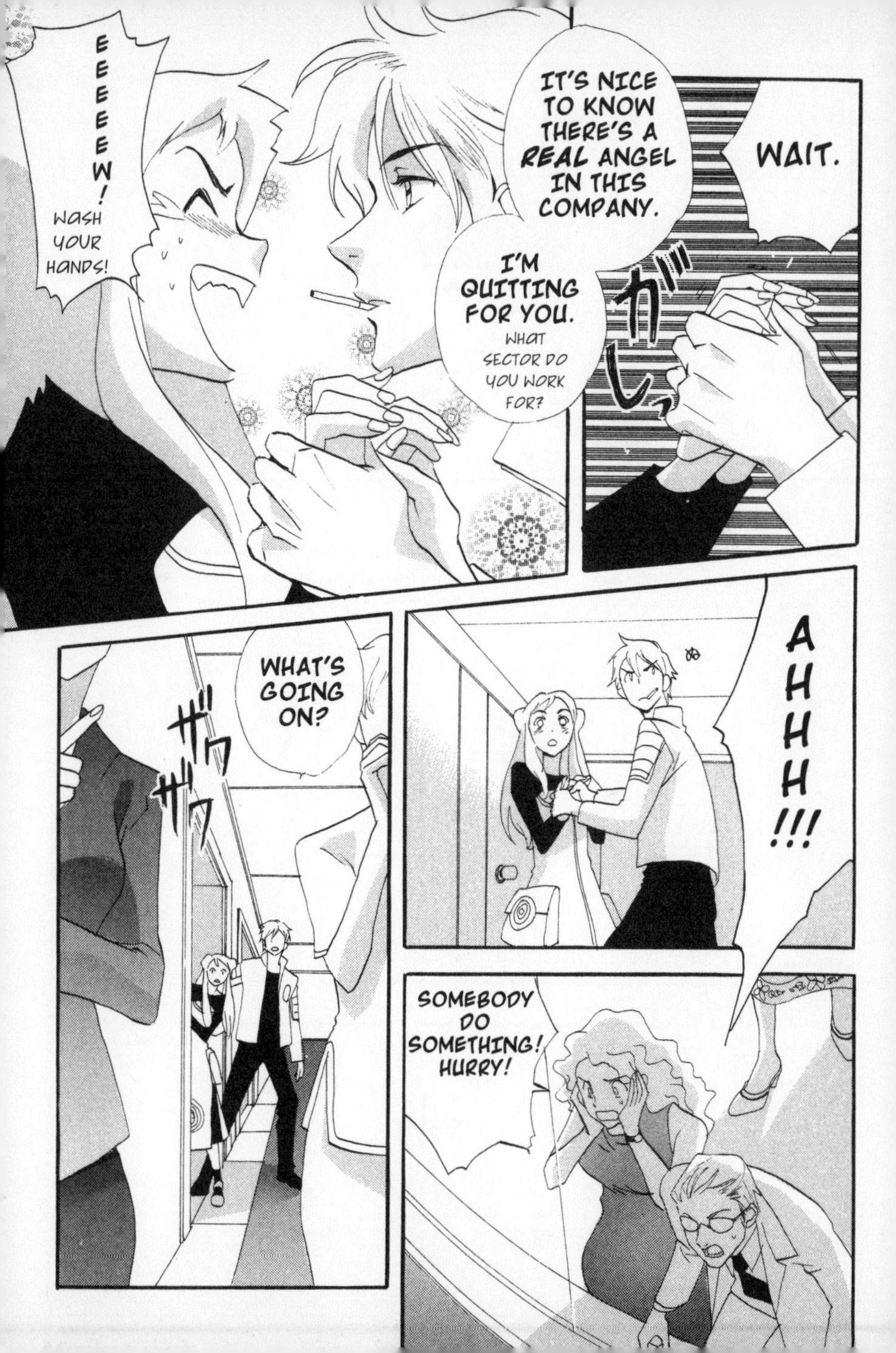
WAIT.
がし
IT'S NICE TO KNOW THERE'S A REAL ANGEL IN THIS COMPANY.
I'M QUITTING FOR YOU. WHAT SECTOR DO YOU WORK FOR?
EEEEEEW! WASH YOUR HANDS!
AHHHH!!!
SOMEBODY DO SOMETHING! HURRY!
WHAT'S GOING ON?
ザワザワ

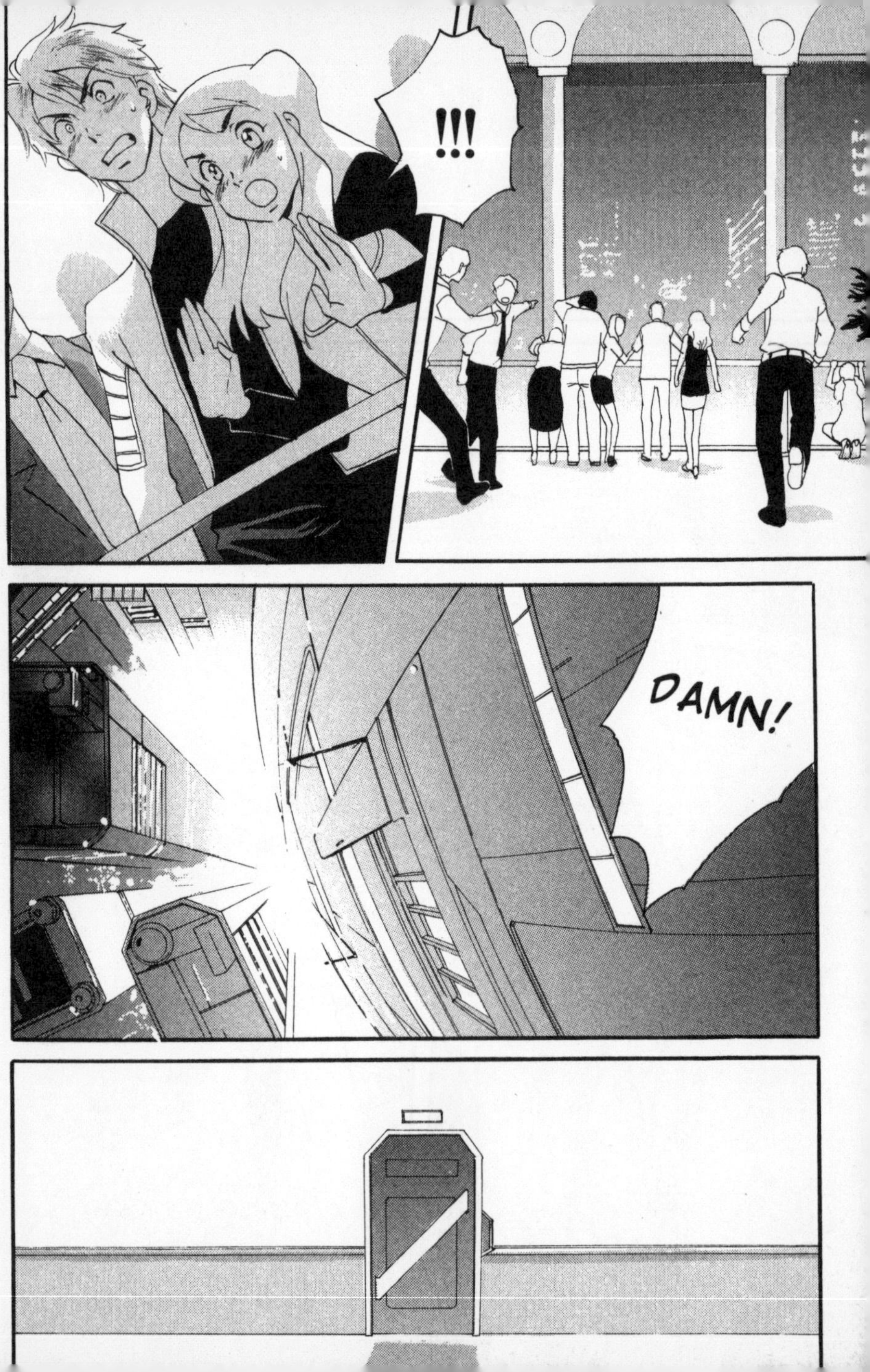
!!!
DAMN!

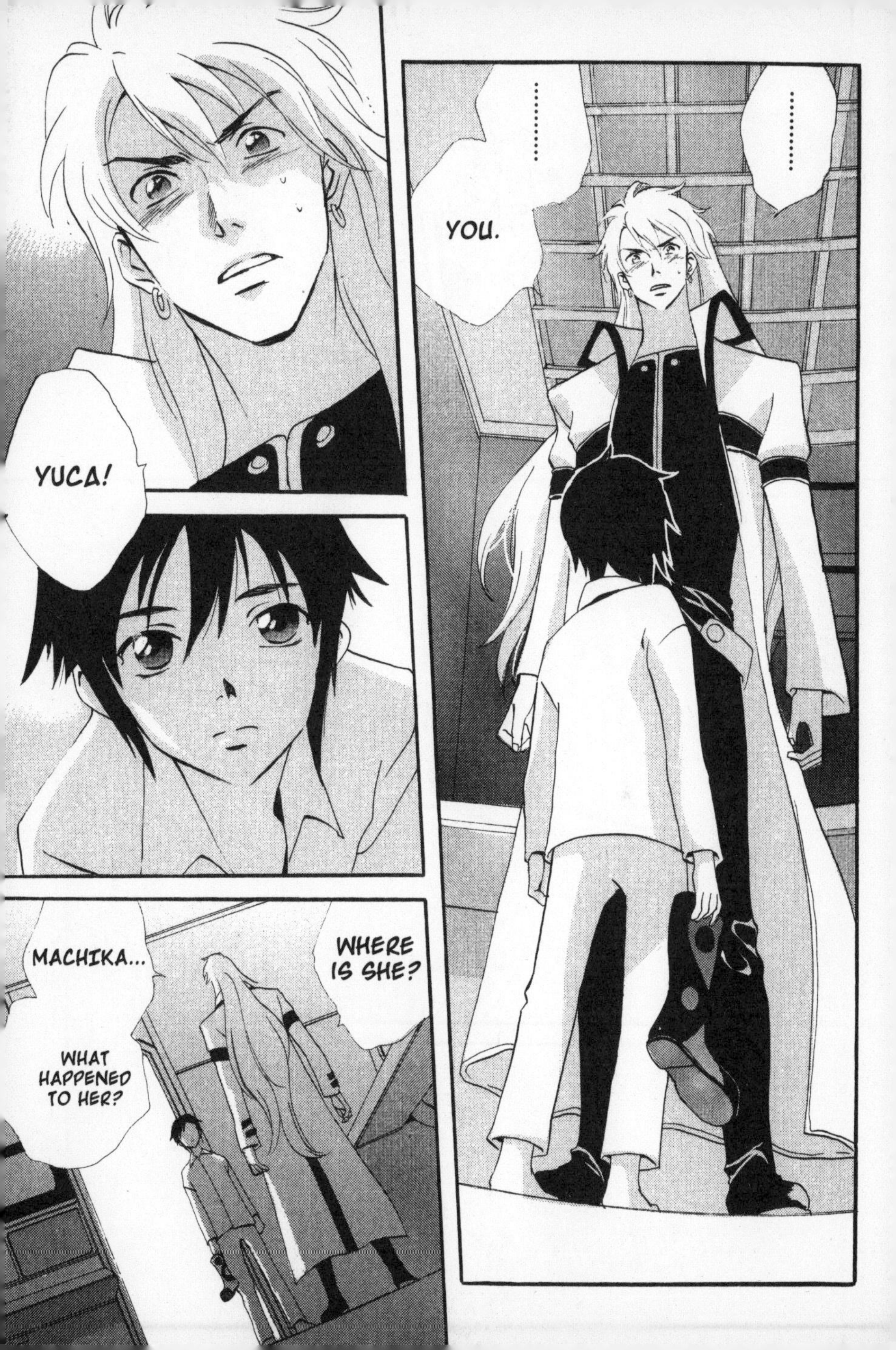

......
......
YOU.
YUCA!
MACHIKA...
WHERE IS SHE?
WHAT HAPPENED TO HER?

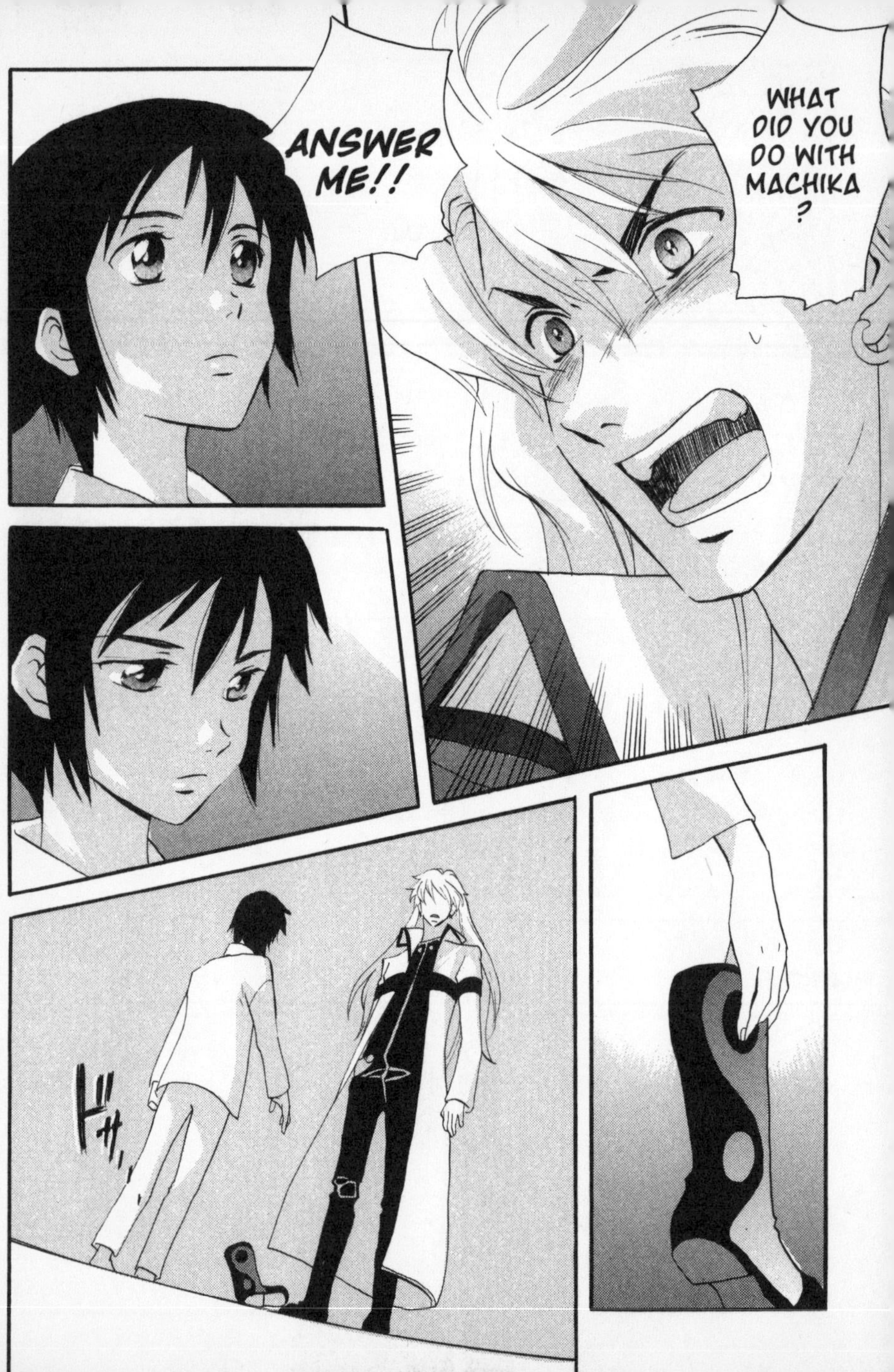
WHAT DID YOU DO WITH MACHIKA ?
ANSWER ME!!
ドサ

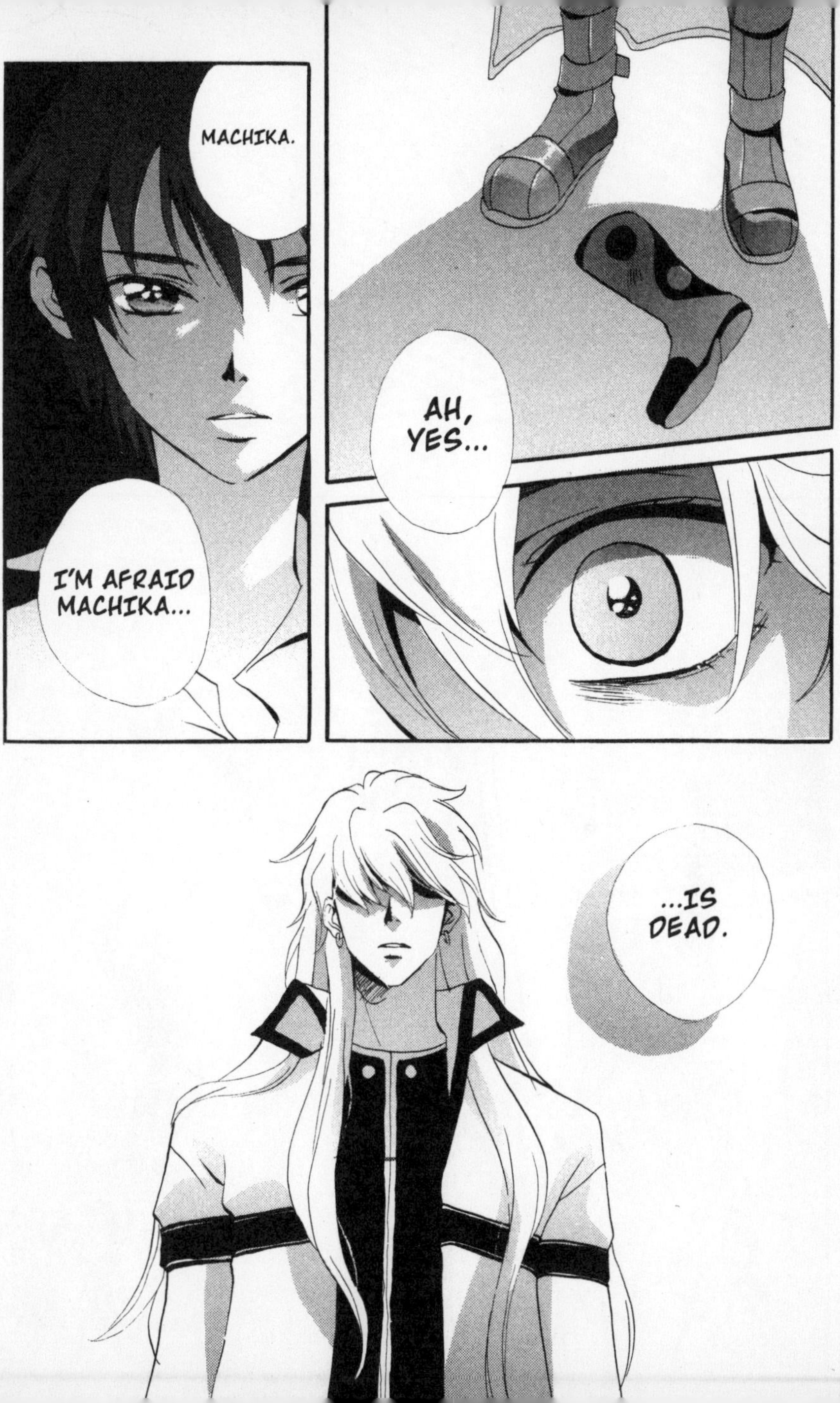
AH, YES...
MACHIKA.
I'M AFRAID MACHIKA...
...IS DEAD.

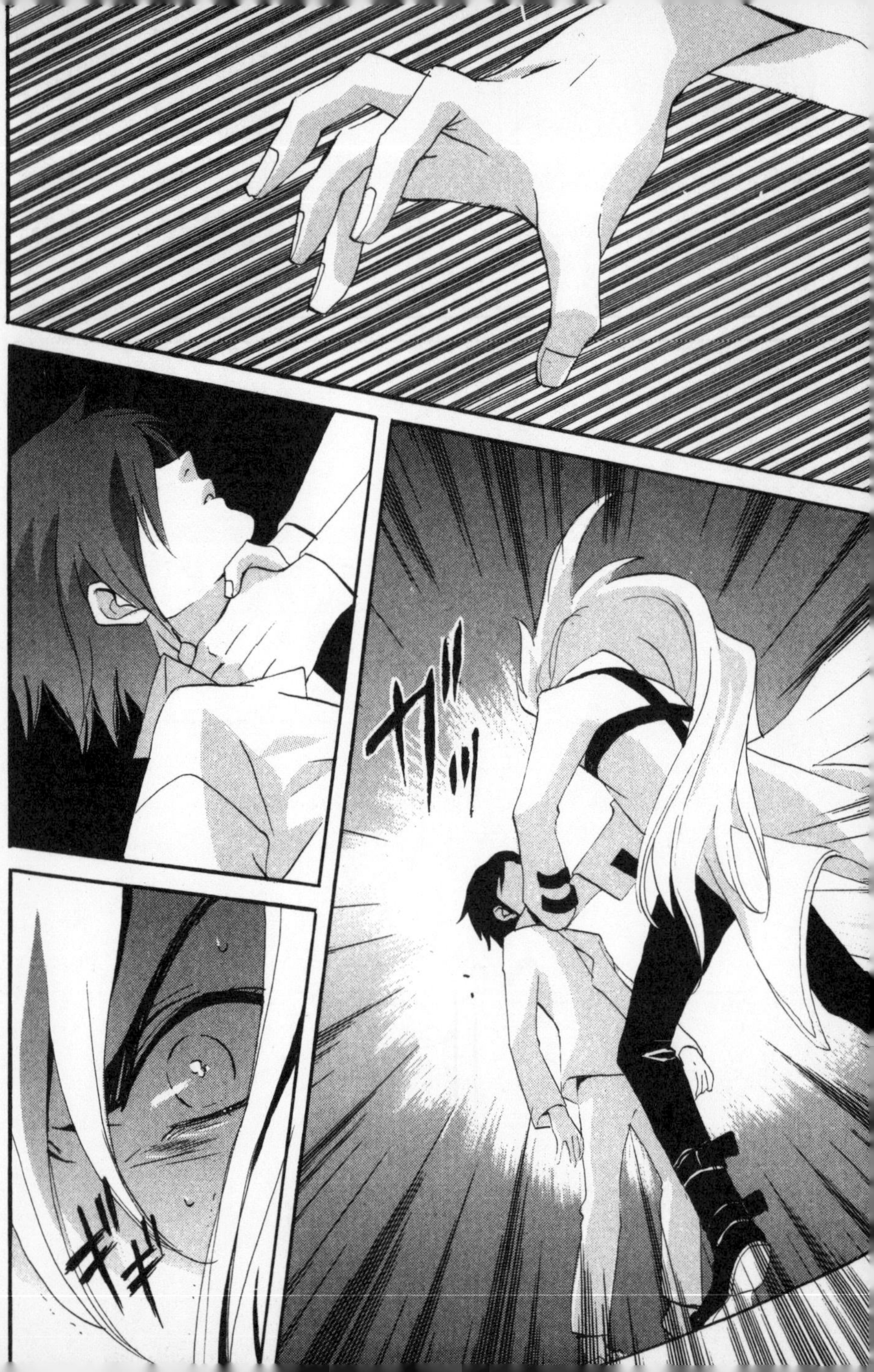
ガッ
ギギ

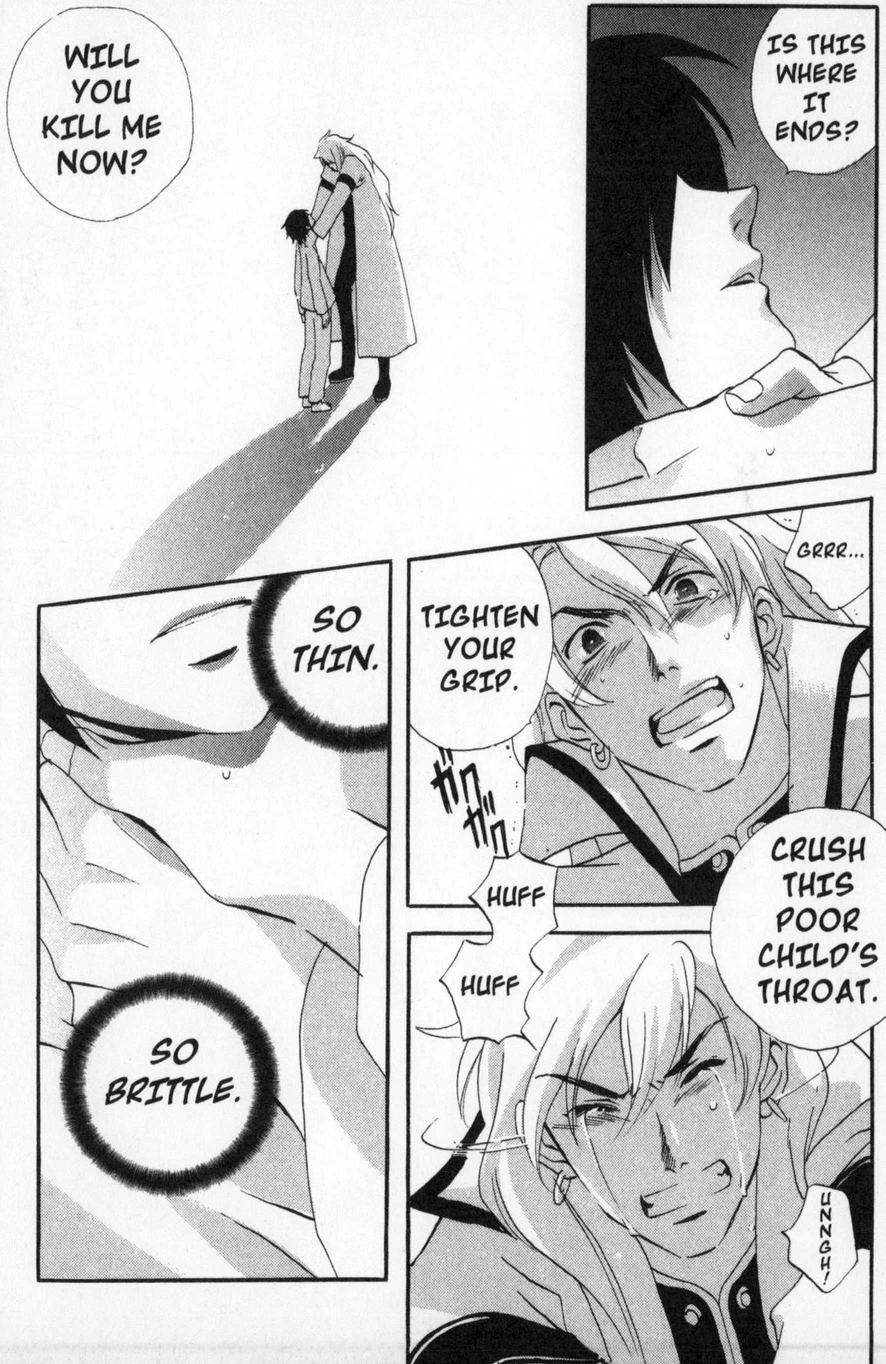
IS THIS WHERE IT ENDS?
WILL YOU KILL ME NOW?
GRRR...
TIGHTEN YOUR GRIP.
CRUSH THIS POOR CHILD'S THROAT.
HUFF
HUFF
UNNGH!
SO THIN.
SO BRITTLE.

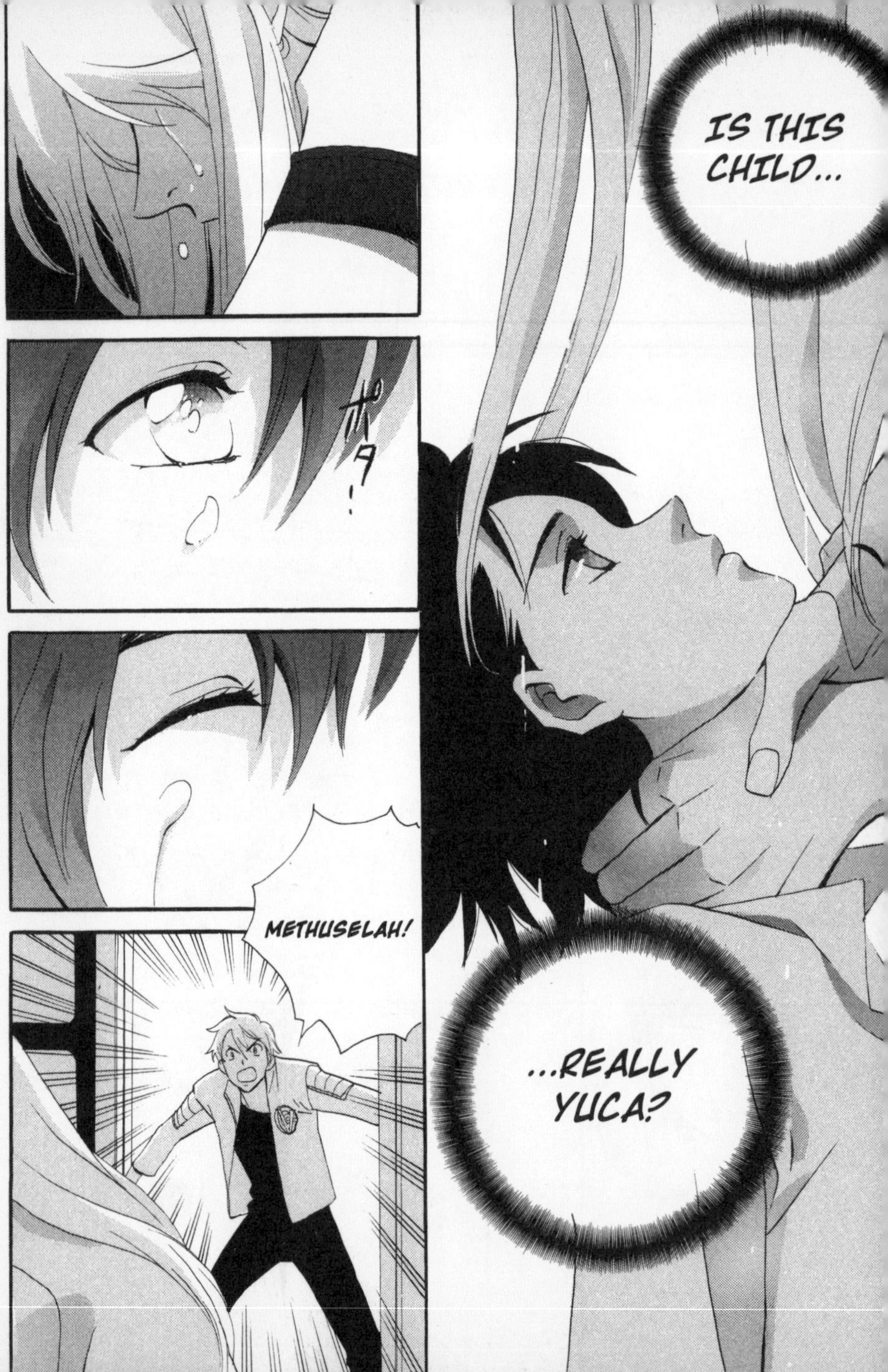
IS THIS CHILD...
...REALLY YUCA?
ポタ!
METHUSELAH!

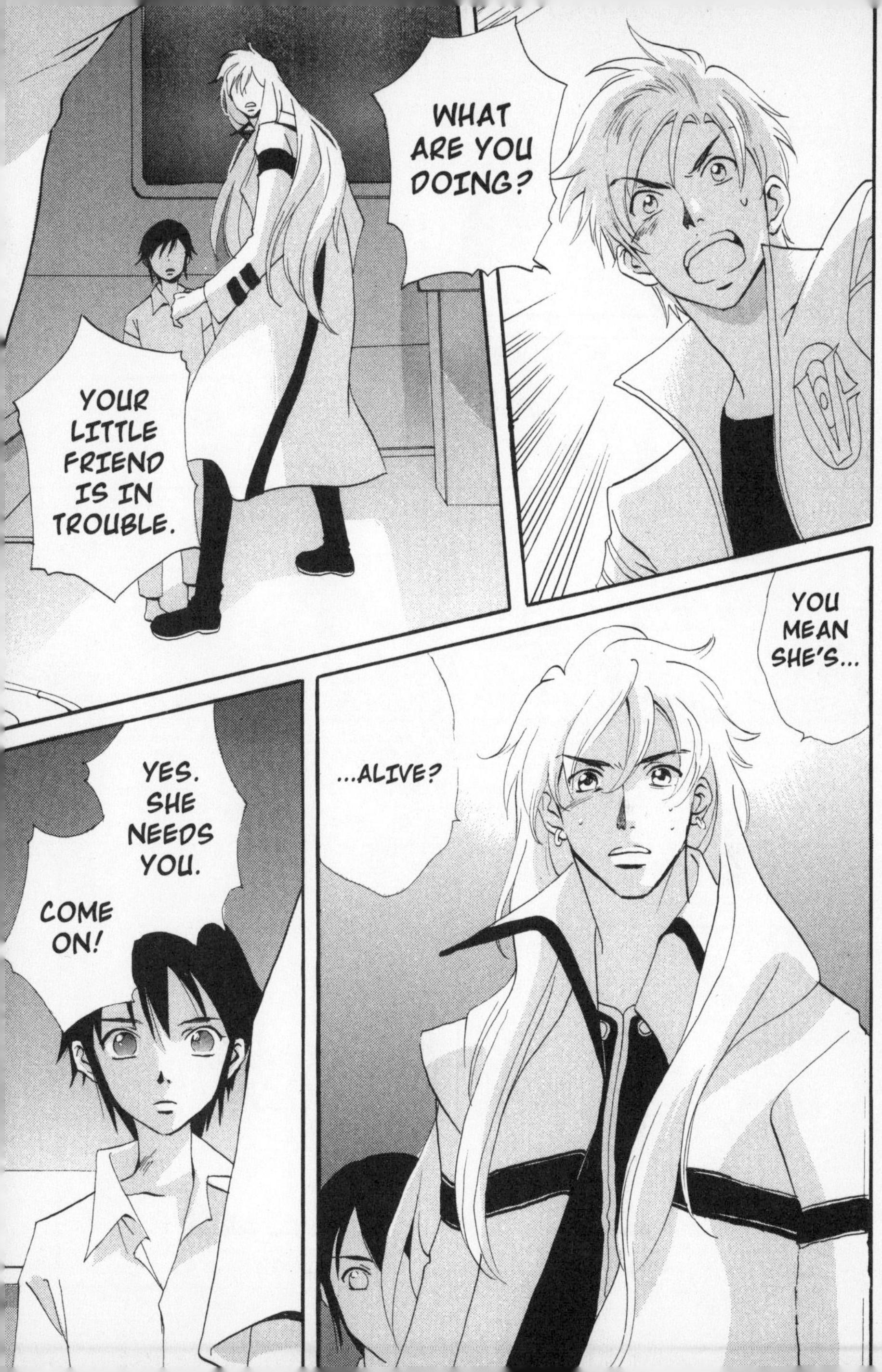
WHAT ARE YOU DOING?
YOUR LITTLE FRIEND IS IN TROUBLE.
YOU MEAN SHE'S...
...ALIVE?
YES. SHE NEEDS YOU.
COME ON!

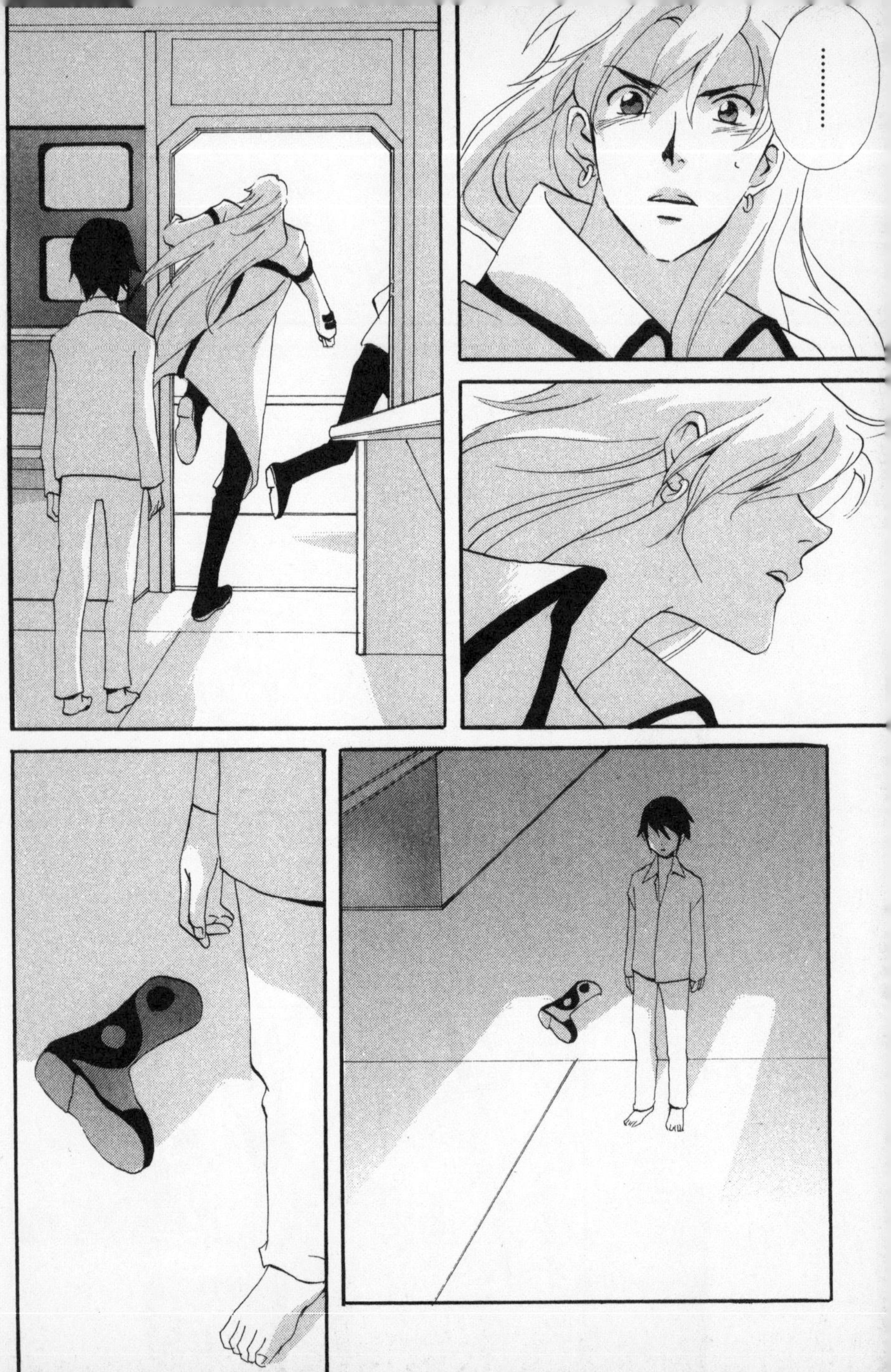
……

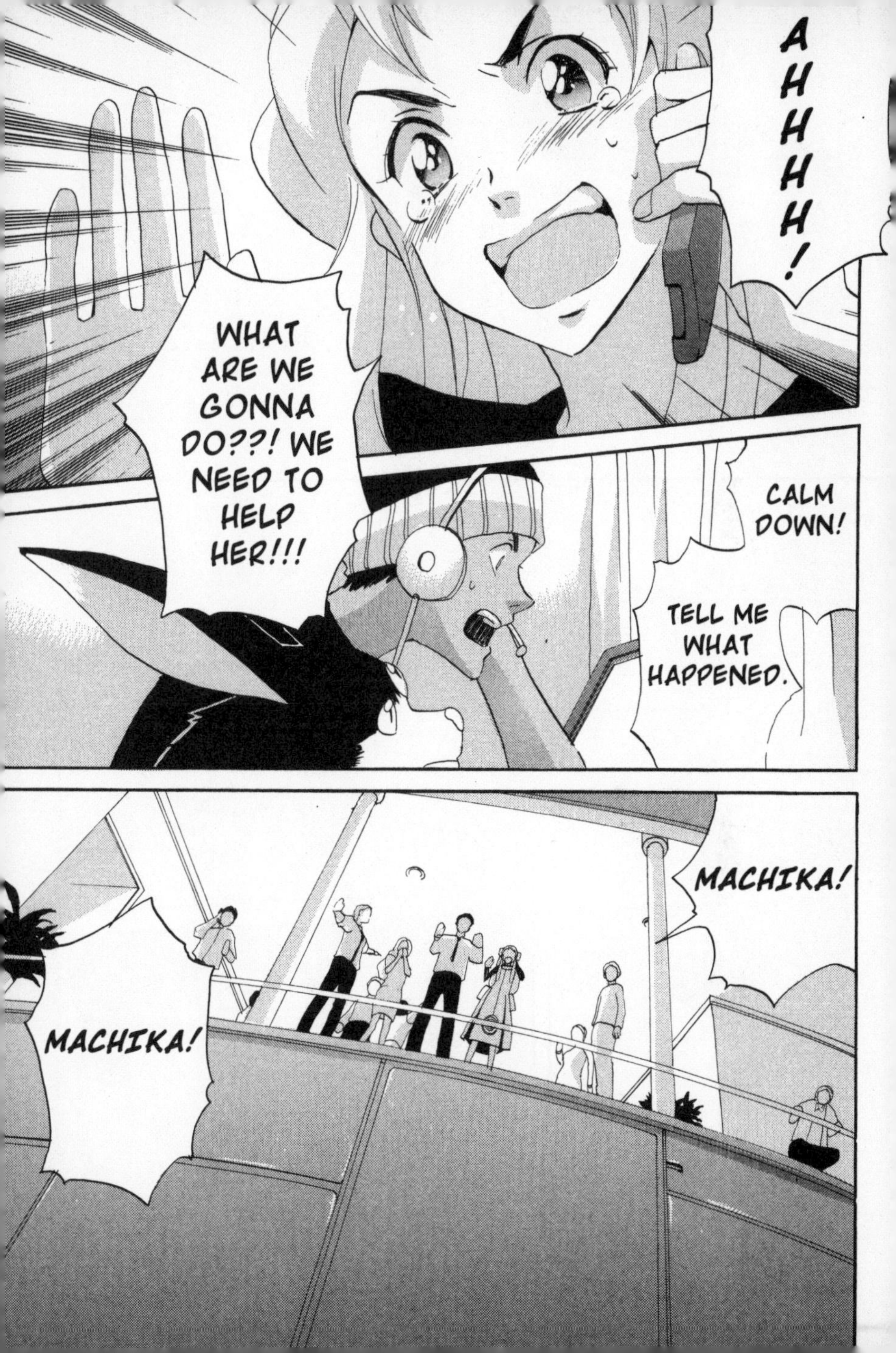
AHHHH!
WHAT ARE WE GONNA DO??! WE NEED TO HELP HER!!!
CALM DOWN!
TELL ME WHAT HAPPENED.
MACHIKA!
MACHIKA!

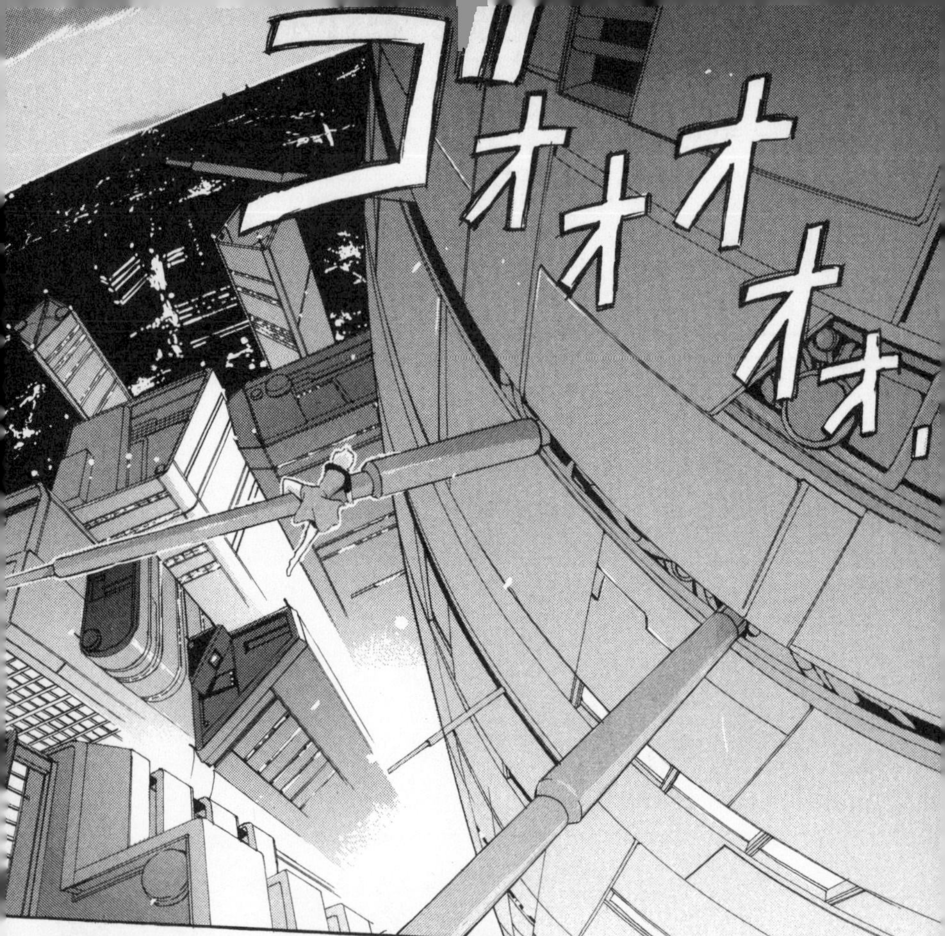
ゴオォオオォ…

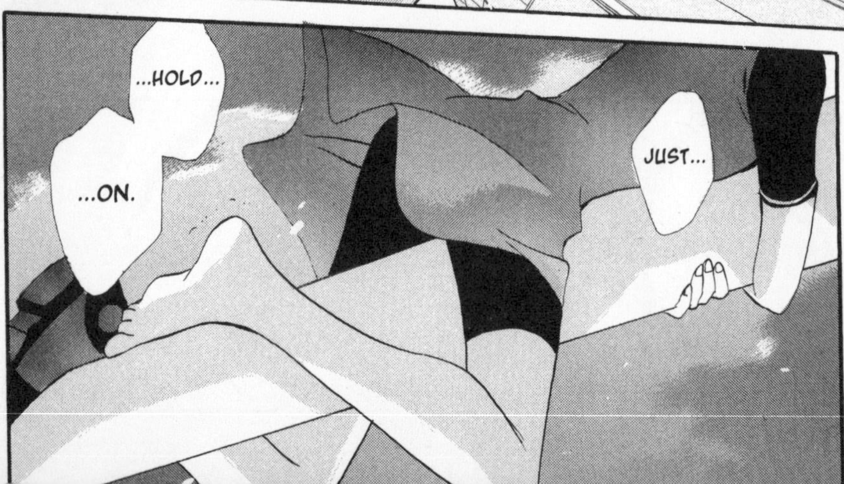
JUST...
...HOLD...
...ON.

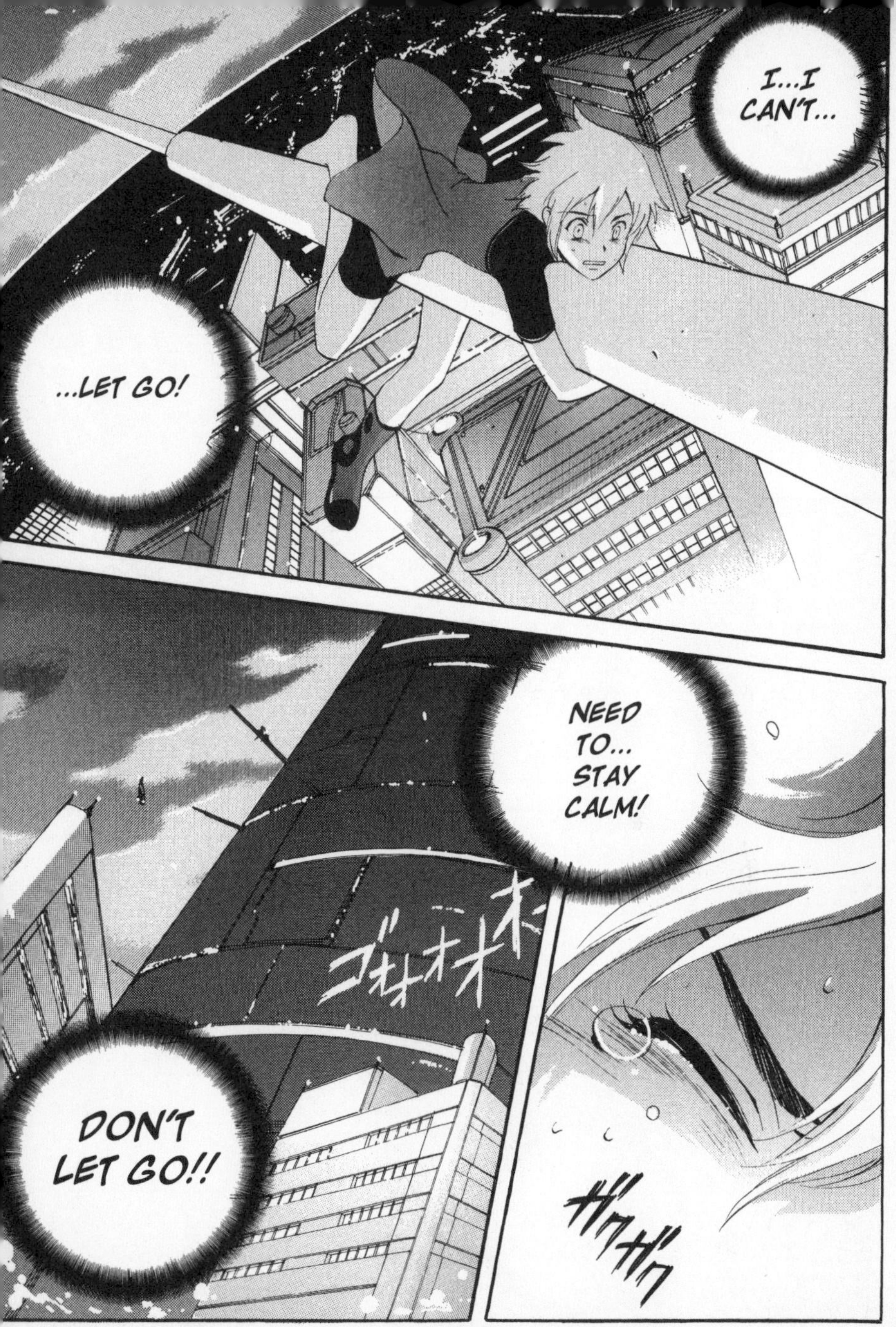
I...I CAN'T...
...LET GO!
NEED TO... STAY CALM!
ガクガク
ゴォォォォ
DON'T LET GO!!

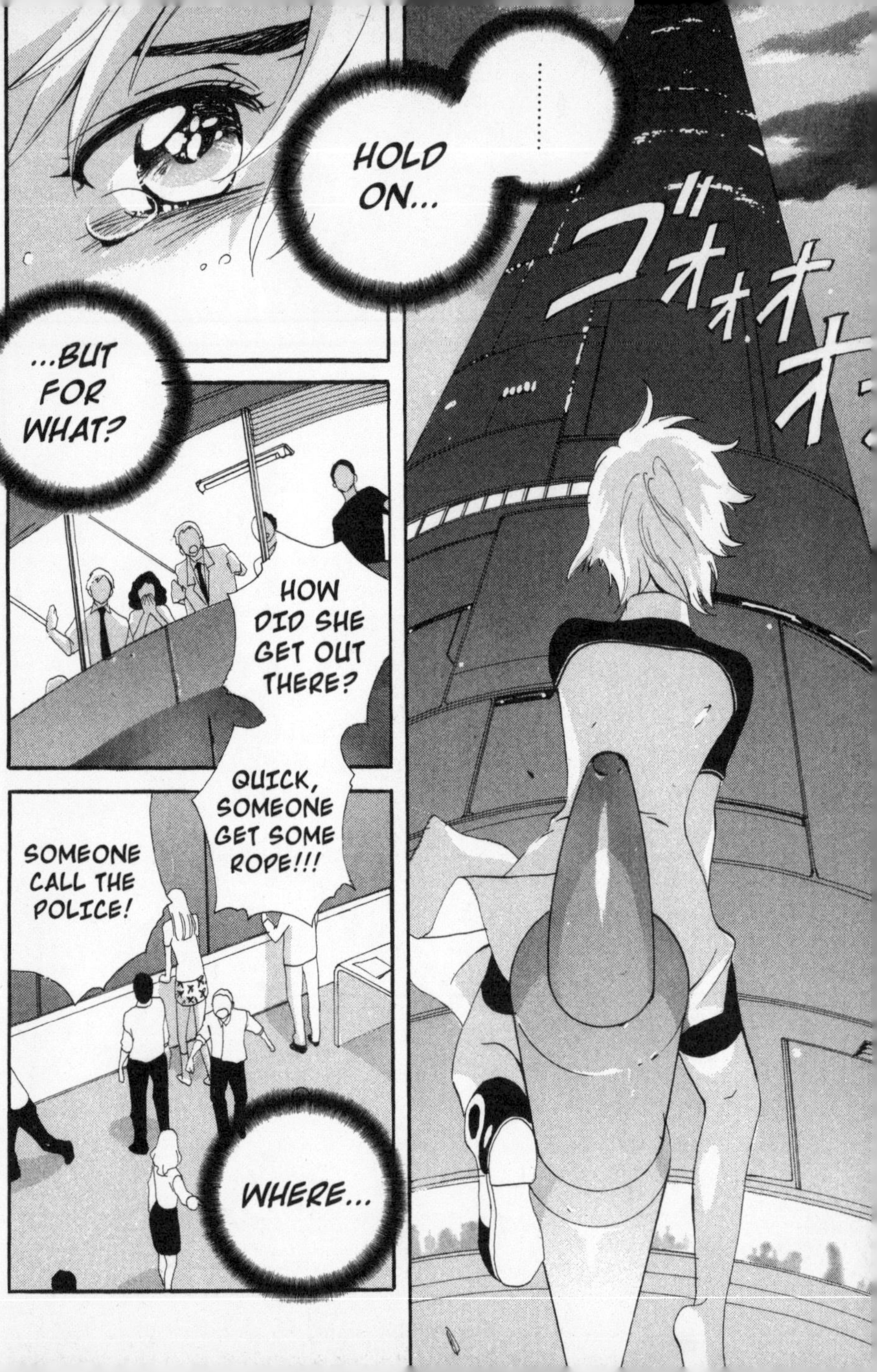
......
HOLD ON...
ゴオオオオー
...BUT FOR WHAT?
HOW DID SHE GET OUT THERE?
QUICK, SOMEONE GET SOME ROPE!!!
SOMEONE CALL THE POLICE!
WHERE...

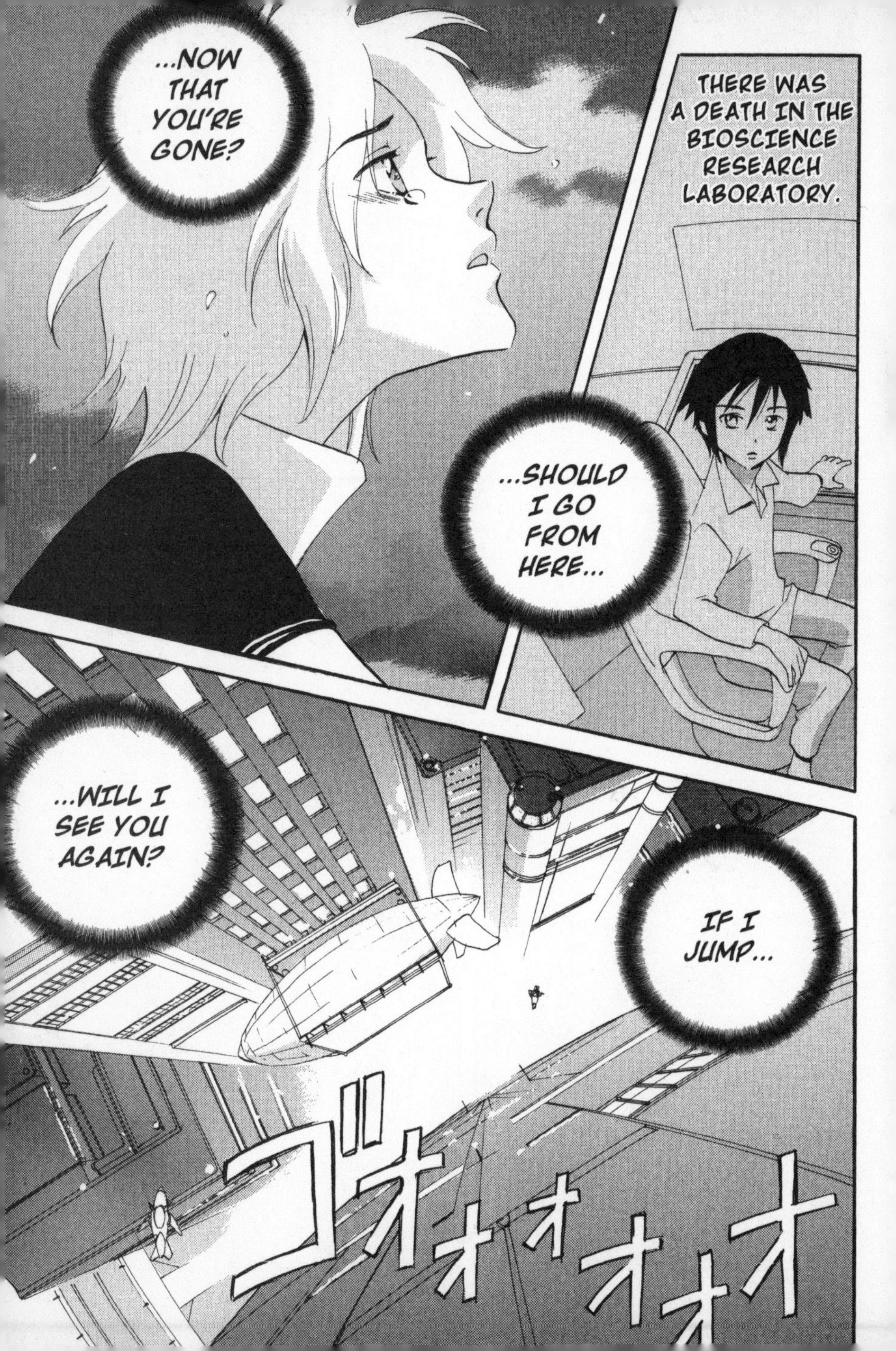
THERE WAS A DEATH IN THE BIOSCIENCE RESEARCH LABORATORY.
...SHOULD I GO FROM HERE...
...NOW THAT YOU'RE GONE?
IF I JUMP...
...WILL I SEE YOU AGAIN?
ゴオオオオオ

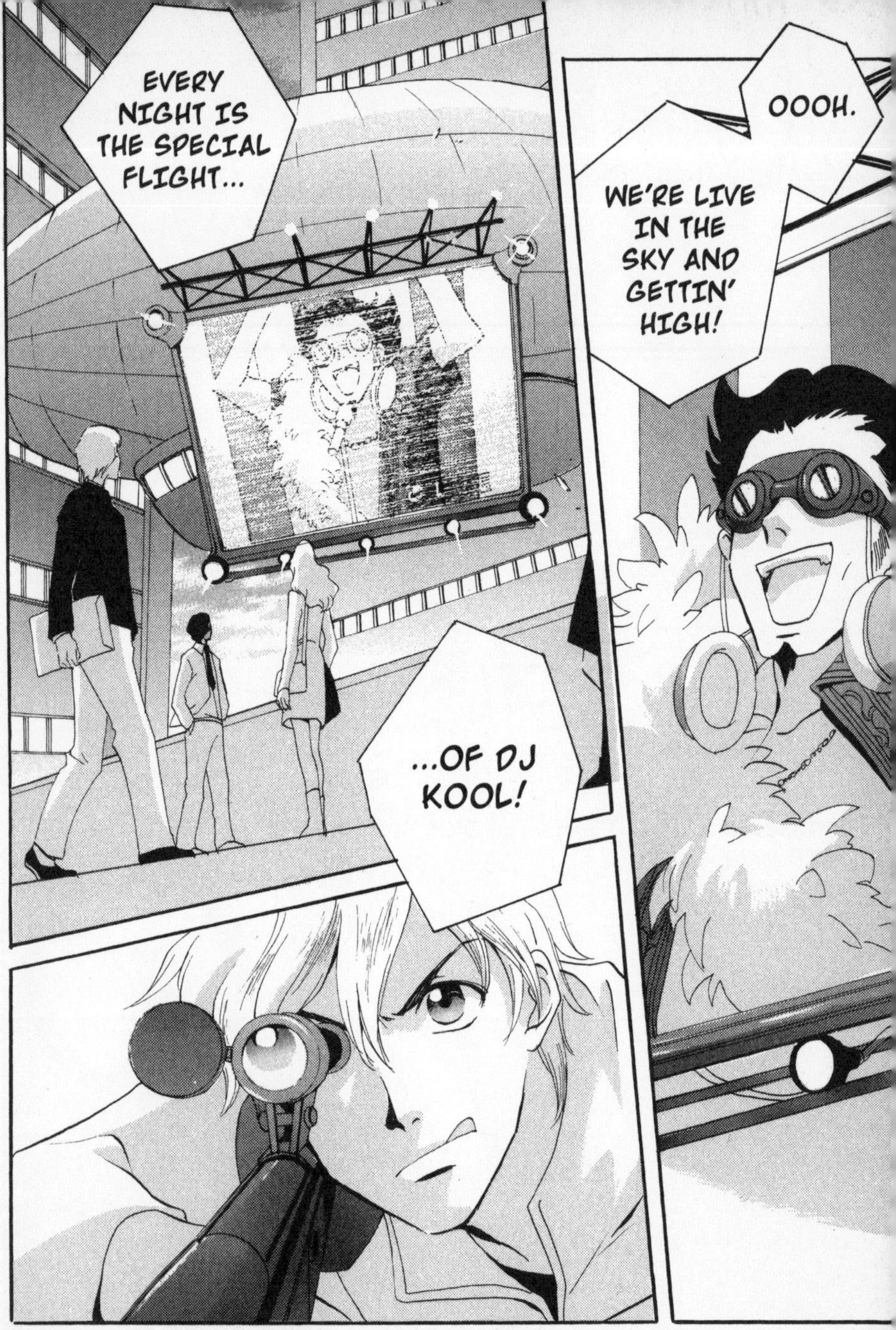
OOOH.
WE'RE LIVE IN THE SKY AND GETTIN' HIGH!
EVERY NIGHT IS THE SPECIAL FLIGHT...
...OF DJ KOOL!

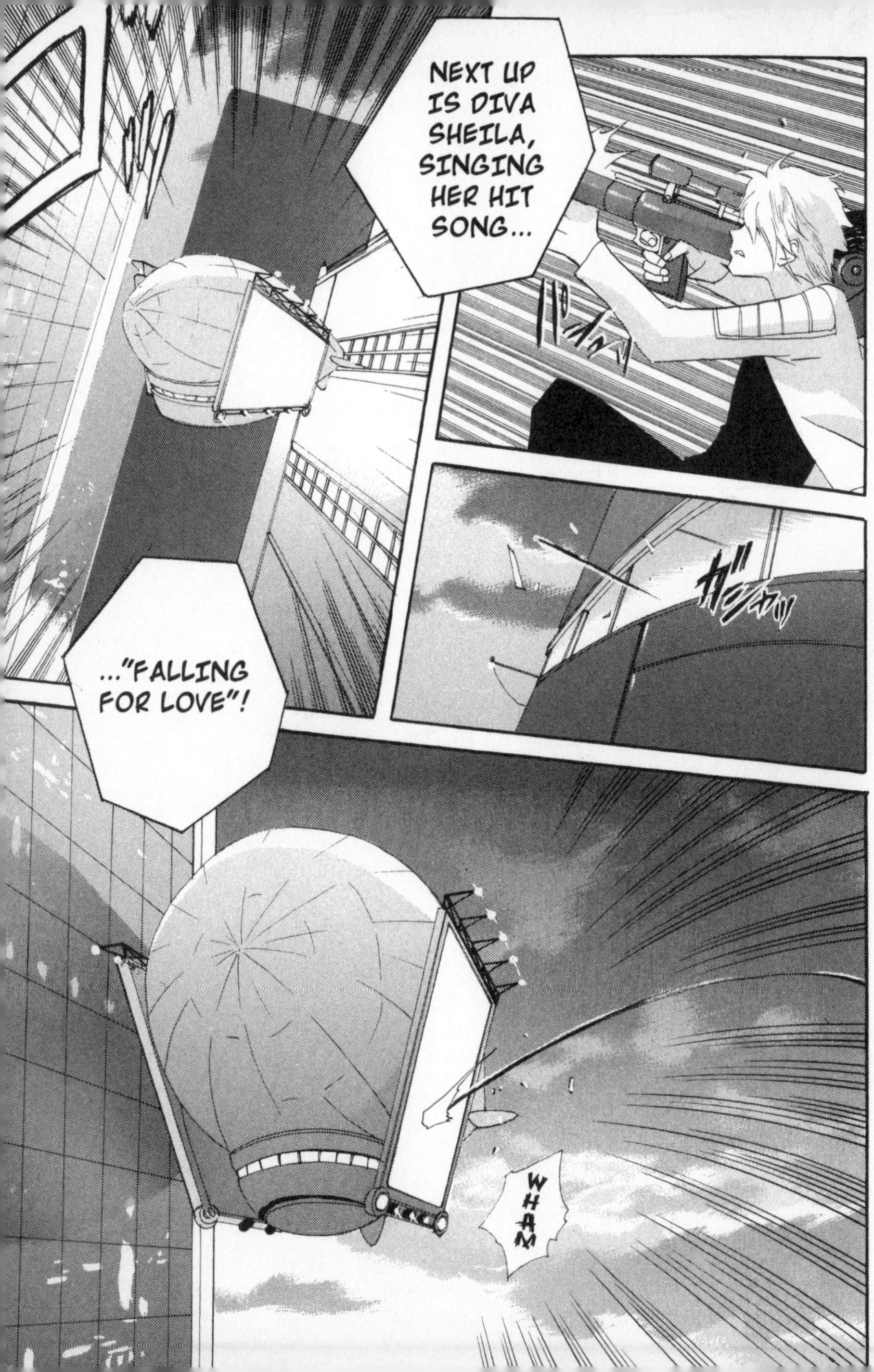
NEXT UP IS DIVA SHEILA, SINGING HER HIT SONG...
..."FALLING FOR LOVE"!
WHAM

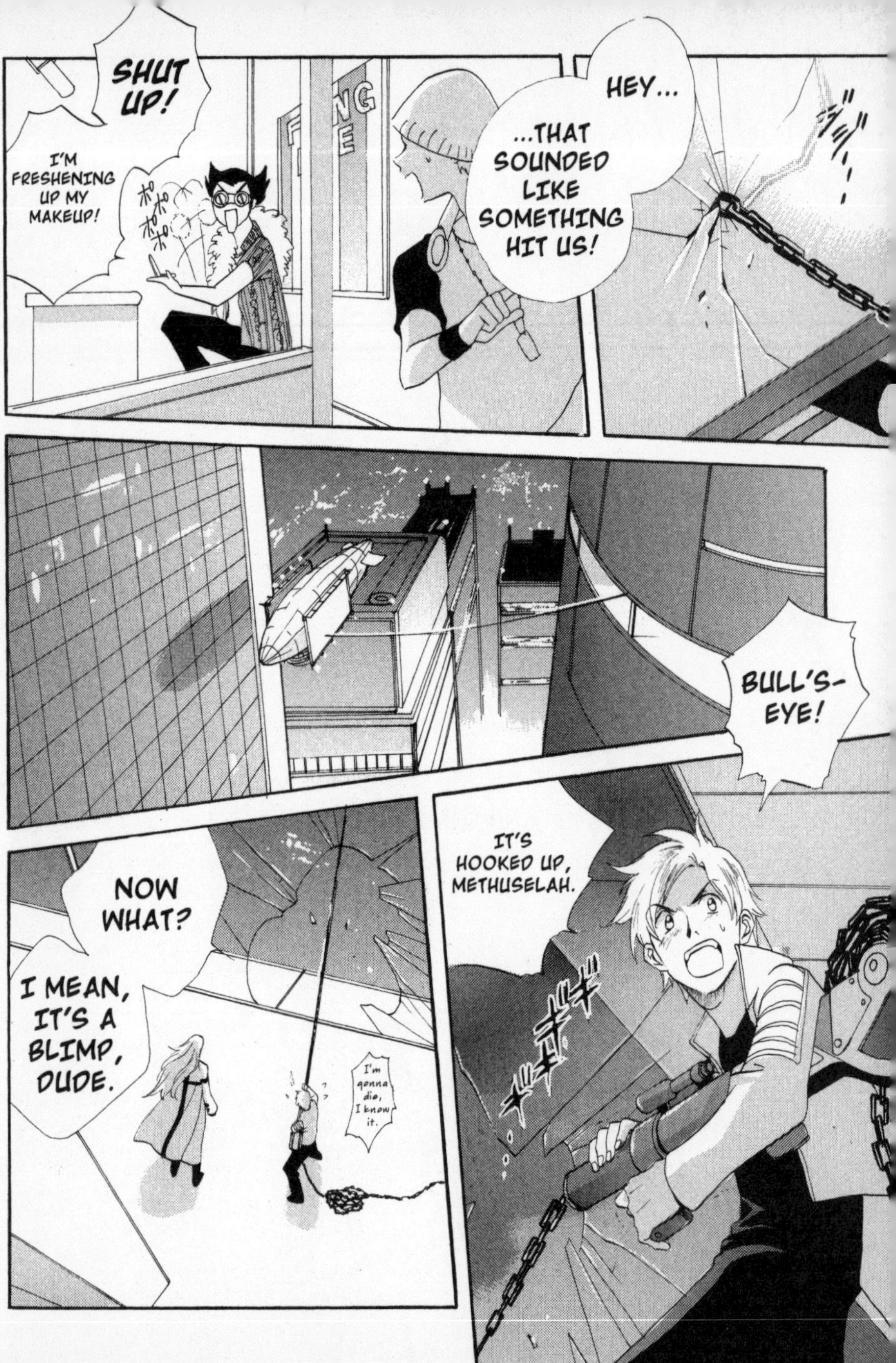
HEY...
...THAT SOUNDED LIKE SOMETHING HIT US!
SHUT UP!
I'M FRESHENING UP MY MAKEUP!
BULL'S-EYE!
IT'S HOOKED UP, METHUSELAH.
NOW WHAT?
I MEAN, IT'S A BLIMP, DUDE.
I'm gonna die, I know it.

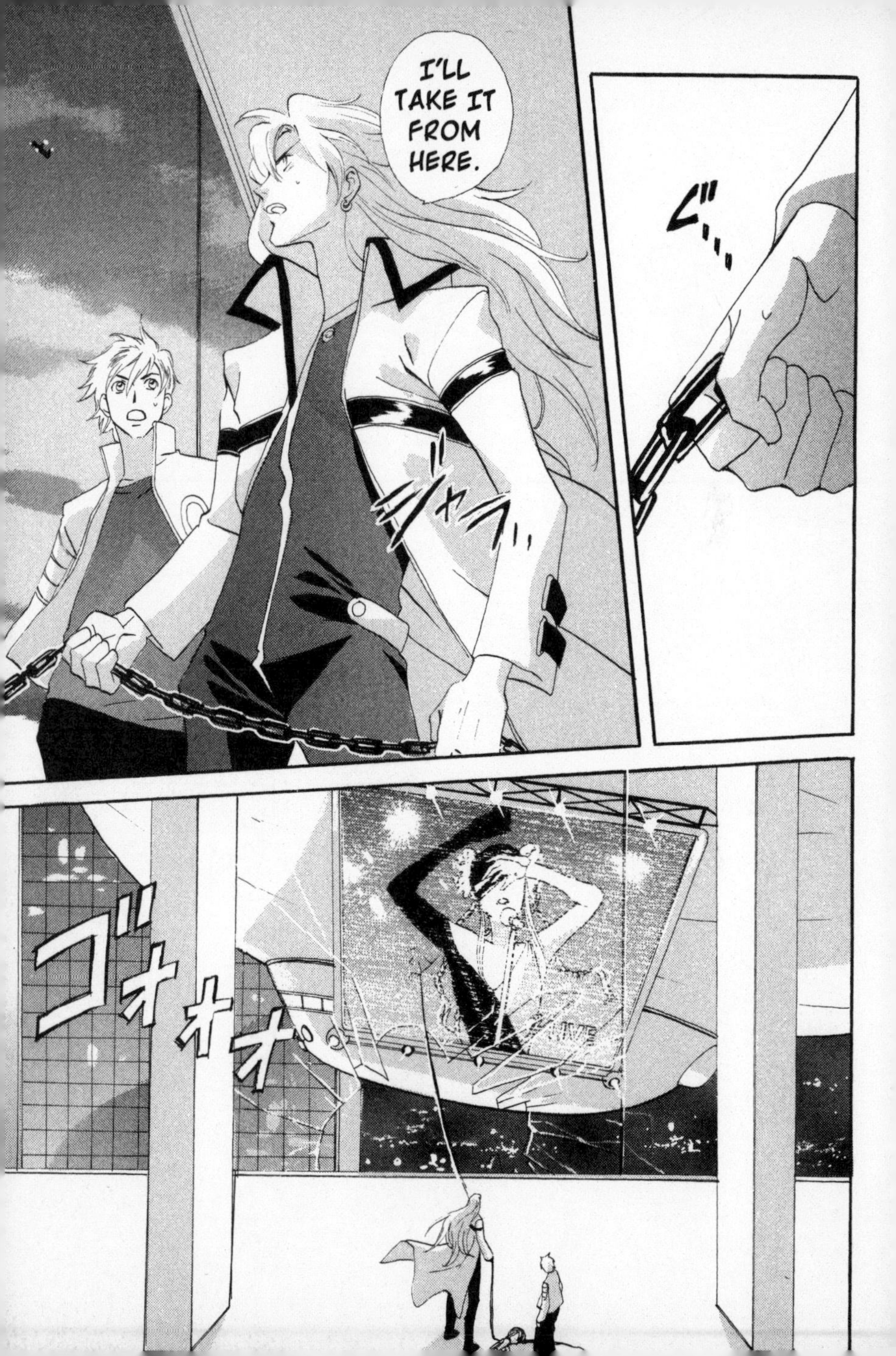
ぐ…
I'LL TAKE IT FROM HERE.
ジャラ
ゴォオオ…

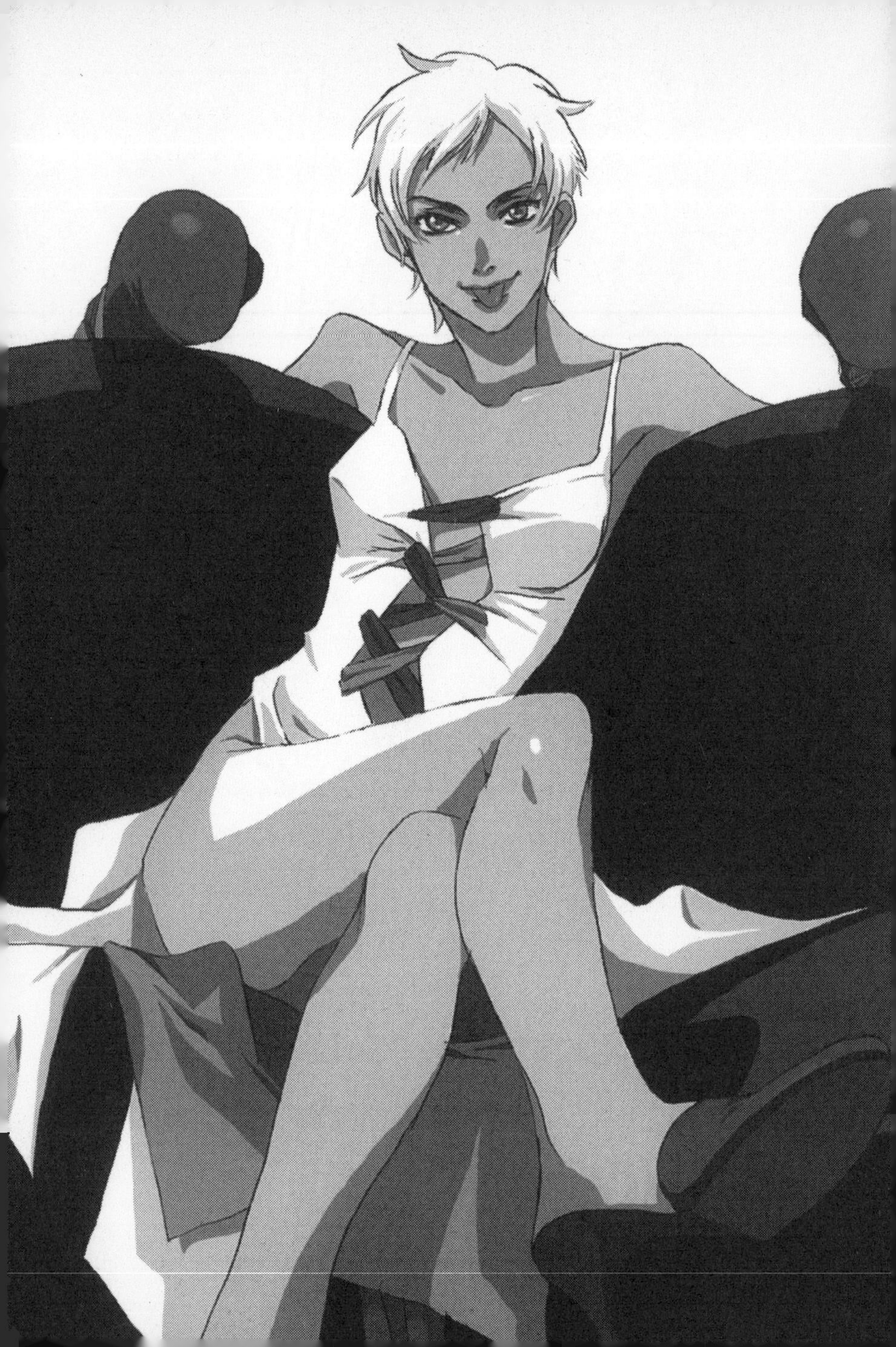

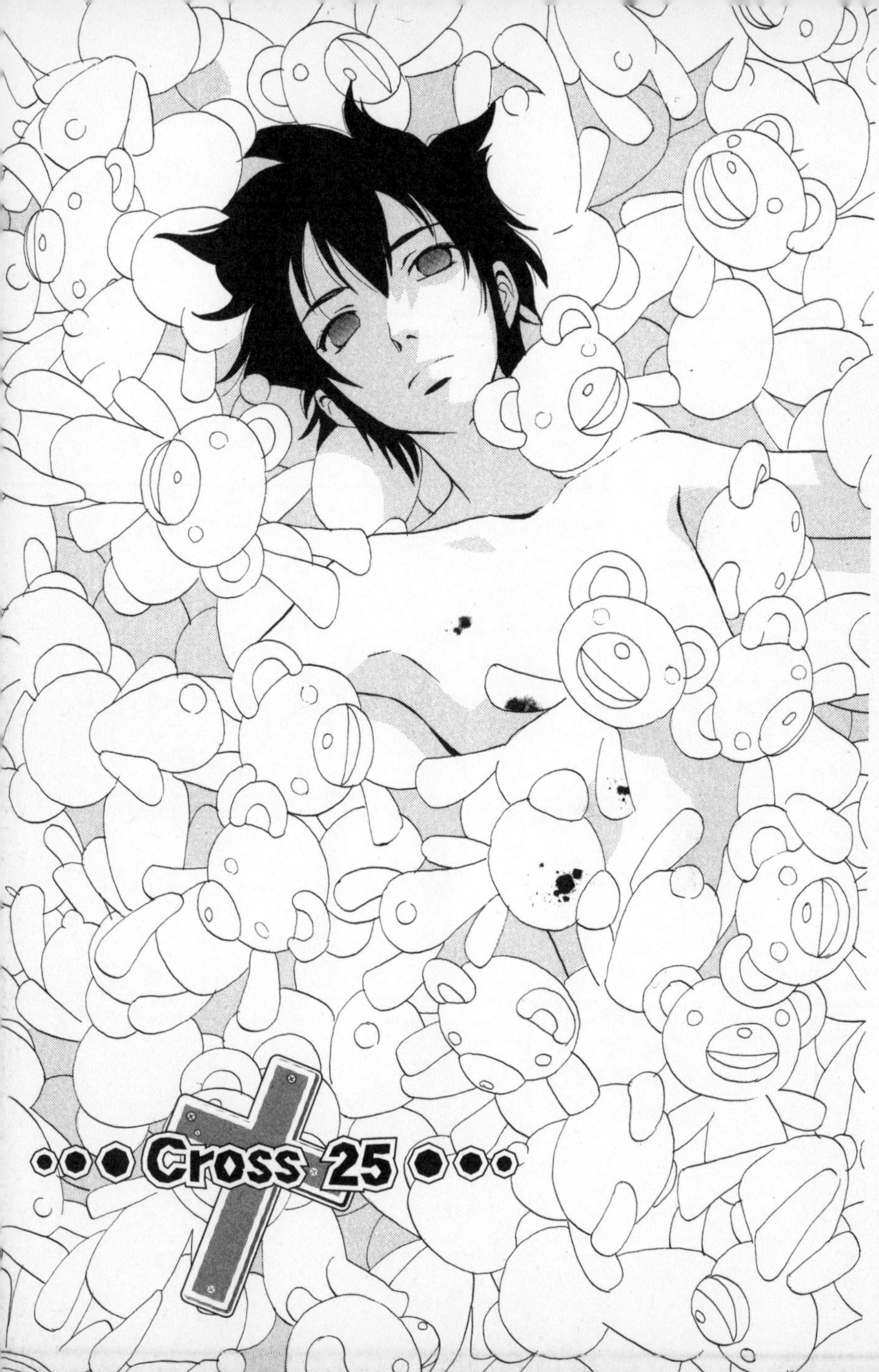
Cross 25

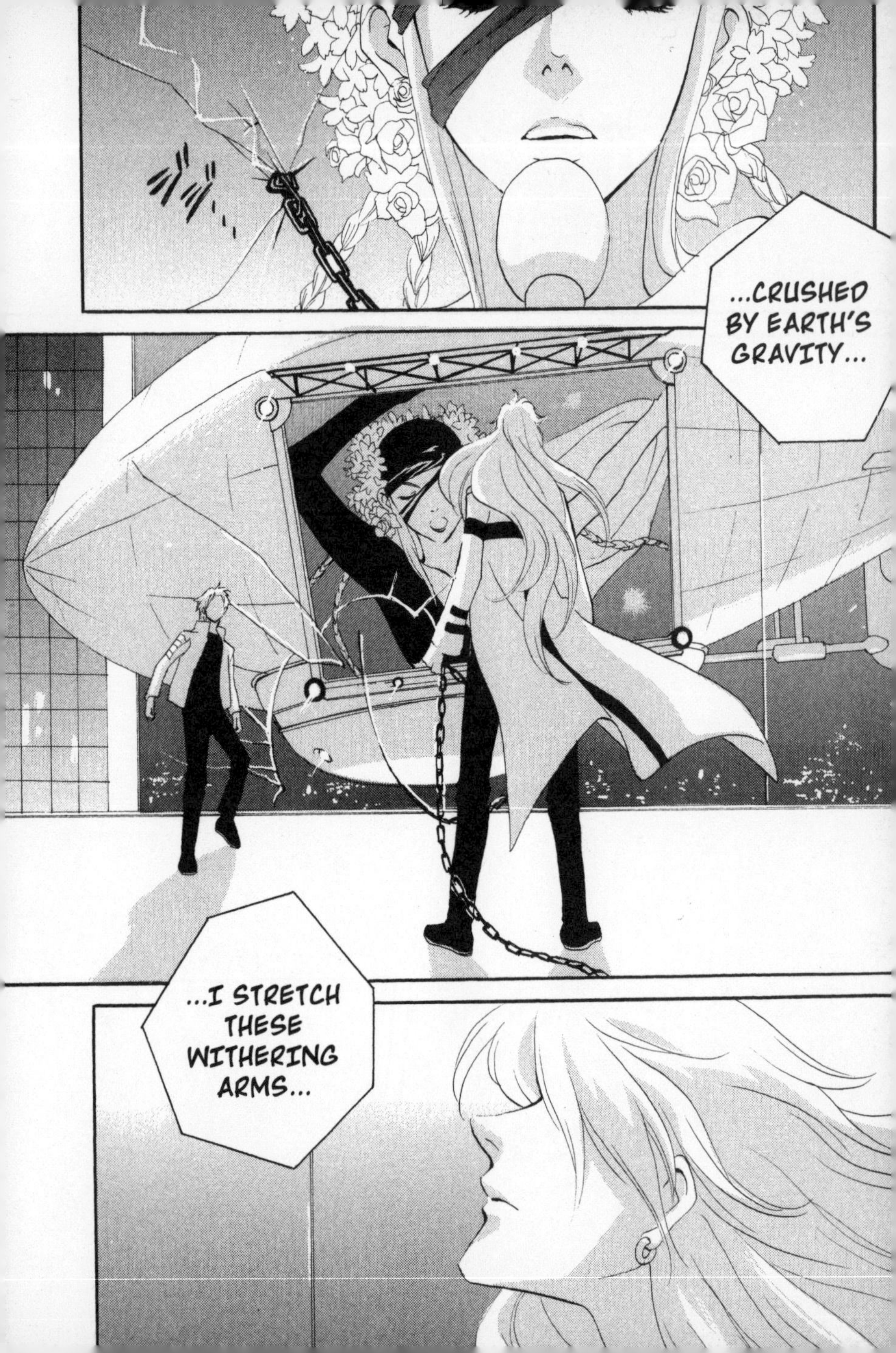
...CRUSHED BY EARTH'S GRAVITY...
...I STRETCH THESE WITHERING ARMS...

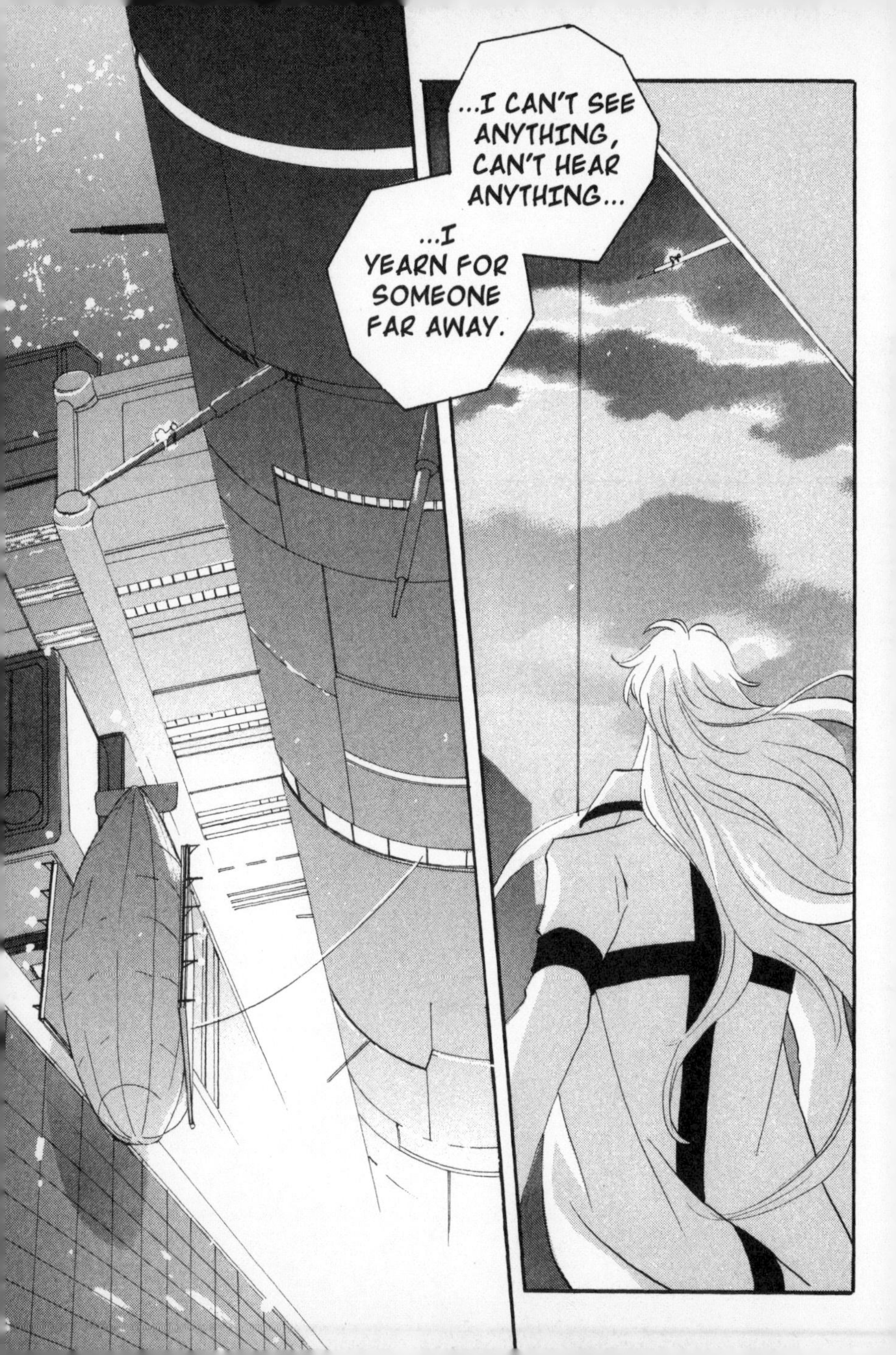
...I CAN'T SEE ANYTHING, CAN'T HEAR ANYTHING...
...I YEARN FOR SOMEONE FAR AWAY.

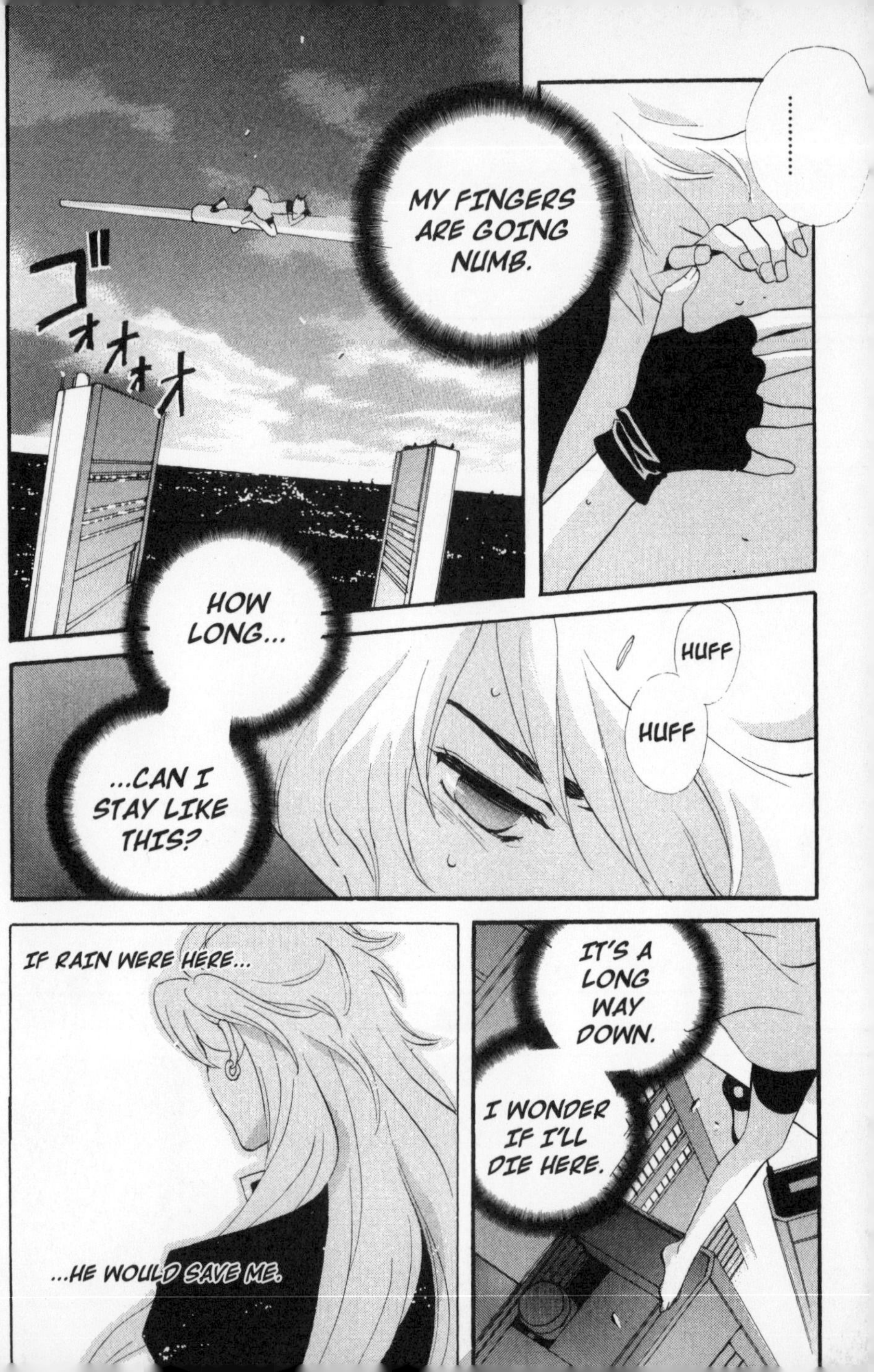
……
MY FINGERS ARE GOING NUMB.
ゴォォォォ
HUFF
HUFF
HOW LONG...
...CAN I STAY LIKE THIS?
IT'S A LONG WAY DOWN.
I WONDER IF I'LL DIE HERE.
IF RAIN WERE HERE...
...HE WOULD SAVE ME.

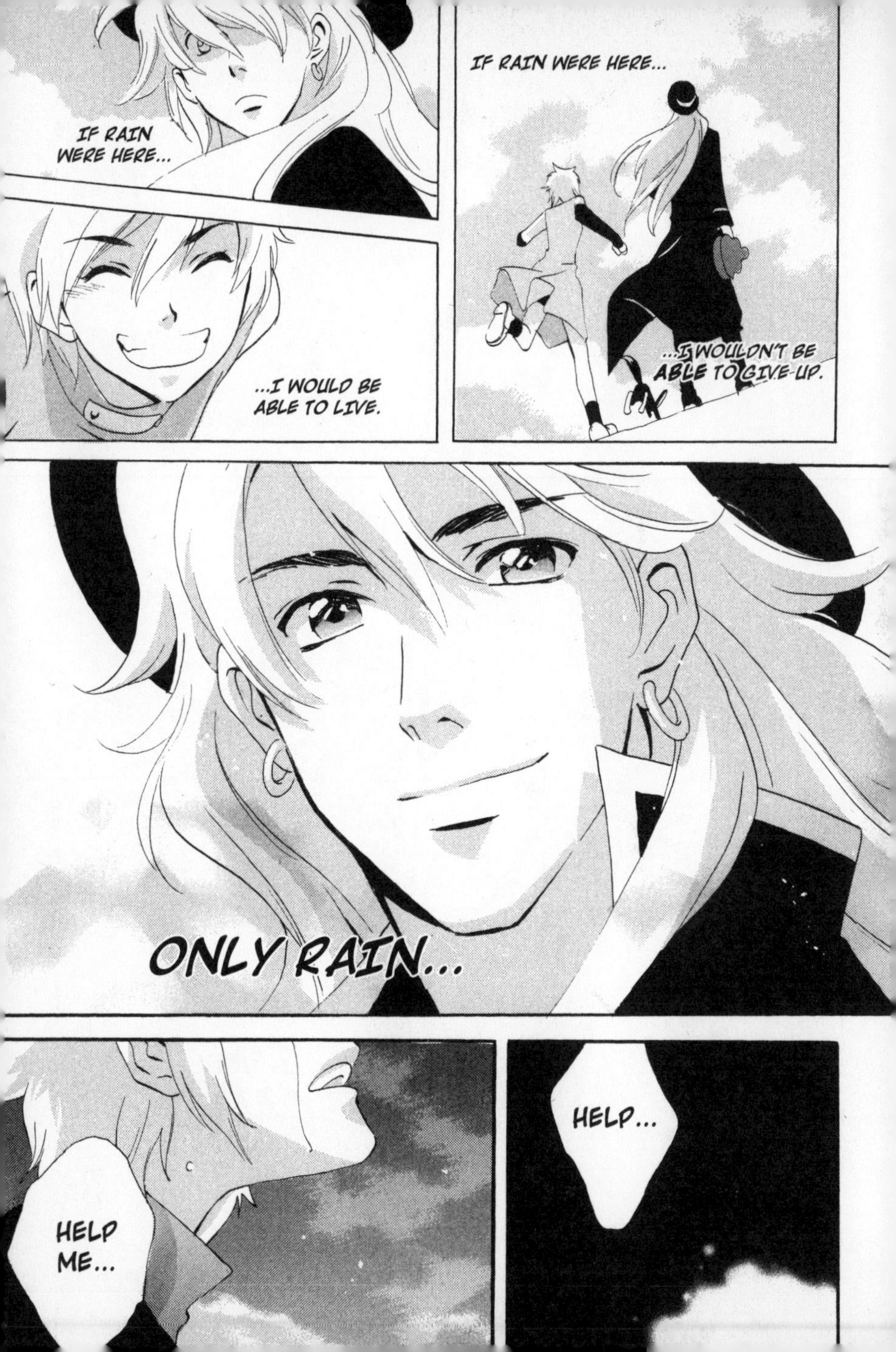
IF RAIN WERE HERE...
...I WOULDN'T BE ABLE TO GIVE UP.
IF RAIN WERE HERE...
...I WOULD BE ABLE TO LIVE.
ONLY RAIN...
HELP...
HELP ME...

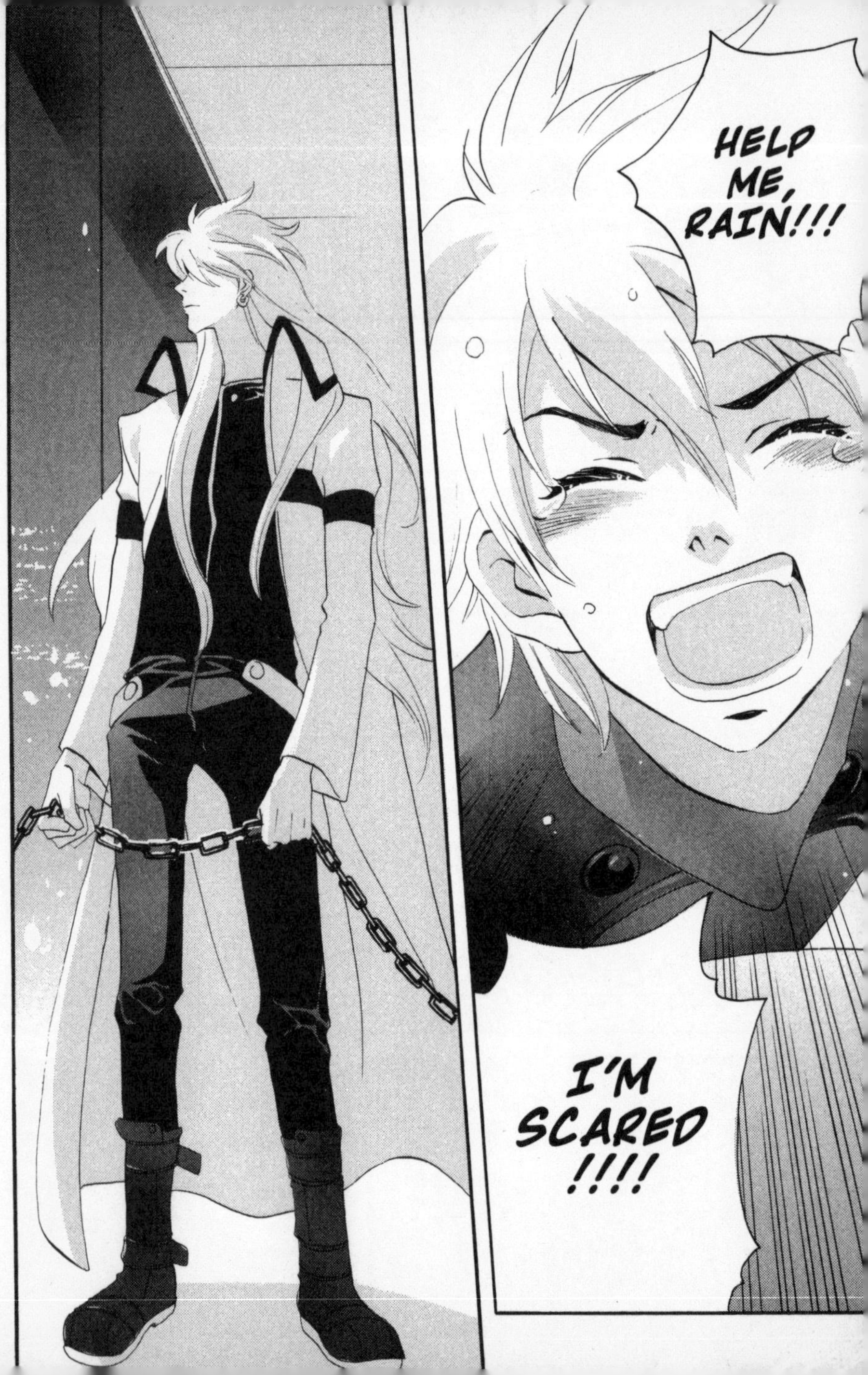
HELP ME, RAIN!!!
I'M SCARED !!!!

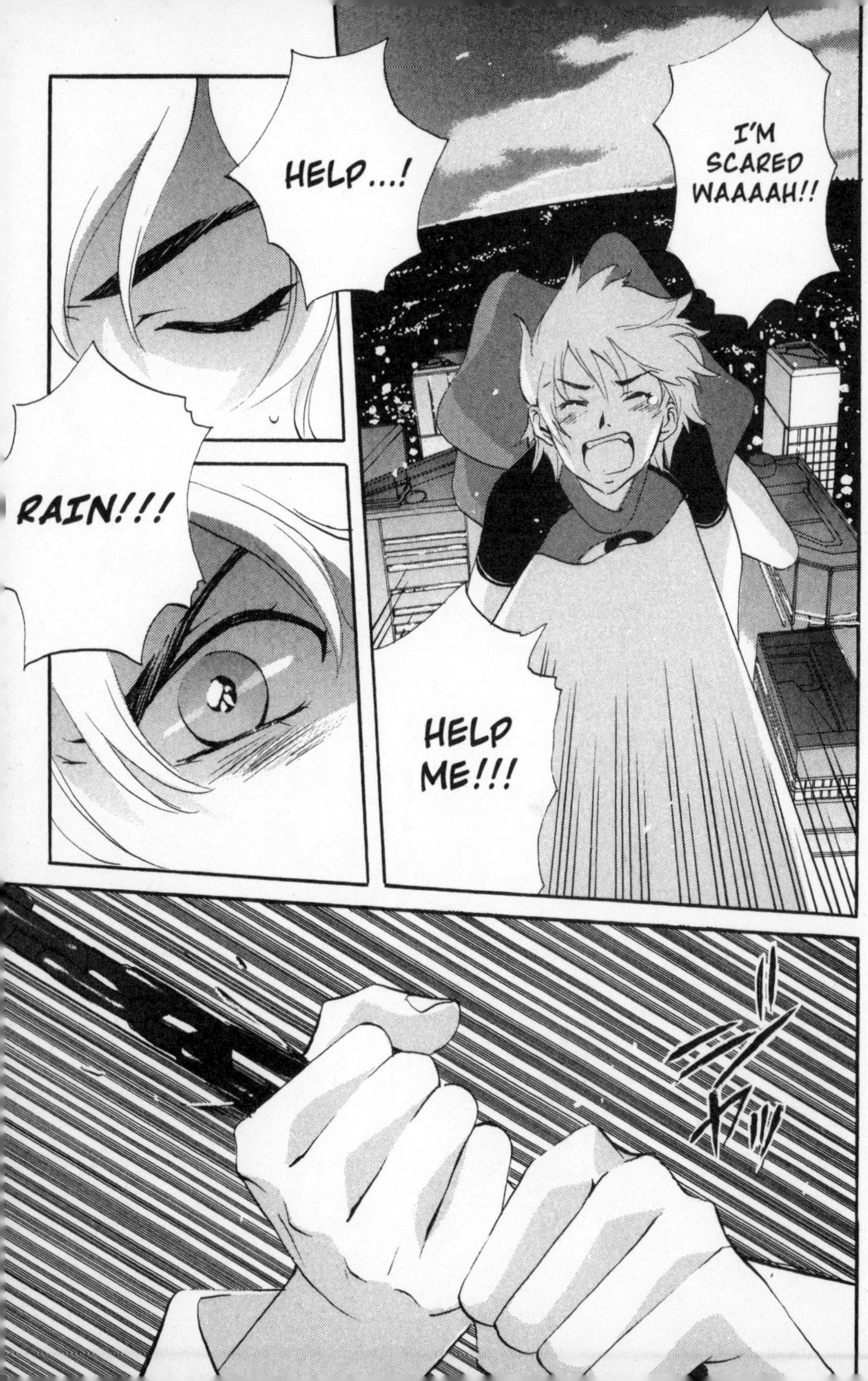
I'M SCARED WAAAAH!!
HELP...!
HELP ME!!!
RAIN!!!

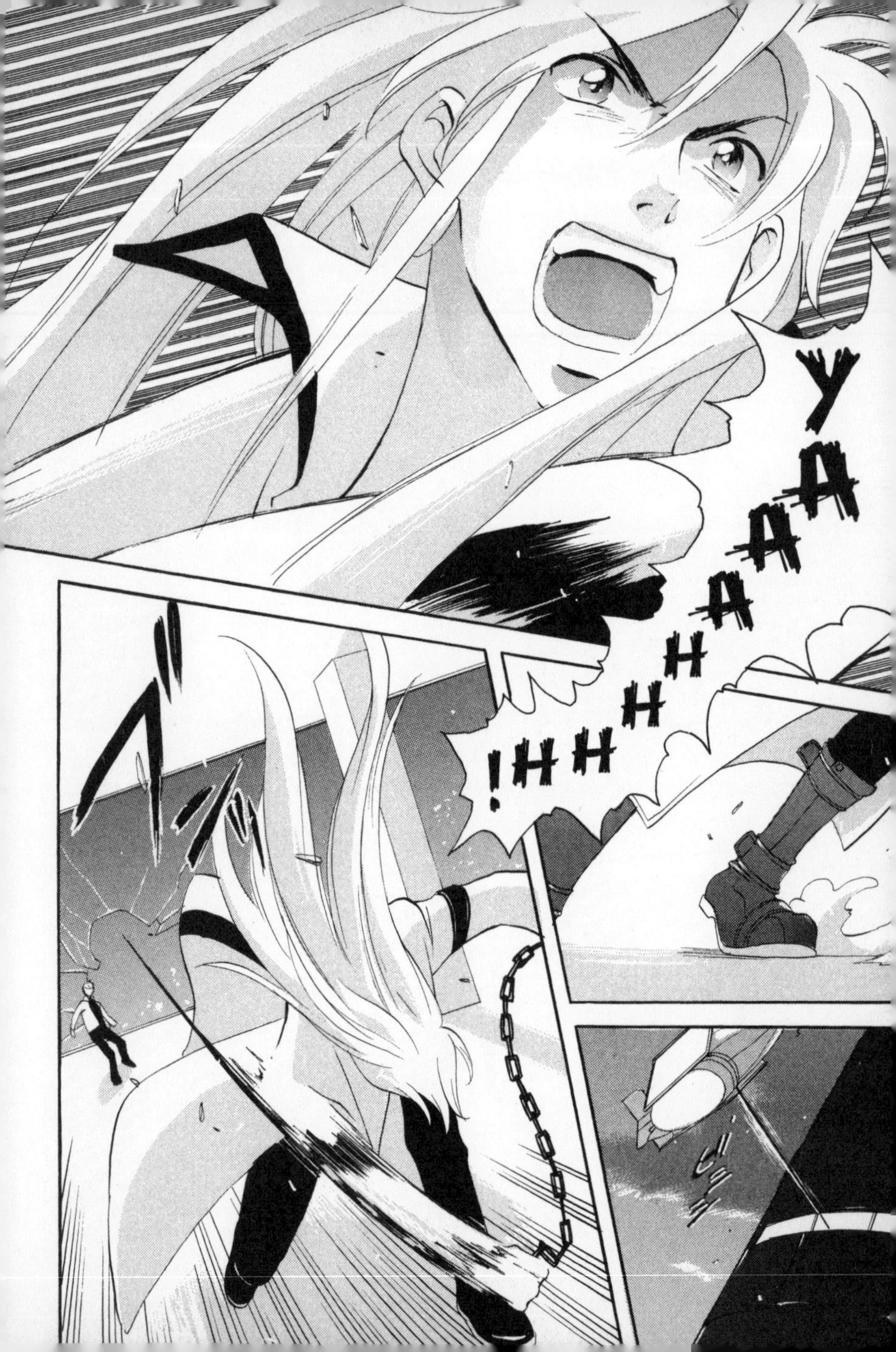
YAAAHHHH!

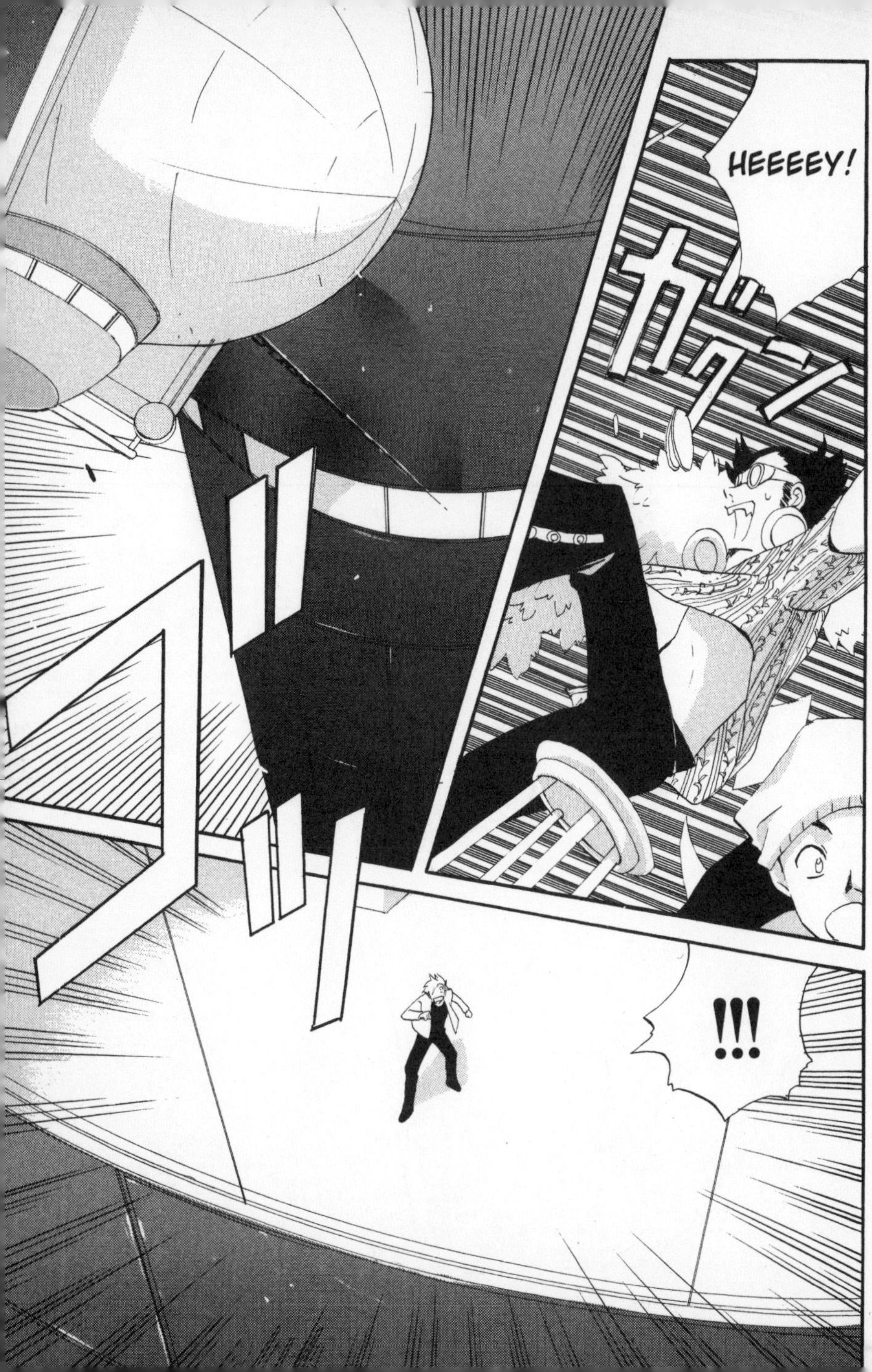
HEEEEY!
!!!

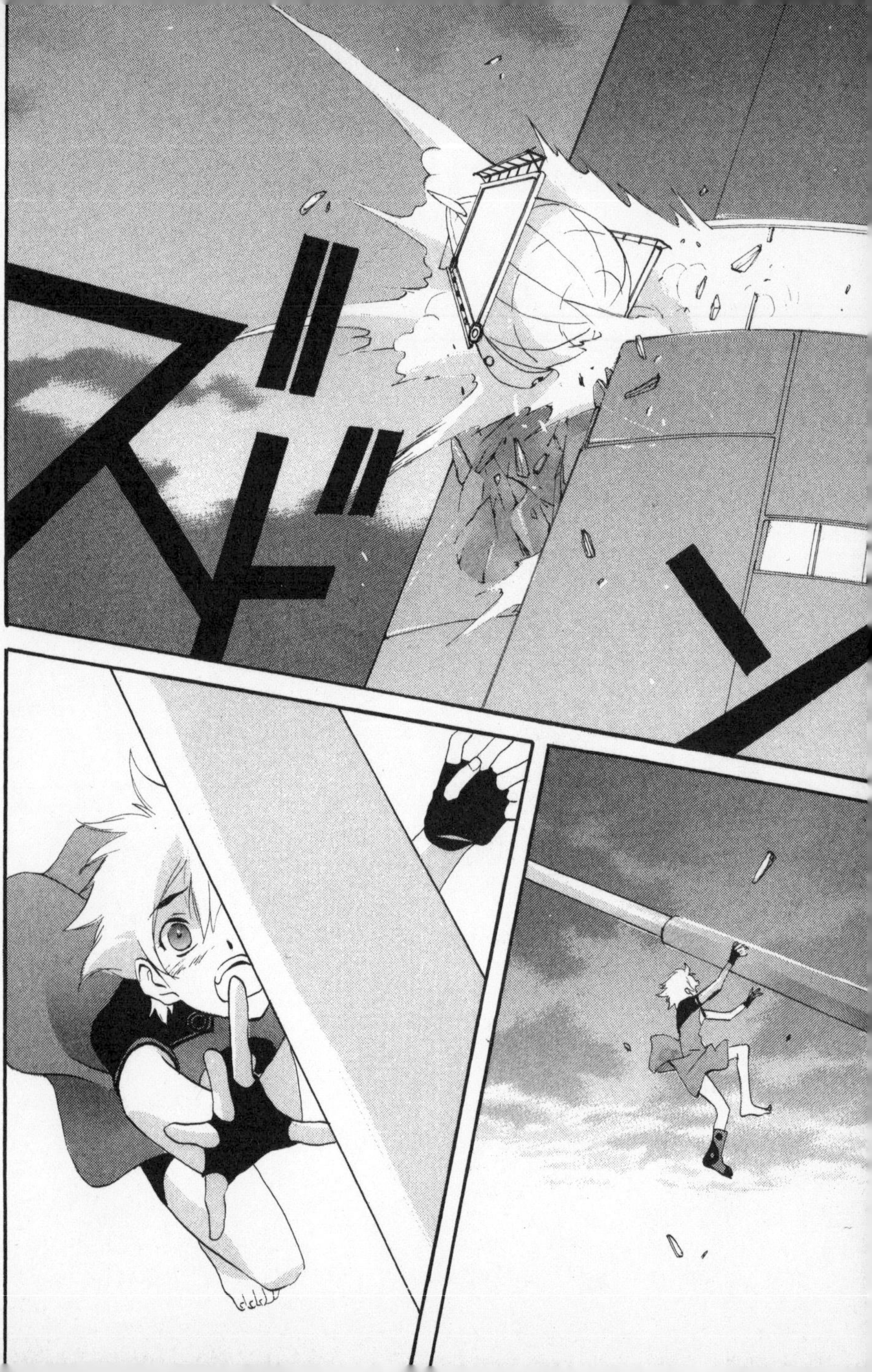
ズドー

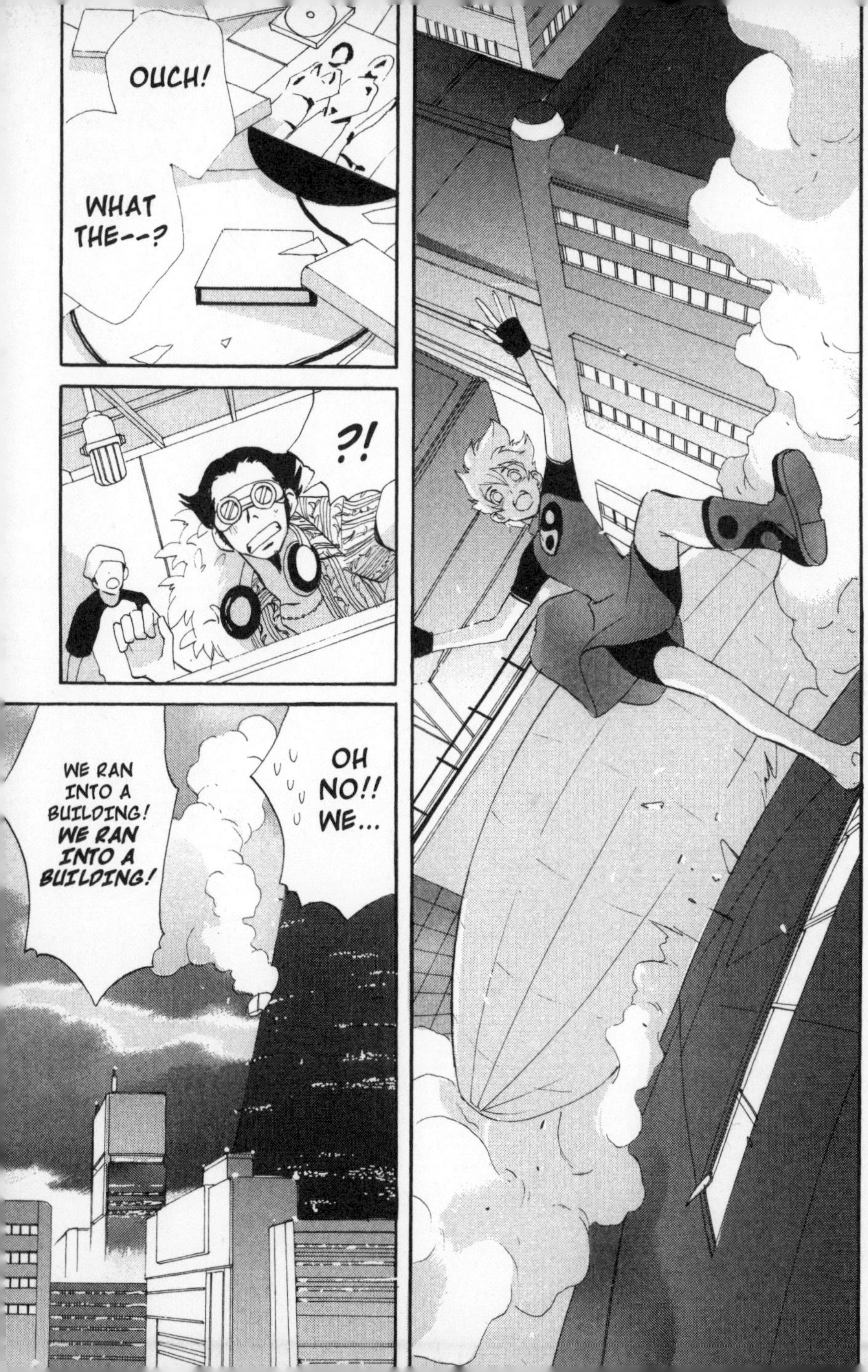
OUCH!
WHAT THE--?
?!
OH NO!! WE...
WE RAN INTO A BUILDING! WE RAN INTO A BUILDING!

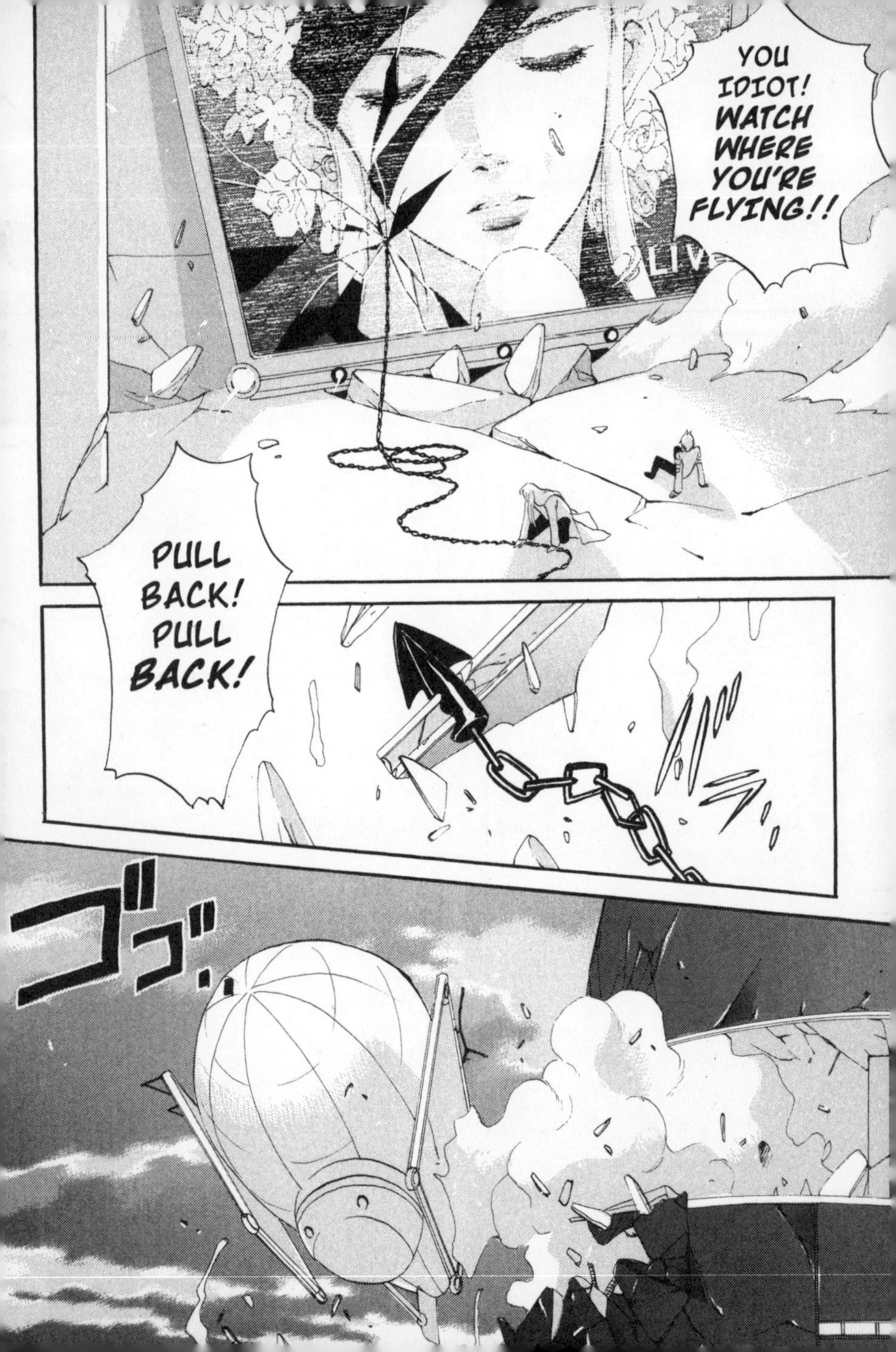
YOU IDIOT! WATCH WHERE YOU'RE FLYING!!
PULL BACK! PULL BACK!
ゴゴ

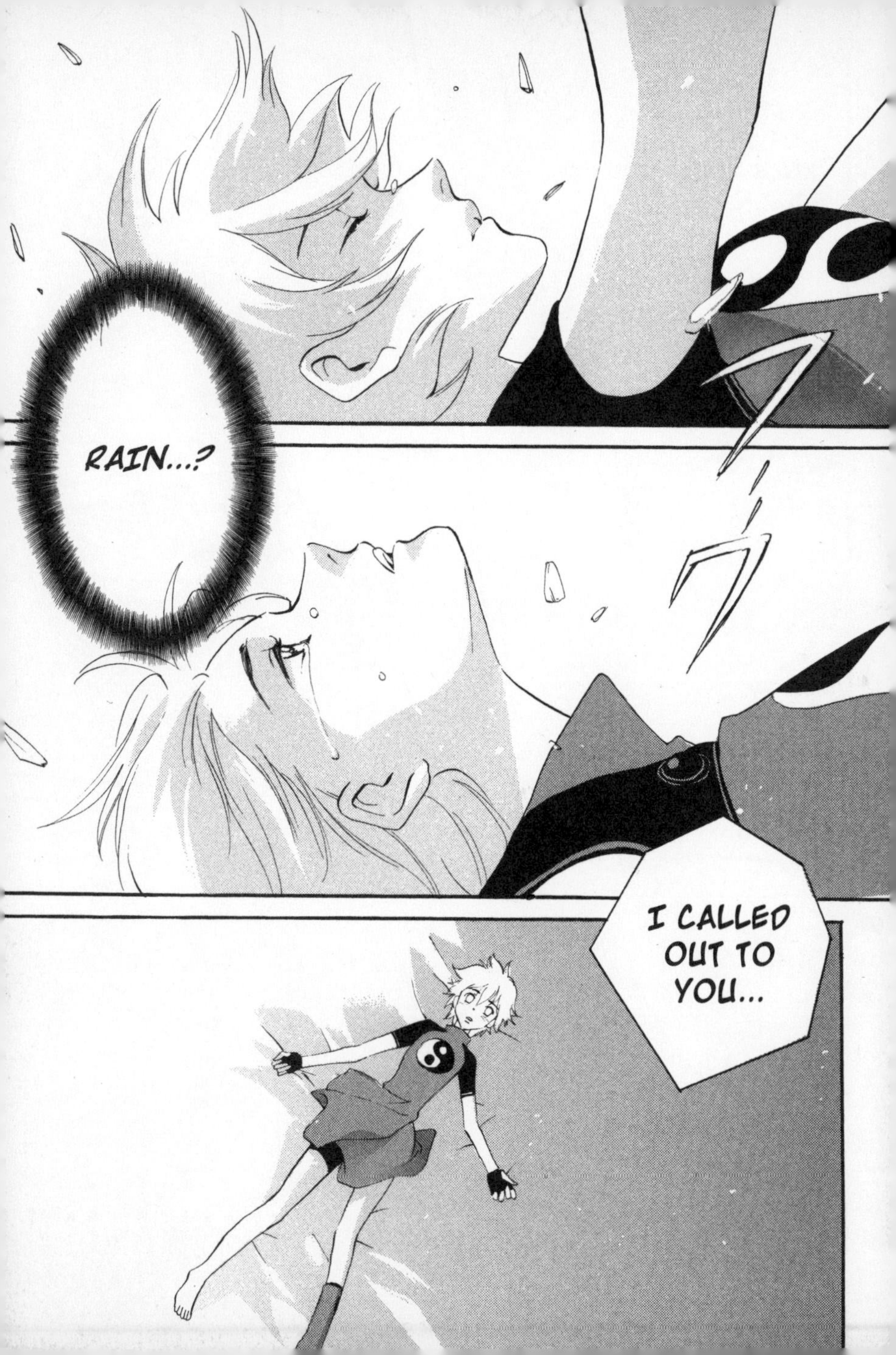
RAIN...?
I CALLED OUT TO YOU...

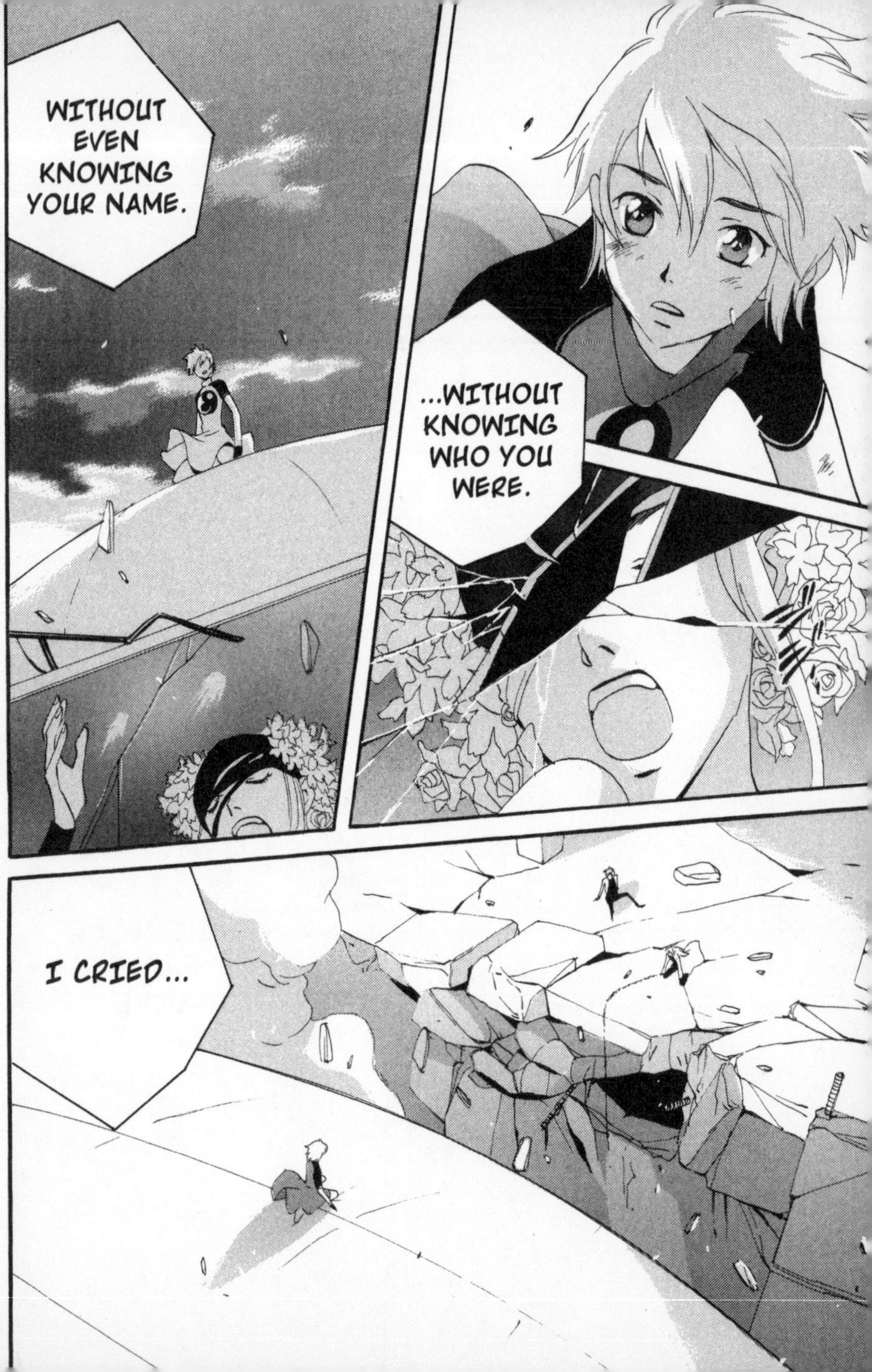
WITHOUT EVEN KNOWING YOUR NAME.
...WITHOUT KNOWING WHO YOU WERE.
I CRIED...

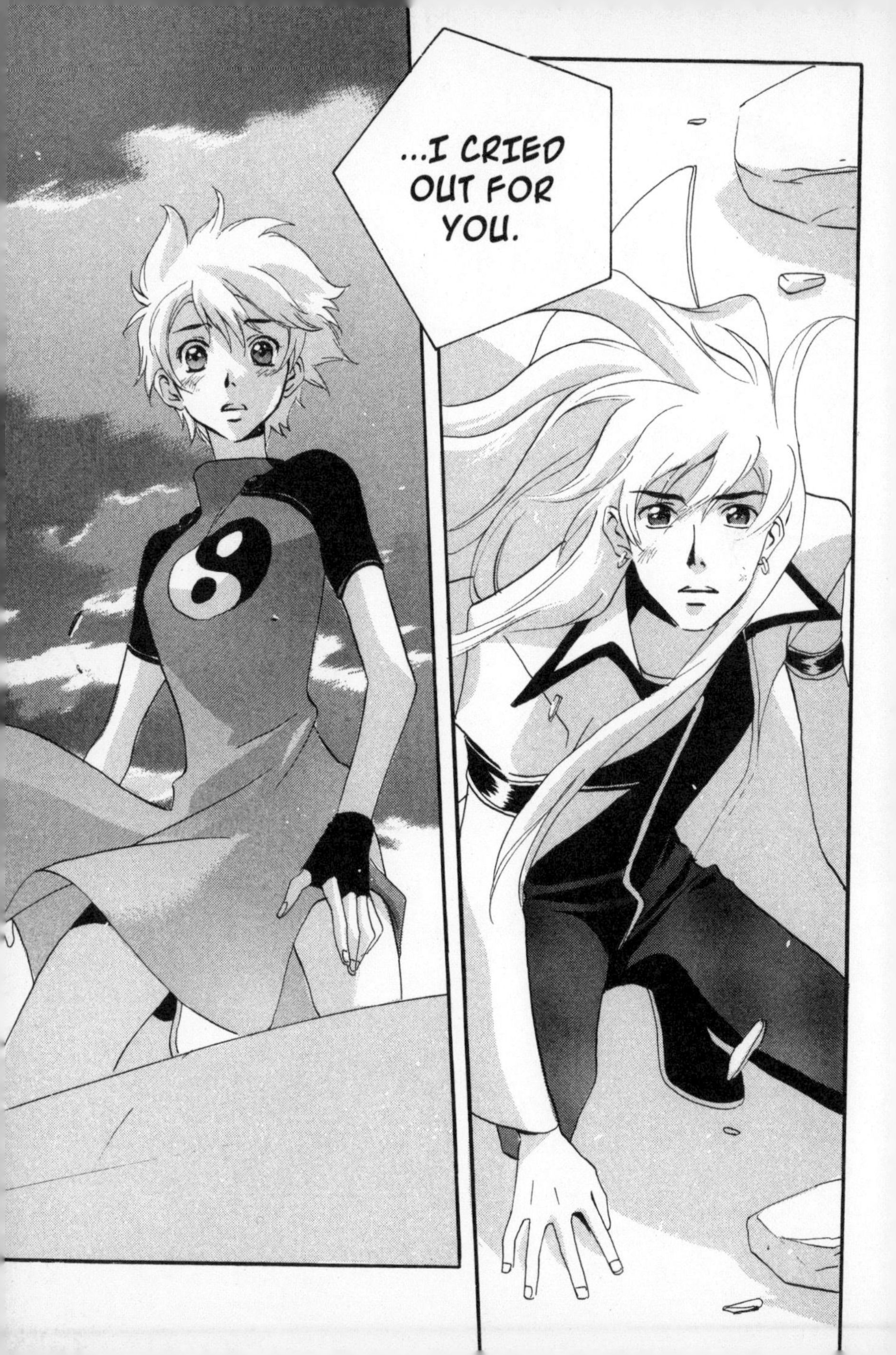
...I CRIED OUT FOR YOU.

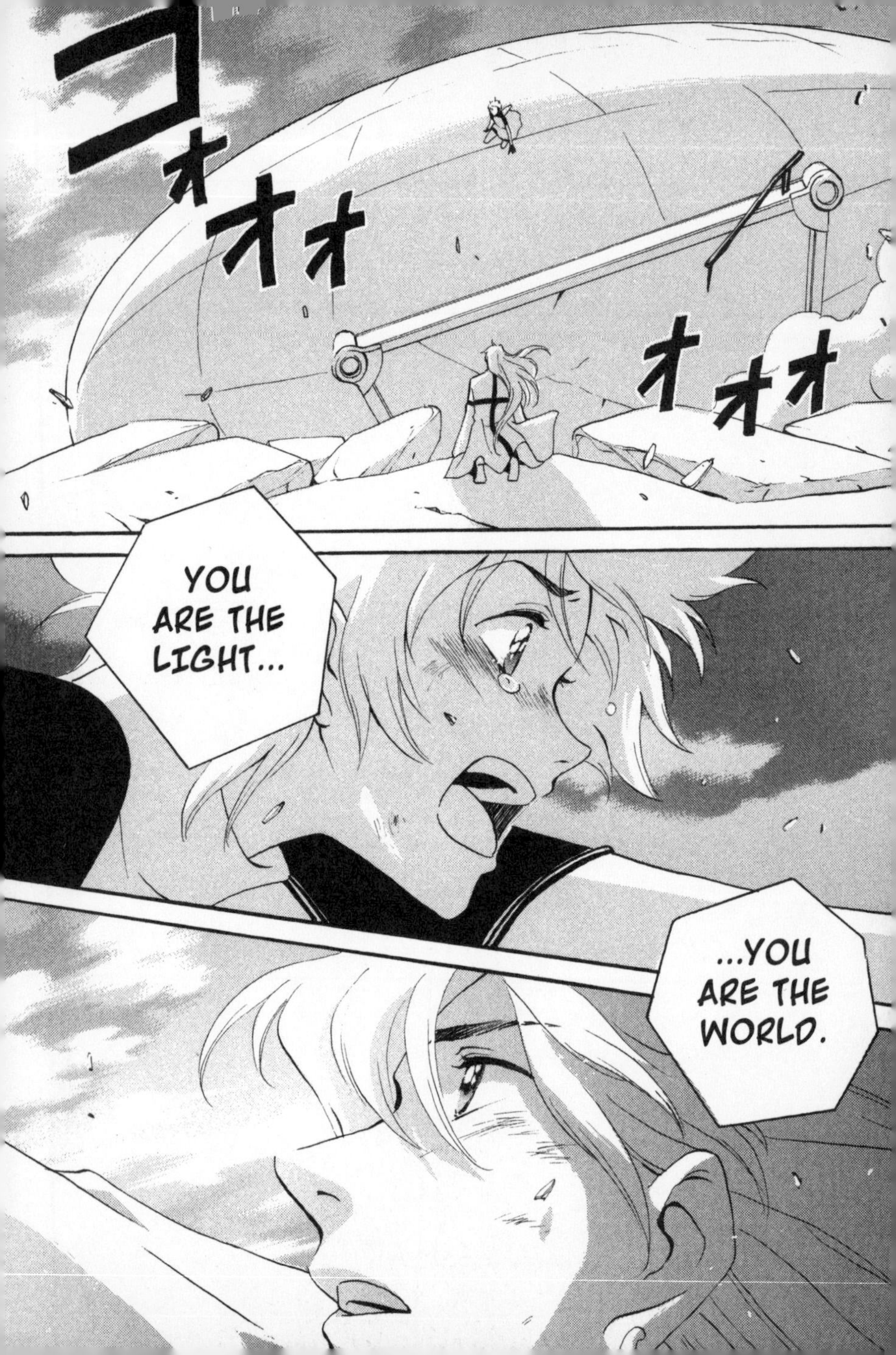
ゴオオオ
オオオ
YOU ARE THE LIGHT...
...YOU ARE THE WORLD.

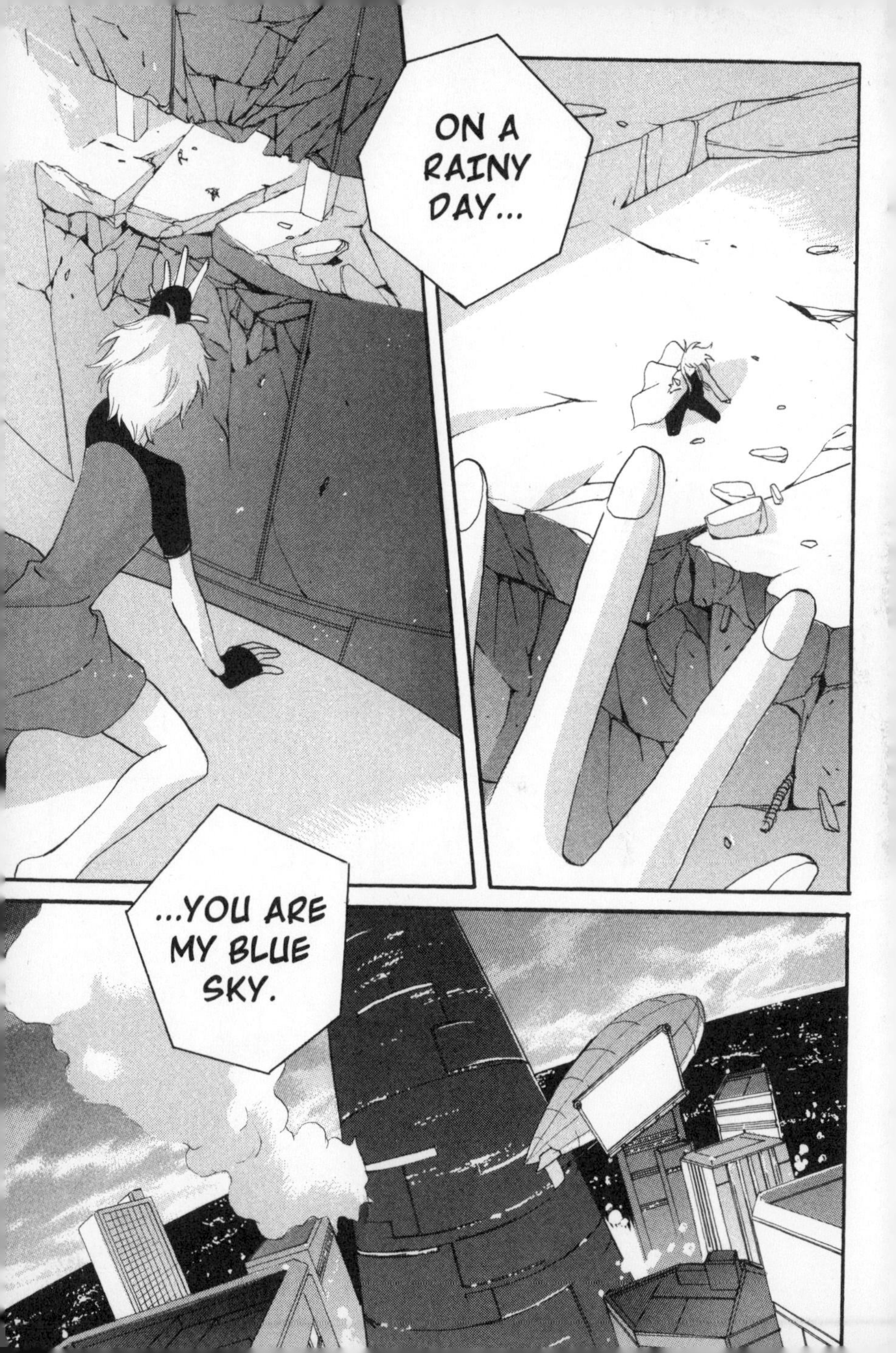
ON A RAINY DAY...
...YOU ARE MY BLUE SKY.

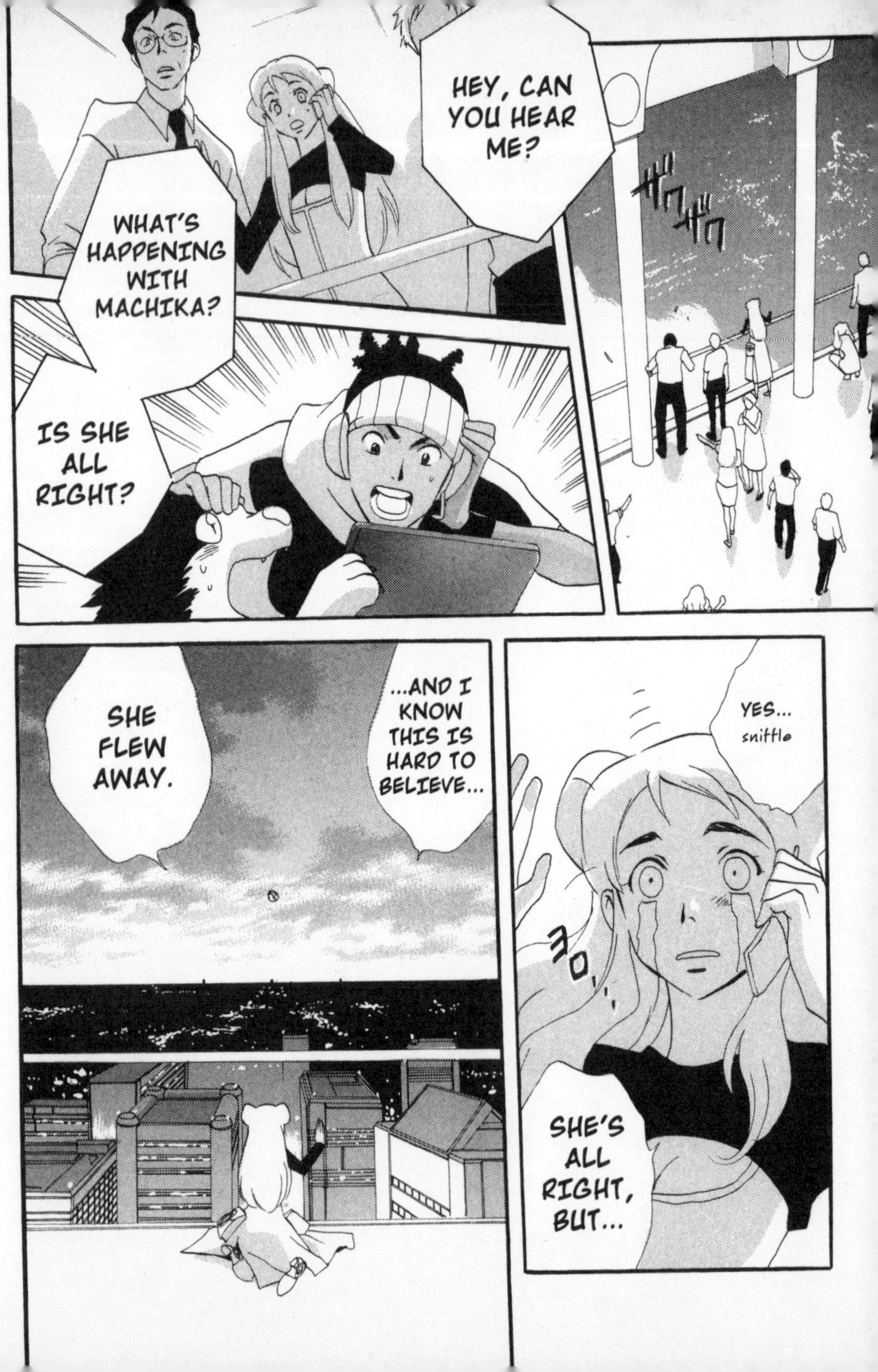
ザワザワ
HEY, CAN YOU HEAR ME?
WHAT'S HAPPENING WITH MACHIKA?
IS SHE ALL RIGHT?
YES... sniffle
ヨロ
SHE'S ALL RIGHT, BUT...
...AND I KNOW THIS IS HARD TO BELIEVE...
SHE FLEW AWAY.

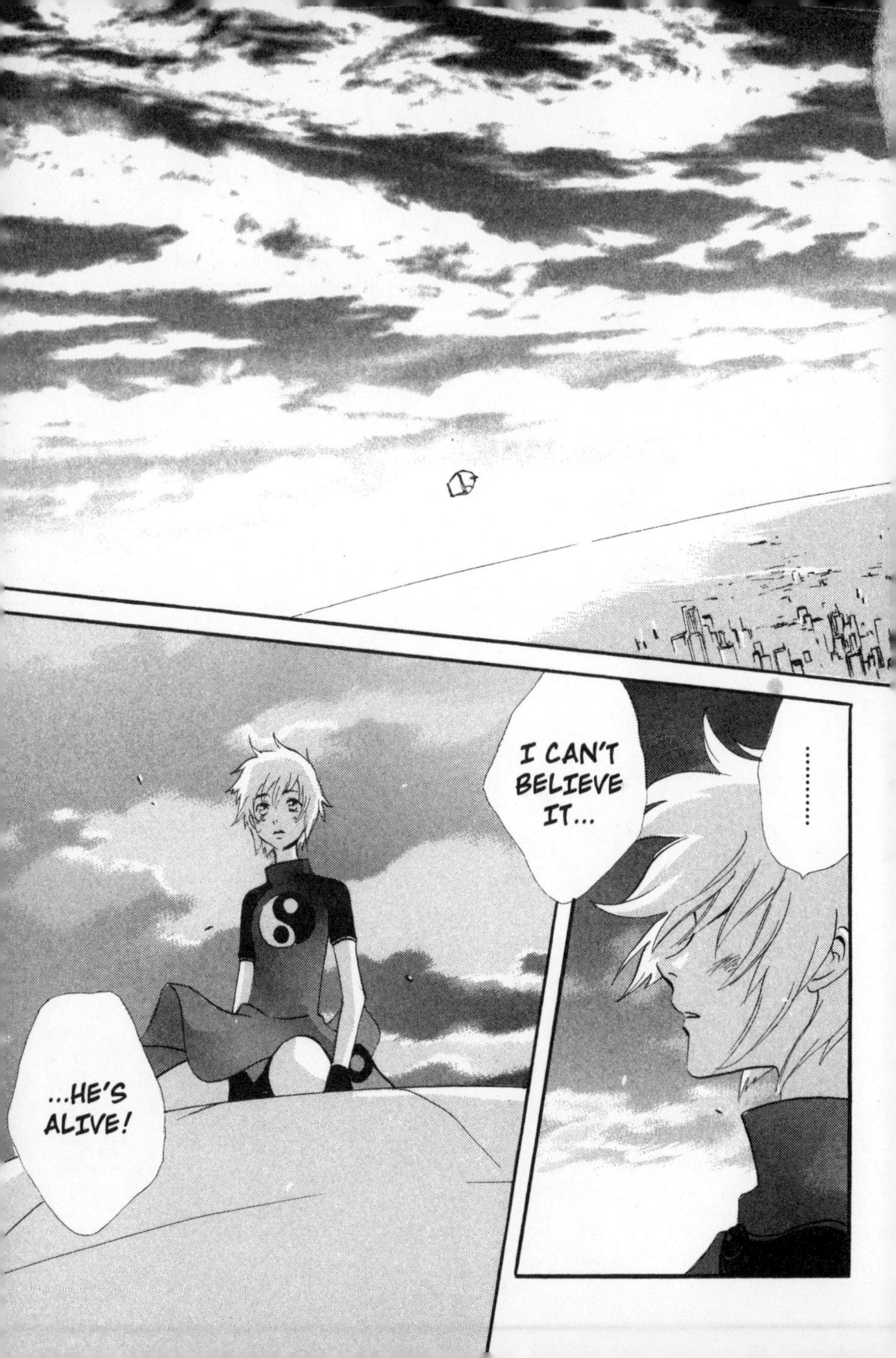
......
I CAN'T BELIEVE IT...
...HE'S ALIVE!

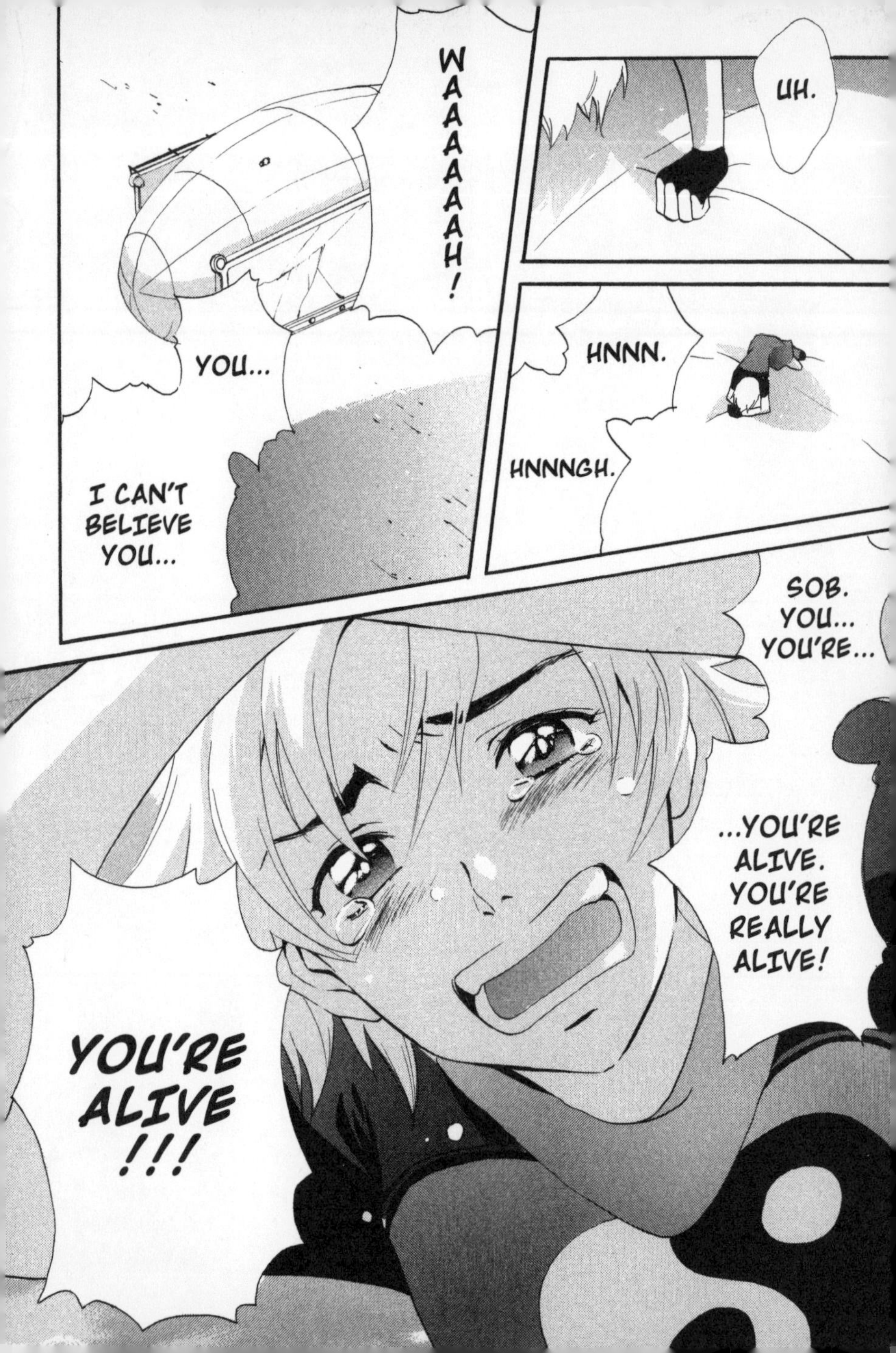
UH.
HNNN.
HNNNGH.
WAAAAAAH!
YOU...
I CAN'T BELIEVE YOU...
SOB. YOU... YOU'RE...
...YOU'RE ALIVE. YOU'RE REALLY ALIVE!
YOU'RE ALIVE!!!

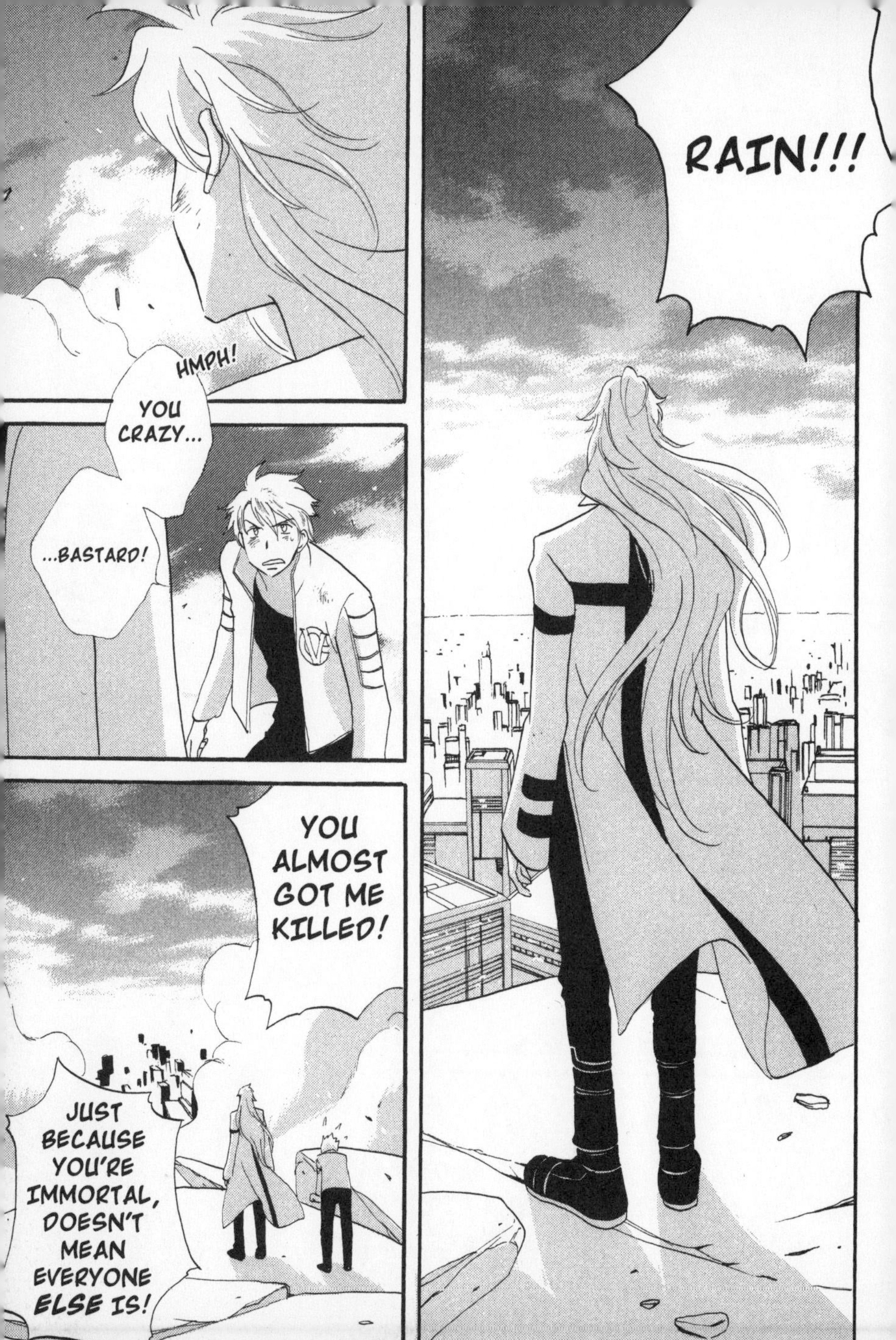
RAIN!!!
HMPH!
YOU CRAZY...
...BASTARD!
YOU ALMOST GOT ME KILLED!
JUST BECAUSE YOU'RE IMMORTAL, DOESN'T MEAN EVERYONE ELSE IS!

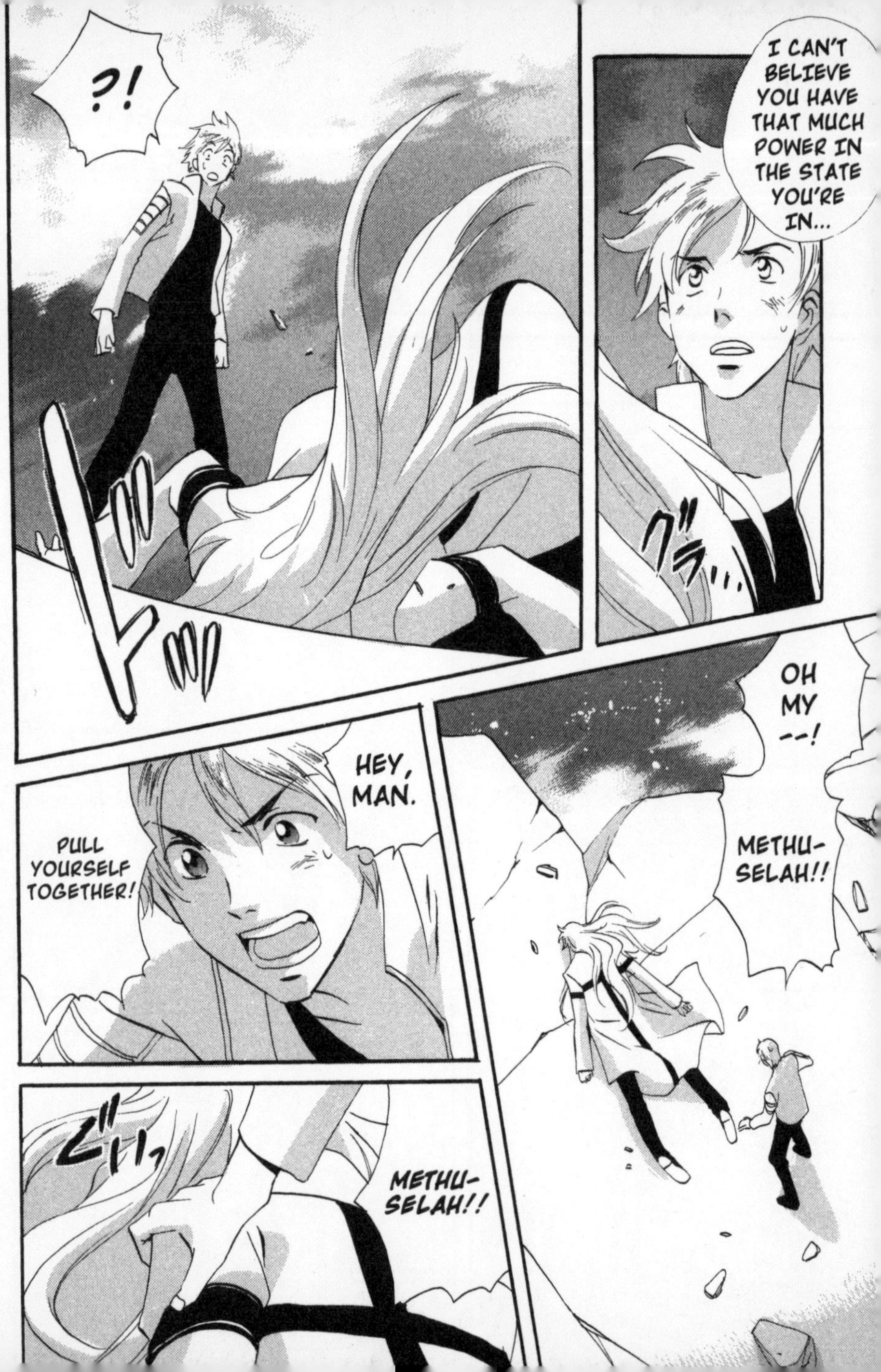
I CAN'T BELIEVE YOU HAVE THAT MUCH POWER IN THE STATE YOU'RE IN...
?!
OH MY --!
METHU-SELAH!!
HEY, MAN.
PULL YOURSELF TOGETHER!
METHU-SELAH!!

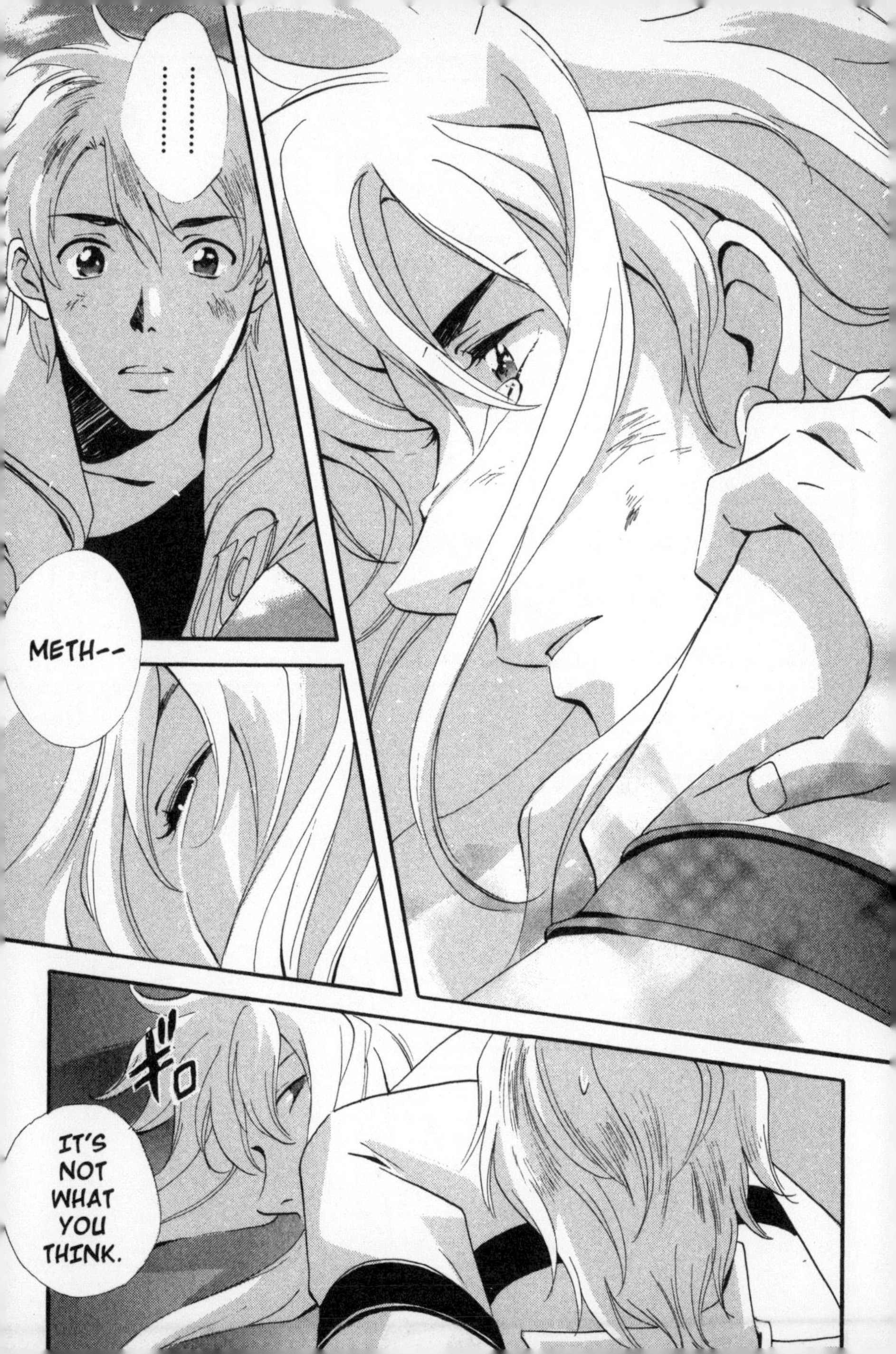
......
METH--
ギロ
IT'S NOT WHAT YOU THINK.

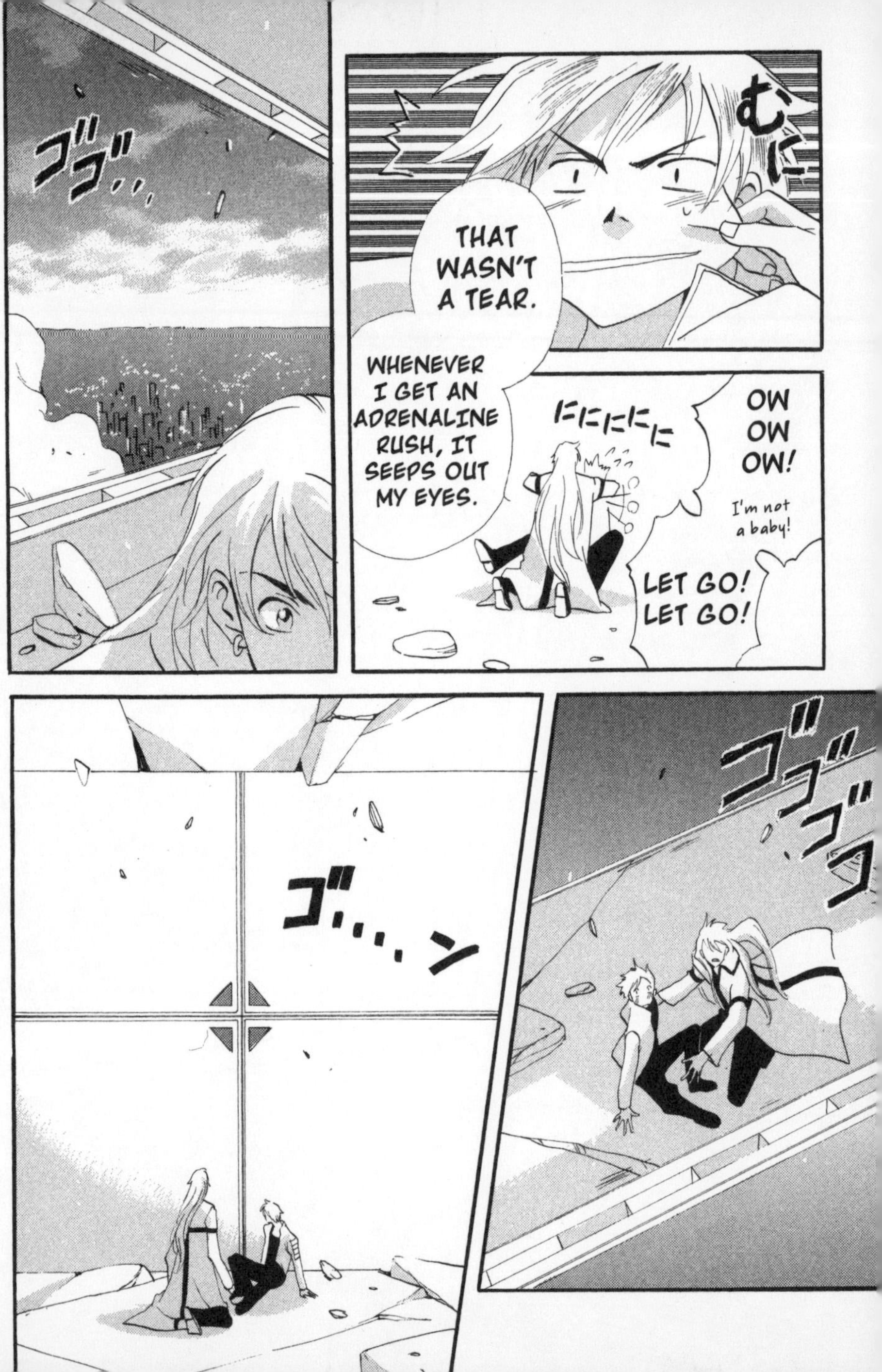
むに
THAT WASN'T A TEAR.
WHENEVER I GET AN ADRENALINE RUSH, IT SEEPS OUT MY EYES.
にににに
OW OW OW!
I'm not a baby!
LET GO! LET GO!
ゴゴ…
ゴゴゴゴ
ゴ…ン

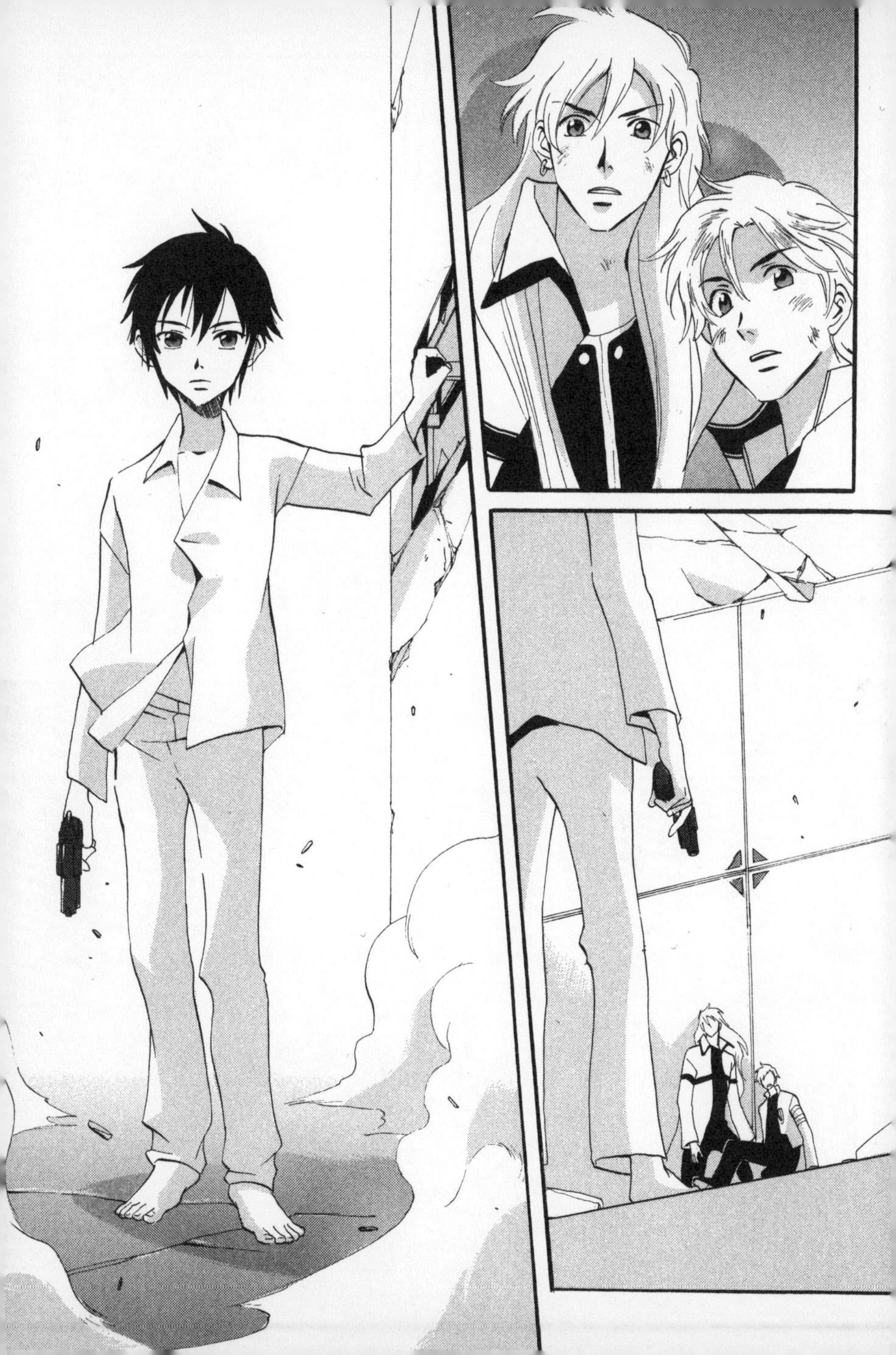

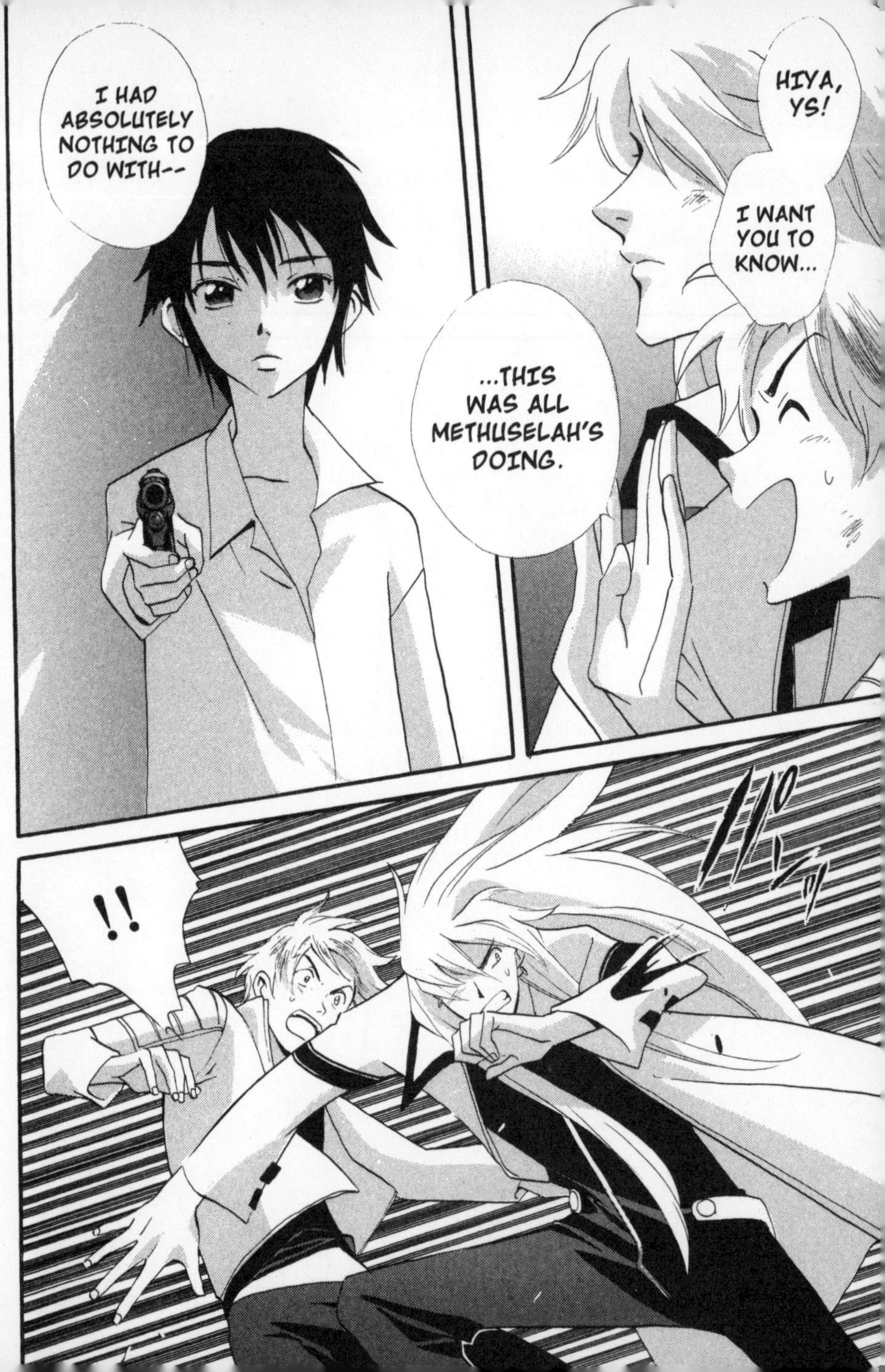
HIYA, YS!
I WANT YOU TO KNOW...
...THIS WAS ALL METHUSELAH'S DOING.
I HAD ABSOLUTELY NOTHING TO DO WITH--
!!

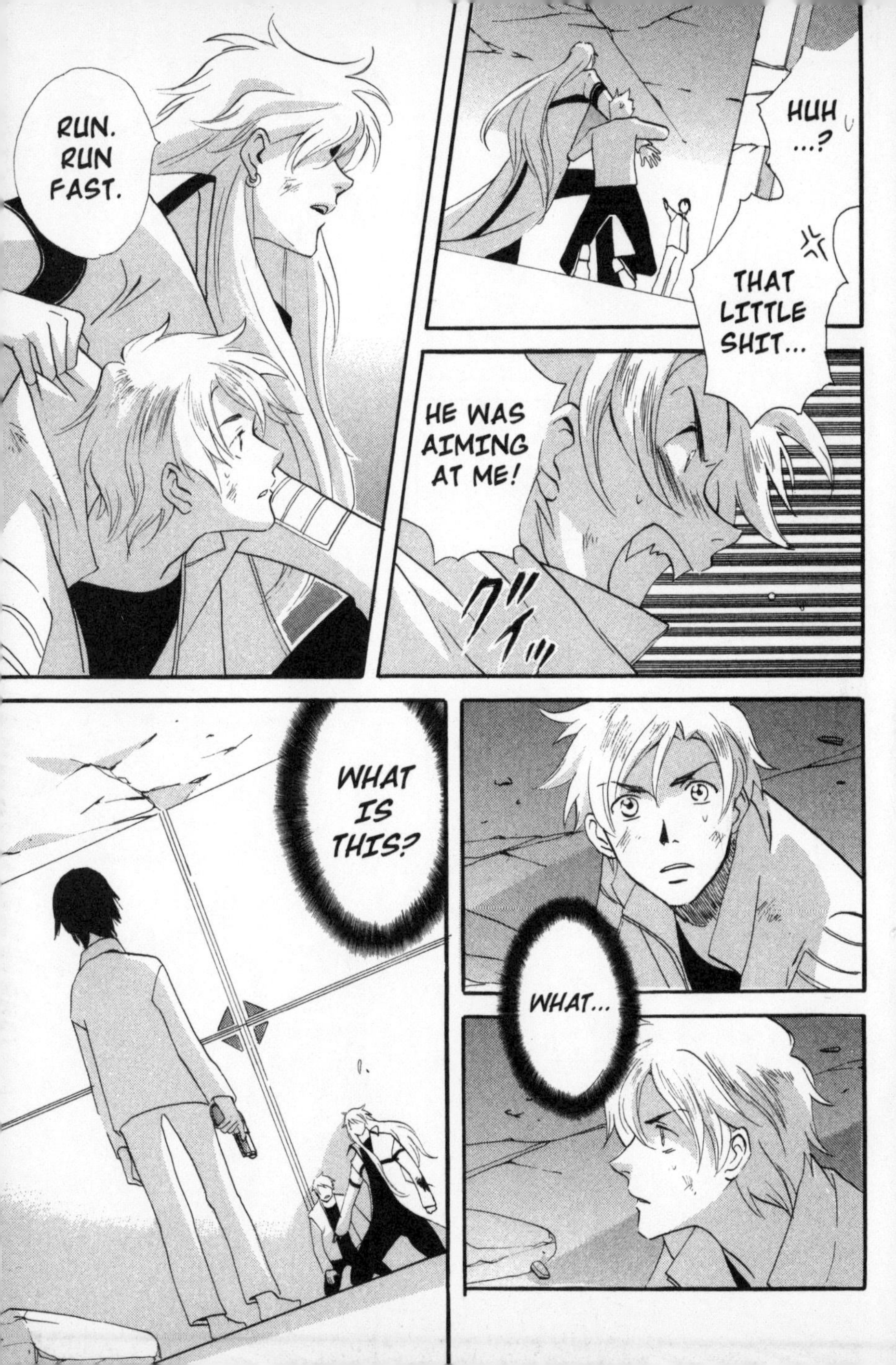
HUH ...?
THAT LITTLE SHIT...
HE WAS AIMING AT ME!
グイッ
RUN. RUN FAST.
WHAT...
WHAT IS THIS?

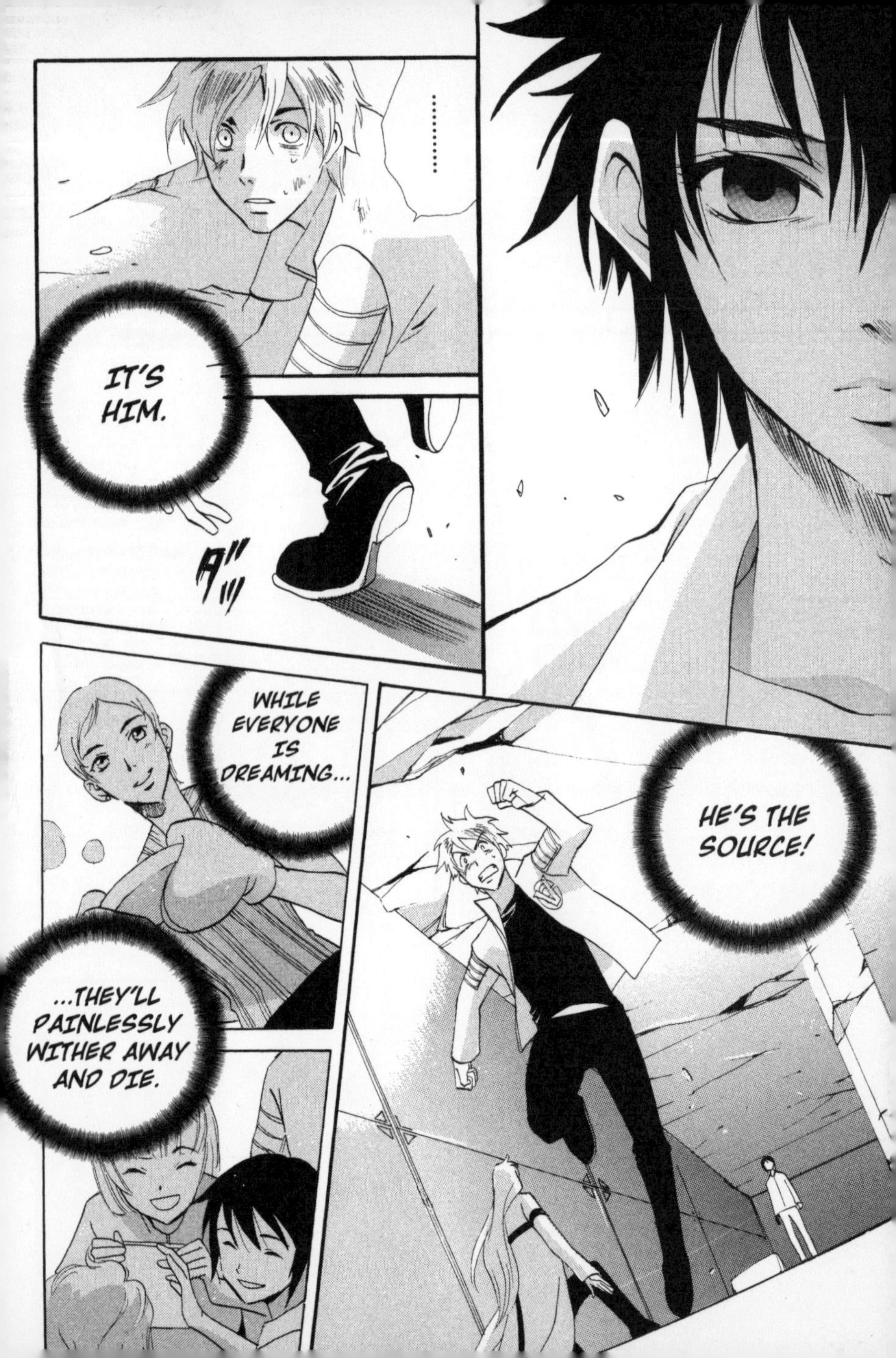
......
IT'S HIM.
ダッ
HE'S THE SOURCE!
WHILE EVERYONE IS DREAMING...
...THEY'LL PAINLESSLY WITHER AWAY AND DIE.

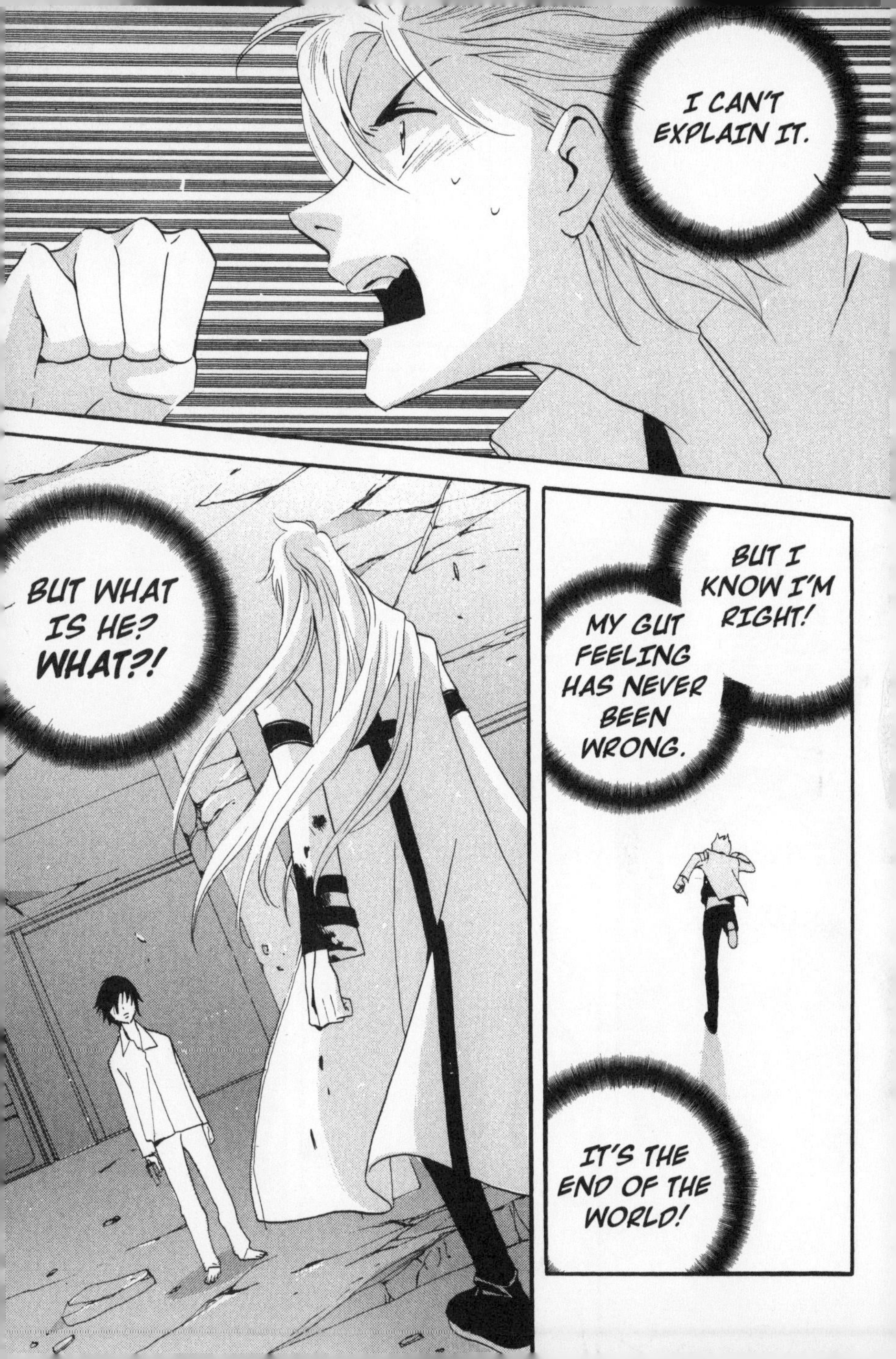
I CAN'T EXPLAIN IT.
BUT I KNOW I'M RIGHT!
MY GUT FEELING HAS NEVER BEEN WRONG.
IT'S THE END OF THE WORLD!
BUT WHAT IS HE? WHAT?!

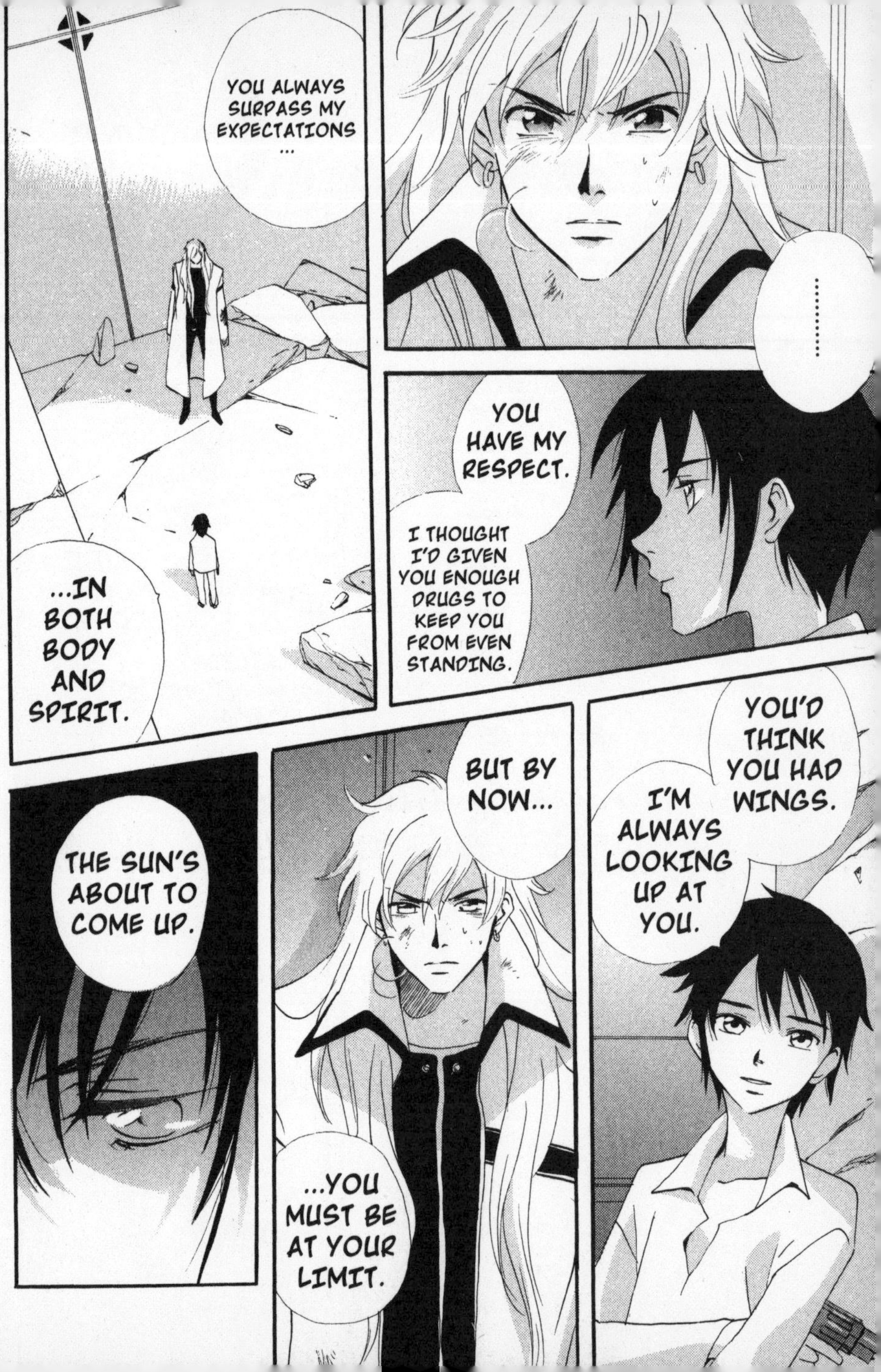
YOU ALWAYS SURPASS MY EXPECTATIONS ...
...IN BOTH BODY AND SPIRIT.
......
YOU HAVE MY RESPECT.
I THOUGHT I'D GIVEN YOU ENOUGH DRUGS TO KEEP YOU FROM EVEN STANDING.
YOU'D THINK YOU HAD WINGS.
I'M ALWAYS LOOKING UP AT YOU.
BUT BY NOW...
...YOU MUST BE AT YOUR LIMIT.
THE SUN'S ABOUT TO COME UP.

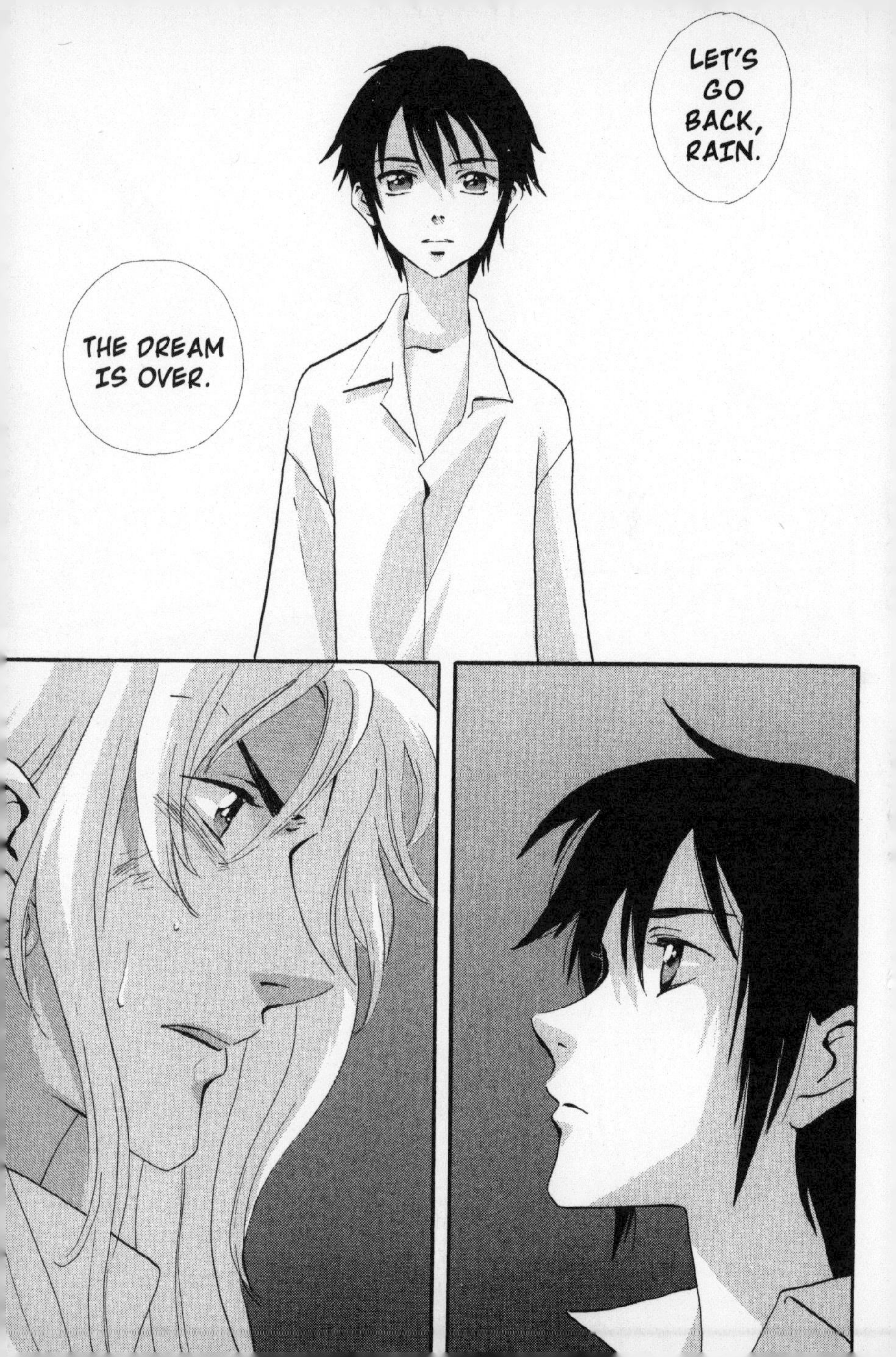
LET'S GO BACK, RAIN.
THE DREAM IS OVER.

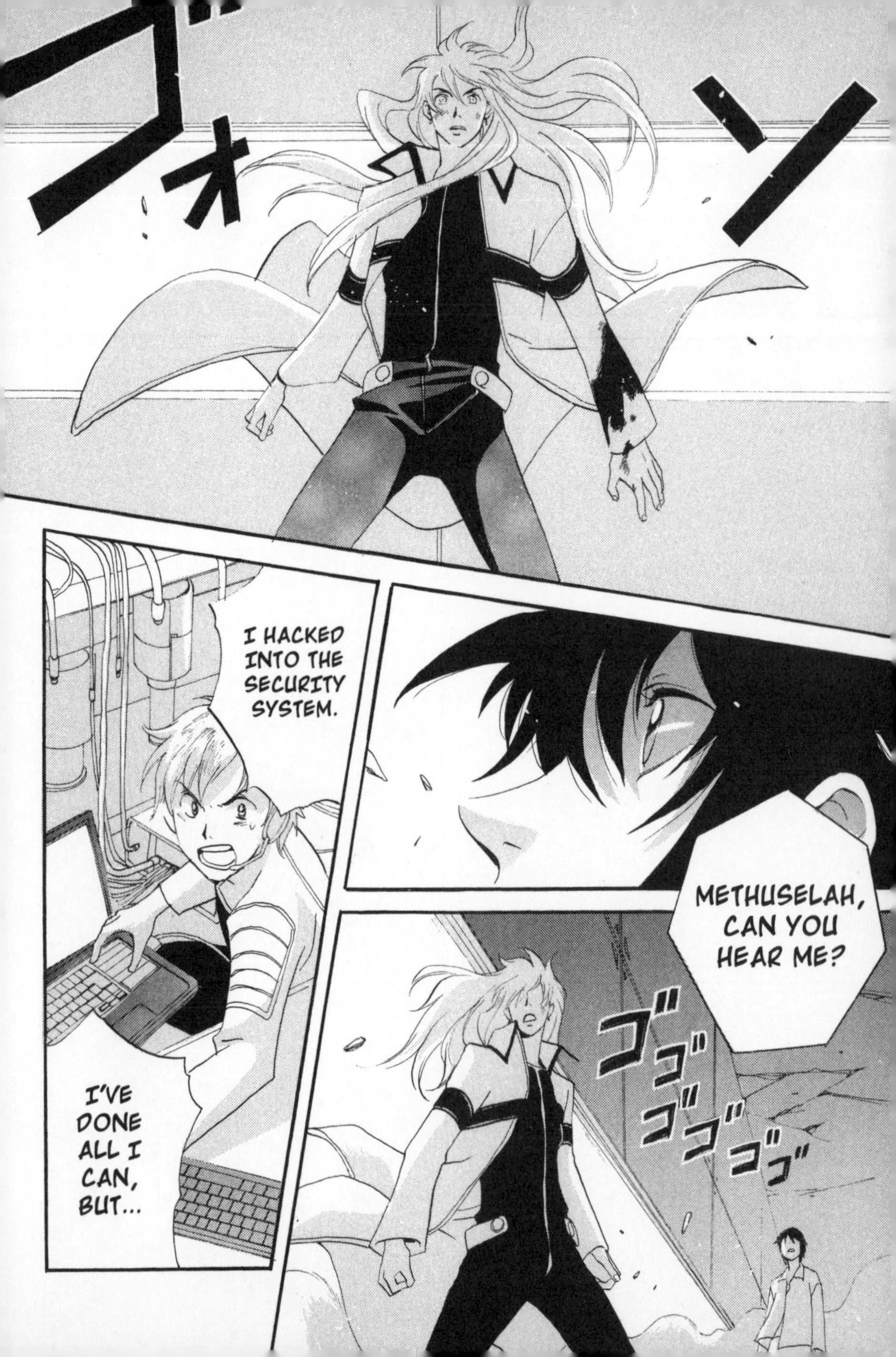
ゴオン
I HACKED INTO THE SECURITY SYSTEM.
I'VE DONE ALL I CAN, BUT...
METHUSELAH, CAN YOU HEAR ME?
ゴゴゴゴゴゴ

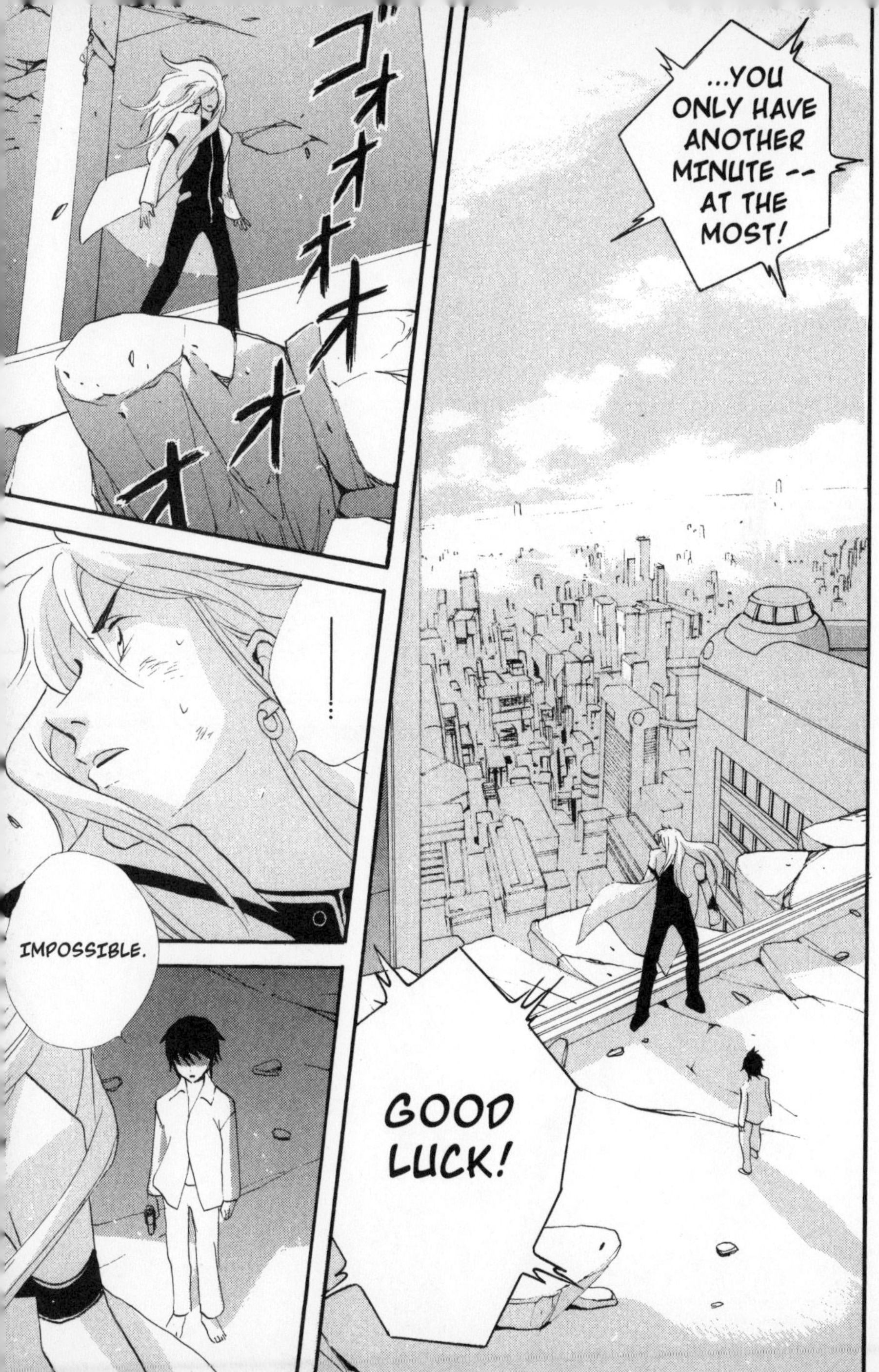
...YOU ONLY HAVE ANOTHER MINUTE -- AT THE MOST!
GOOD LUCK!
ゴオオオオオ
—...
IMPOSSIBLE.

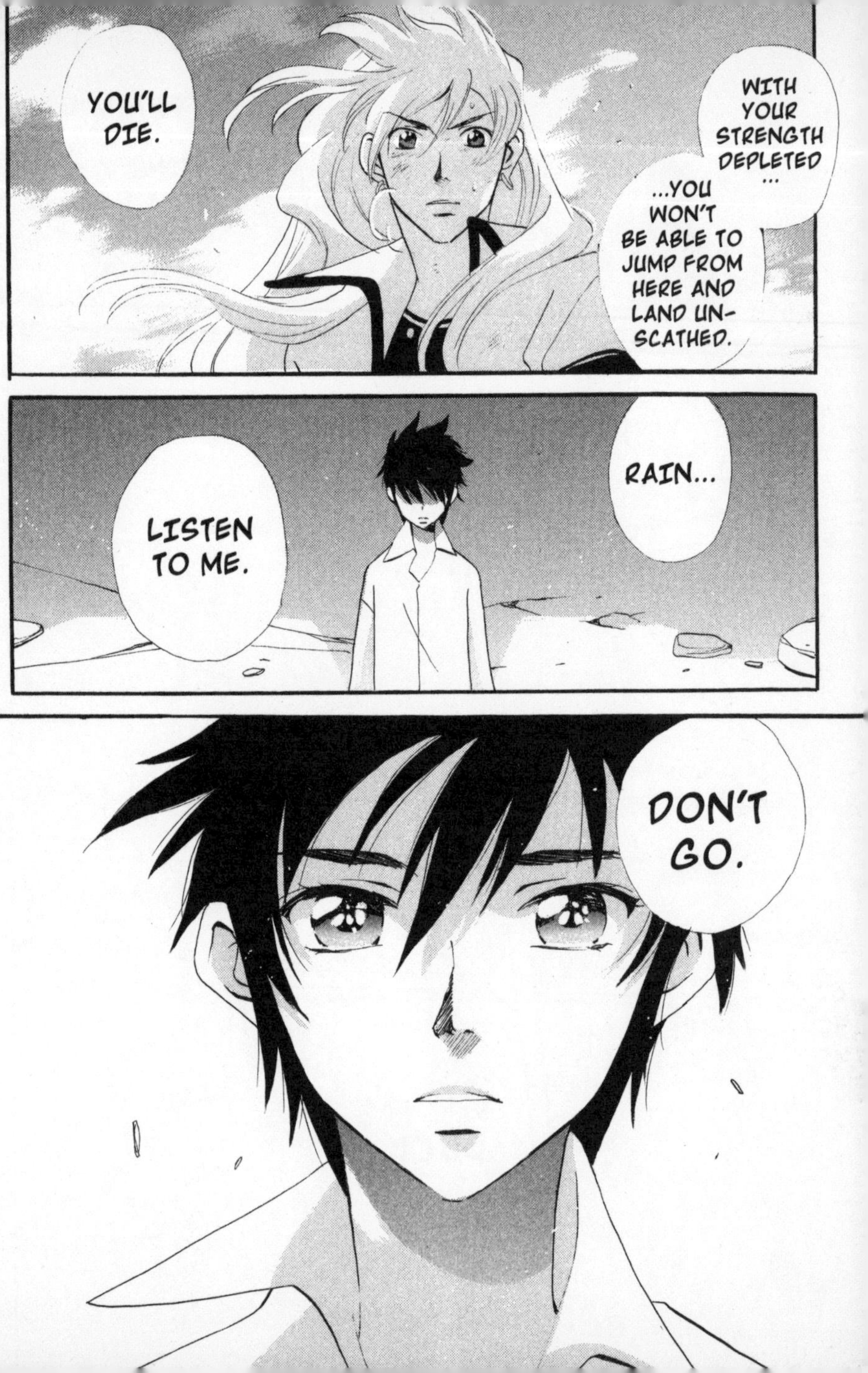
WITH YOUR STRENGTH DEPLETED...
...YOU WON'T BE ABLE TO JUMP FROM HERE AND LAND UN-SCATHED.
YOU'LL DIE.
RAIN...
LISTEN TO ME.
DON'T GO.

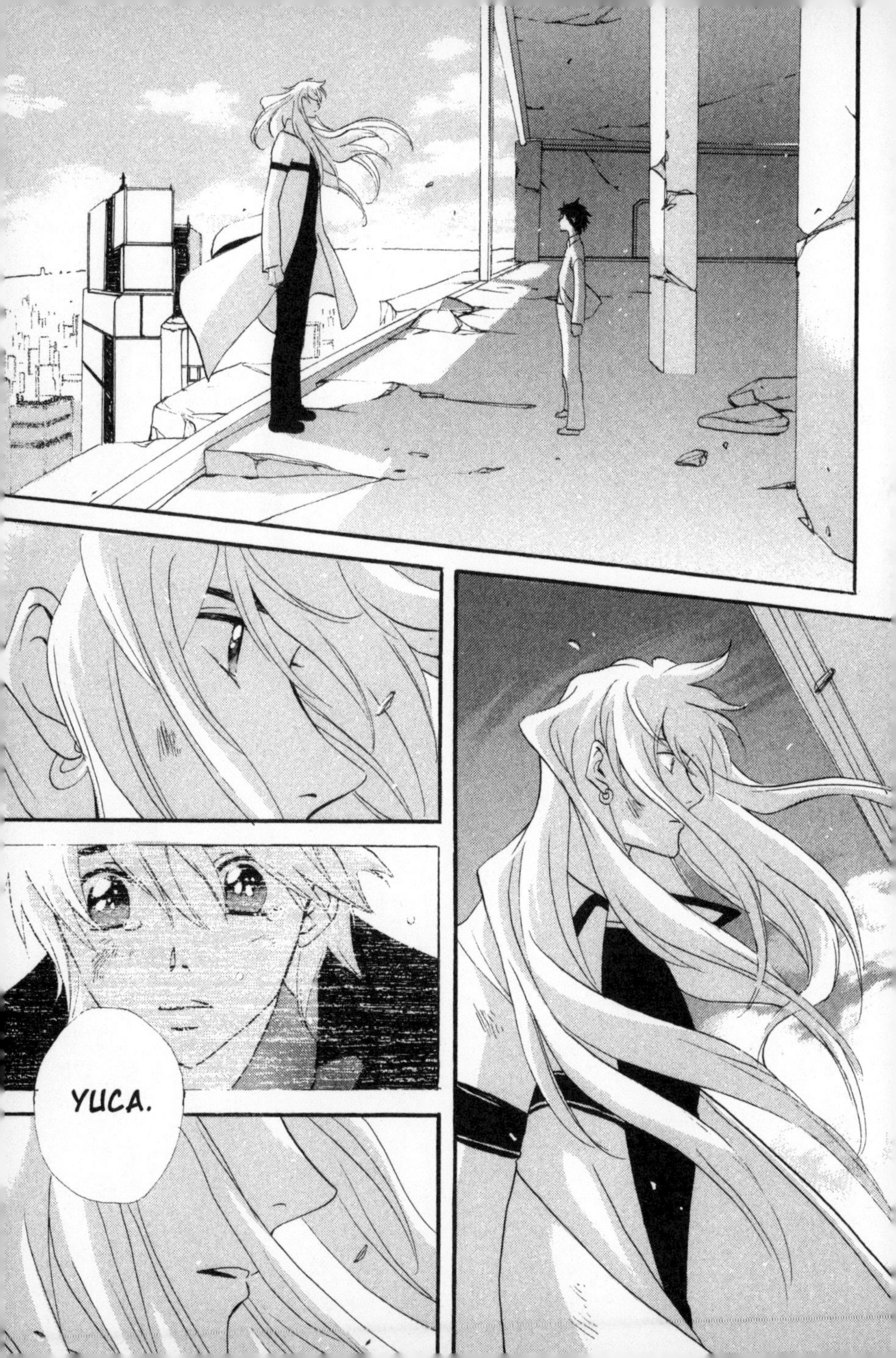
YUCA.

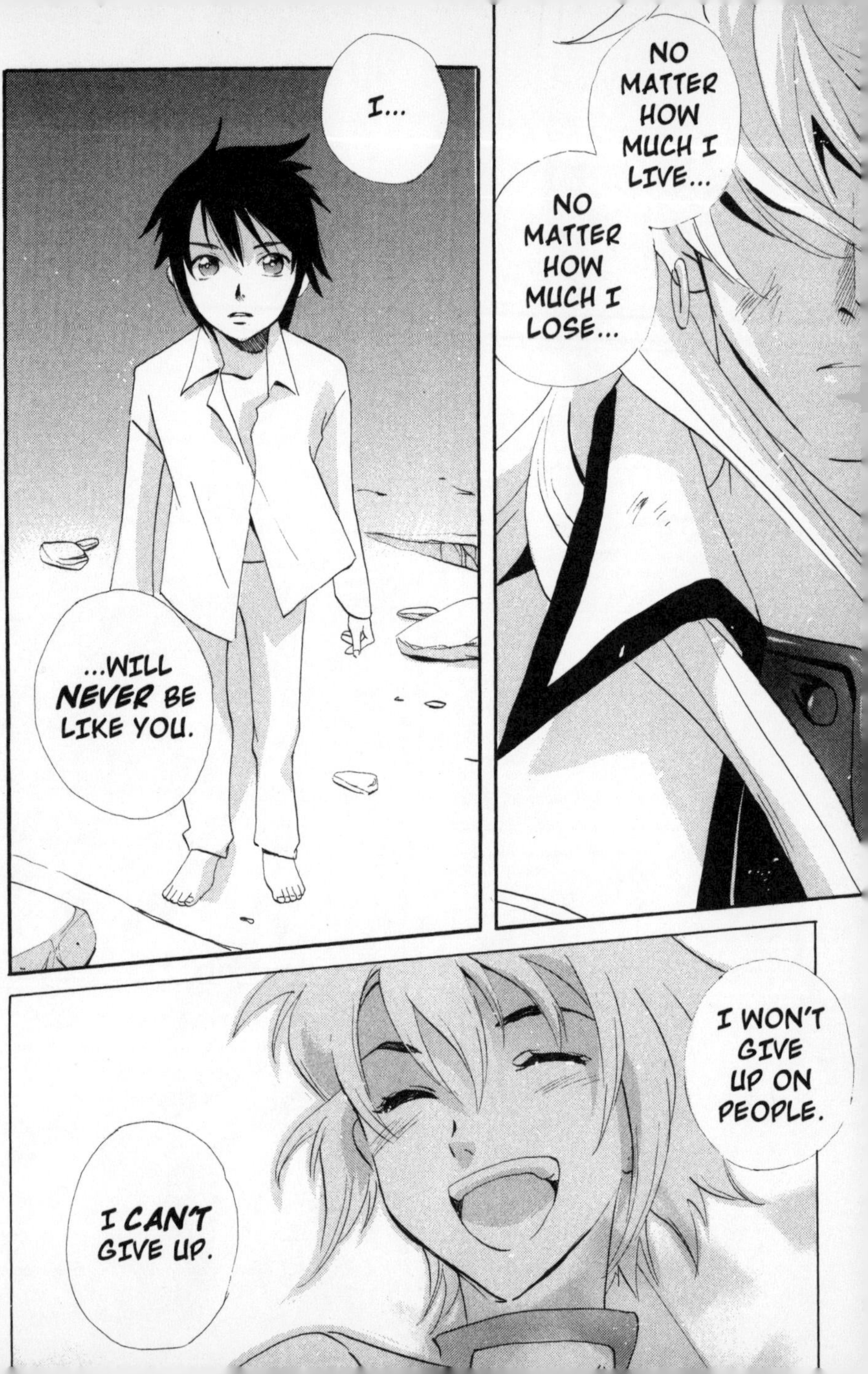
NO MATTER HOW MUCH I LIVE...
NO MATTER HOW MUCH I LOSE...
I...
...WILL NEVER BE LIKE YOU.
I WON'T GIVE UP ON PEOPLE.
I CAN'T GIVE UP.

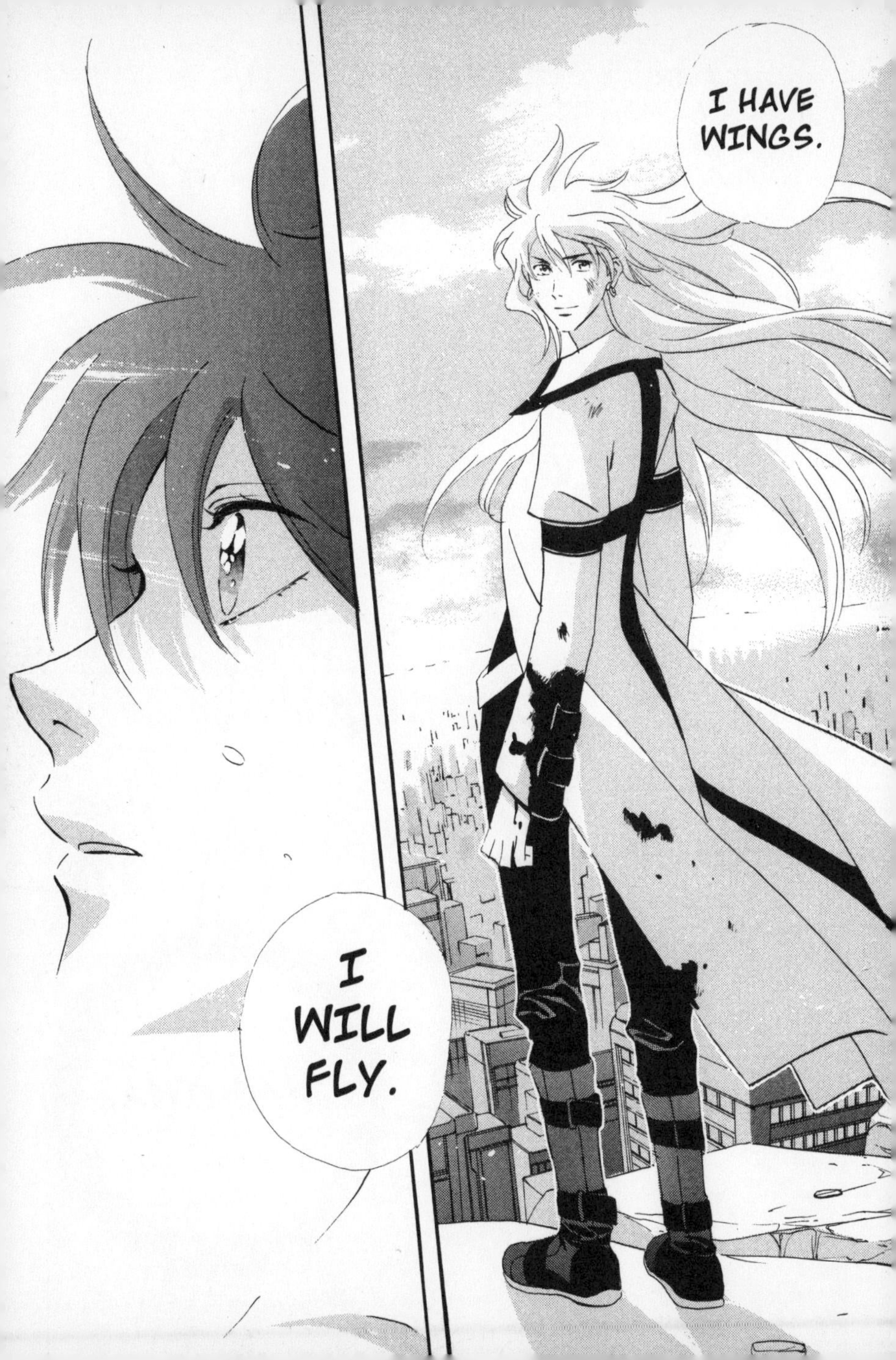
I HAVE WINGS.
I WILL FLY.

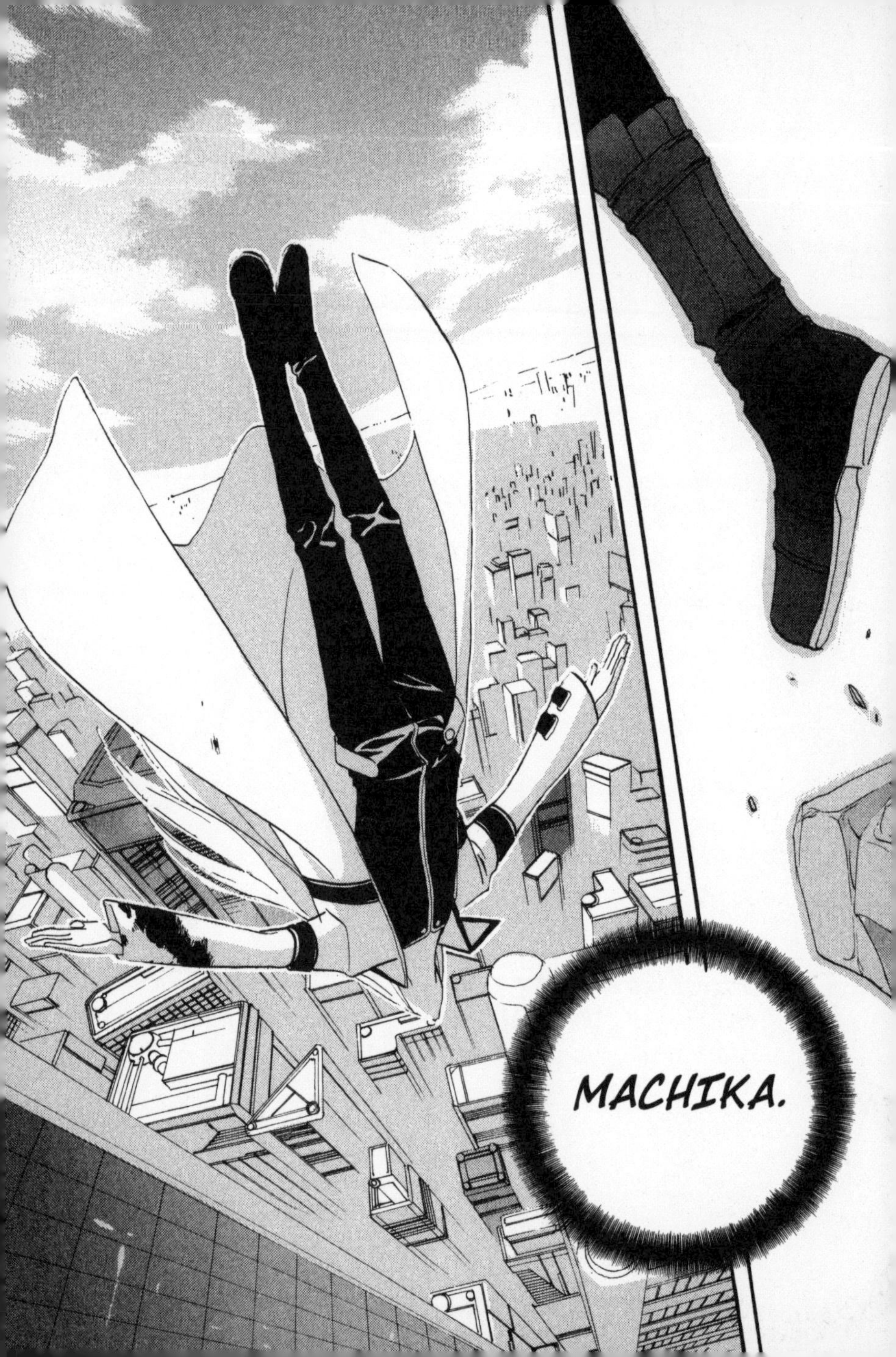
MACHIKA.

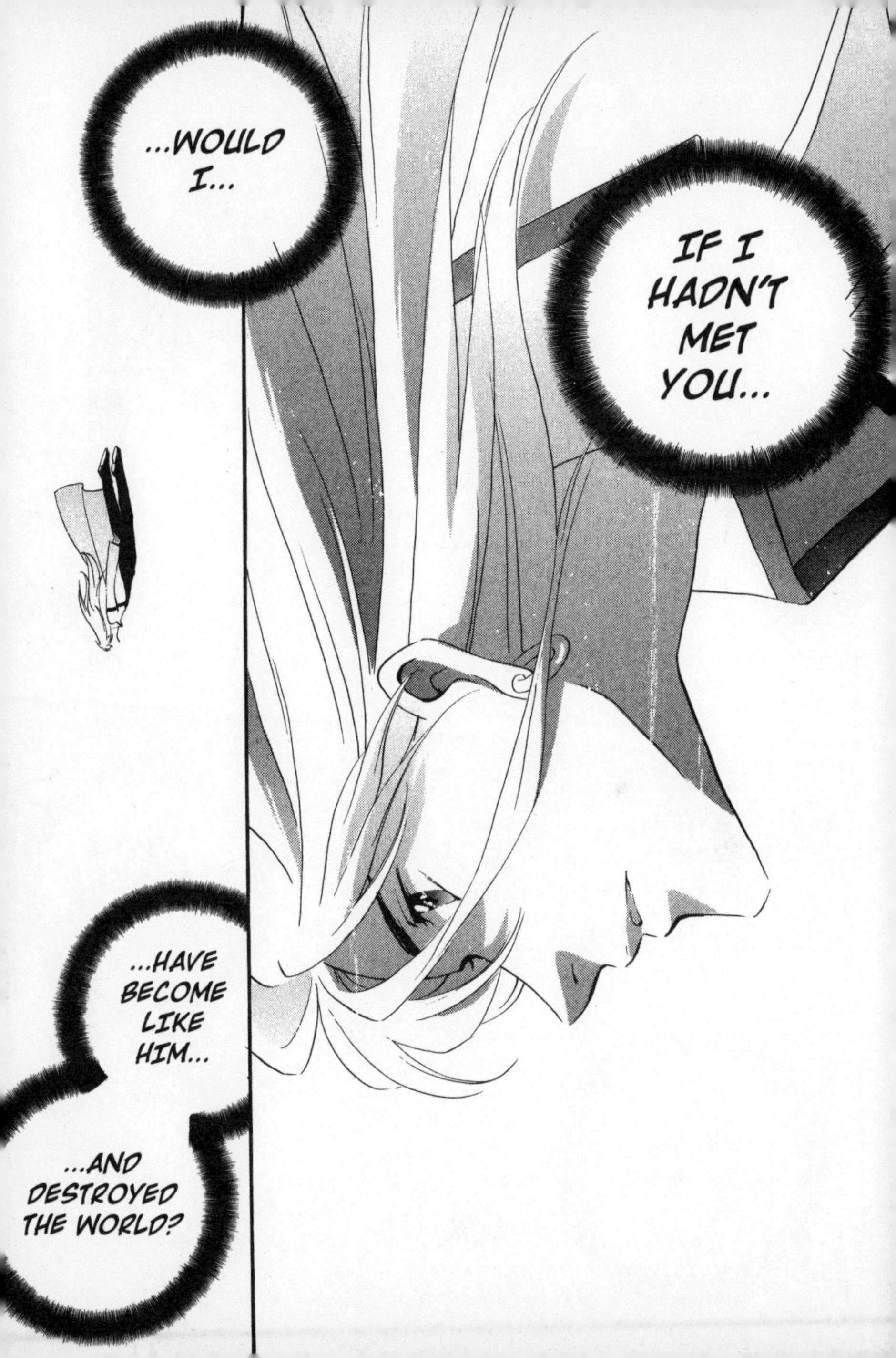
IF I HADN'T MET YOU...
...WOULD I...
...HAVE BECOME LIKE HIM...
...AND DESTROYED THE WORLD?

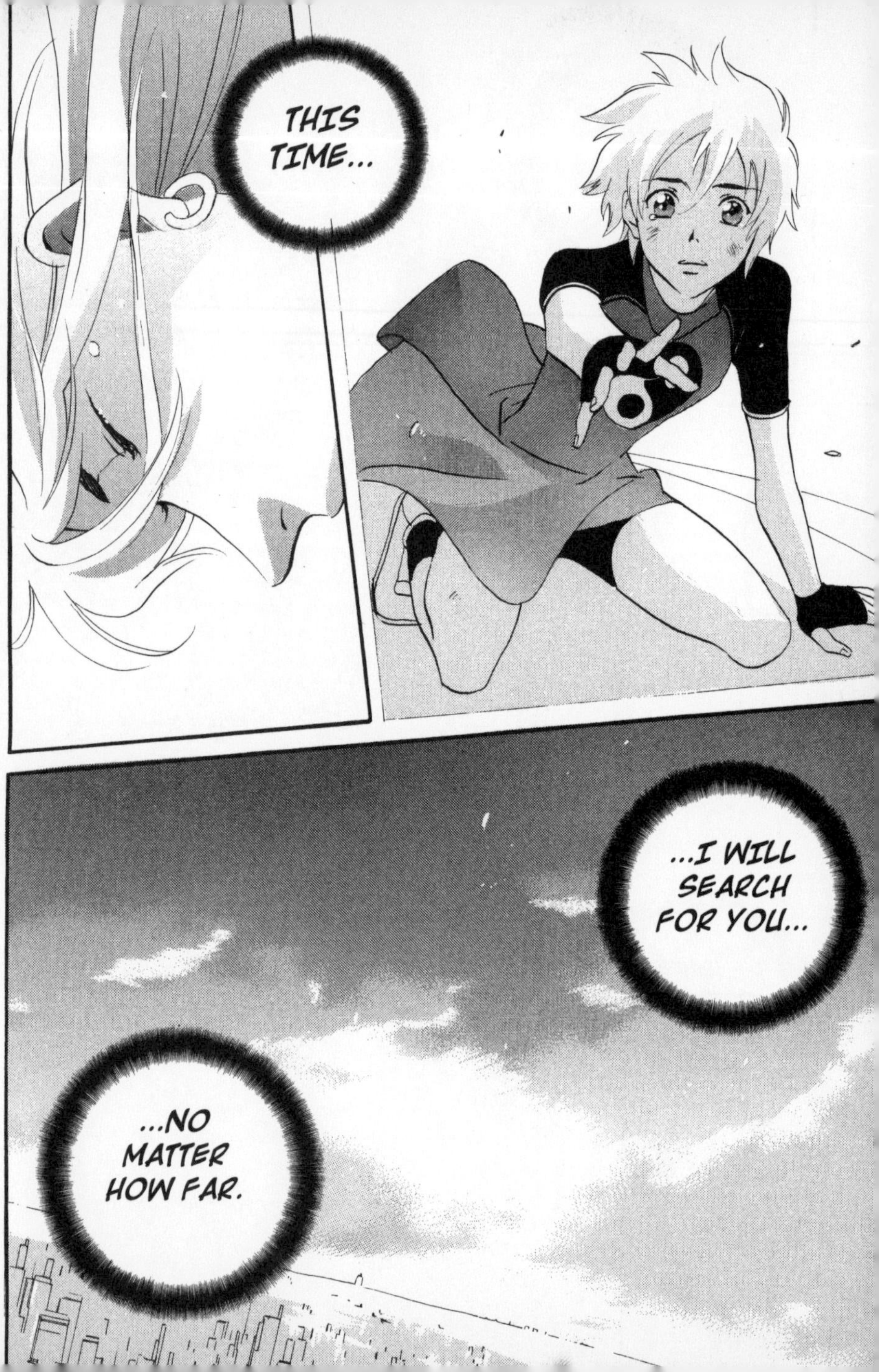
THIS TIME...
...I WILL SEARCH FOR YOU...
...NO MATTER HOW FAR.

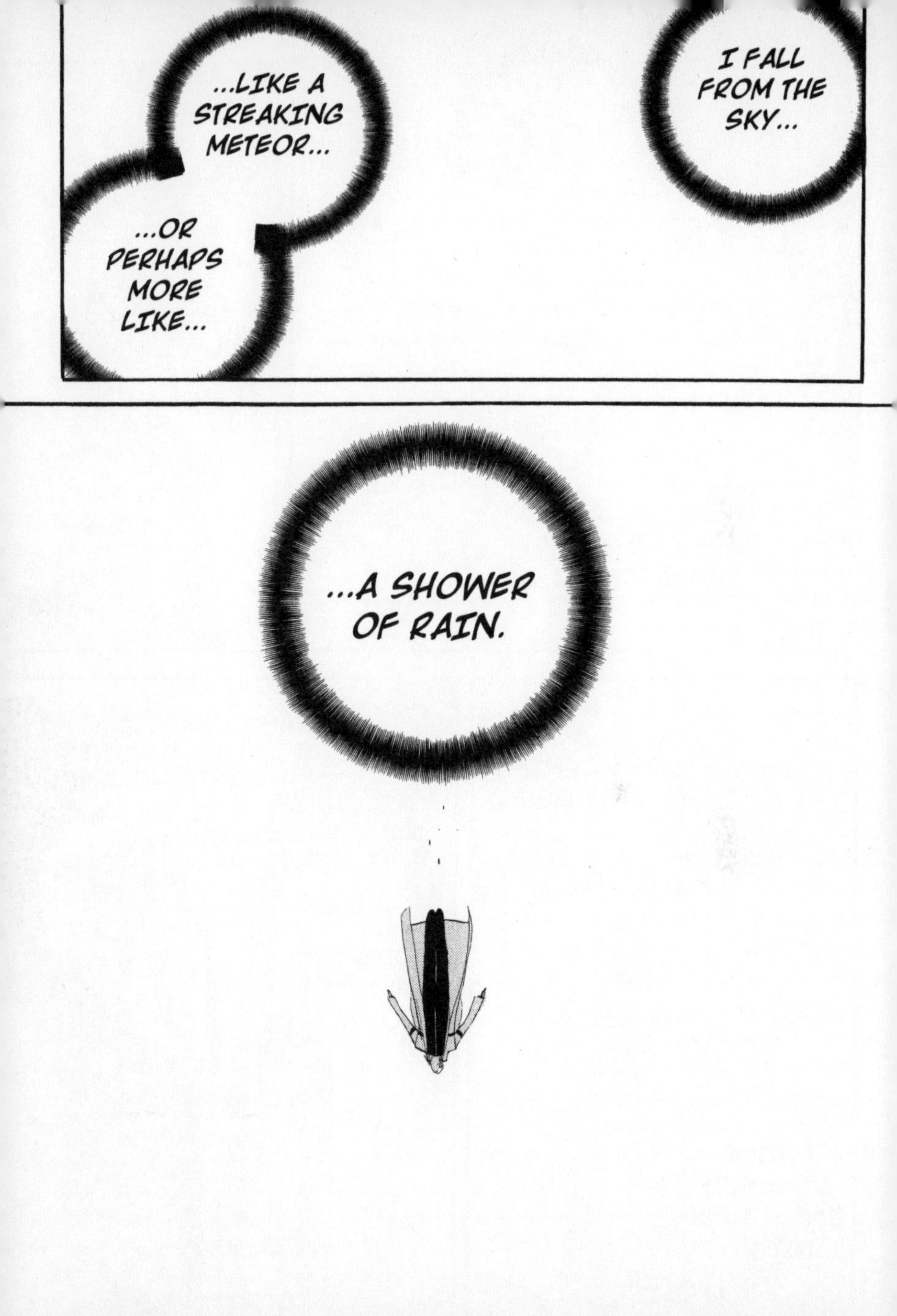
I FALL FROM THE SKY...
...LIKE A STREAKING METEOR...
...OR PERHAPS MORE LIKE...
...A SHOWER OF RAIN.

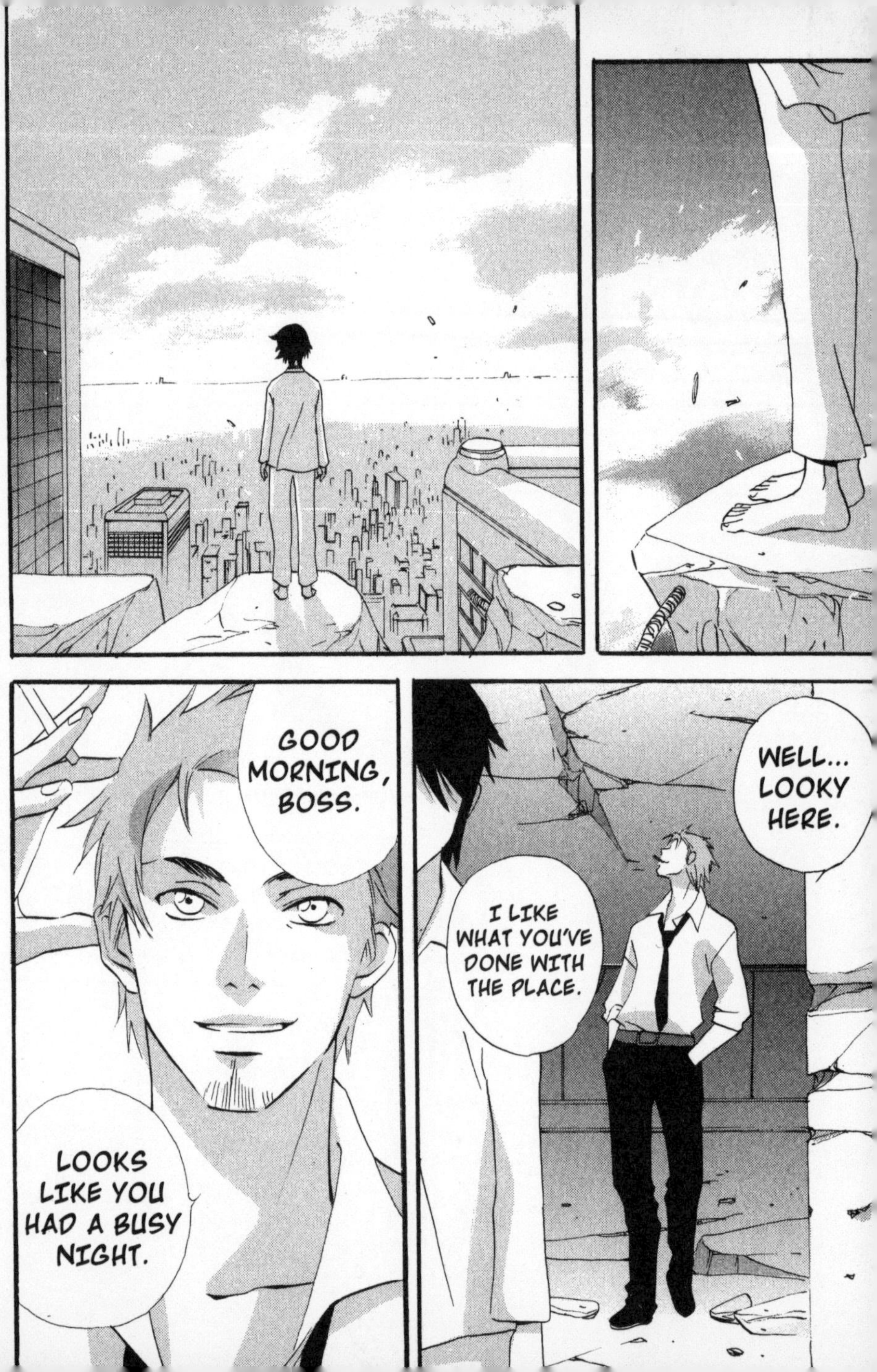
WELL... LOOKY HERE.
I LIKE WHAT YOU'VE DONE WITH THE PLACE.
GOOD MORNING, BOSS.
LOOKS LIKE YOU HAD A BUSY NIGHT.

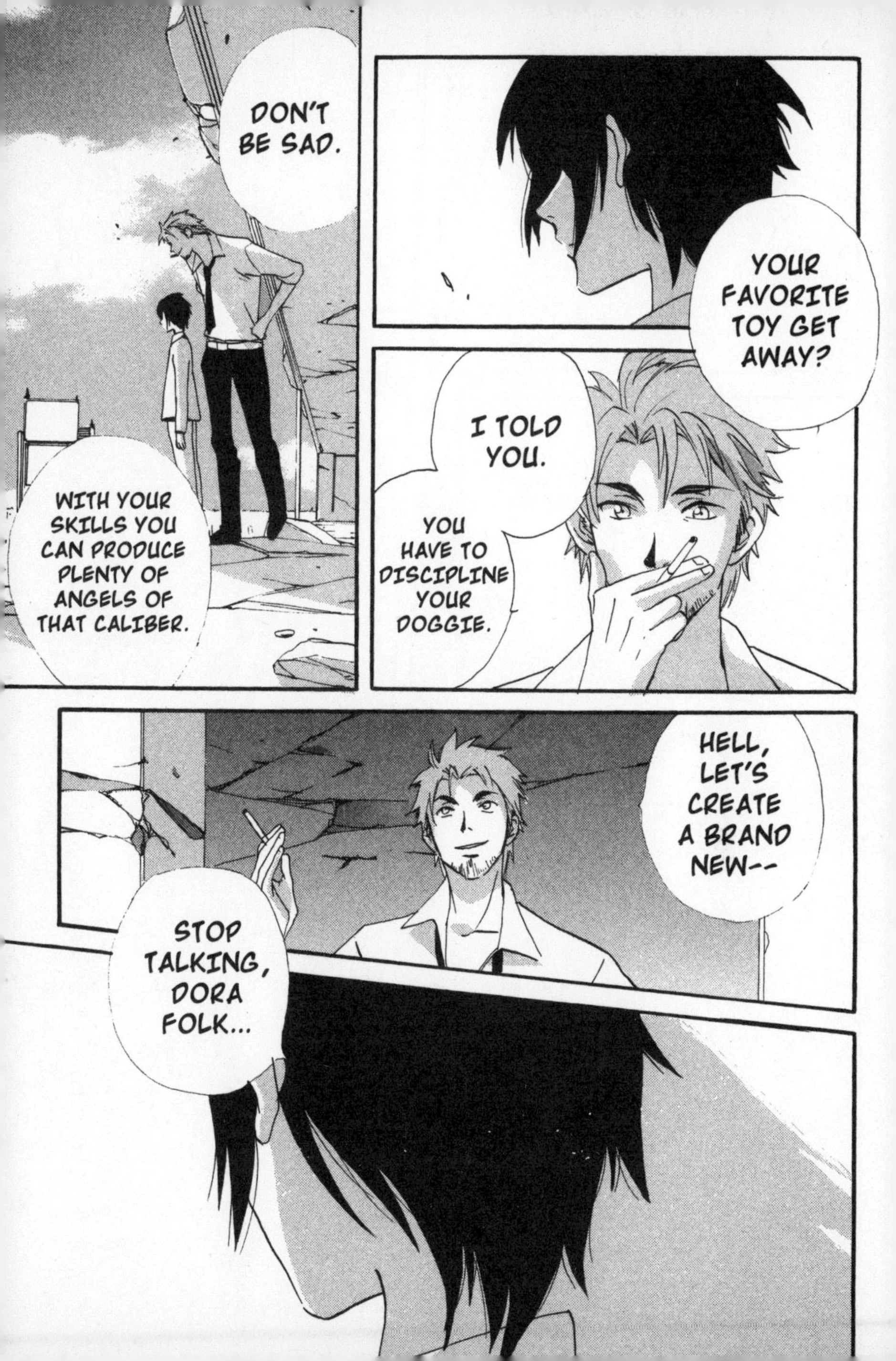
YOUR FAVORITE TOY GET AWAY?
I TOLD YOU.
YOU HAVE TO DISCIPLINE YOUR DOGGIE.
DON'T BE SAD.
WITH YOUR SKILLS YOU CAN PRODUCE PLENTY OF ANGELS OF THAT CALIBER.
HELL, LET'S CREATE A BRAND NEW--
STOP TALKING, DORA FOLK...

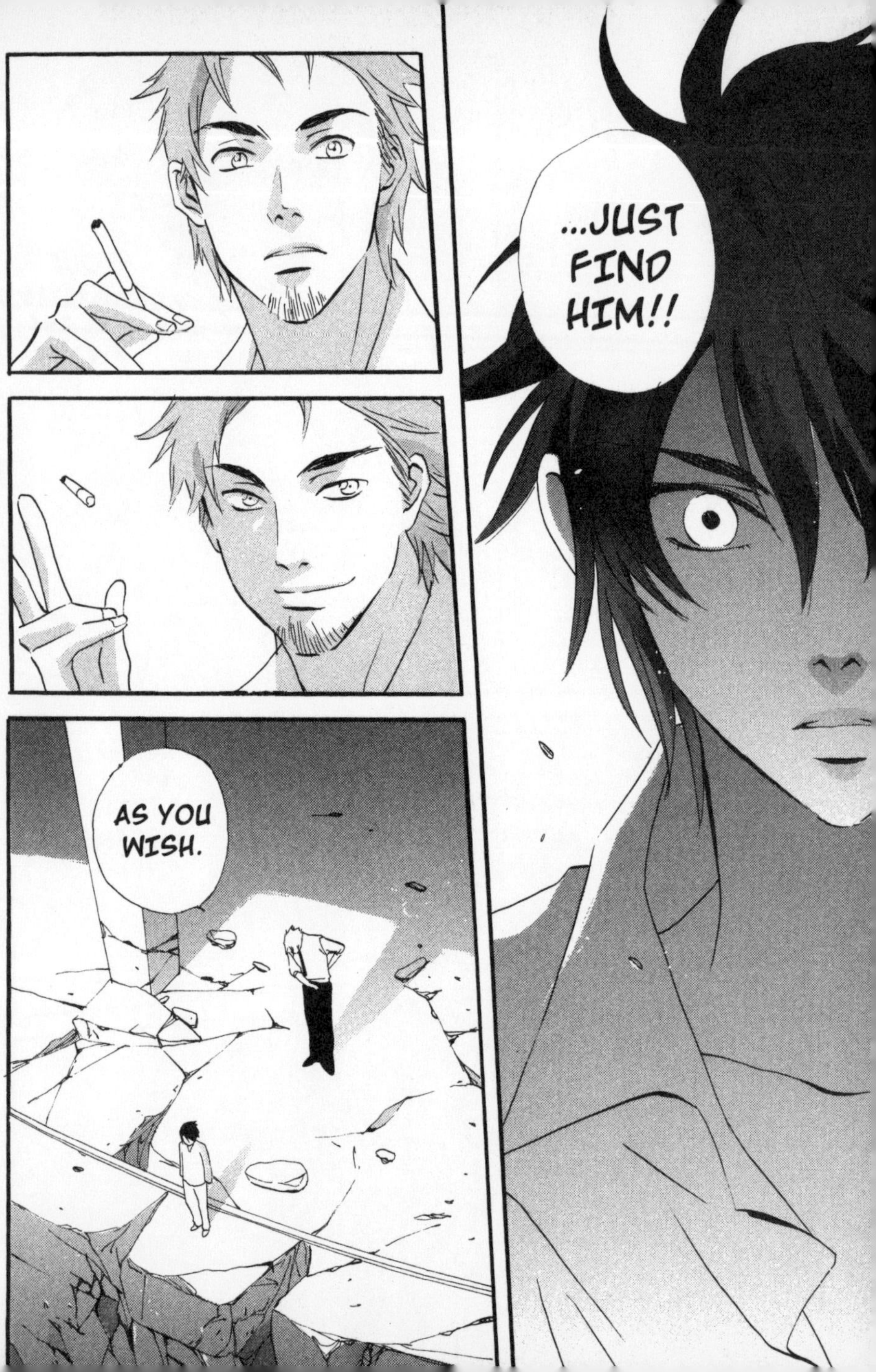
...JUST FIND HIM!!
AS YOU WISH.

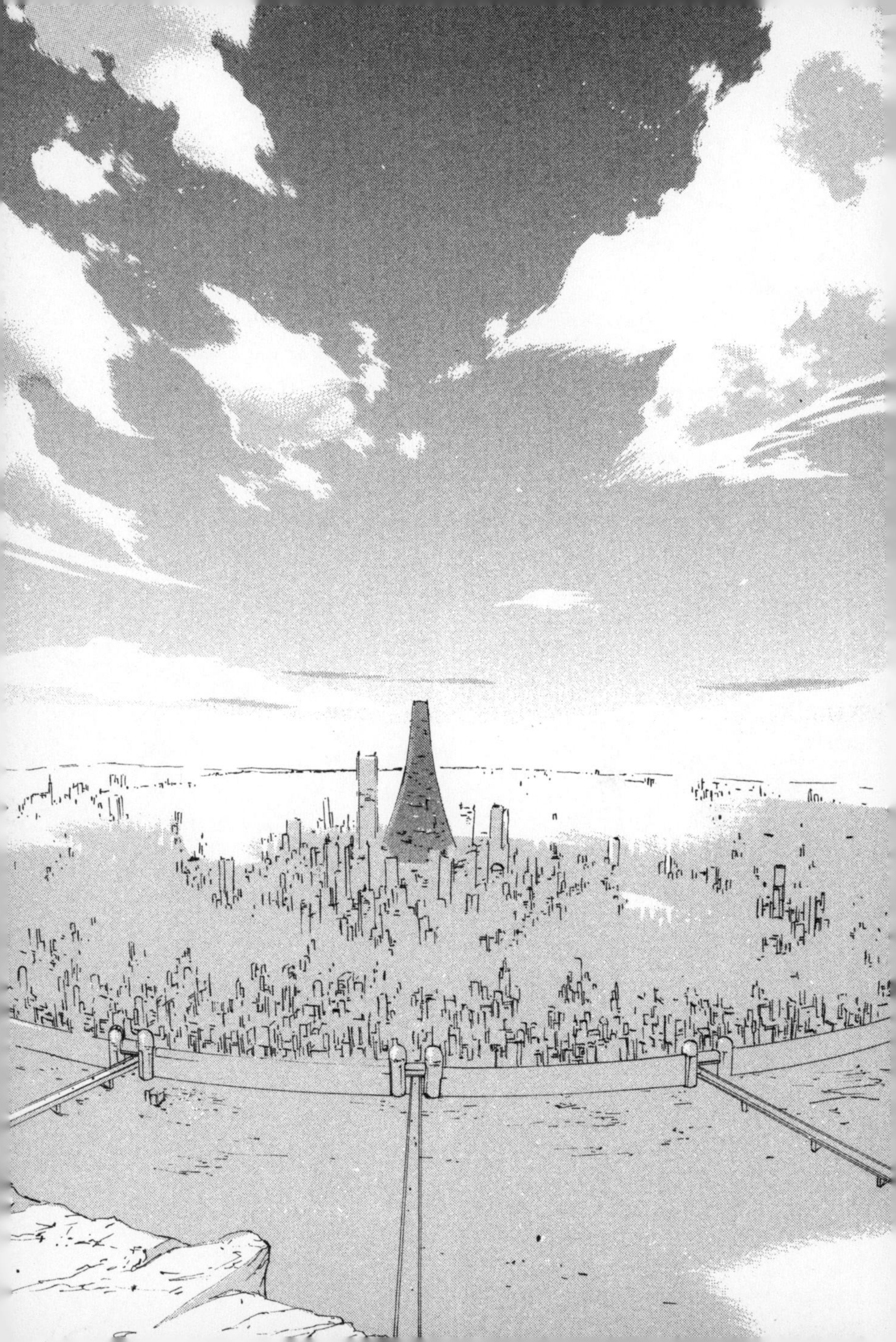

Back Stage Mini

Oyaji and Nekomimi

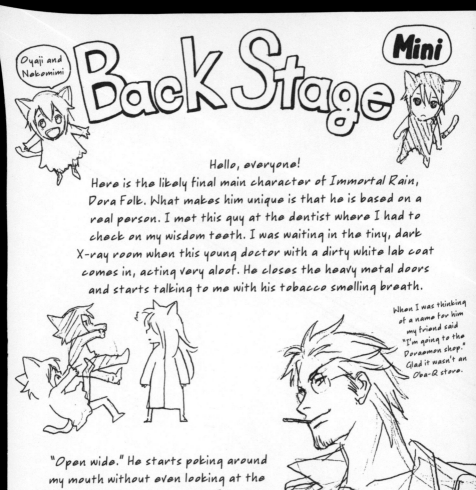

Hello, everyone!

Here is the likely final main character of Immortal Rain, Dora Folk. What makes him unique is that he is based on a real person. I met this guy at the dentist where I had to check on my wisdom teeth. I was waiting in the tiny, dark X-ray room when this young doctor with a dirty white lab coat comes in, acting very aloof. He closes the heavy metal doors and starts talking to me with his tobacco smelling breath.

When I was thinking of a name for him my friend said "I'm going to the Doraemon shop." Glad it wasn't an Oba-Q store.

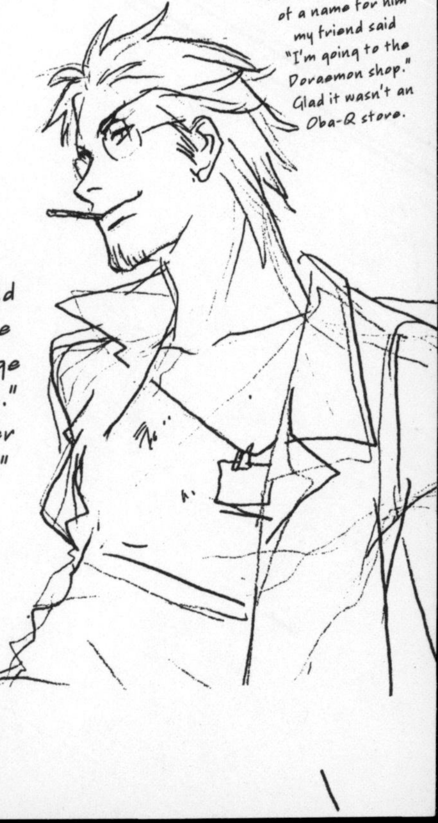

"Open wide." He starts poking around my mouth without even looking at the X-ray. With tears in my eyes, I manage to say, "Ahhh, it won't go in anymore." He replies, "No, it'll go in much deeper or I won't be able to take them out."

It was kind of perverted...

Anyway, now my wisdom teeth look like this.

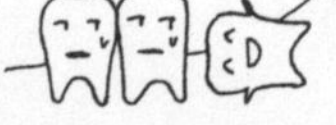

Moreover, I'm so busy I haven't had time to have them taken out. Uh, what was I talking about? Guess I better get started on the next chapter. Enjoy, see ya! - Kaori Ozaki.

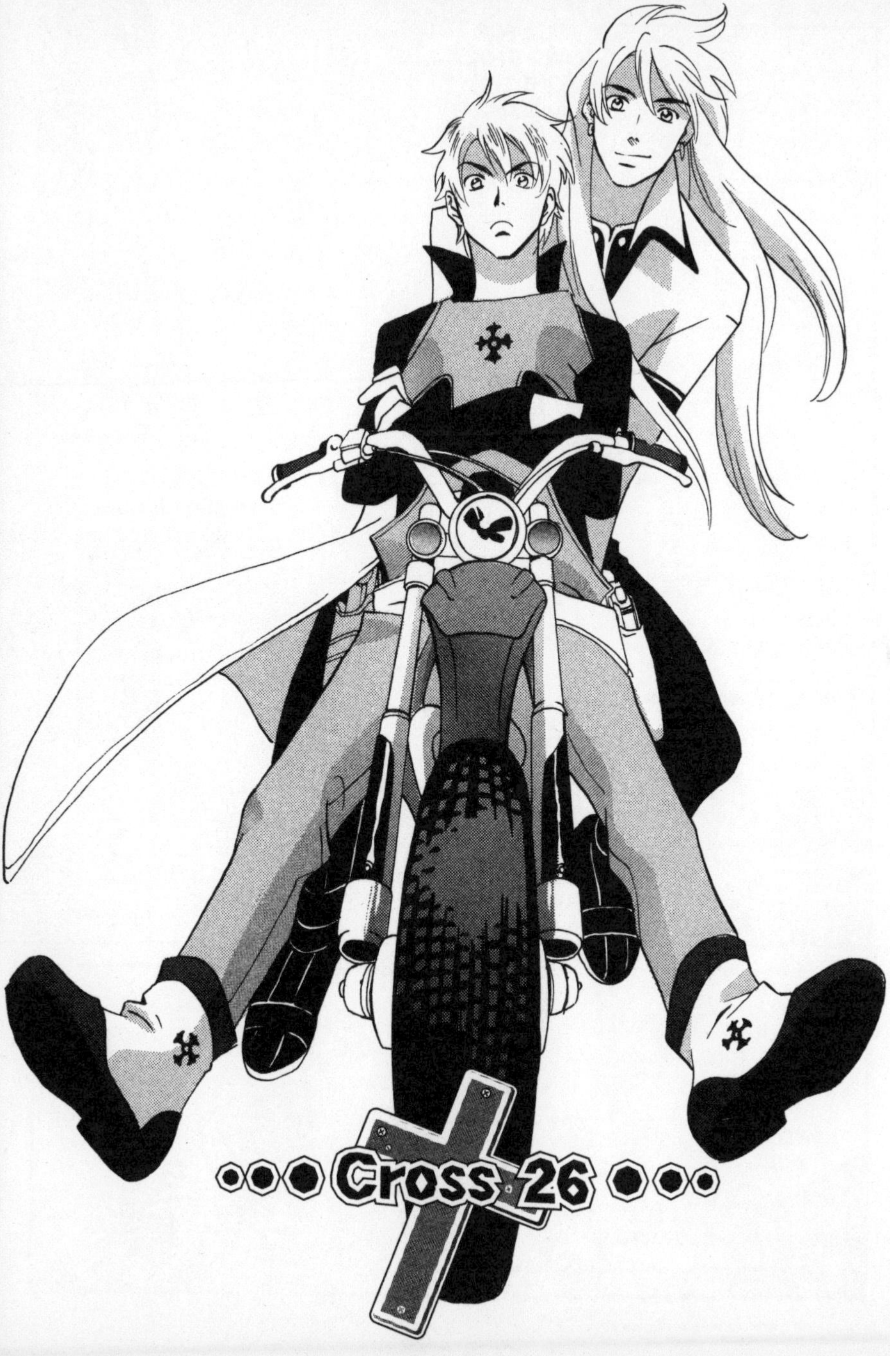
Cross 26

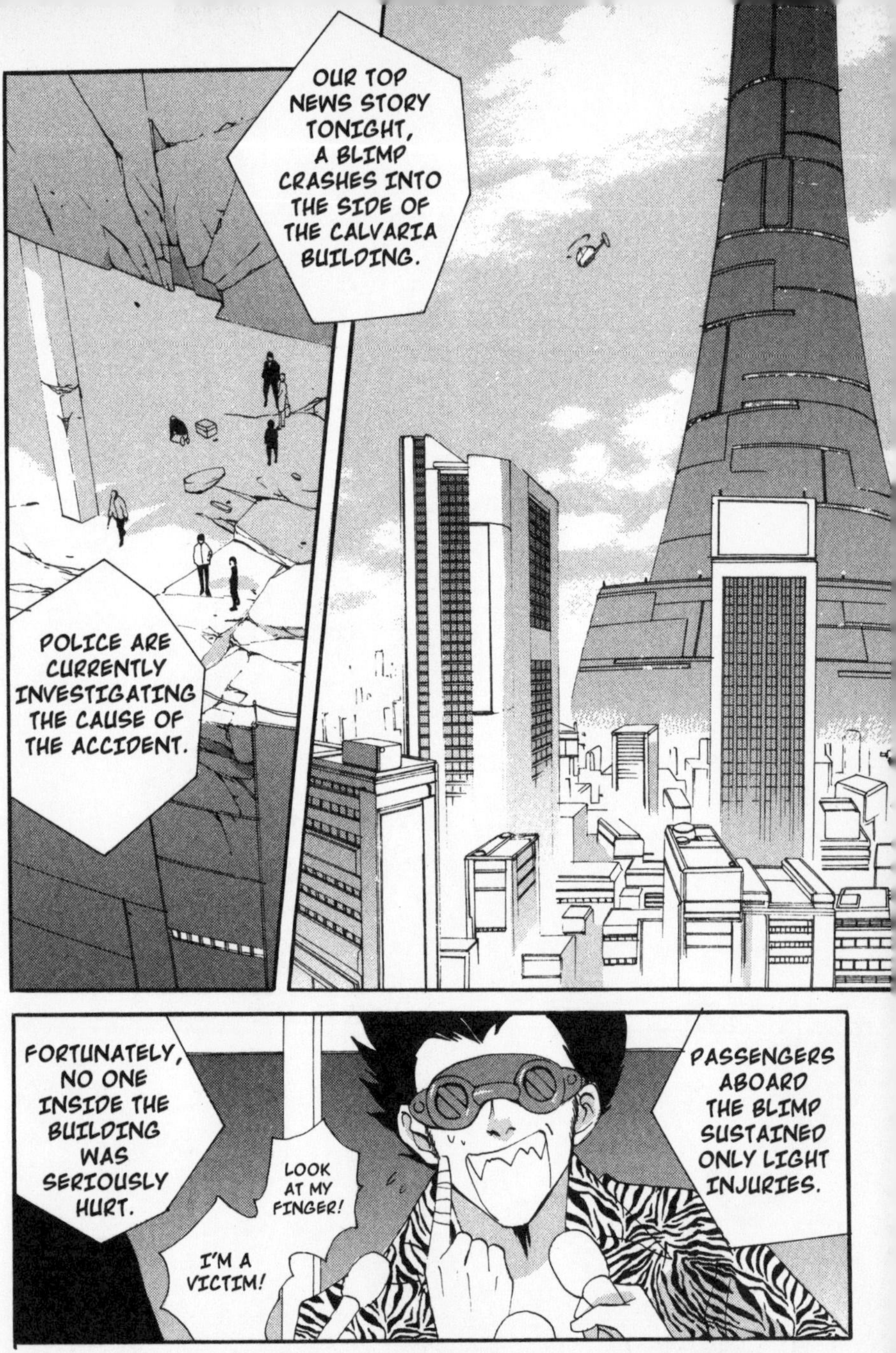
OUR TOP NEWS STORY TONIGHT, A BLIMP CRASHES INTO THE SIDE OF THE CALVARIA BUILDING.
POLICE ARE CURRENTLY INVESTIGATING THE CAUSE OF THE ACCIDENT.
FORTUNATELY, NO ONE INSIDE THE BUILDING WAS SERIOUSLY HURT.
LOOK AT MY FINGER!
I'M A VICTIM!
PASSENGERS ABOARD THE BLIMP SUSTAINED ONLY LIGHT INJURIES.

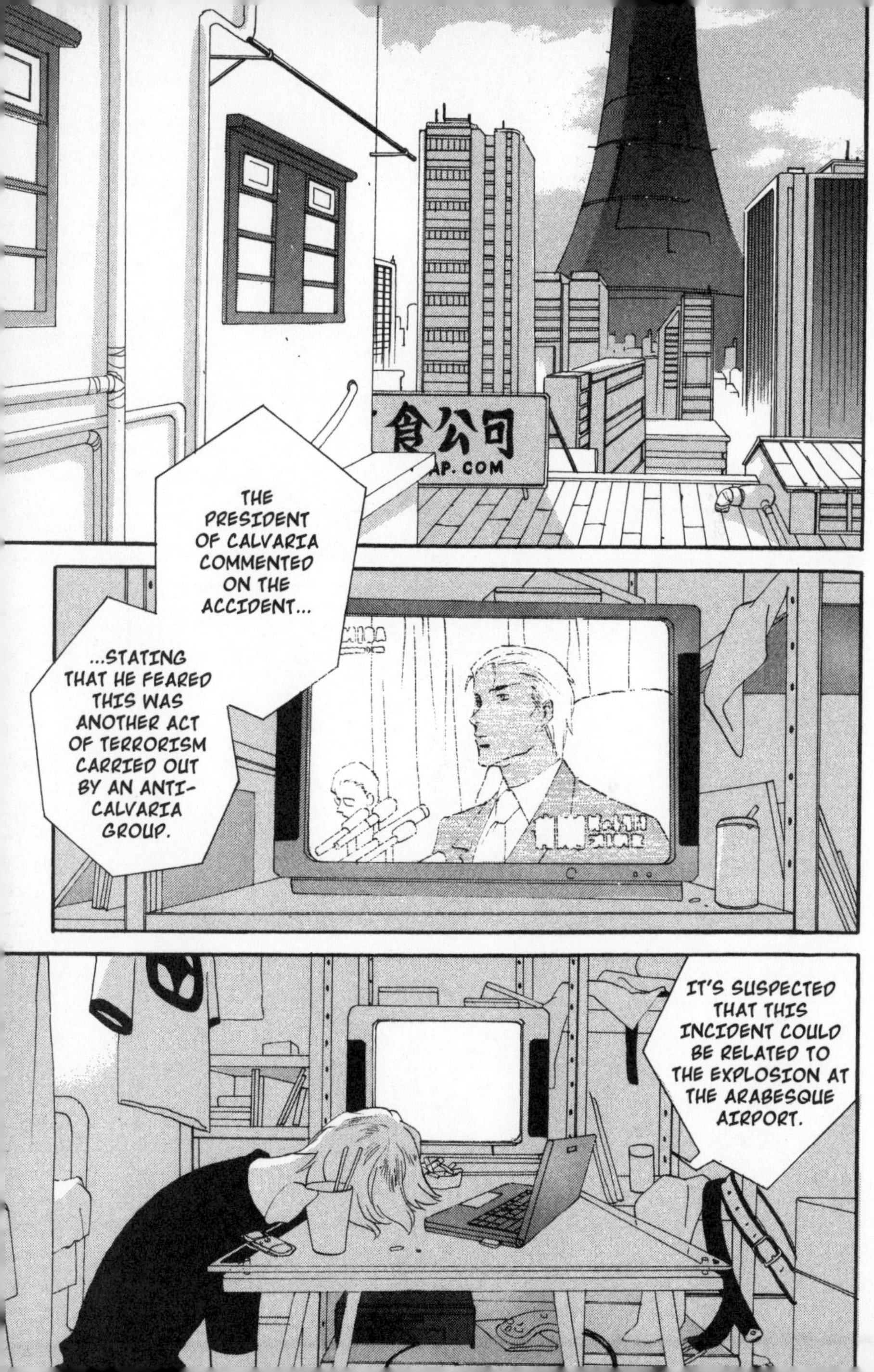
食公司
AP.COM
THE PRESIDENT OF CALVARIA COMMENTED ON THE ACCIDENT...
...STATING THAT HE FEARED THIS WAS ANOTHER ACT OF TERRORISM CARRIED OUT BY AN ANTI-CALVARIA GROUP.
IT'S SUSPECTED THAT THIS INCIDENT COULD BE RELATED TO THE EXPLOSION AT THE ARABESQUE AIRPORT.

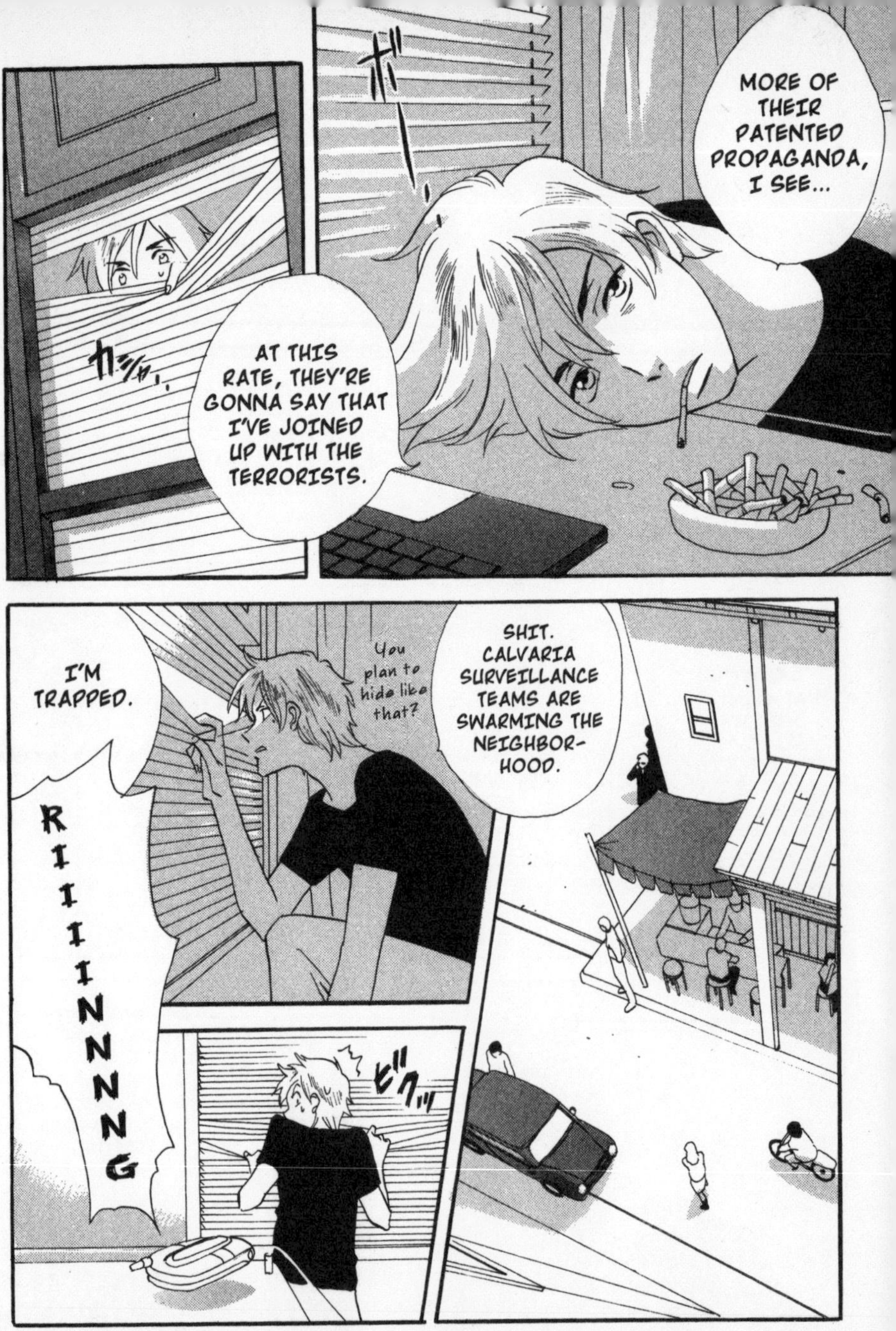
MORE OF THEIR PATENTED PROPAGANDA, I SEE...
AT THIS RATE, THEY'RE GONNA SAY THAT I'VE JOINED UP WITH THE TERRORISTS.
SHIT. CALVARIA SURVEILLANCE TEAMS ARE SWARMING THE NEIGHBOR-HOOD.
You plan to hide like that?
I'M TRAPPED.
RIIIINNNG

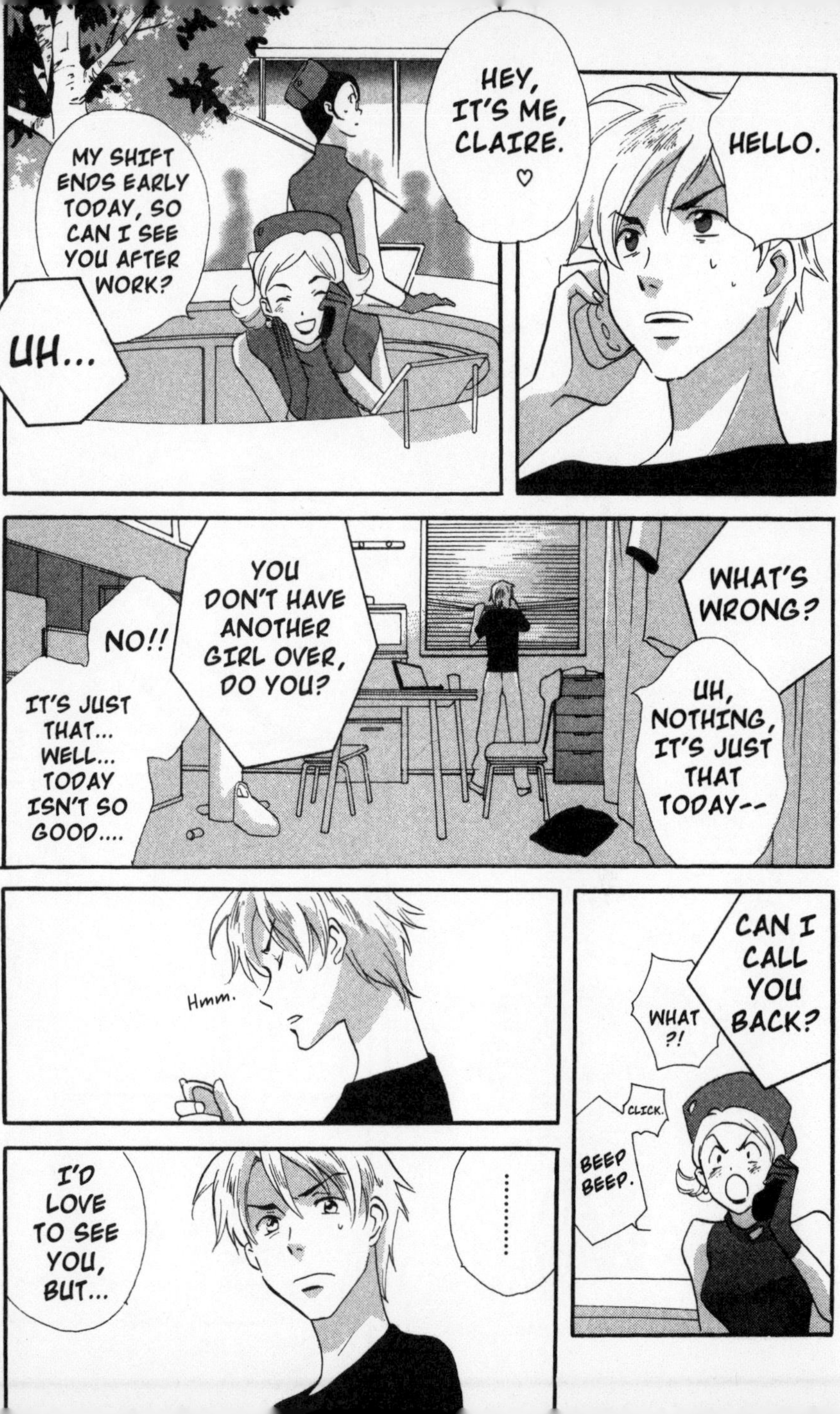
HELLO.
HEY, IT'S ME, CLAIRE. ♡
MY SHIFT ENDS EARLY TODAY, SO CAN I SEE YOU AFTER WORK?
UH...
WHAT'S WRONG?
UH, NOTHING, IT'S JUST THAT TODAY--
YOU DON'T HAVE ANOTHER GIRL OVER, DO YOU?
NO!!
IT'S JUST THAT... WELL... TODAY ISN'T SO GOOD....
Hmm.
....
I'D LOVE TO SEE YOU, BUT...
CAN I CALL YOU BACK?
WHAT ?!
CLICK.
BEEP BEEP.

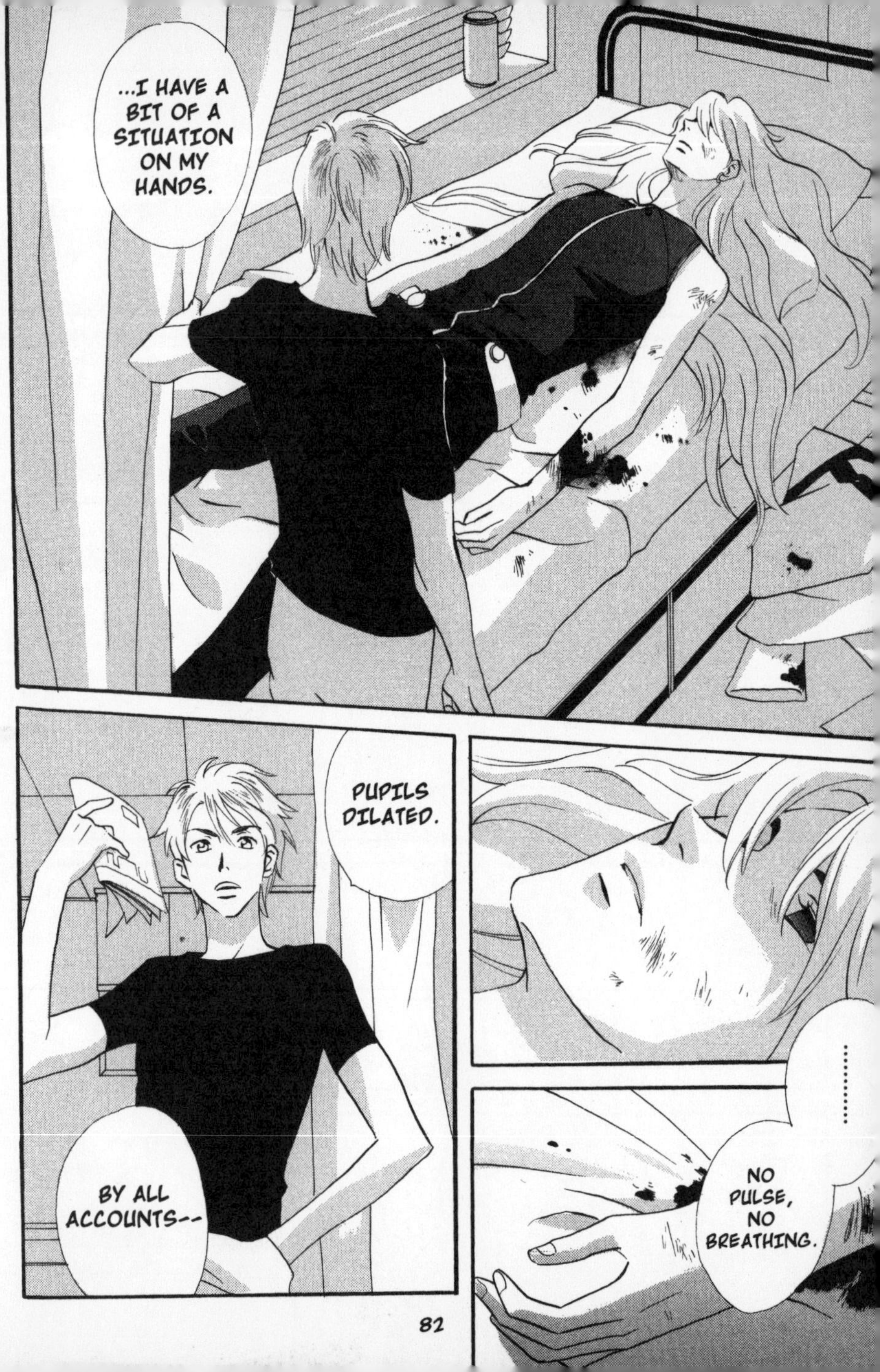
...I HAVE A BIT OF A SITUATION ON MY HANDS.
PUPILS DILATED.
......
NO PULSE, NO BREATHING.
BY ALL ACCOUNTS--

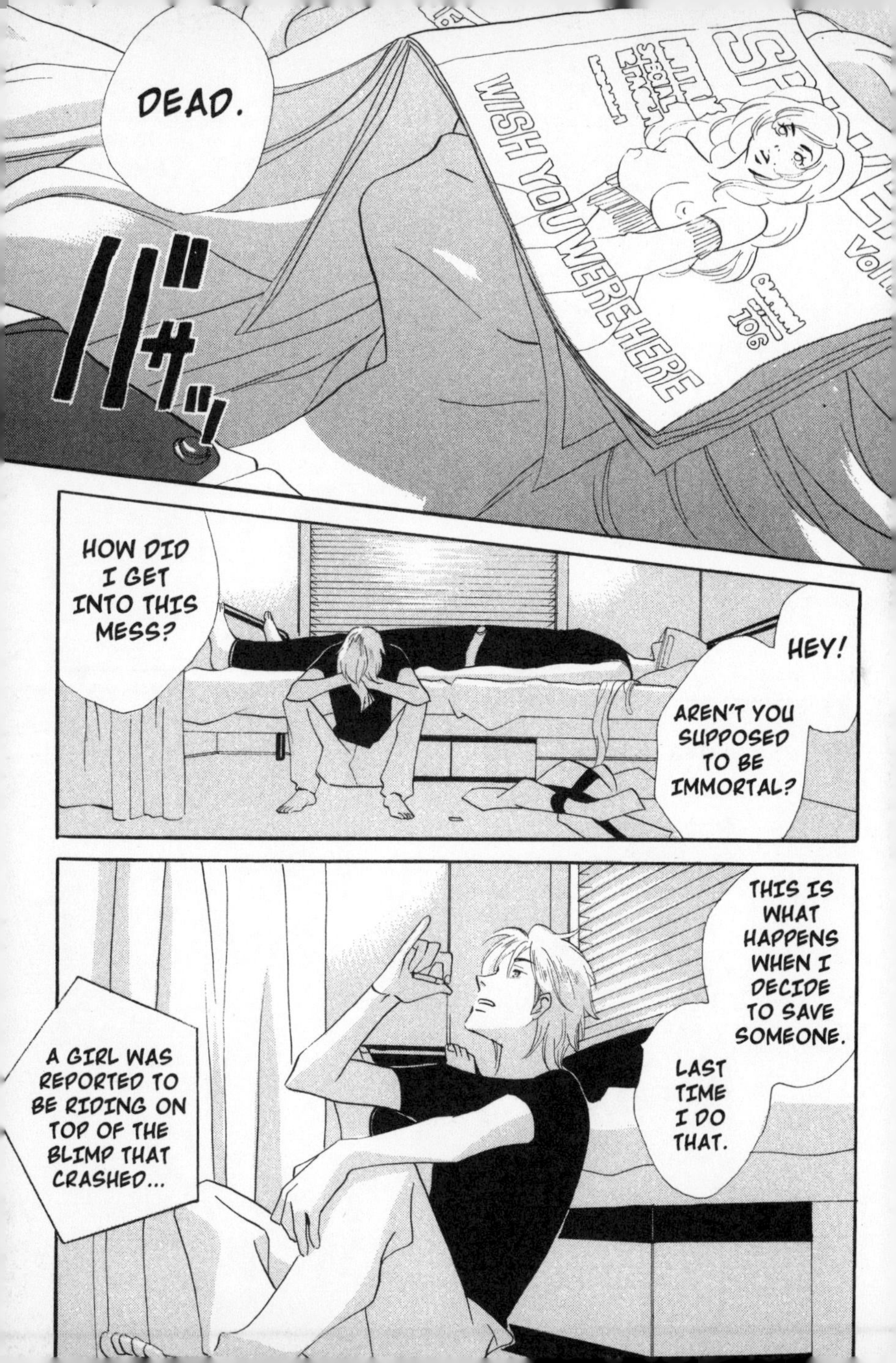
WISH YOUWERE HERE
106
DEAD.
バザッ
HEY!
AREN'T YOU SUPPOSED TO BE IMMORTAL?
HOW DID I GET INTO THIS MESS?
THIS IS WHAT HAPPENS WHEN I DECIDE TO SAVE SOMEONE.
LAST TIME I DO THAT.
A GIRL WAS REPORTED TO BE RIDING ON TOP OF THE BLIMP THAT CRASHED...

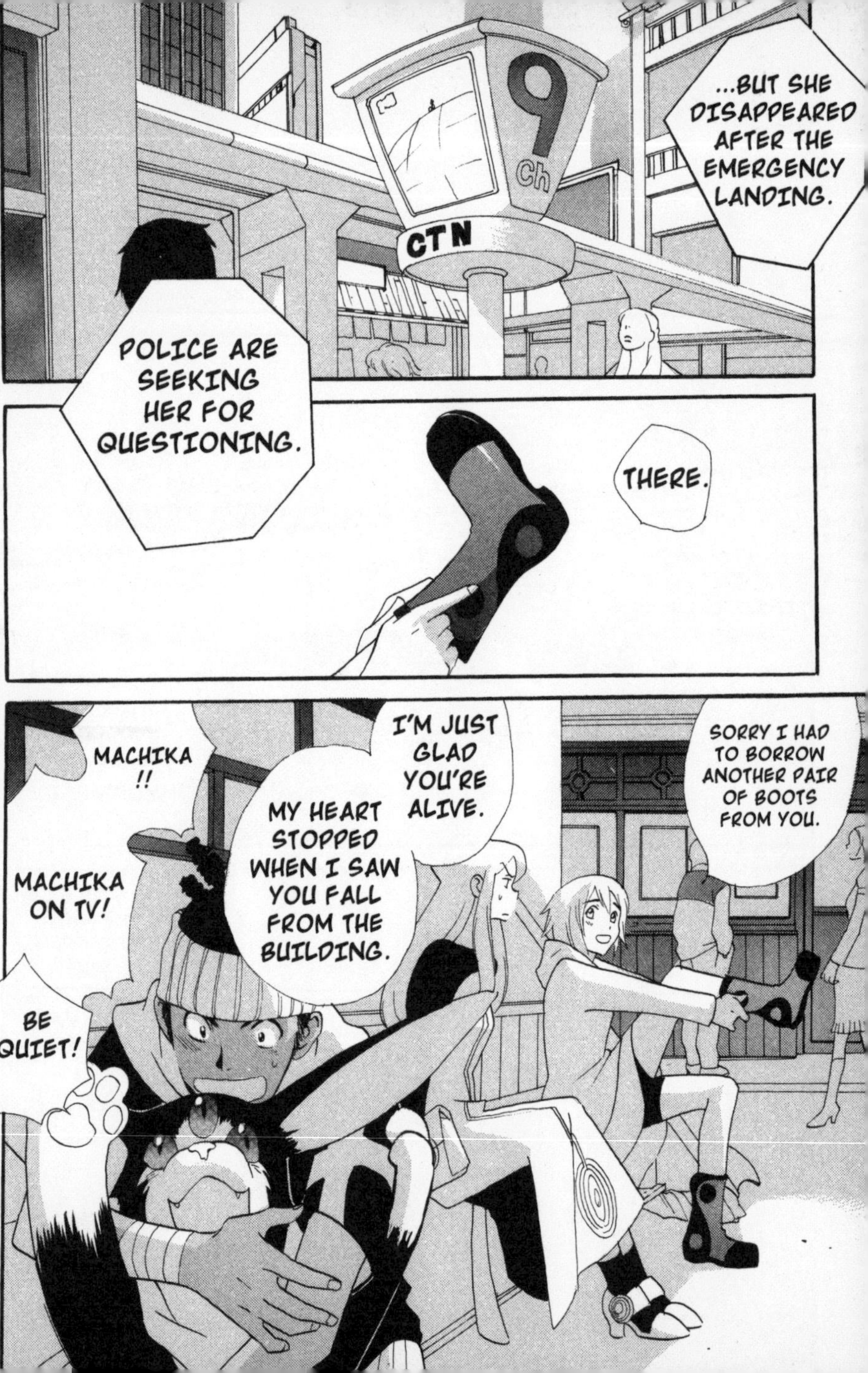
...BUT SHE DISAPPEARED AFTER THE EMERGENCY LANDING.
POLICE ARE SEEKING HER FOR QUESTIONING.
THERE.
SORRY I HAD TO BORROW ANOTHER PAIR OF BOOTS FROM YOU.
I'M JUST GLAD YOU'RE ALIVE.
MY HEART STOPPED WHEN I SAW YOU FALL FROM THE BUILDING.
MACHIKA !!
MACHIKA ON TV!
BE QUIET!
CTN
9 Ch

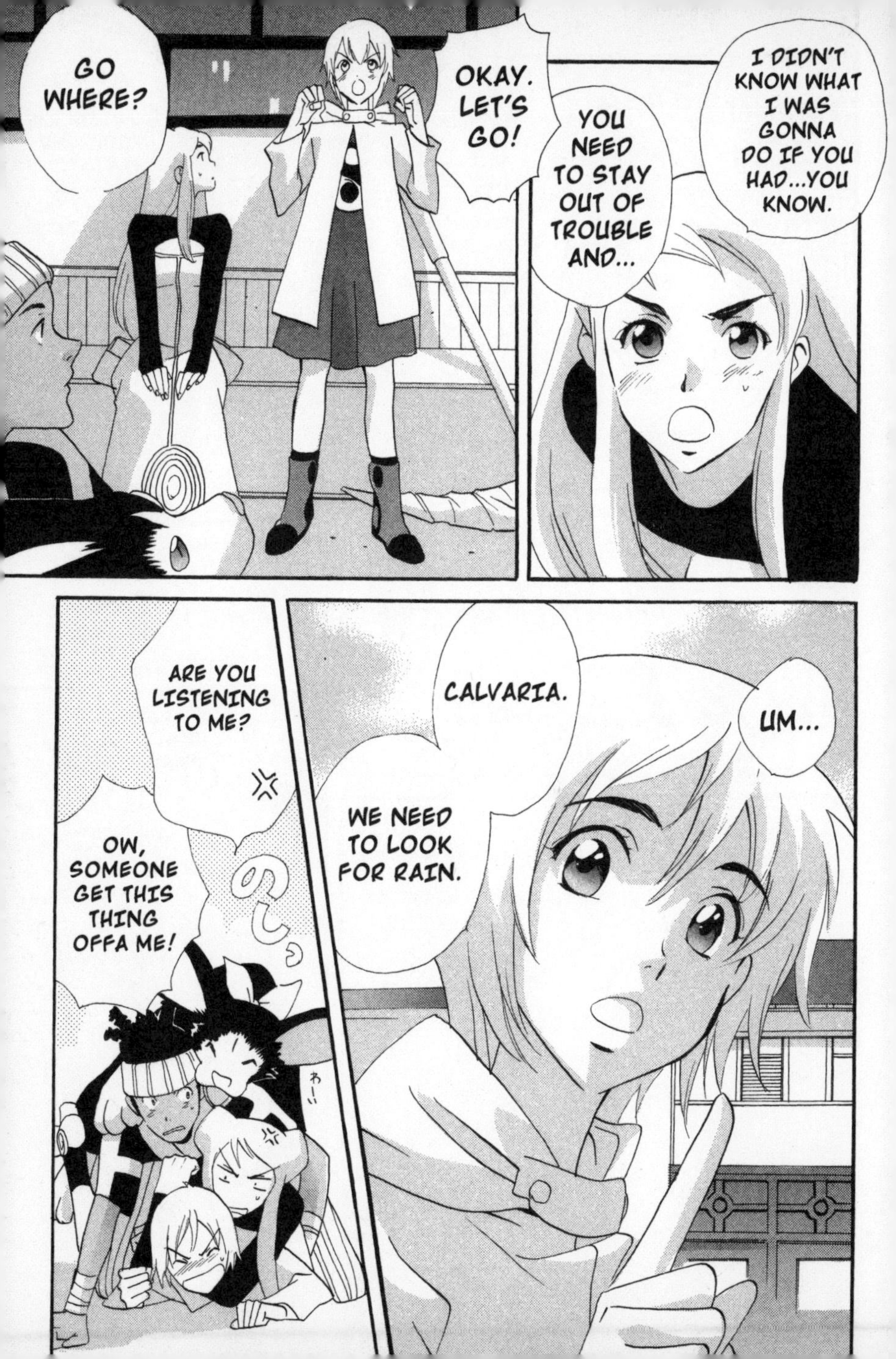
I DIDN'T KNOW WHAT I WAS GONNA DO IF YOU HAD...YOU KNOW.
YOU NEED TO STAY OUT OF TROUBLE AND...
OKAY. LET'S GO!
GO WHERE?
UM...
CALVARIA.
WE NEED TO LOOK FOR RAIN.
ARE YOU LISTENING TO ME?
OW, SOMEONE GET THIS THING OFFA ME!

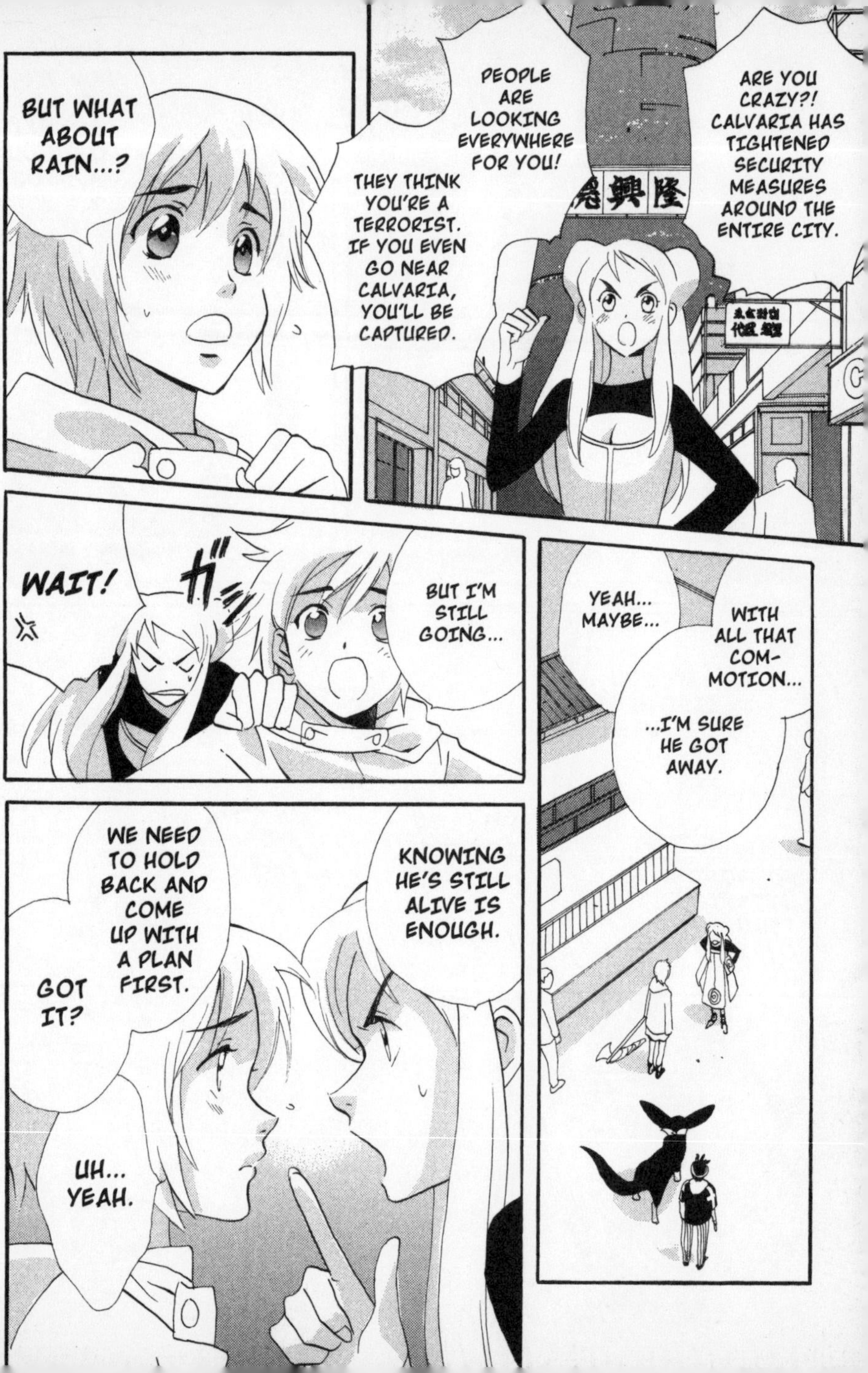
ARE YOU CRAZY?! CALVARIA HAS TIGHTENED SECURITY MEASURES AROUND THE ENTIRE CITY.
PEOPLE ARE LOOKING EVERYWHERE FOR YOU!
THEY THINK YOU'RE A TERRORIST. IF YOU EVEN GO NEAR CALVARIA, YOU'LL BE CAPTURED.
BUT WHAT ABOUT RAIN...?
YEAH... MAYBE...
WITH ALL THAT COM-MOTION...
...I'M SURE HE GOT AWAY.
BUT I'M STILL GOING...
WAIT!
KNOWING HE'S STILL ALIVE IS ENOUGH.
WE NEED TO HOLD BACK AND COME UP WITH A PLAN FIRST.
GOT IT?
UH... YEAH.

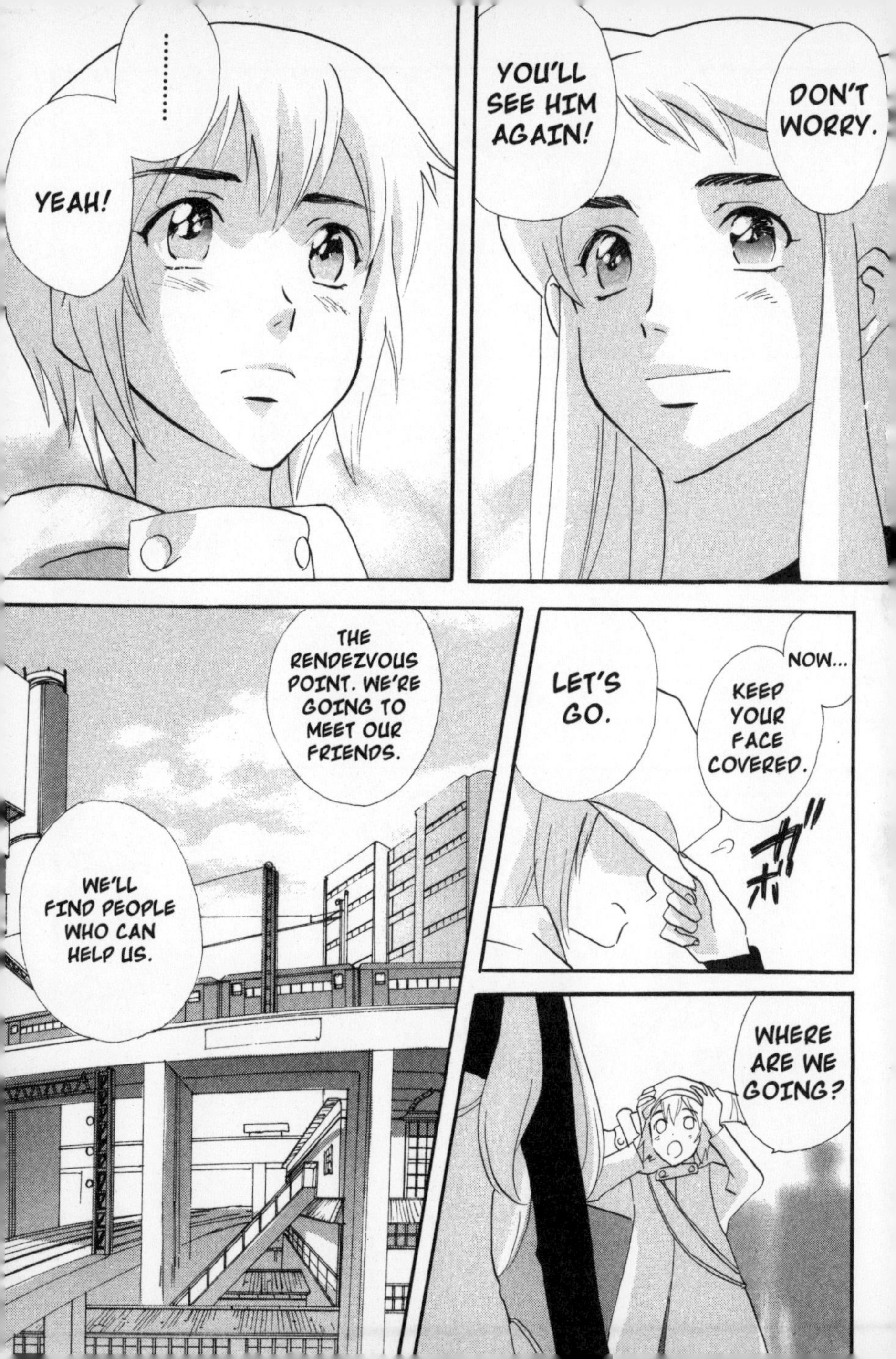
DON'T WORRY.
YOU'LL SEE HIM AGAIN!
......
YEAH!
NOW... KEEP YOUR FACE COVERED.
LET'S GO.
ガボ
WHERE ARE WE GOING?
THE RENDEZVOUS POINT. WE'RE GOING TO MEET OUR FRIENDS.
WE'LL FIND PEOPLE WHO CAN HELP US.

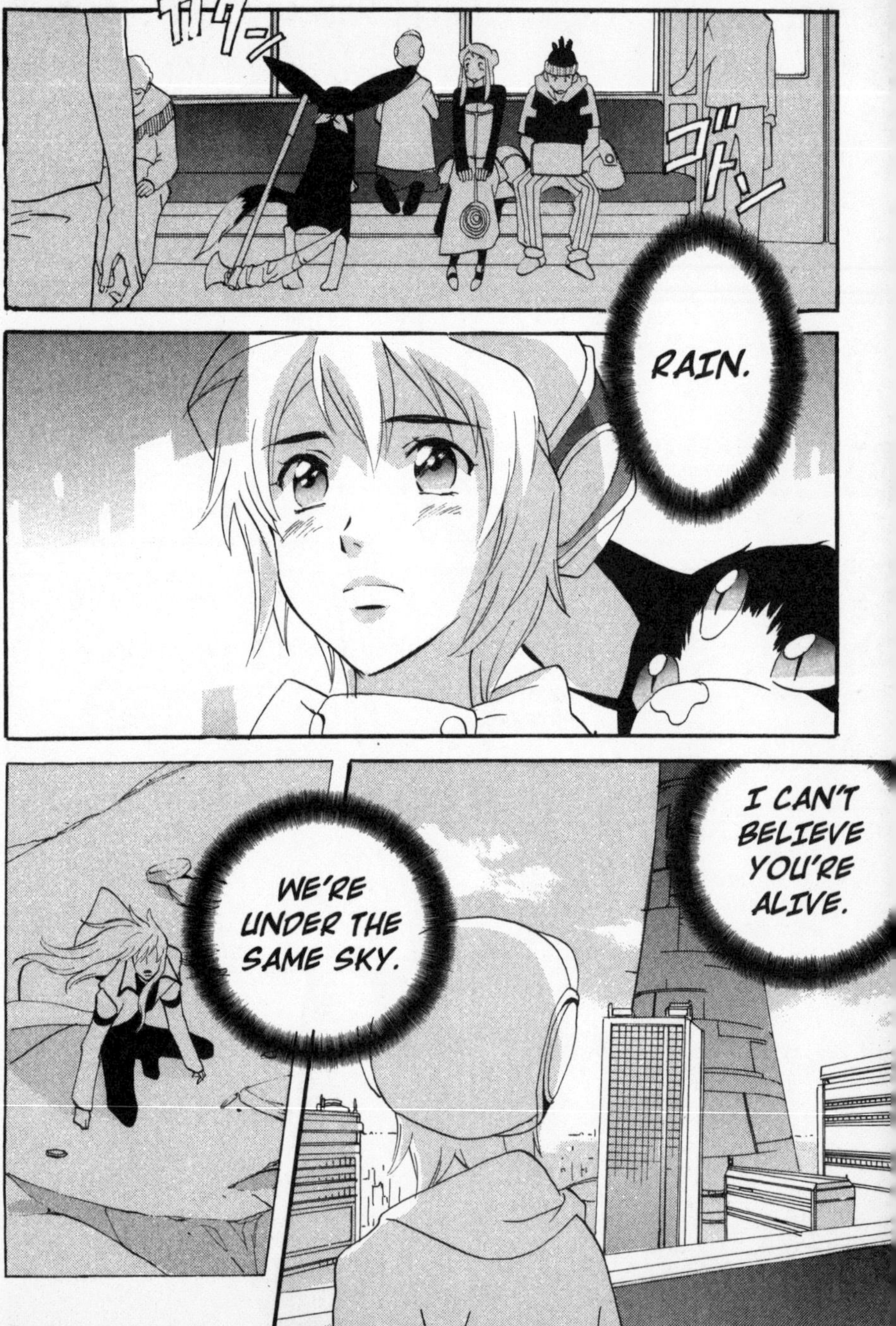
ゴトン
ガターン
RAIN.
I CAN'T BELIEVE YOU'RE ALIVE.
WE'RE UNDER THE SAME SKY.

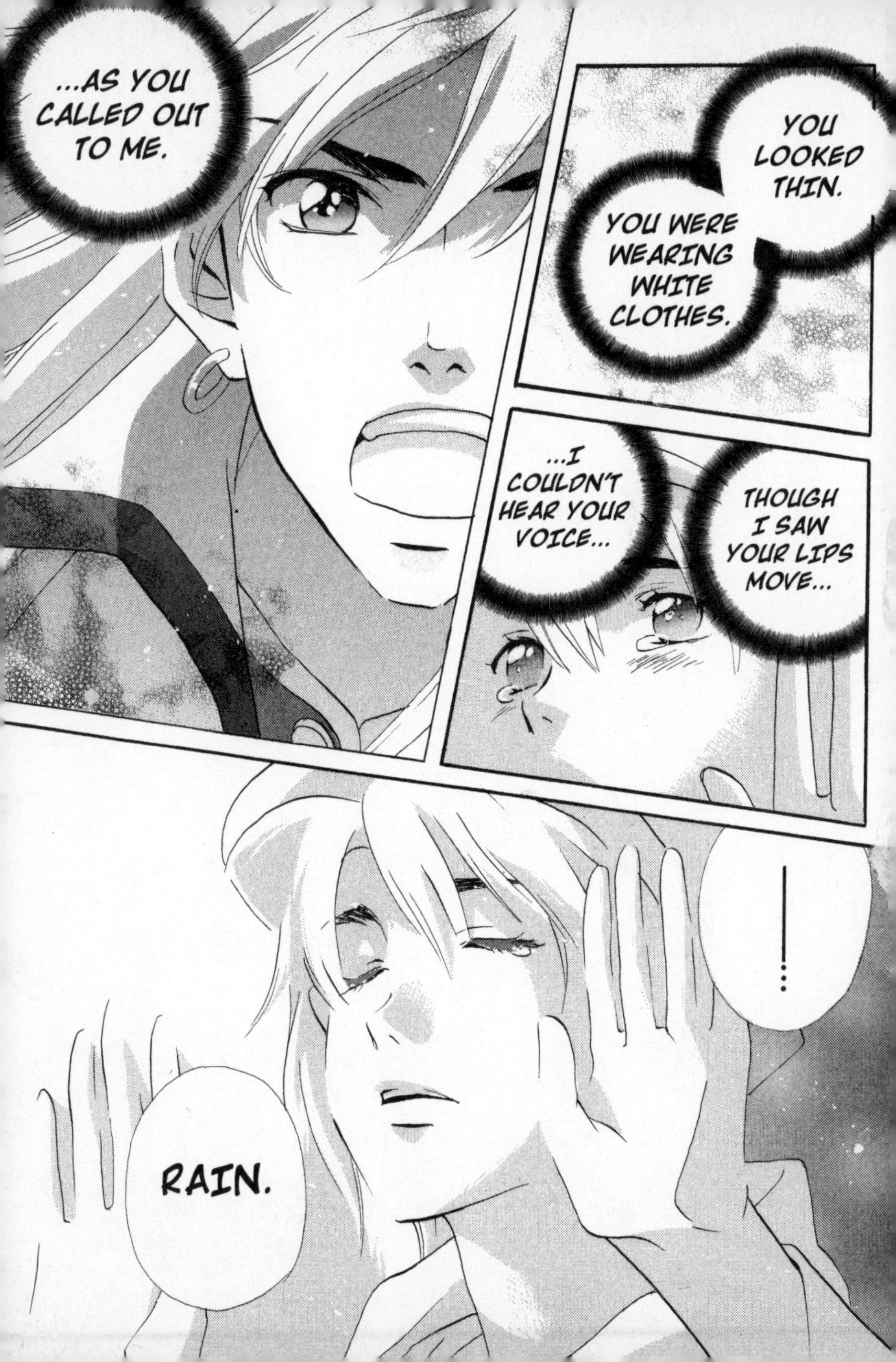
YOU LOOKED THIN.
YOU WERE WEARING WHITE CLOTHES.
THOUGH I SAW YOUR LIPS MOVE...
...I COULDN'T HEAR YOUR VOICE...
...AS YOU CALLED OUT TO ME.
!......
RAIN.

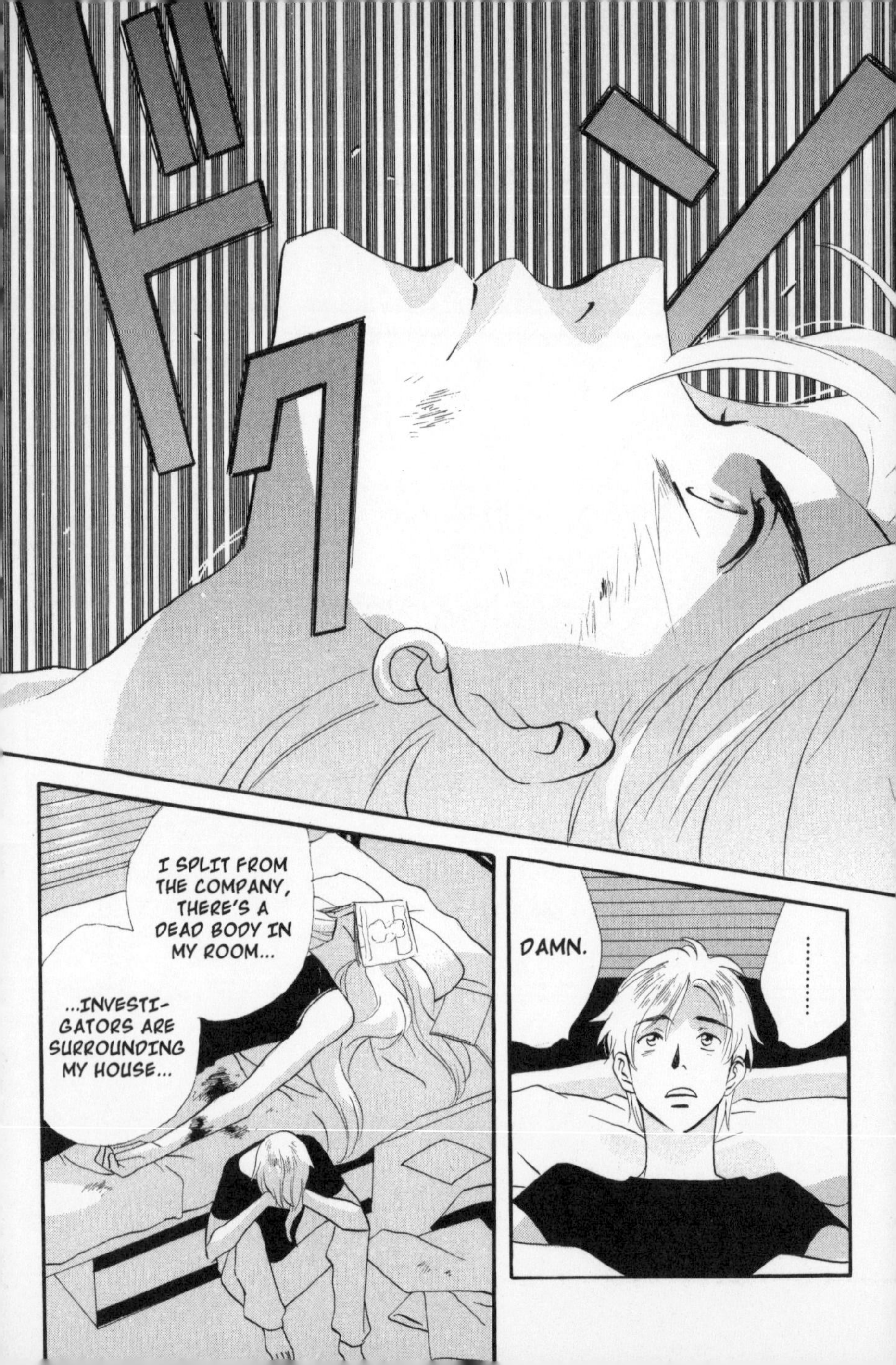

ドクン
......
DAMN.
I SPLIT FROM THE COMPANY, THERE'S A DEAD BODY IN MY ROOM...
...INVESTI- GATORS ARE SURROUNDING MY HOUSE...

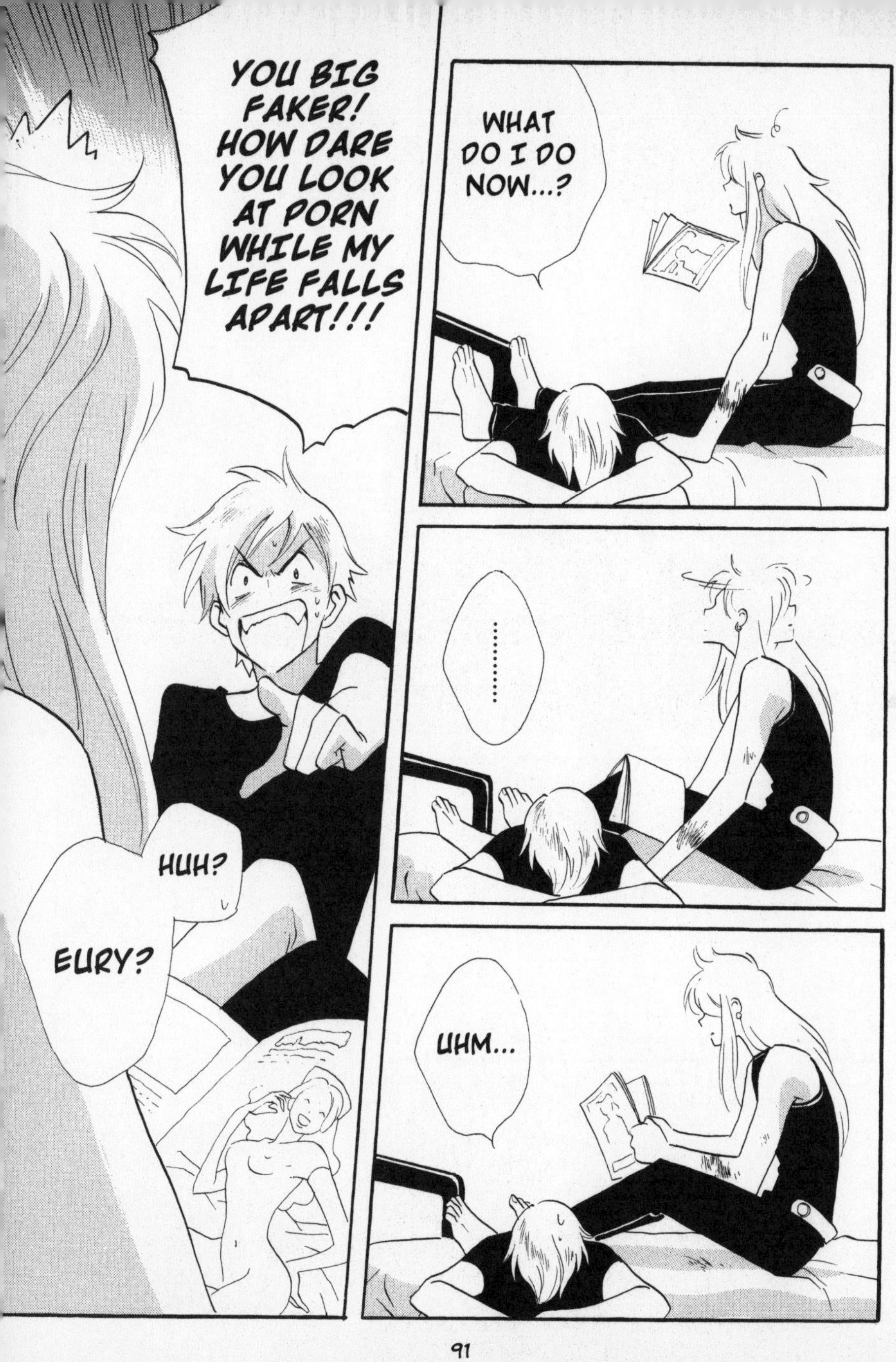
WHAT DO I DO NOW...?
....
UHM...
YOU BIG FAKER! HOW DARE YOU LOOK AT PORN WHILE MY LIFE FALLS APART!!!
HUH?
EURY?

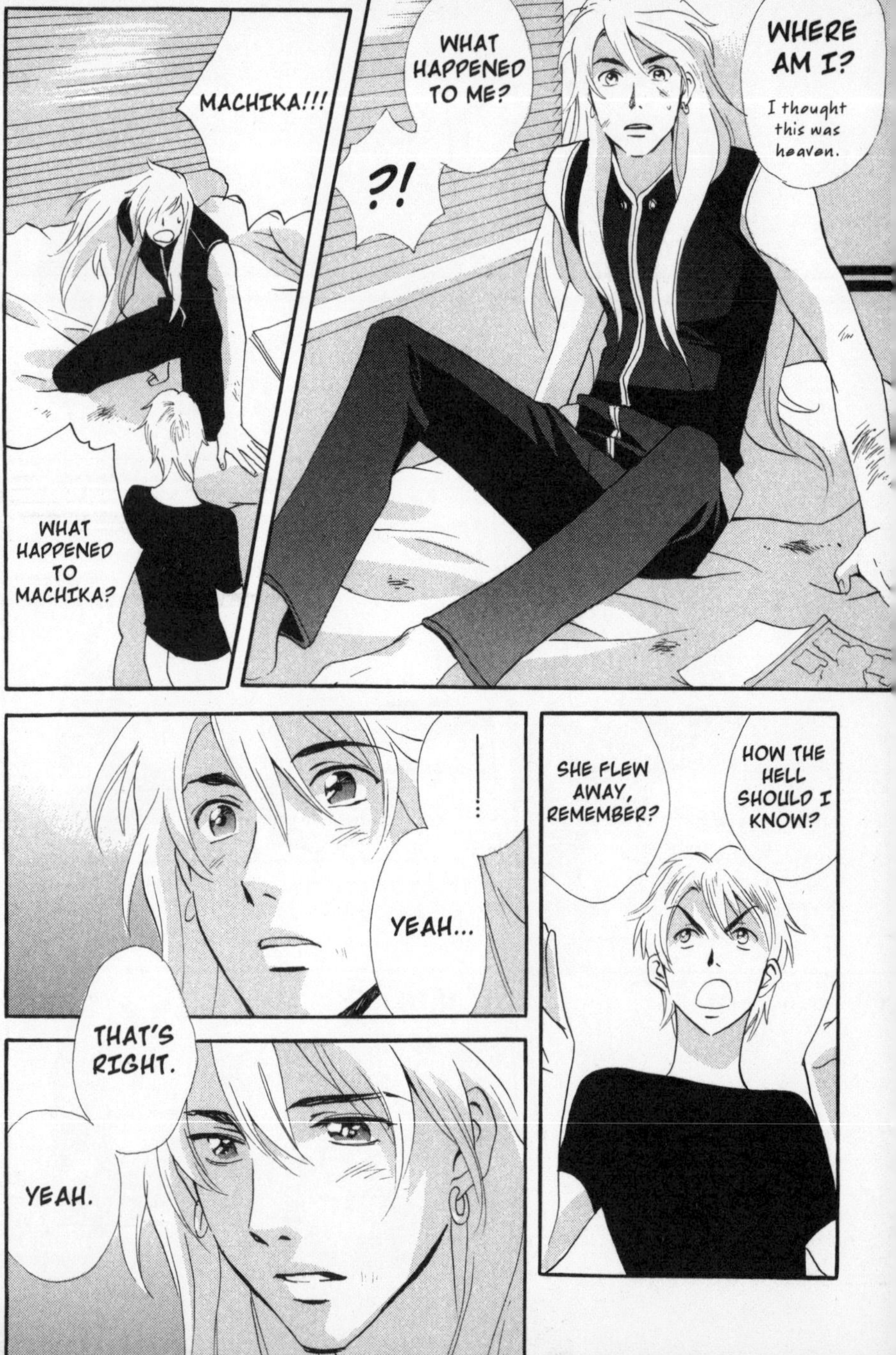
WHERE AM I?
I thought this was heaven.
WHAT HAPPENED TO ME?
?!
MACHIKA!!!
WHAT HAPPENED TO MACHIKA?
HOW THE HELL SHOULD I KNOW?
SHE FLEW AWAY, REMEMBER?
......
YEAH...
THAT'S RIGHT.
YEAH.

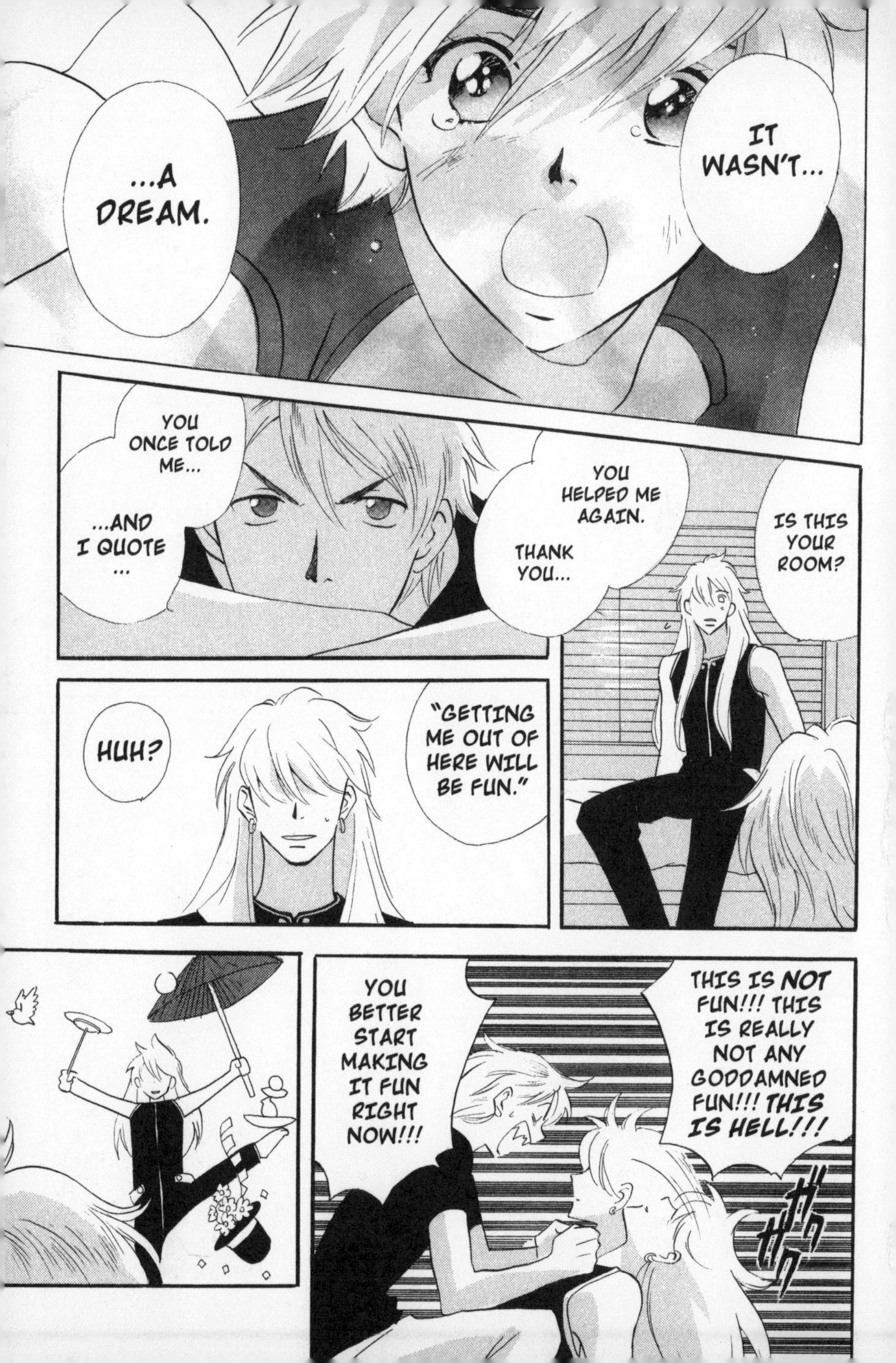
IT WASN'T...
...A DREAM.
IS THIS YOUR ROOM?
YOU HELPED ME AGAIN. THANK YOU...
YOU ONCE TOLD ME...
...AND I QUOTE ...
"GETTING ME OUT OF HERE WILL BE FUN."
HUH?
THIS IS NOT FUN!!! THIS IS REALLY NOT ANY GODDAMNED FUN!!! THIS IS HELL!!!
YOU BETTER START MAKING IT FUN RIGHT NOW!!!

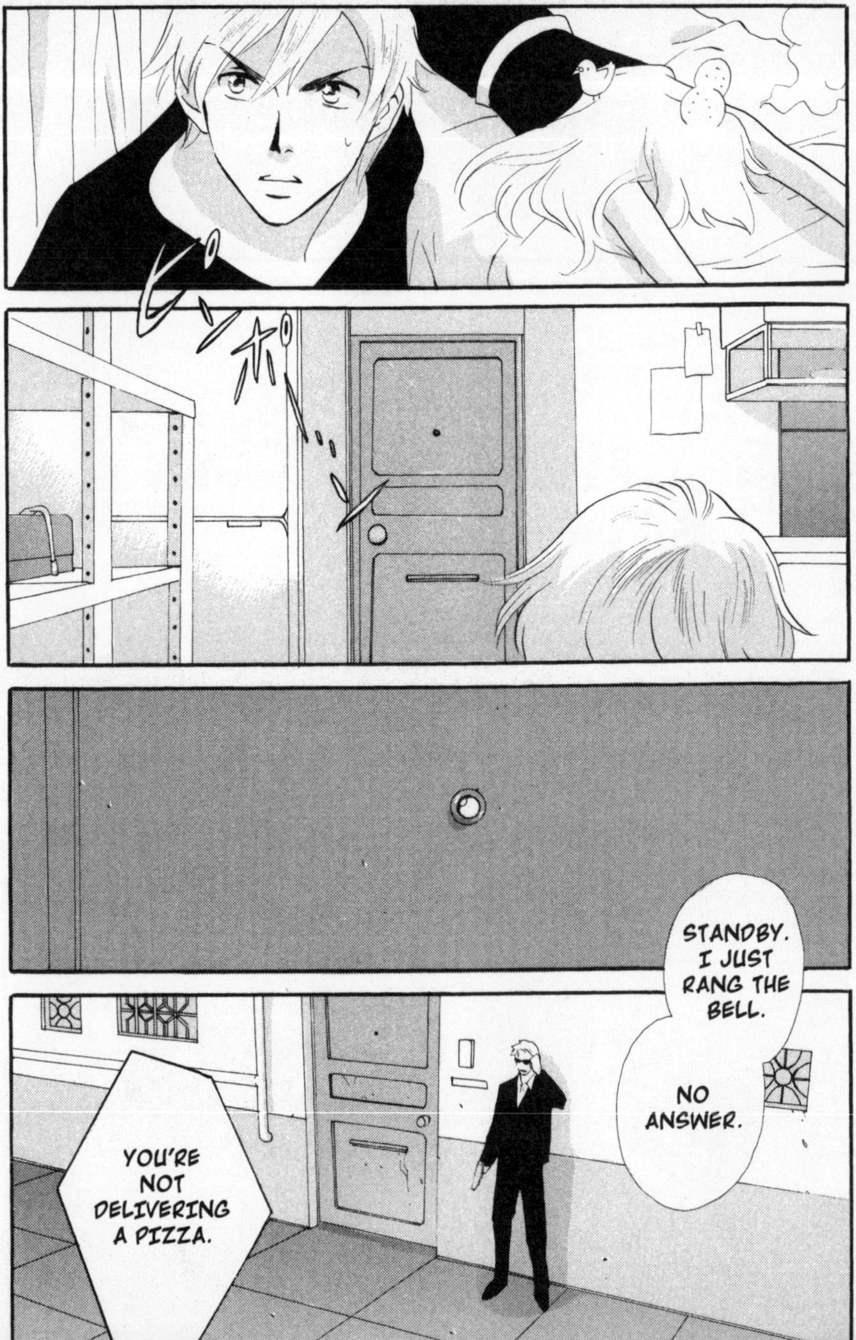
STANDBY. I JUST RANG THE BELL.
NO ANSWER.
YOU'RE NOT DELIVERING A PIZZA.

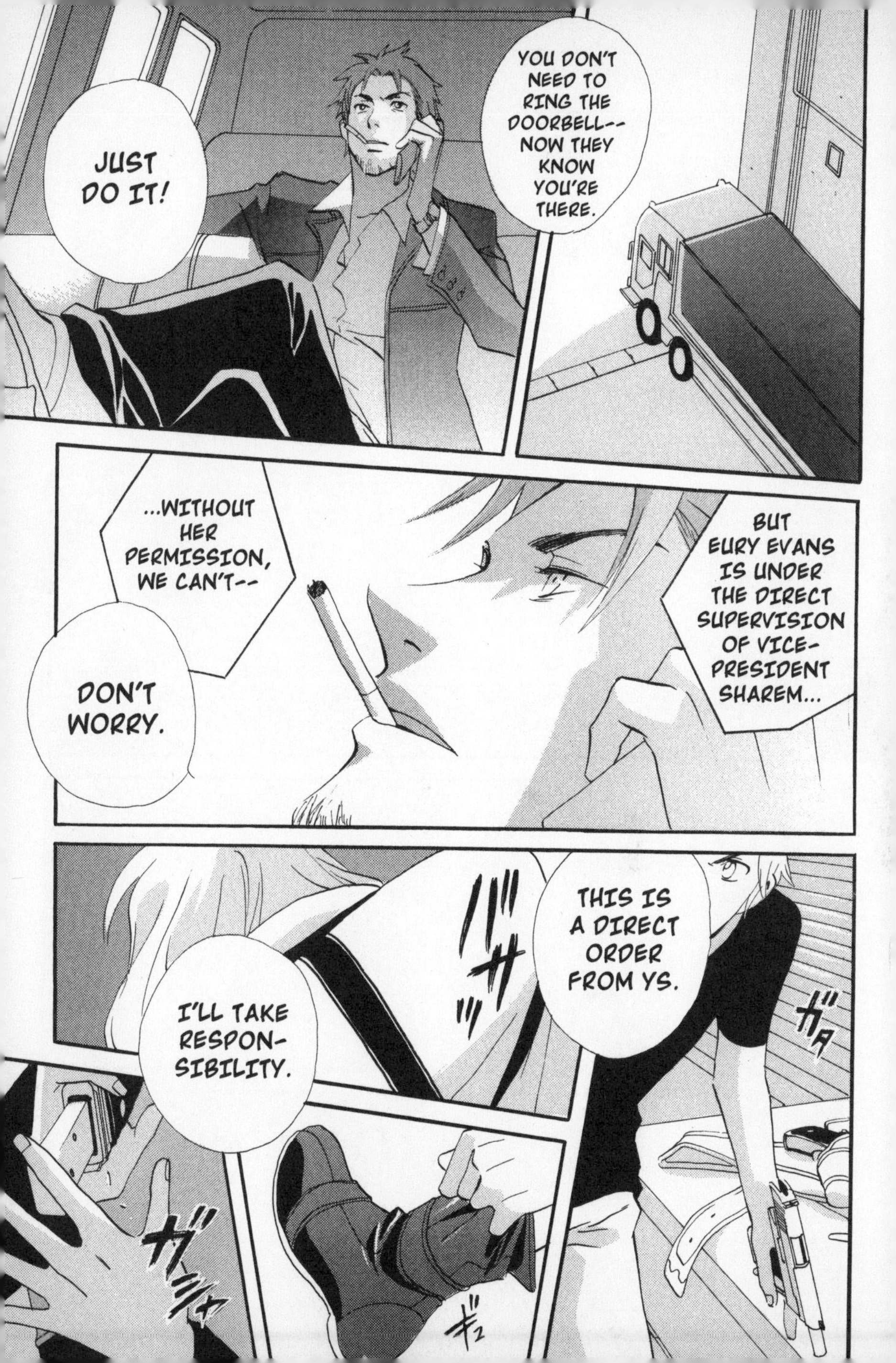
YOU DON'T NEED TO RING THE DOORBELL-- NOW THEY KNOW YOU'RE THERE.
JUST DO IT!
BUT EURY EVANS IS UNDER THE DIRECT SUPERVISION OF VICE-PRESIDENT SHAREM...
...WITHOUT HER PERMISSION, WE CAN'T--
DON'T WORRY.
THIS IS A DIRECT ORDER FROM YS.
I'LL TAKE RESPON-SIBILITY.

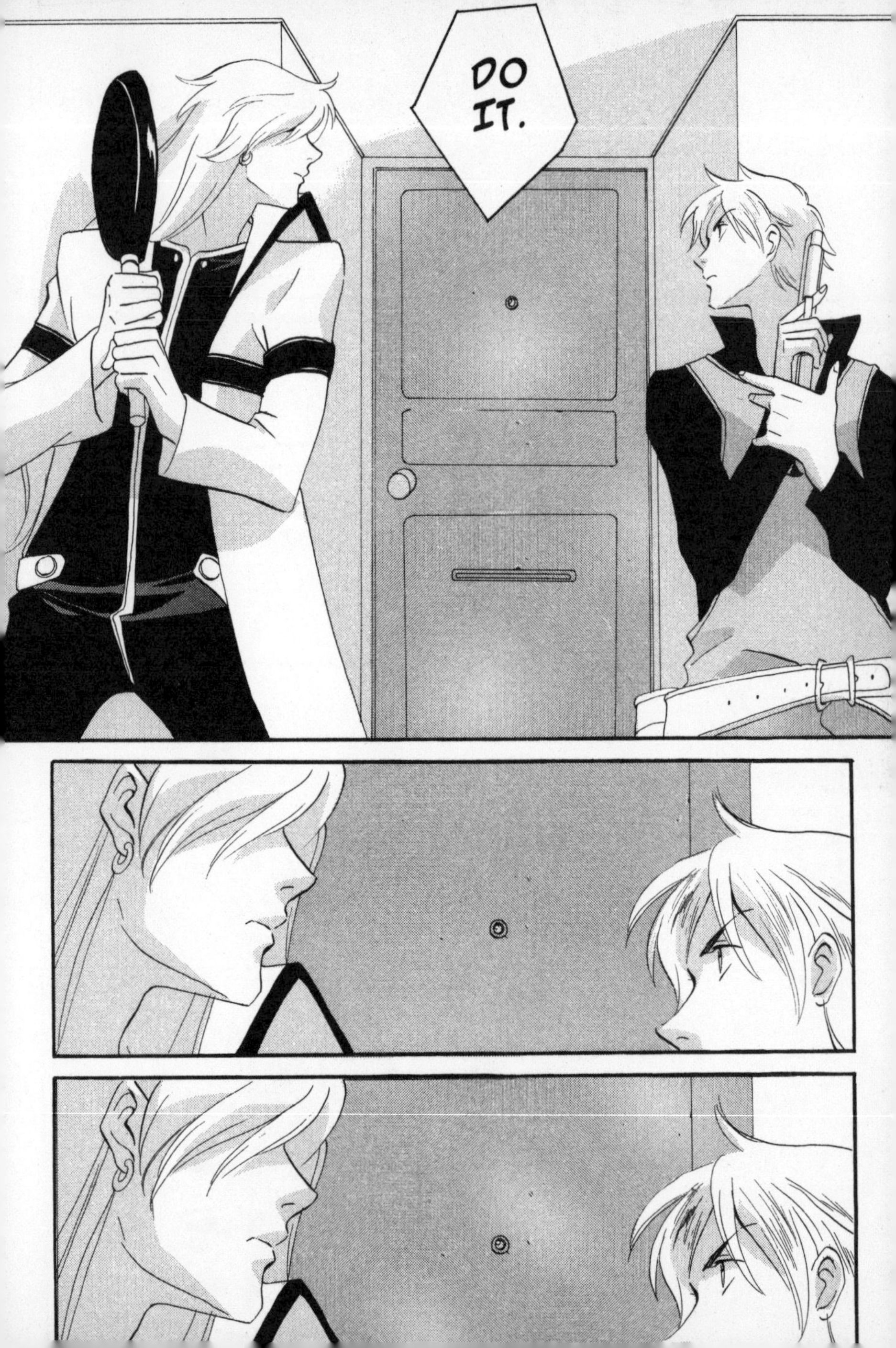
DO IT.

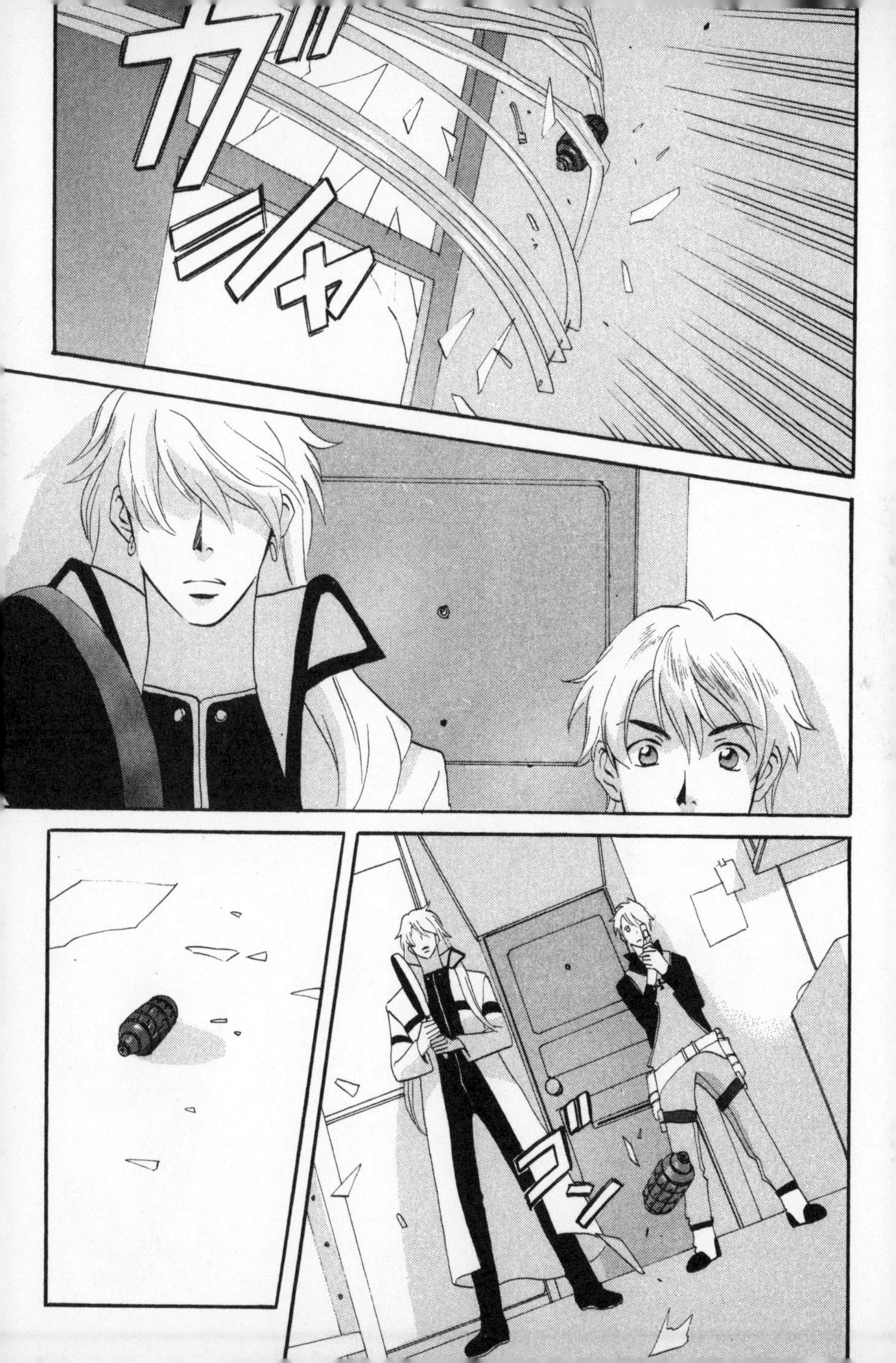
ガシャ
ゴン

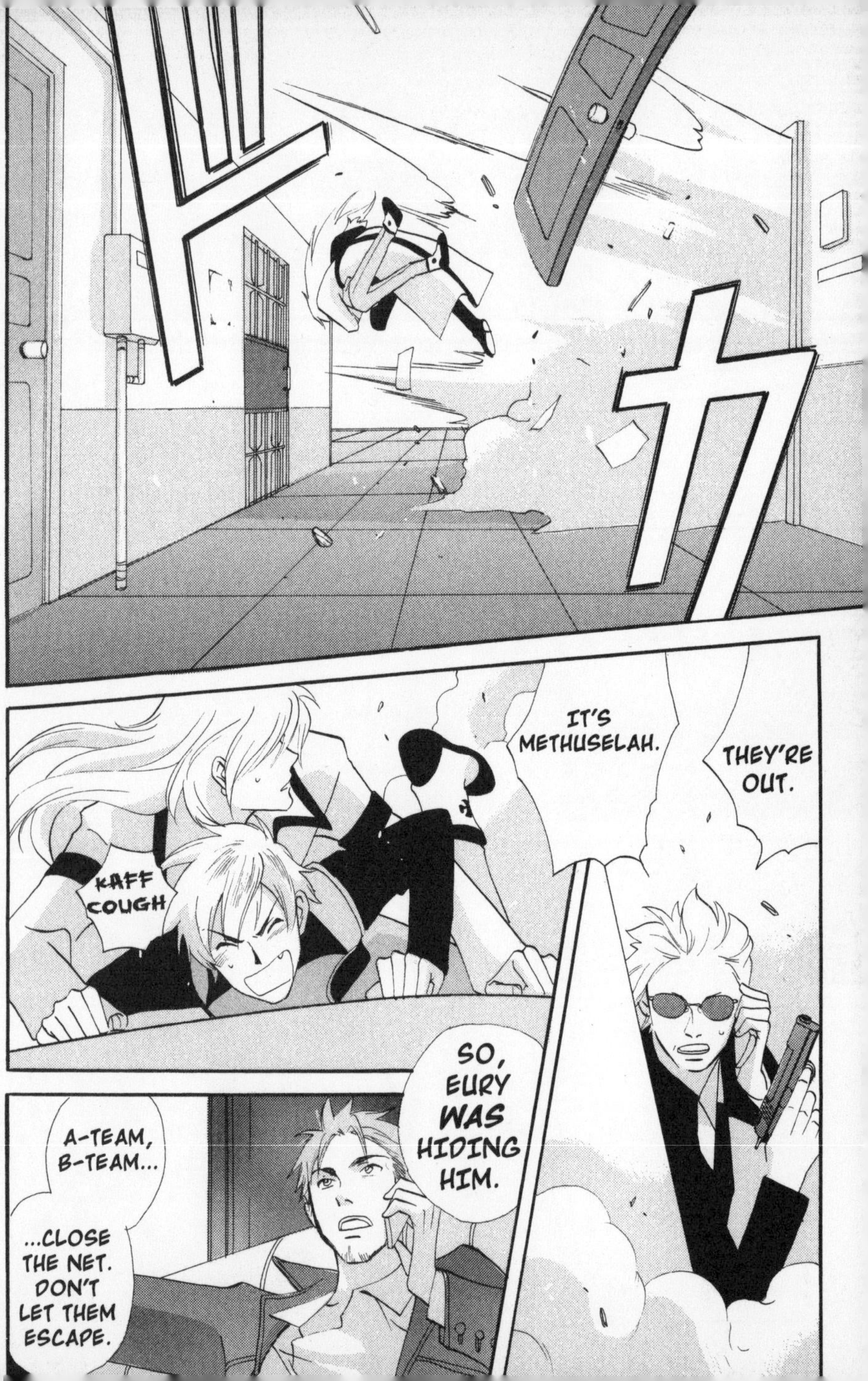
ドカ
THEY'RE OUT.
IT'S METHUSELAH.
KAFF COUGH
SO, EURY WAS HIDING HIM.
A-TEAM, B-TEAM...
...CLOSE THE NET. DON'T LET THEM ESCAPE.

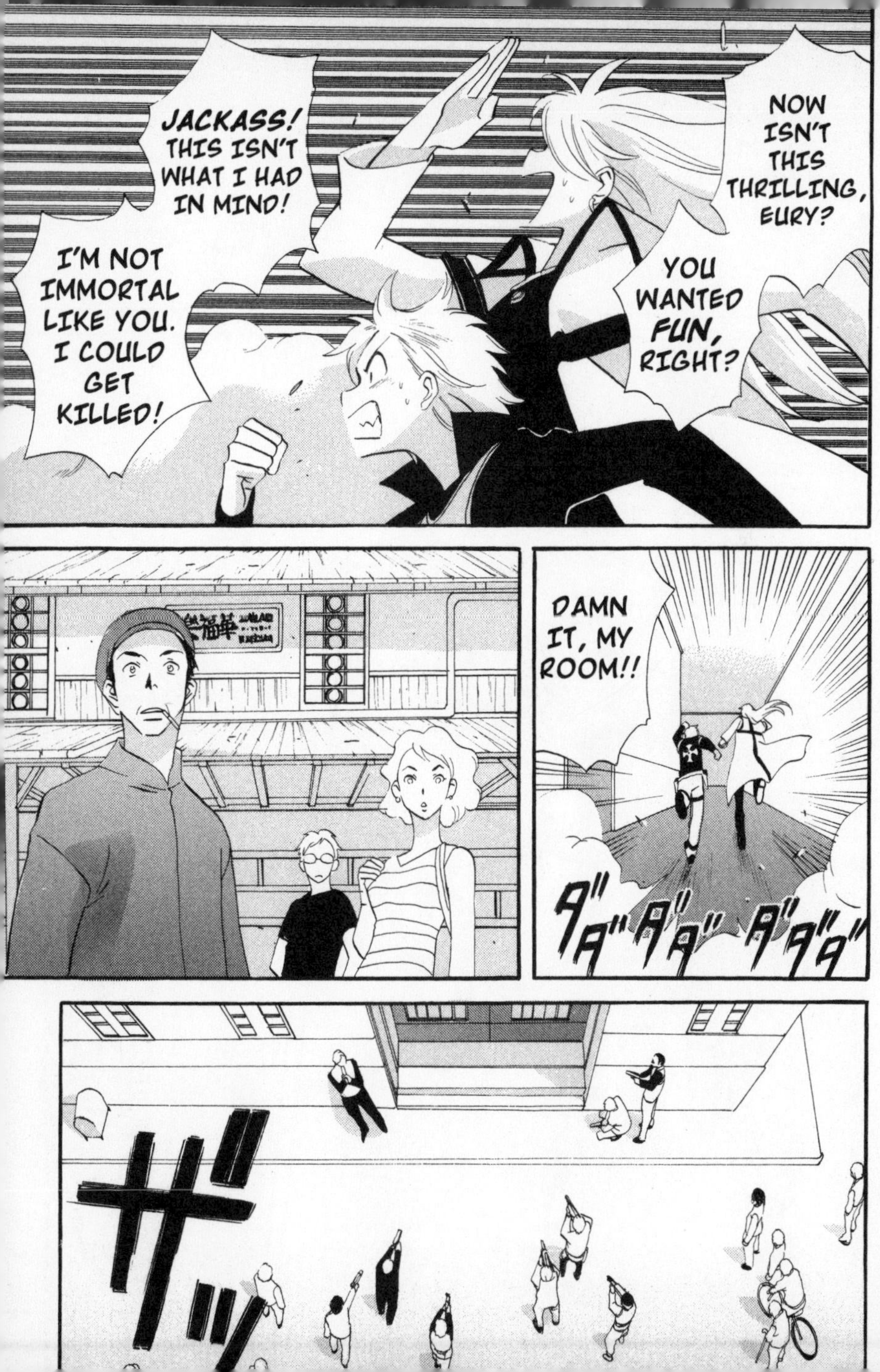
NOW ISN'T THIS THRILLING, EURY?
YOU WANTED FUN, RIGHT?
JACKASS! THIS ISN'T WHAT I HAD IN MIND!
I'M NOT IMMORTAL LIKE YOU. I COULD GET KILLED!
DAMN IT, MY ROOM!!
ダダダダダダ
ザッ

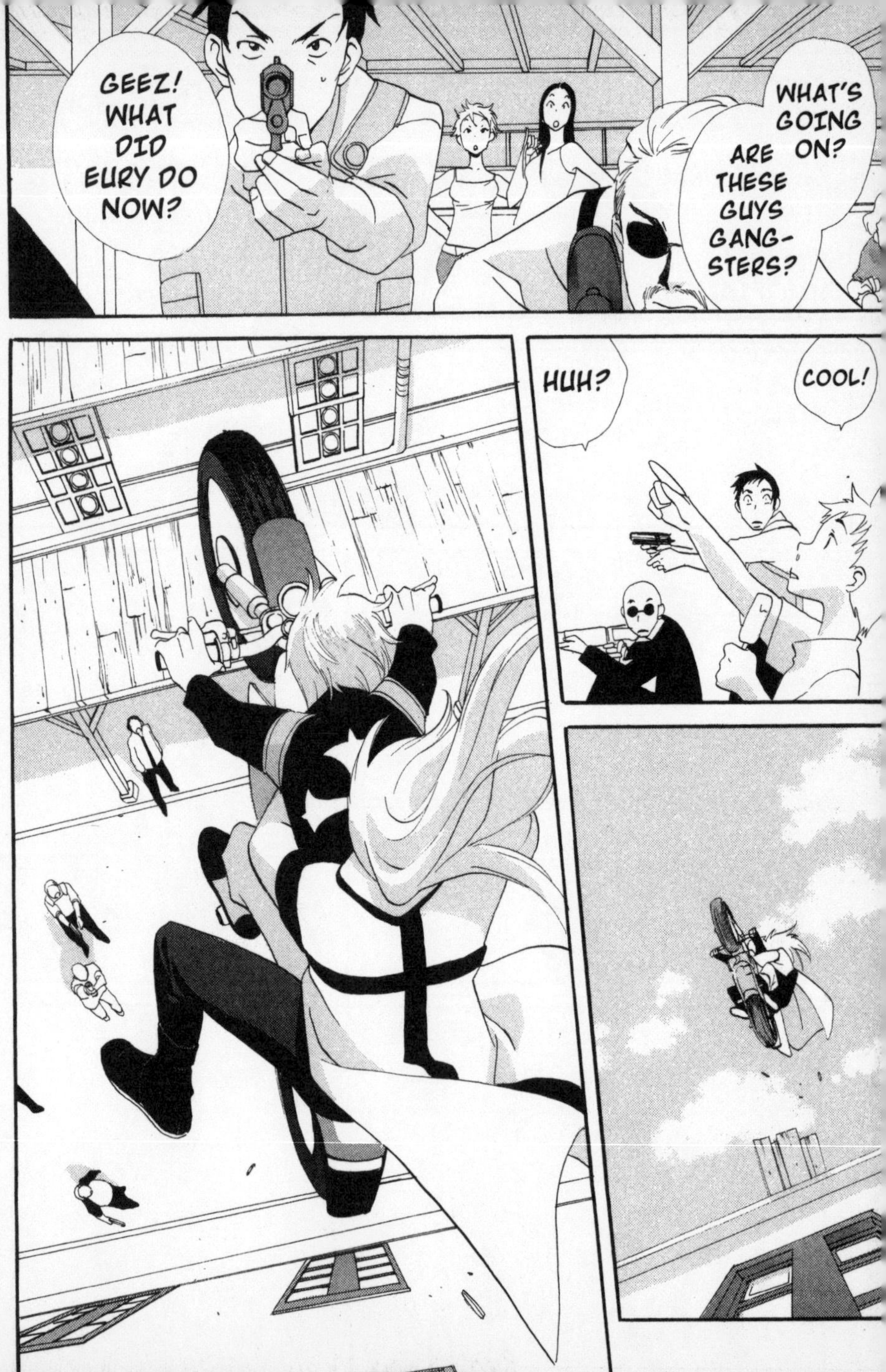
WHAT'S GOING ON? ARE THESE GUYS GANG-STERS?
GEEZ! WHAT DID EURY DO NOW?
COOL!
HUH?

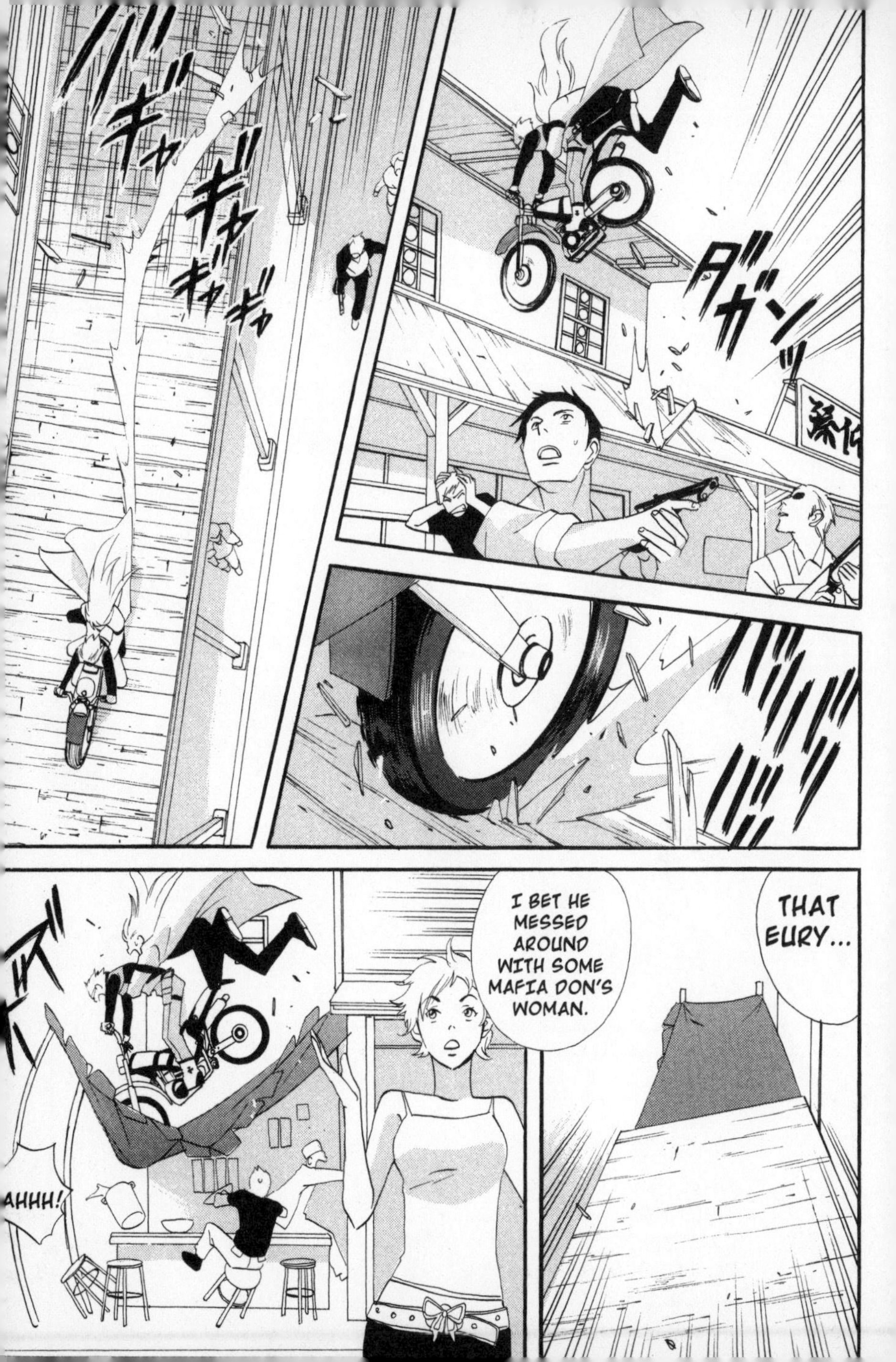
ダガンッ
THAT EURY...
I BET HE MESSED AROUND WITH SOME MAFIA DON'S WOMAN.
AHHH!

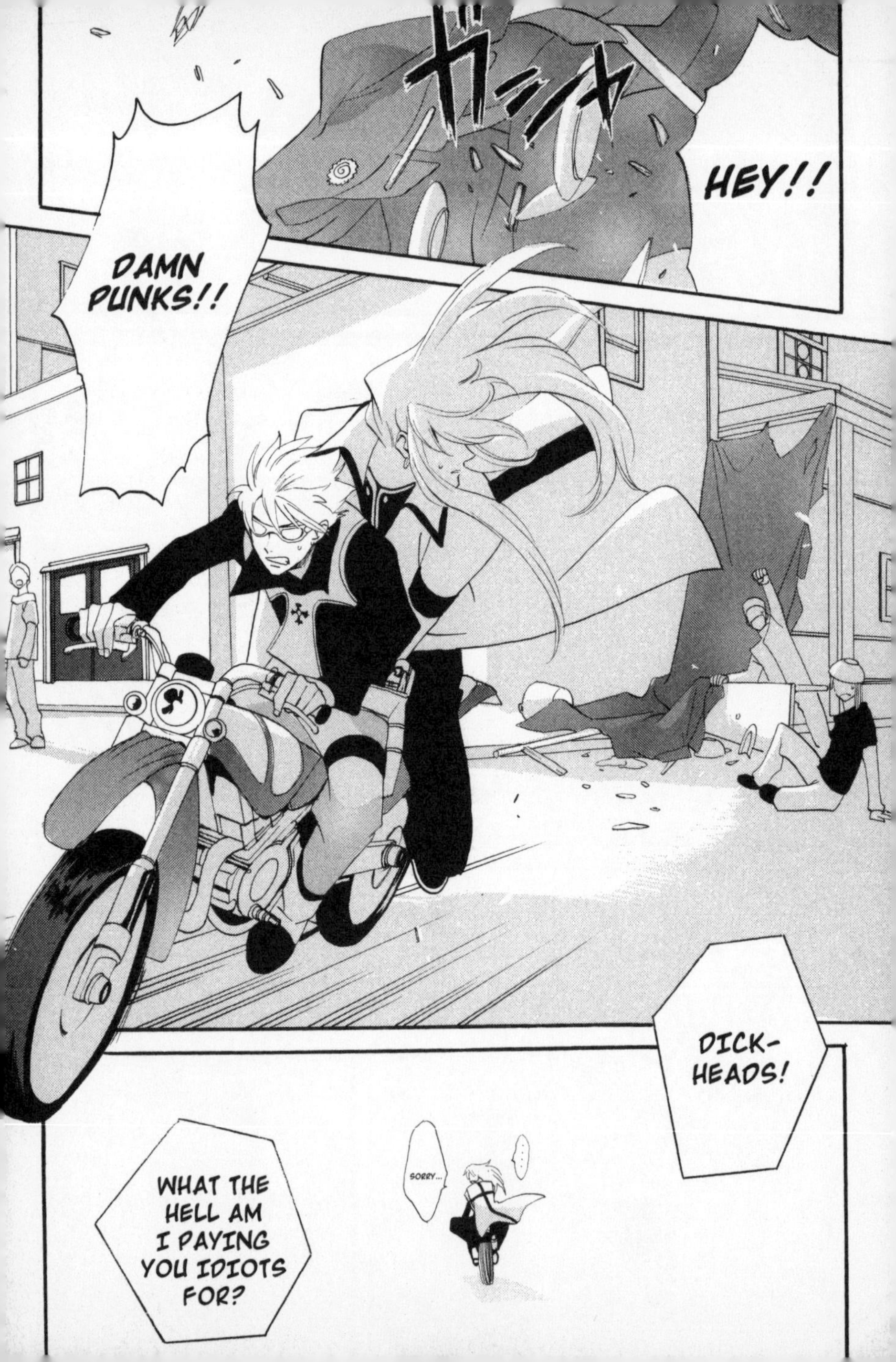
HEY!!
DAMN PUNKS!!
DICK-HEADS!
SORRY...
WHAT THE HELL AM I PAYING YOU IDIOTS FOR?

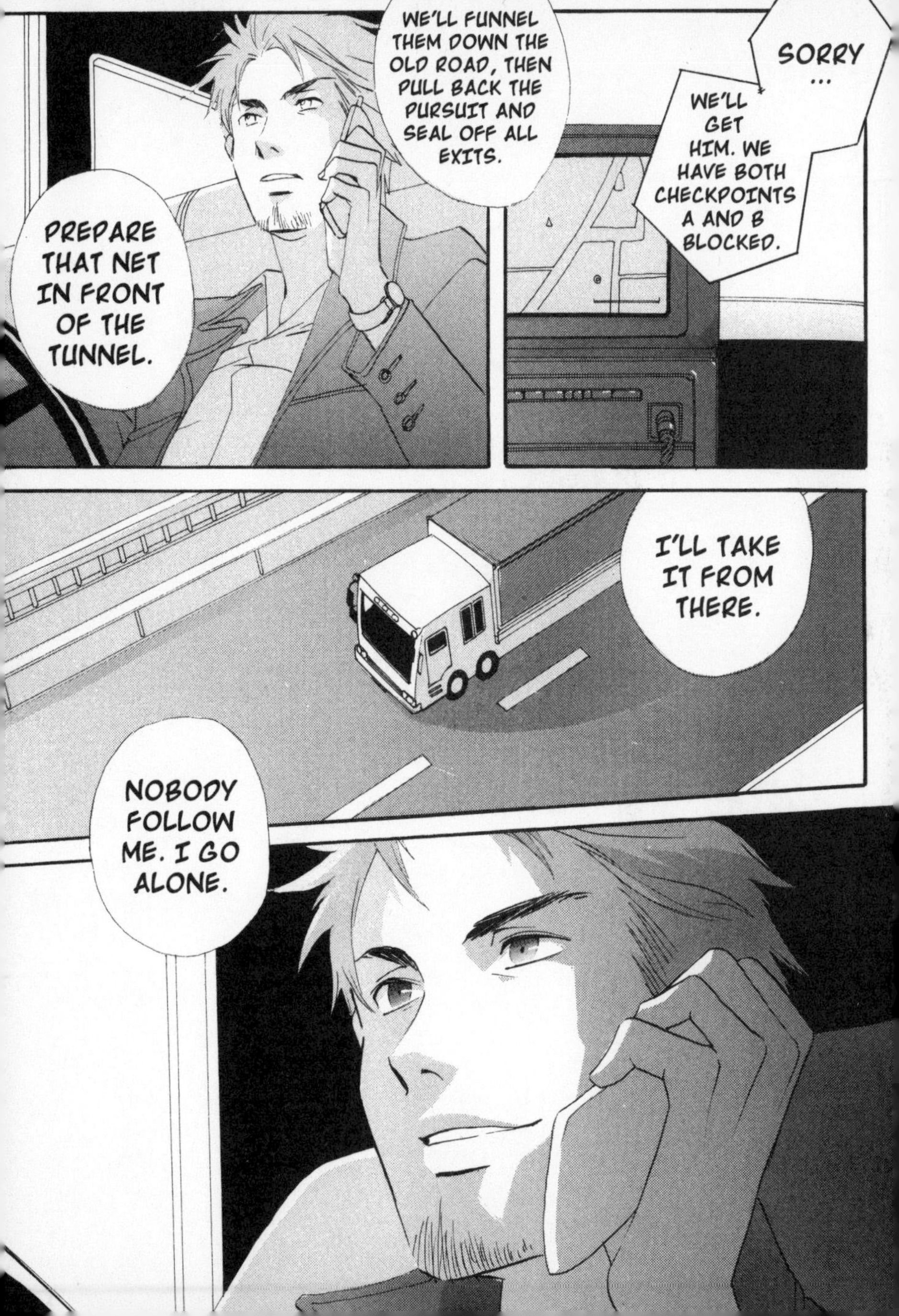
SORRY ...
WE'LL GET HIM. WE HAVE BOTH CHECKPOINTS A AND B BLOCKED.
WE'LL FUNNEL THEM DOWN THE OLD ROAD, THEN PULL BACK THE PURSUIT AND SEAL OFF ALL EXITS.
PREPARE THAT NET IN FRONT OF THE TUNNEL.
I'LL TAKE IT FROM THERE.
NOBODY FOLLOW ME. I GO ALONE.

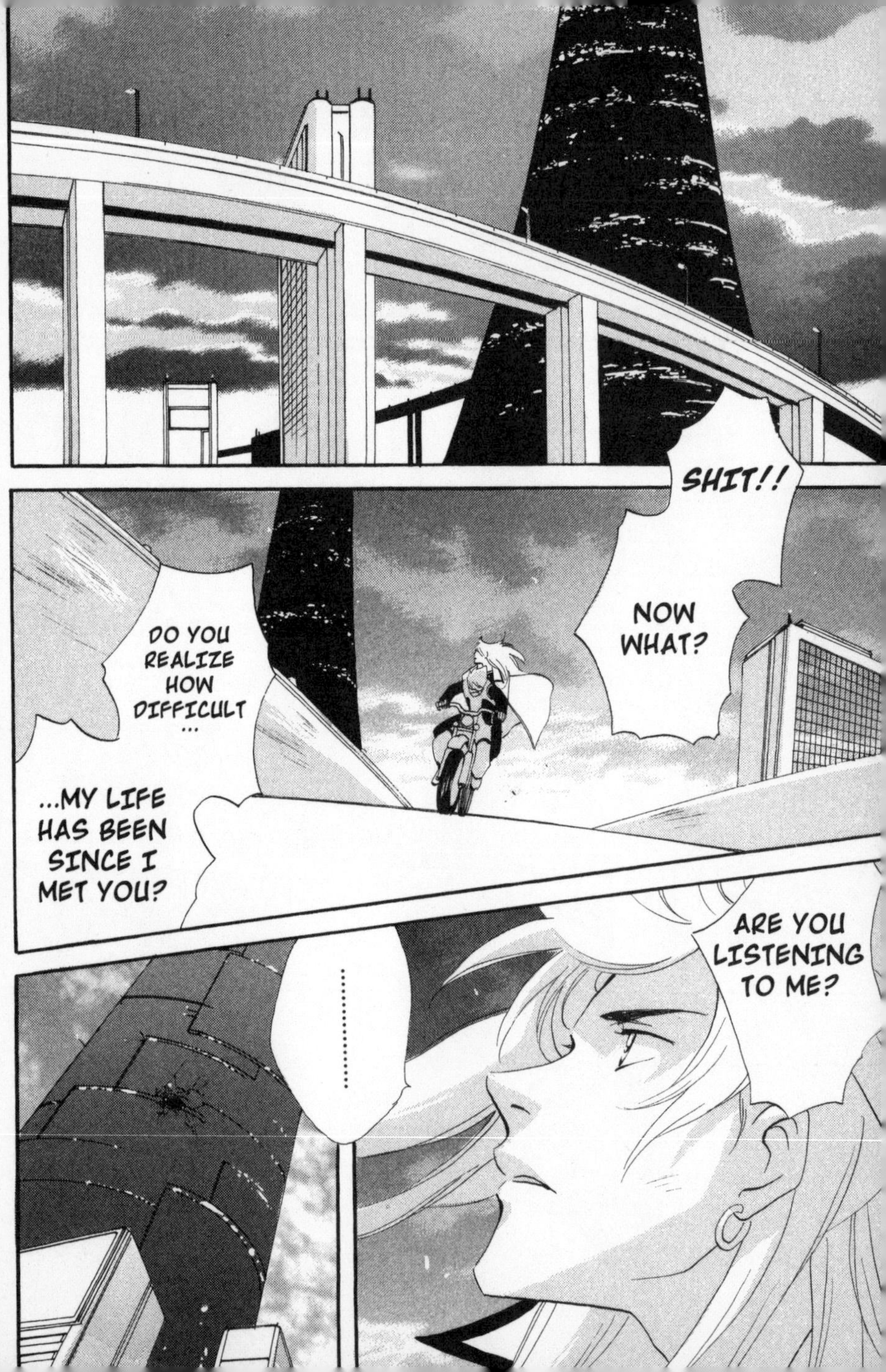
SHIT!!
NOW WHAT?
DO YOU REALIZE HOW DIFFICULT ...
...MY LIFE HAS BEEN SINCE I MET YOU?
ARE YOU LISTENING TO ME?
....

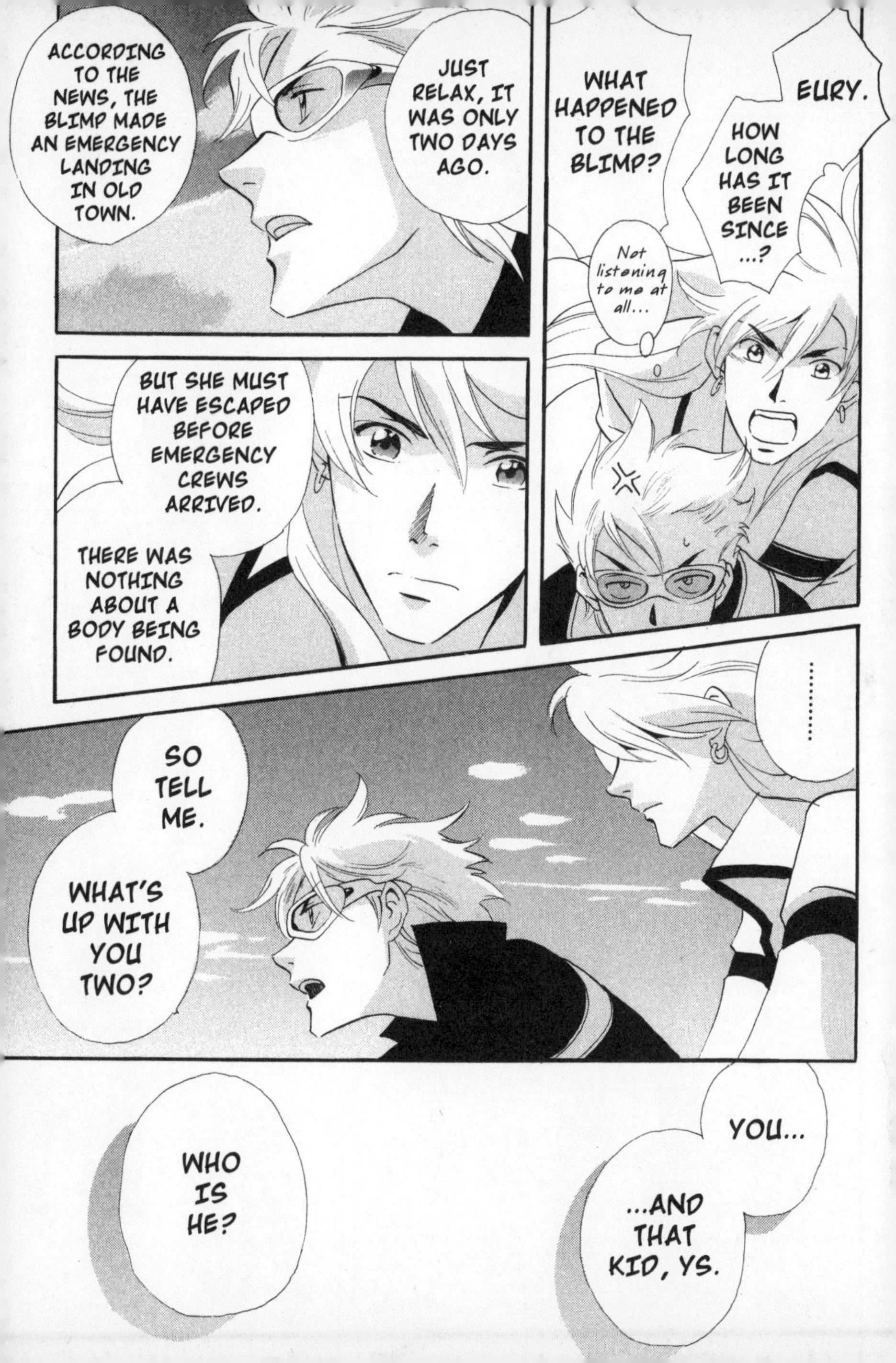
EURY.
HOW LONG HAS IT BEEN SINCE ...?
WHAT HAPPENED TO THE BLIMP?
Not listening to me at all...
JUST RELAX, IT WAS ONLY TWO DAYS AGO.
ACCORDING TO THE NEWS, THE BLIMP MADE AN EMERGENCY LANDING IN OLD TOWN.
BUT SHE MUST HAVE ESCAPED BEFORE EMERGENCY CREWS ARRIVED.
THERE WAS NOTHING ABOUT A BODY BEING FOUND.
......
SO TELL ME.
WHAT'S UP WITH YOU TWO?
YOU...
...AND THAT KID, YS.
WHO IS HE?

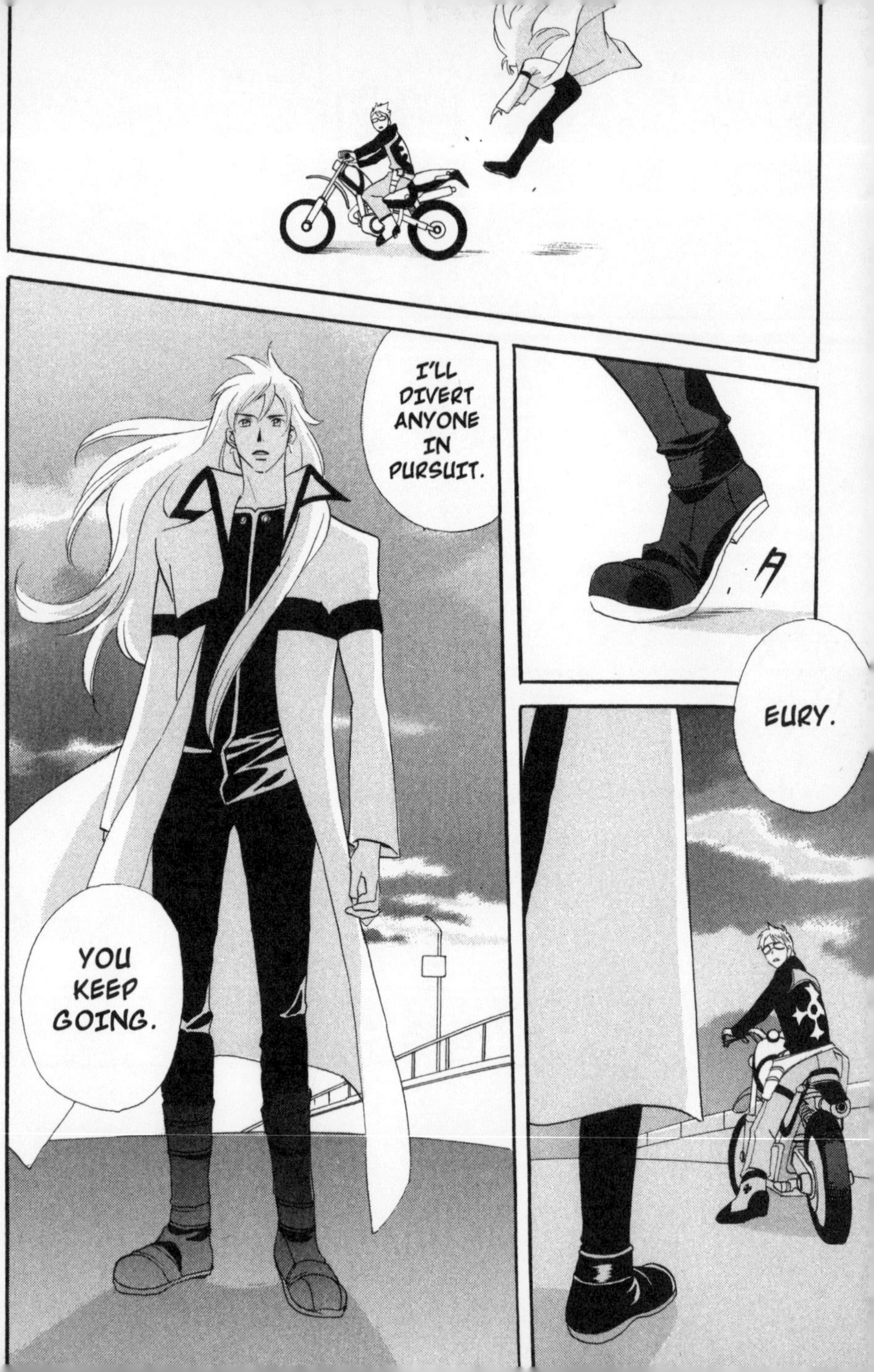
EURY.
I'LL DIVERT ANYONE IN PURSUIT.
YOU KEEP GOING.

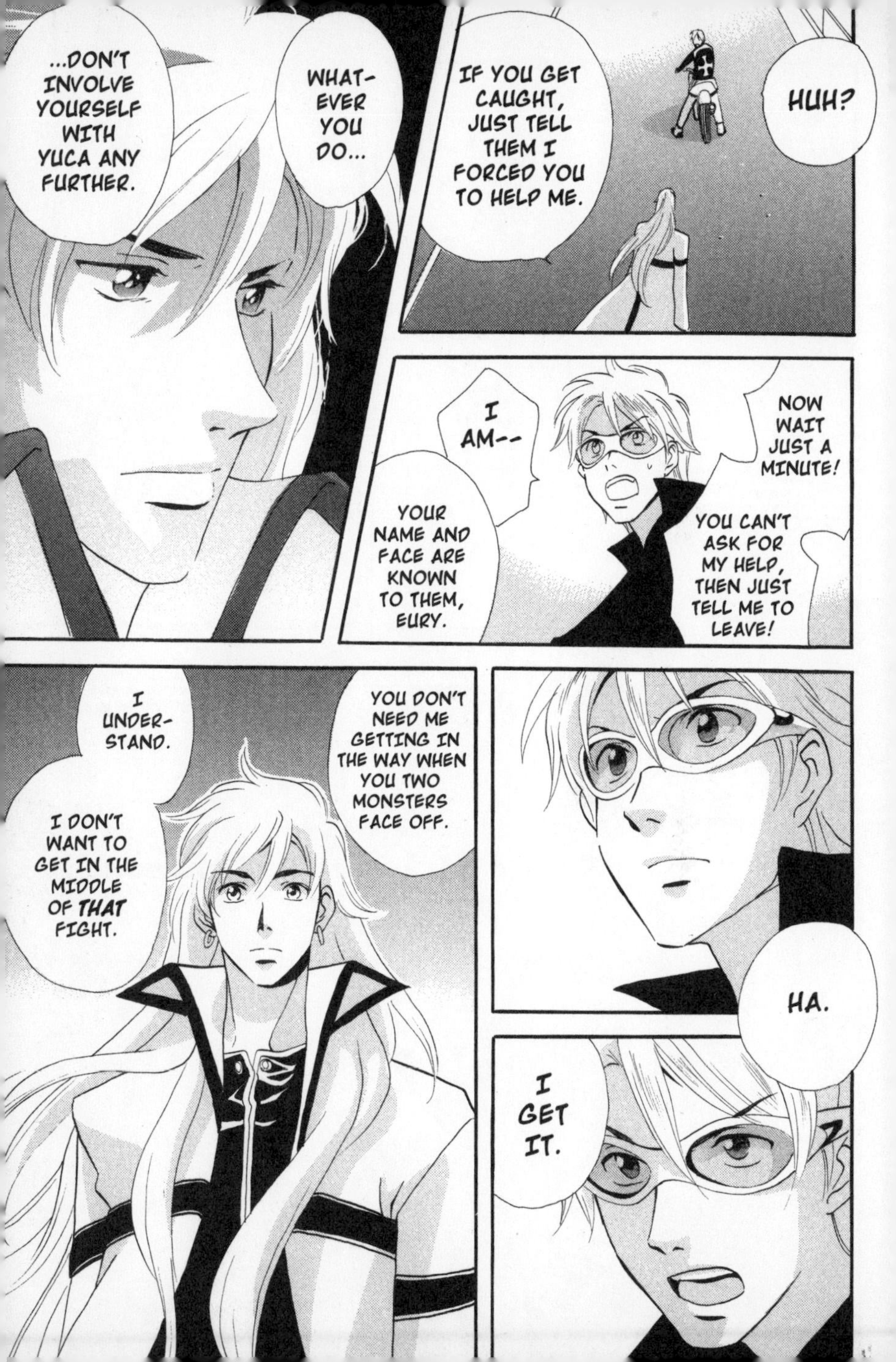
WHAT-EVER YOU DO...
...DON'T INVOLVE YOURSELF WITH YUCA ANY FURTHER.
IF YOU GET CAUGHT, JUST TELL THEM I FORCED YOU TO HELP ME.
HUH?
NOW WAIT JUST A MINUTE!
YOU CAN'T ASK FOR MY HELP, THEN JUST TELL ME TO LEAVE!
I AM--
YOUR NAME AND FACE ARE KNOWN TO THEM, EURY.
I UNDER-STAND.
I DON'T WANT TO GET IN THE MIDDLE OF *THAT* FIGHT.
YOU DON'T NEED ME GETTING IN THE WAY WHEN YOU TWO MONSTERS FACE OFF.
HA.
I GET IT.

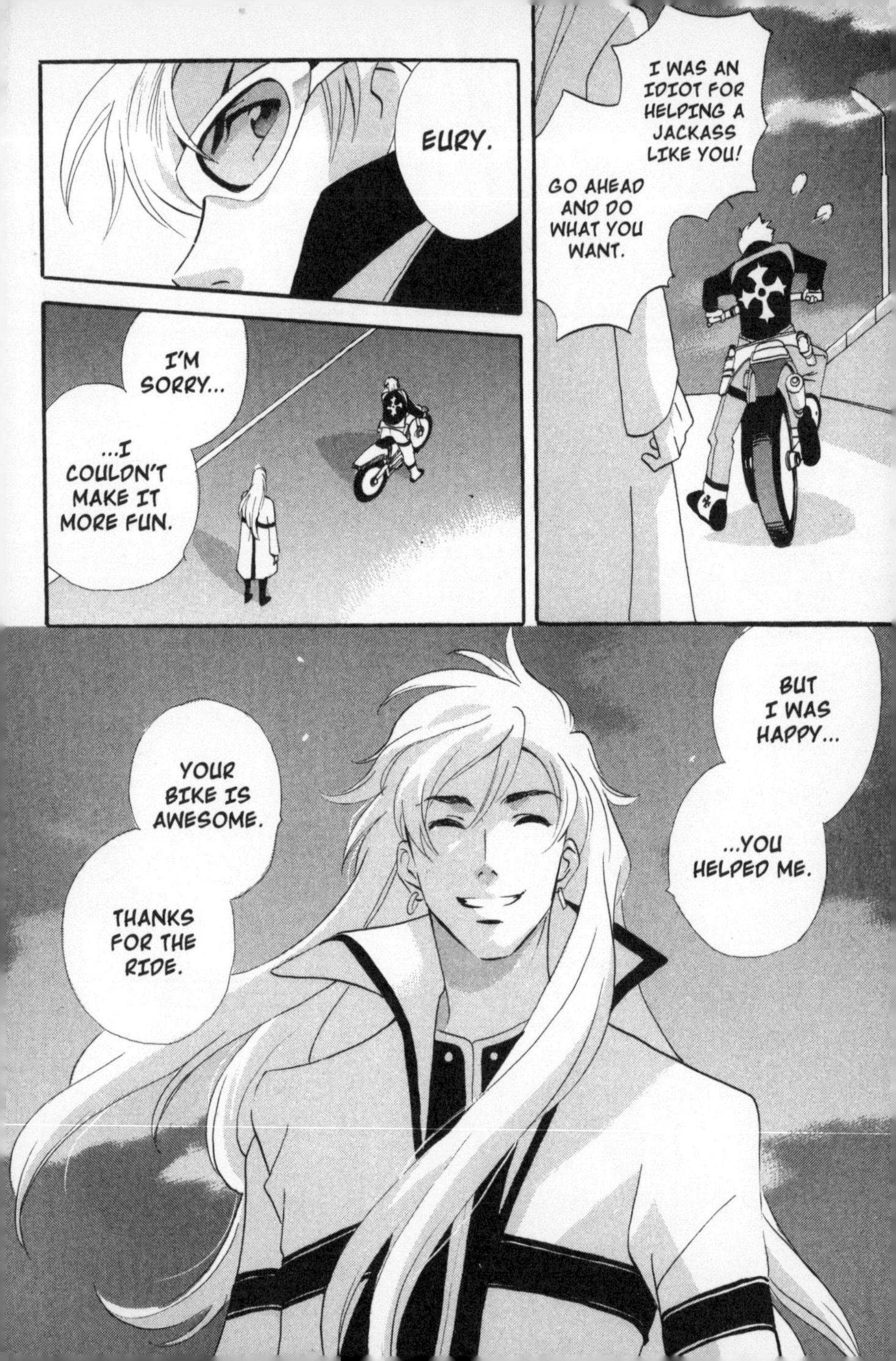
I WAS AN IDIOT FOR HELPING A JACKASS LIKE YOU!
GO AHEAD AND DO WHAT YOU WANT.
EURY.
I'M SORRY...
...I COULDN'T MAKE IT MORE FUN.
BUT I WAS HAPPY...
...YOU HELPED ME.
YOUR BIKE IS AWESOME.
THANKS FOR THE RIDE.

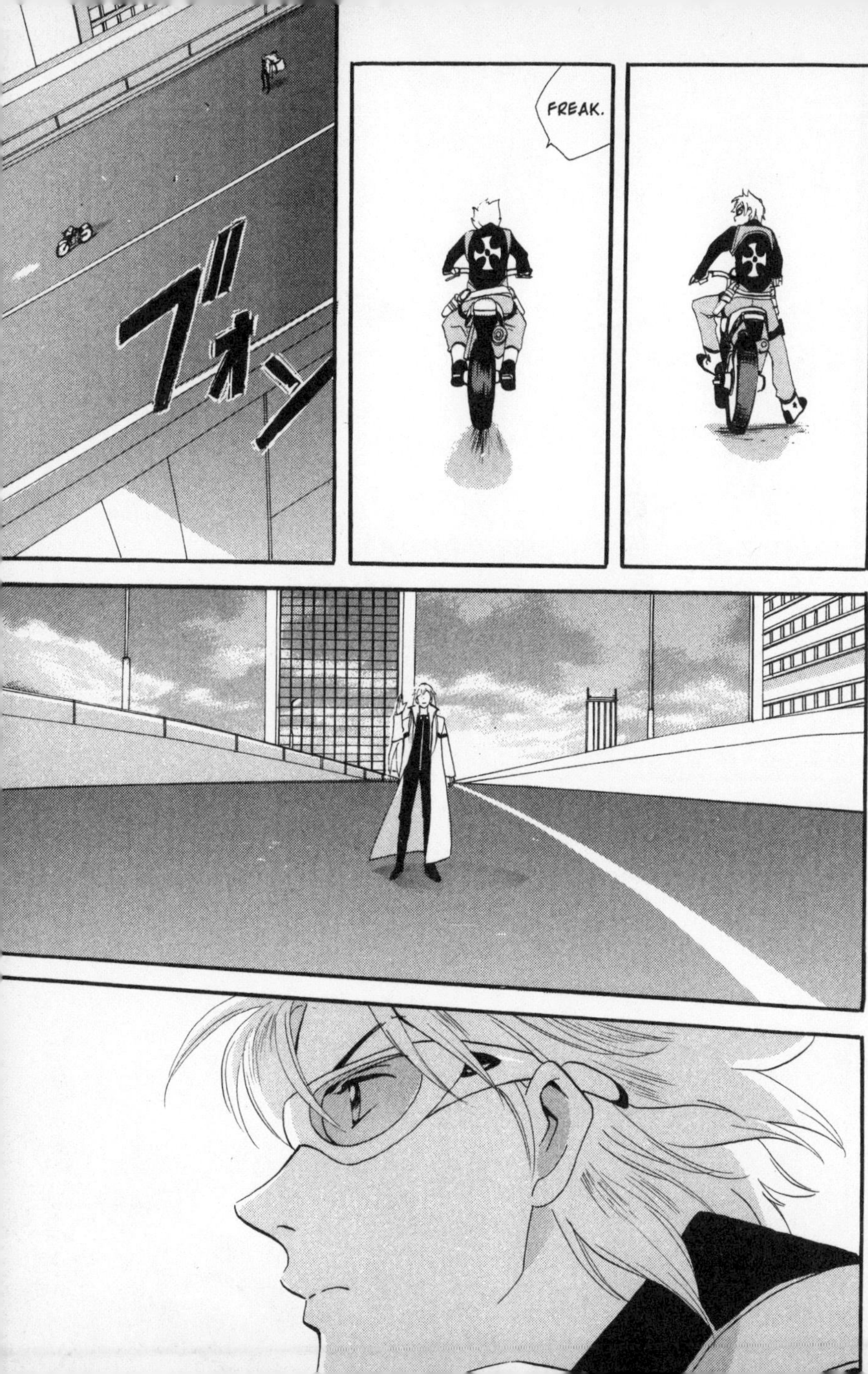
FREAK.
ブォン

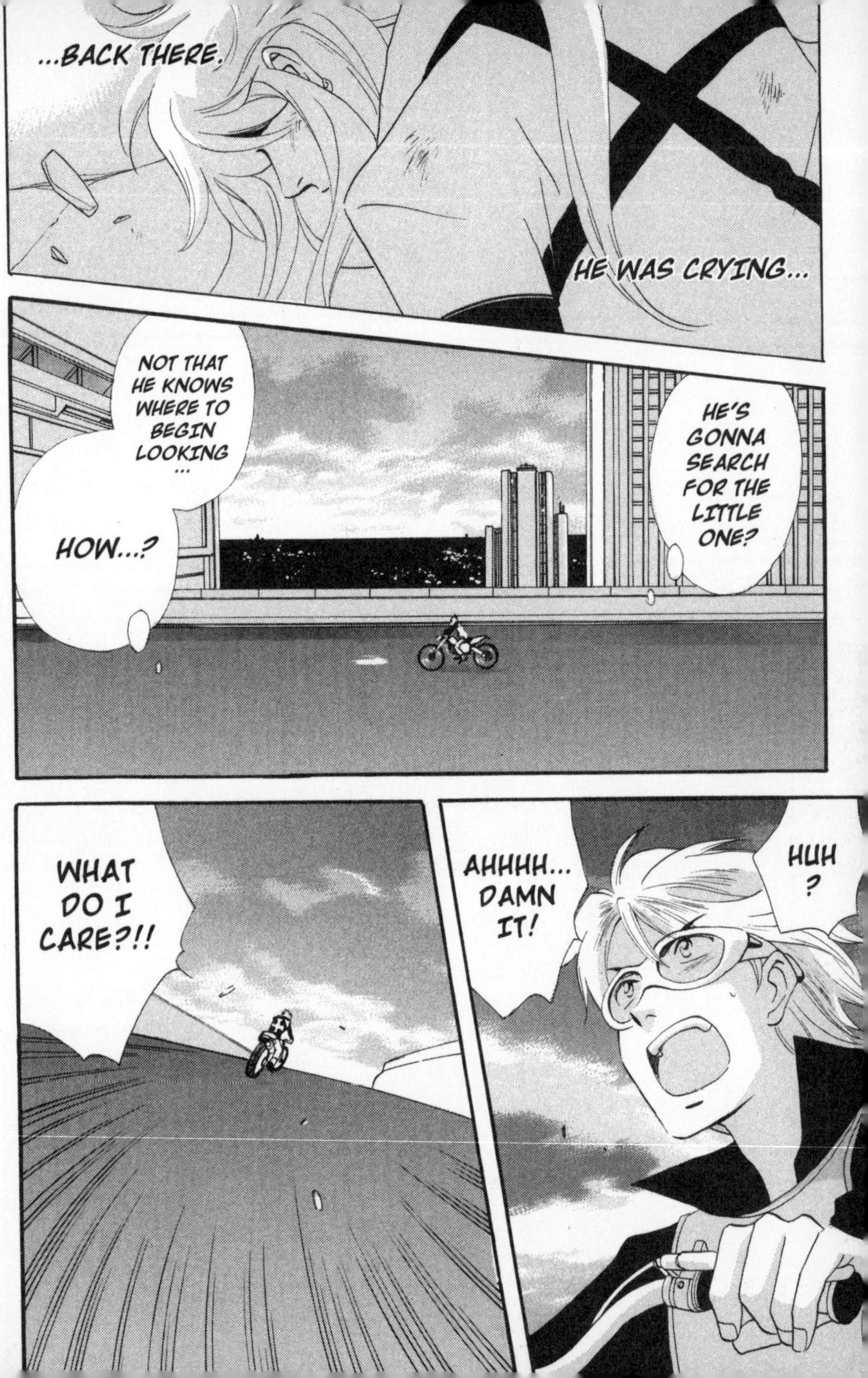
HE WAS CRYING...
...BACK THERE.
HE'S GONNA SEARCH FOR THE LITTLE ONE?
NOT THAT HE KNOWS WHERE TO BEGIN LOOKING...
HOW...?
HUH?
AHHHH... DAMN IT!
WHAT DO I CARE?!!

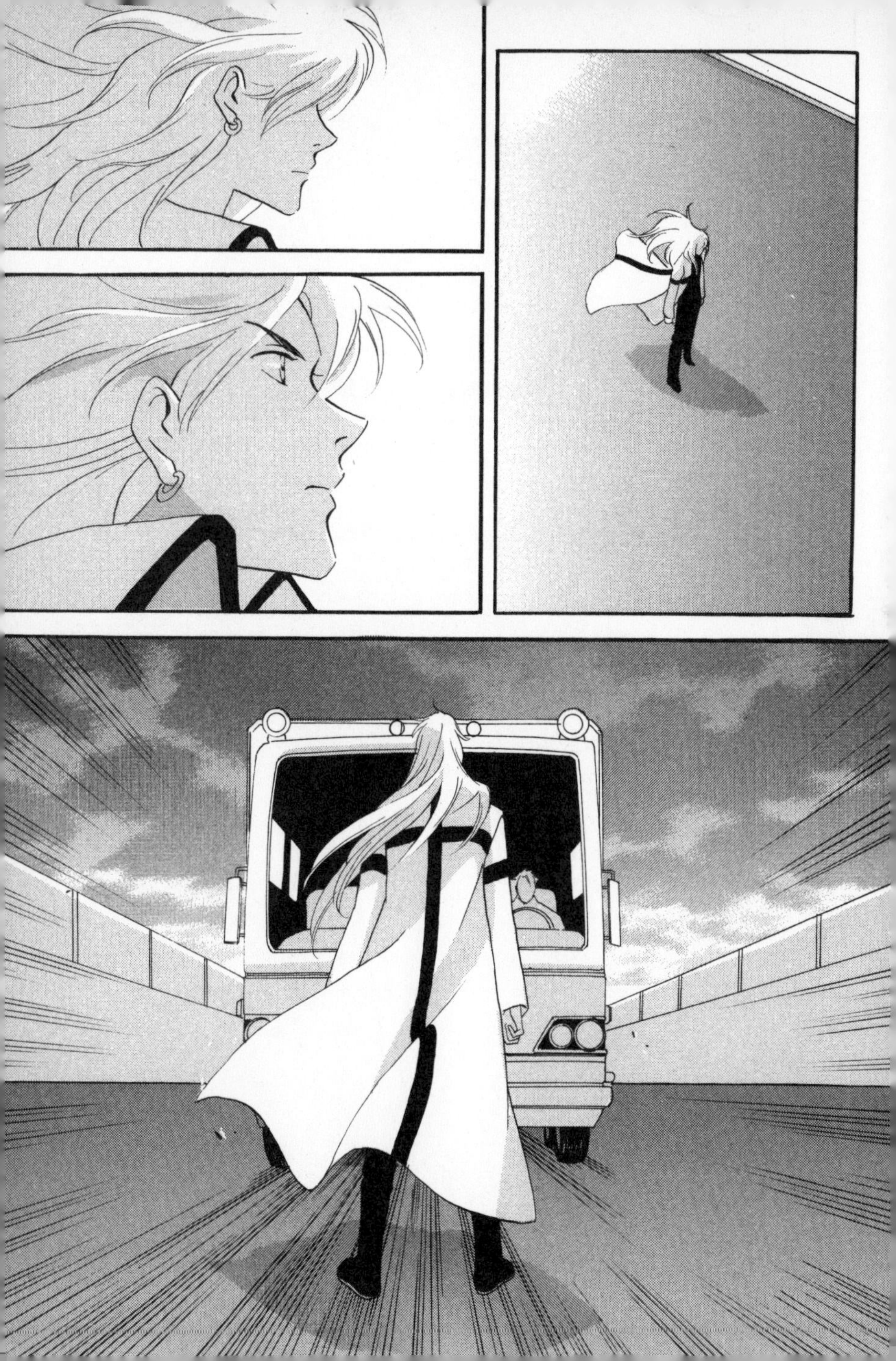

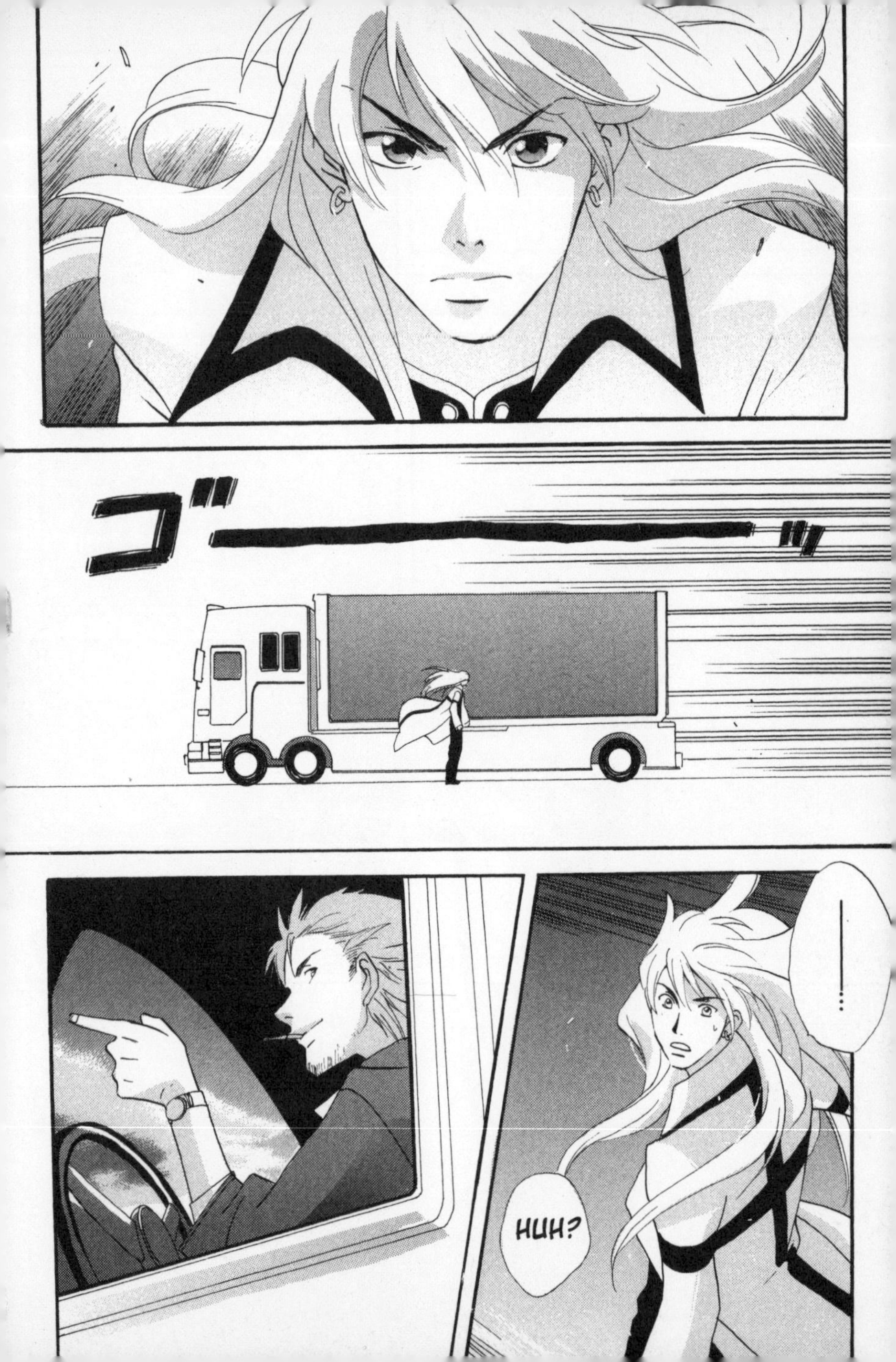
ゴーーーッ
HUH?

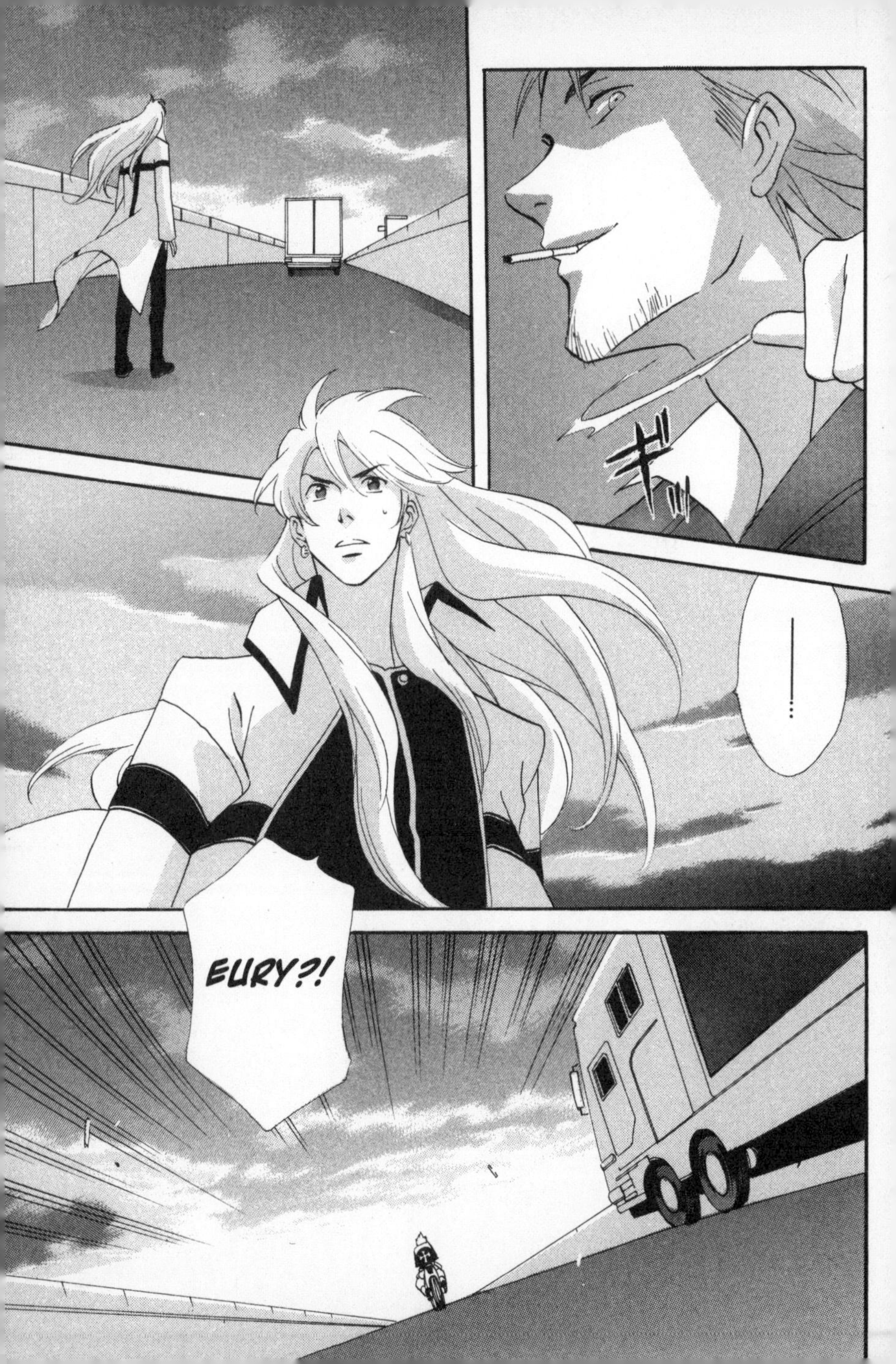
……
EURY?!

Dora Folk

Age:34
Height:186cm
Blood type:O

Command:
Fight
Laugh
Tease

HP..................51

LV.........711/711

Offense
Strength..........89

Defense
Strength.........61

Speed..............38

Cleverness.....79

Luck..............40

Equipment

Weapon: High-powered magnum/
offense strength + 62

Armor: Facial hair / scoundrel + 8

Accessory: Angel blood /
Raise all stats

Deathblow technique command

Eye-Smashing Iron Claw ⇨Ⓟ+Ⓖ

Rib-Breaking Body Blow ↘Ⓟ

Testicle Knee Smash ⇩⇨Ⓚ+Ⓖ

A character as merciless and savage as a wild animal.
He's not afraid to break the rules. He'll do anything
to win -- even punch a woman or knock over a child!

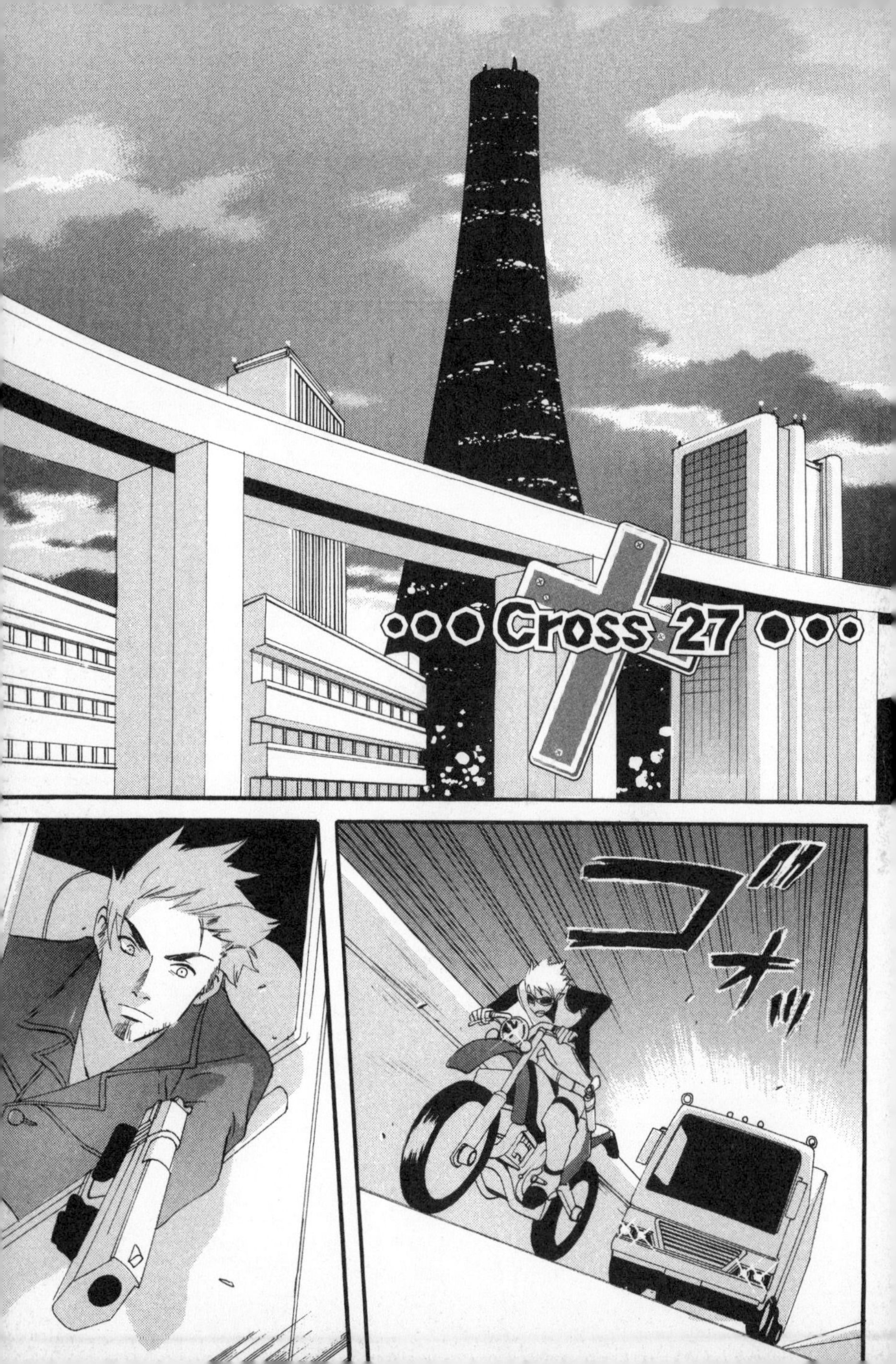
Cross 27
ゴオッ

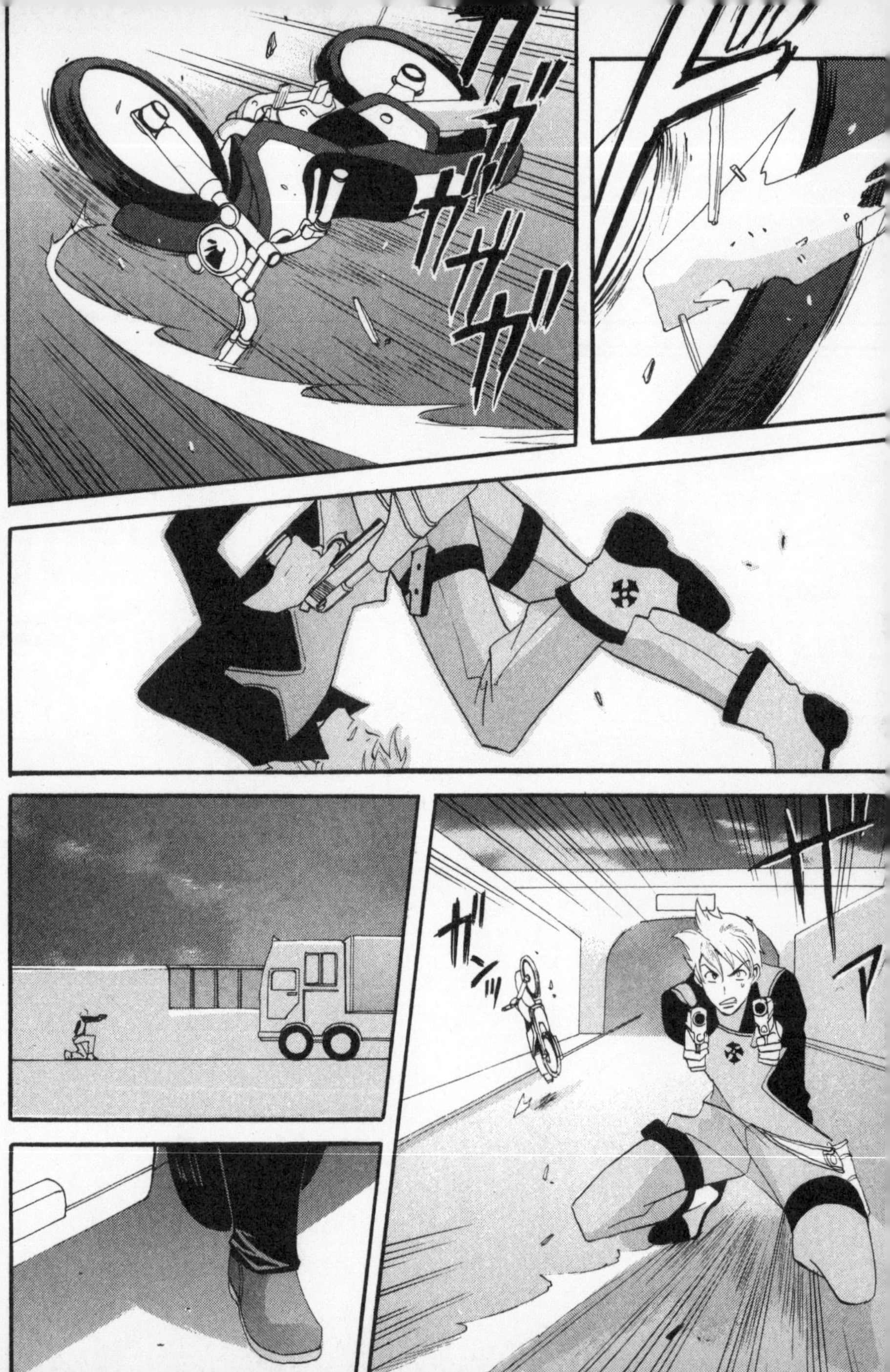

ガガザザガ
ザァ
ザーンッ

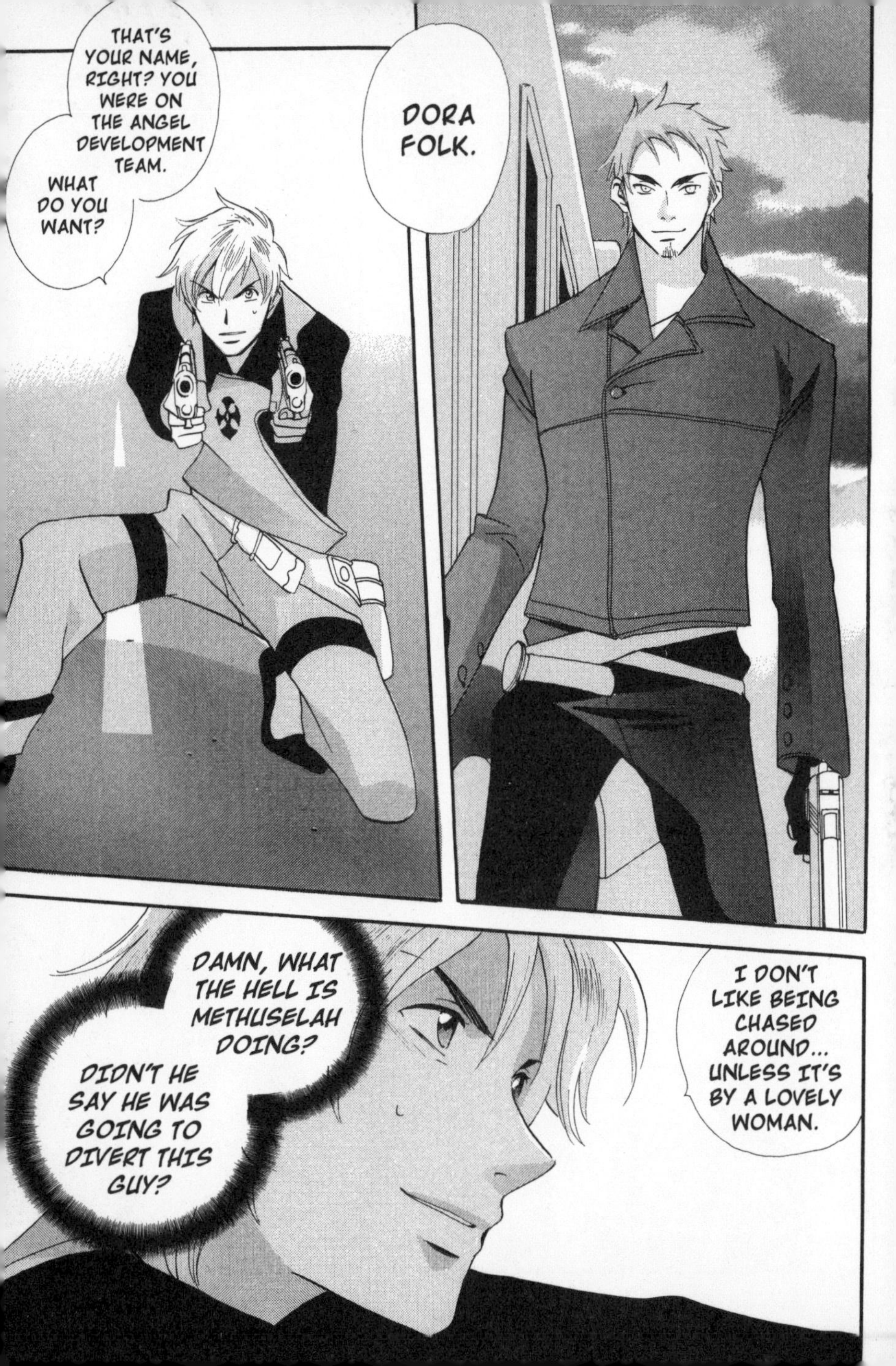
DORA FOLK.
THAT'S YOUR NAME, RIGHT? YOU WERE ON THE ANGEL DEVELOPMENT TEAM.
WHAT DO YOU WANT?
I DON'T LIKE BEING CHASED AROUND... UNLESS IT'S BY A LOVELY WOMAN.
DAMN, WHAT THE HELL IS METHUSELAH DOING?
DIDN'T HE SAY HE WAS GOING TO DIVERT THIS GUY?

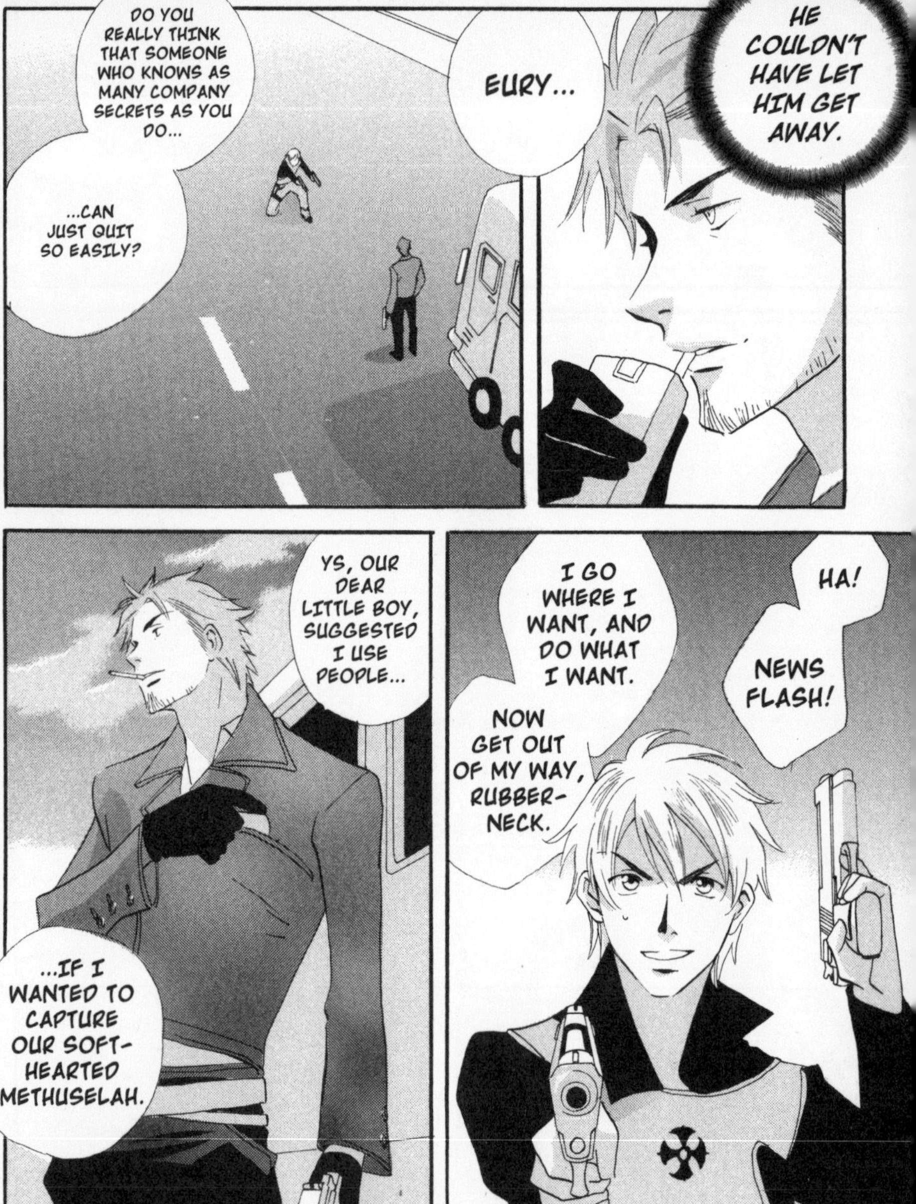
HE COULDN'T HAVE LET HIM GET AWAY.
EURY...
DO YOU REALLY THINK THAT SOMEONE WHO KNOWS AS MANY COMPANY SECRETS AS YOU DO...
...CAN JUST QUIT SO EASILY?
HA!
NEWS FLASH!
I GO WHERE I WANT, AND DO WHAT I WANT.
NOW GET OUT OF MY WAY, RUBBER-NECK.
YS, OUR DEAR LITTLE BOY, SUGGESTED I USE PEOPLE...
...IF I WANTED TO CAPTURE OUR SOFT-HEARTED METHUSELAH.

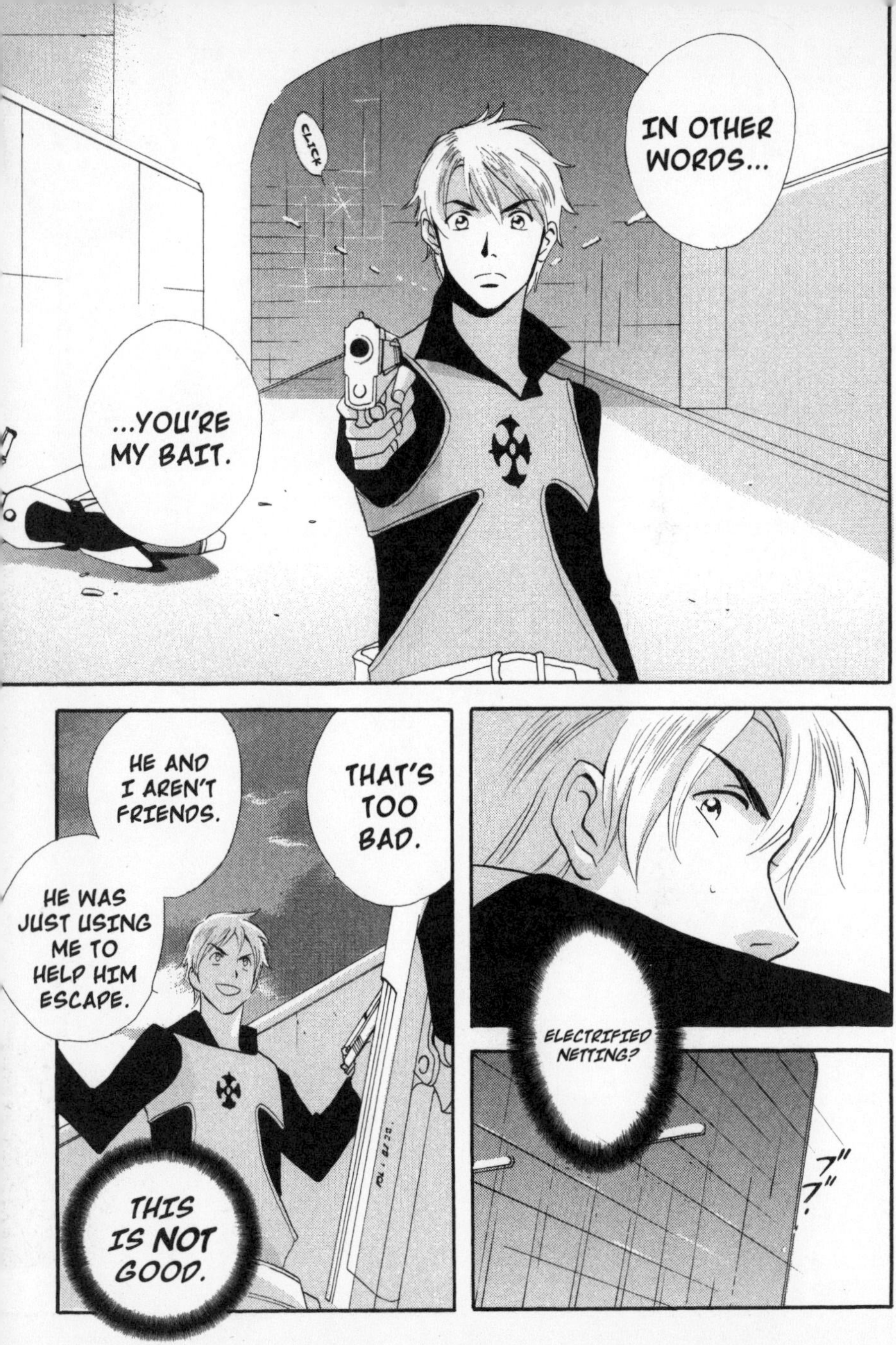
CLICK
IN OTHER WORDS...
...YOU'RE MY BAIT.
ELECTRIFIED NETTING?
THAT'S TOO BAD.
HE AND I AREN'T FRIENDS.
HE WAS JUST USING ME TO HELP HIM ESCAPE.
THIS IS NOT GOOD.

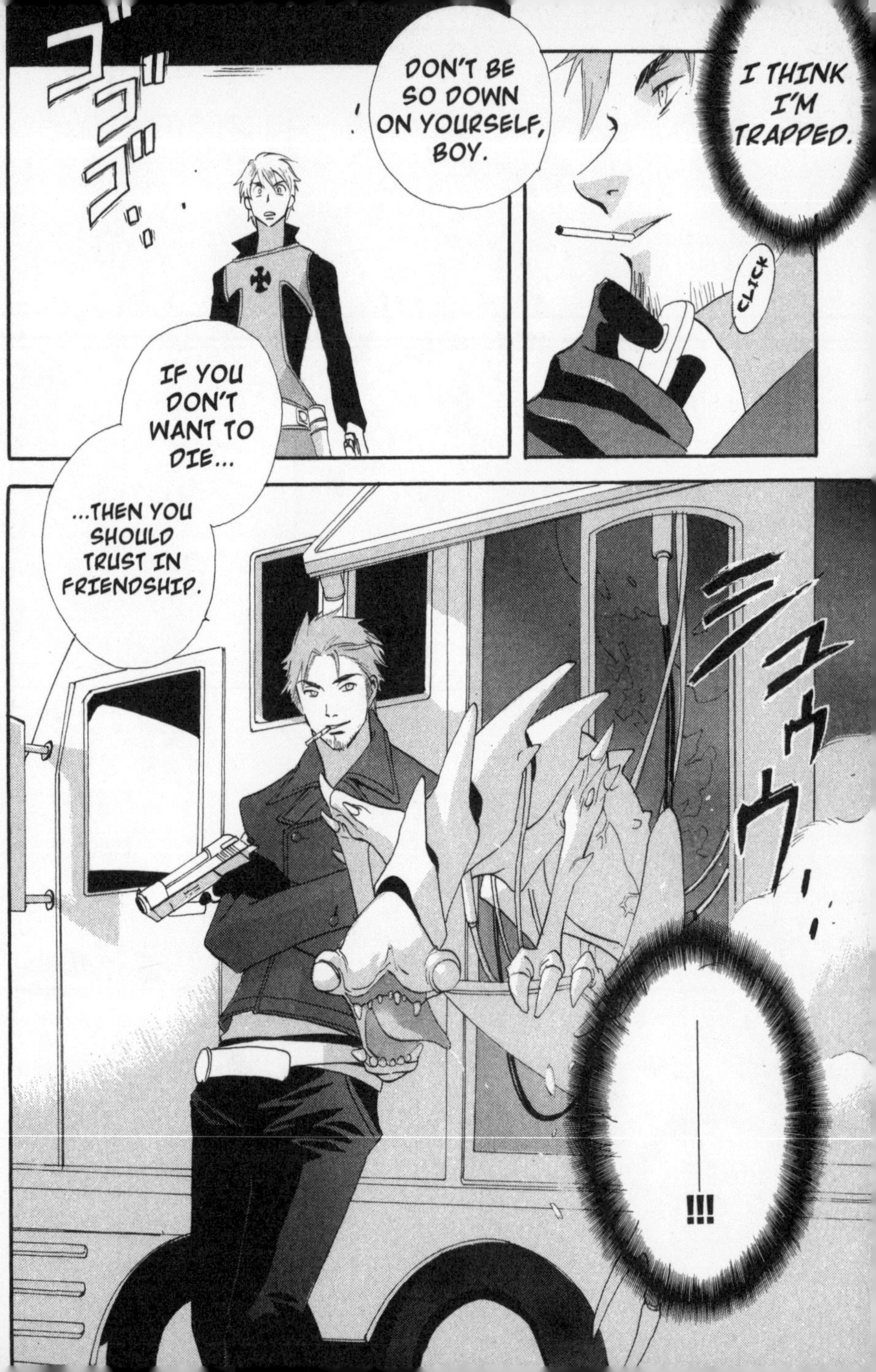
I THINK I'M TRAPPED.
CLICK
DON'T BE SO DOWN ON YOURSELF, BOY.
IF YOU DON'T WANT TO DIE...
...THEN YOU SHOULD TRUST IN FRIENDSHIP.
!!!

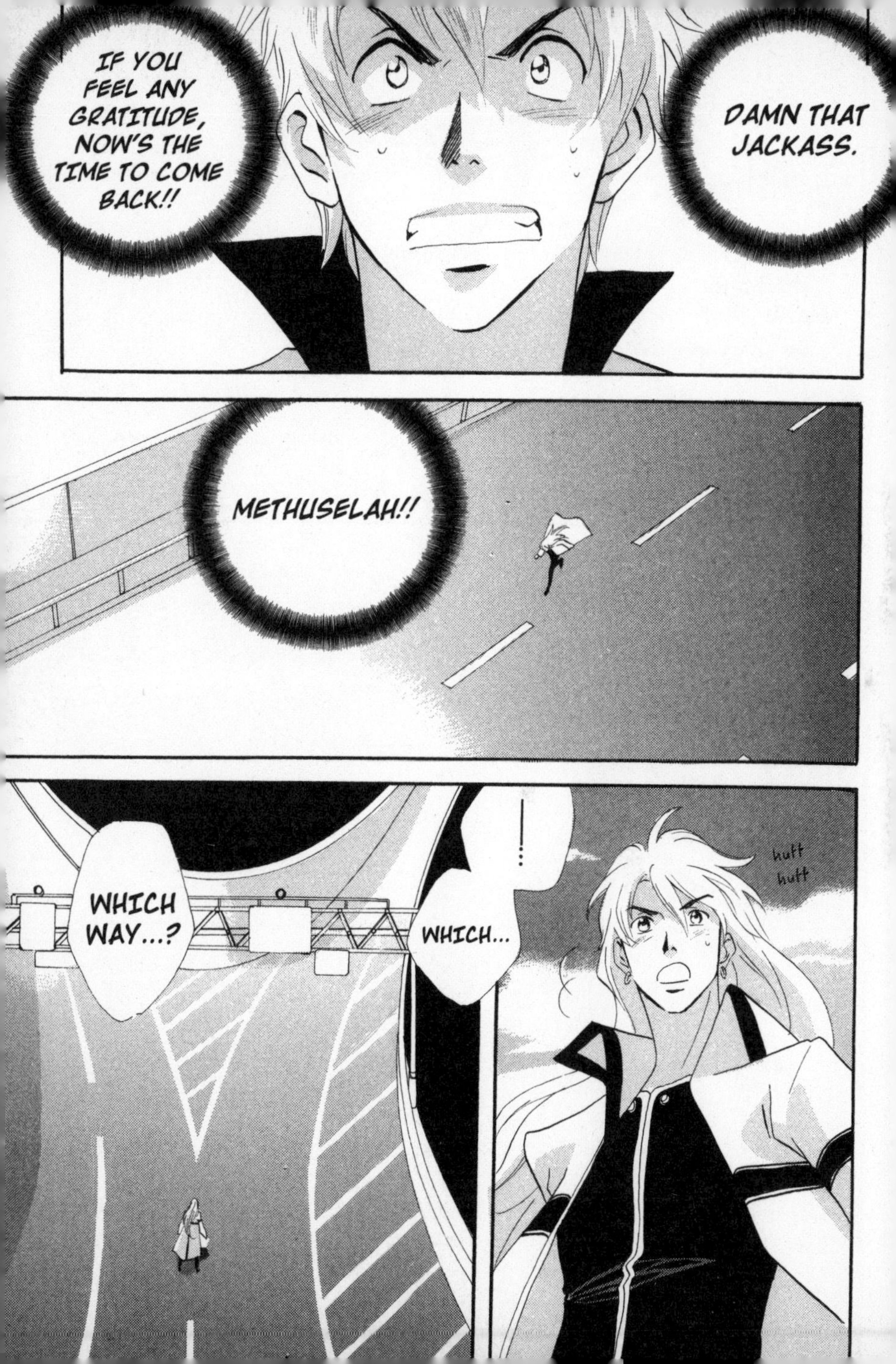
DAMN THAT JACKASS.
IF YOU FEEL ANY GRATITUDE, NOW'S THE TIME TO COME BACK!!
METHUSELAH!!
huff huff
!...
WHICH...
WHICH WAY...?

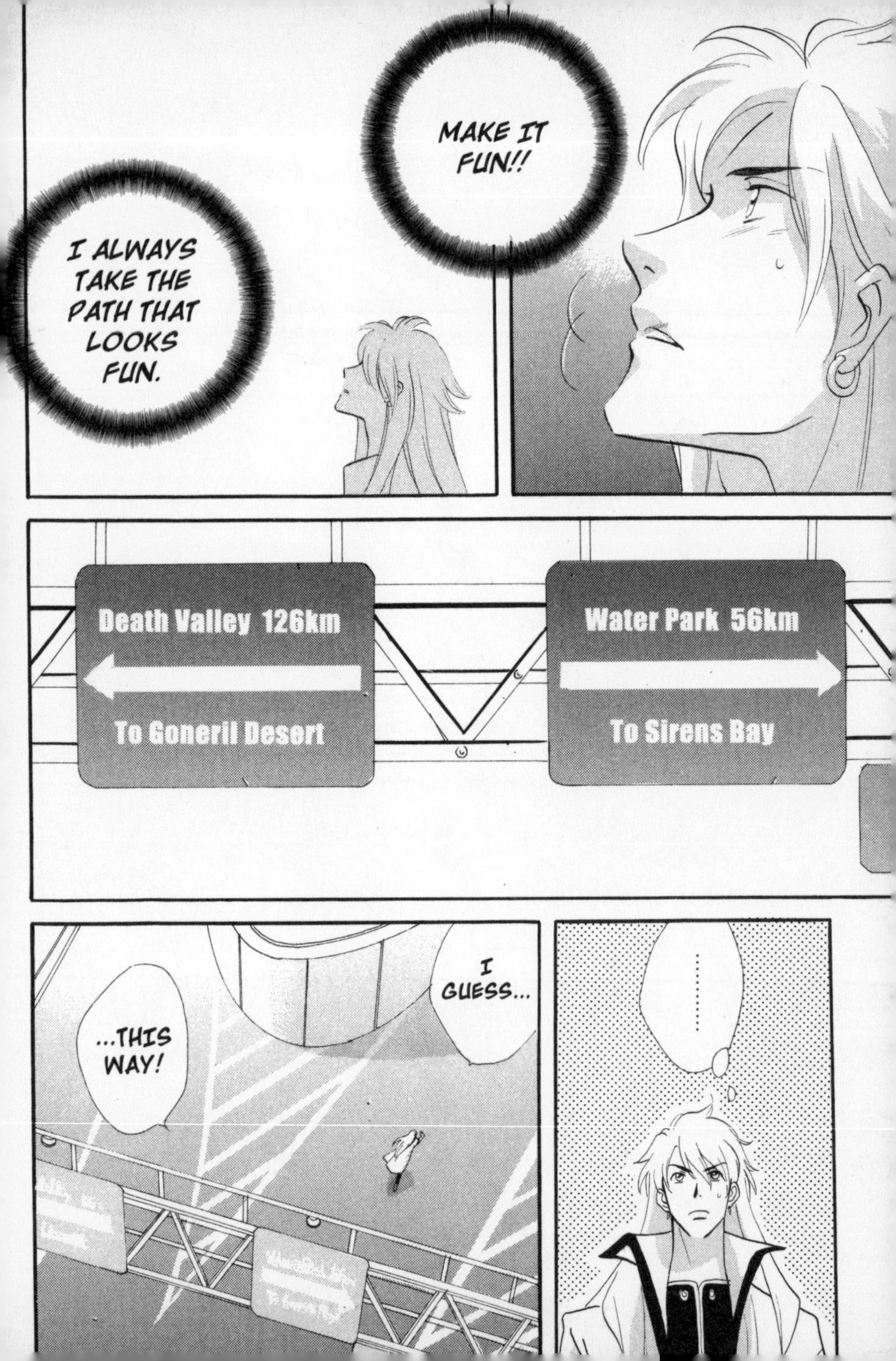
MAKE IT FUN!!
I ALWAYS TAKE THE PATH THAT LOOKS FUN.
Death Valley 126km
To Goneril Desert
Water Park 56km
To Sirens Bay
......
I GUESS...
...THIS WAY!

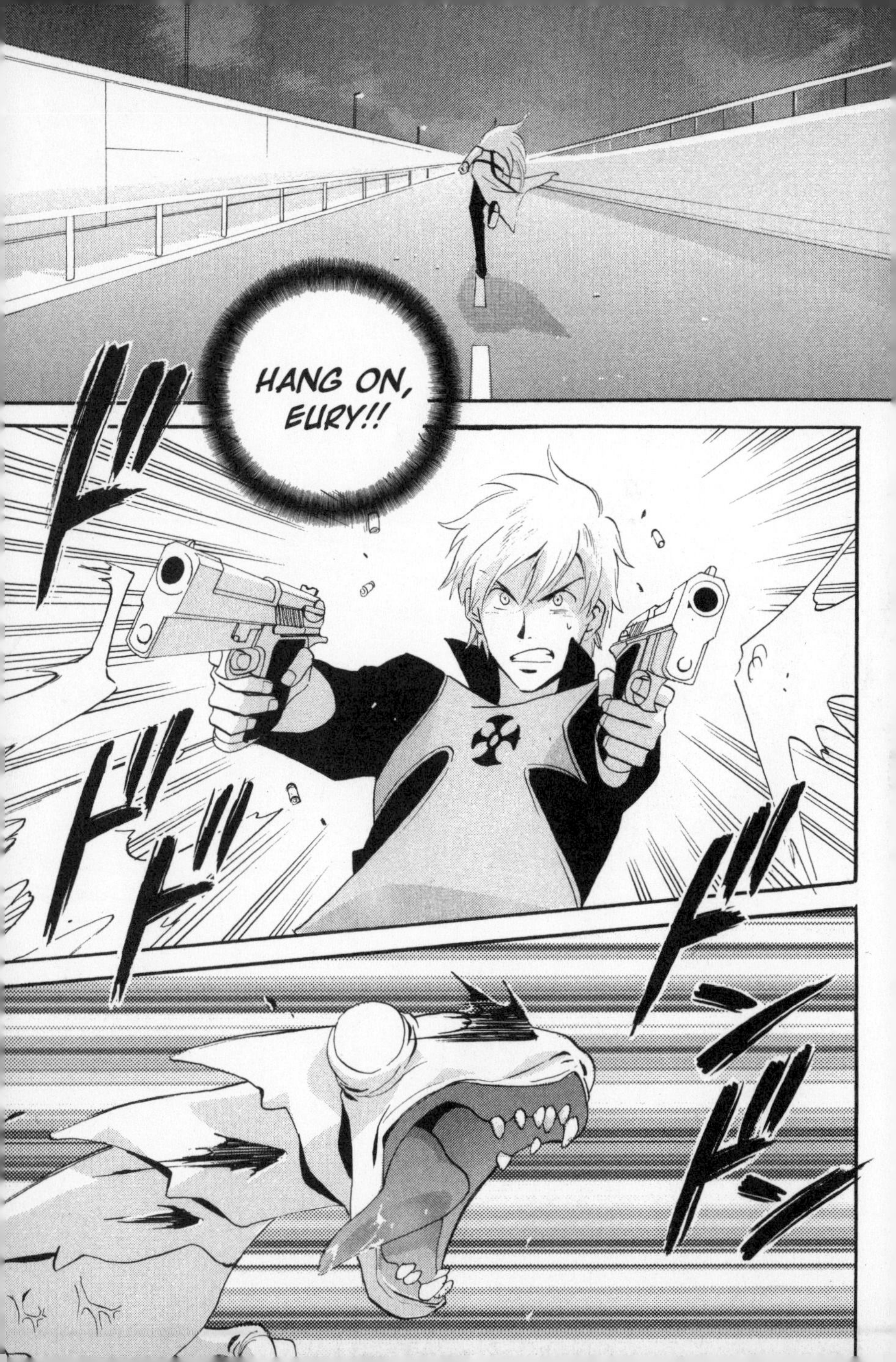
HANG ON, EURY!!
ドドド
ドドドド
ドドド
ドン

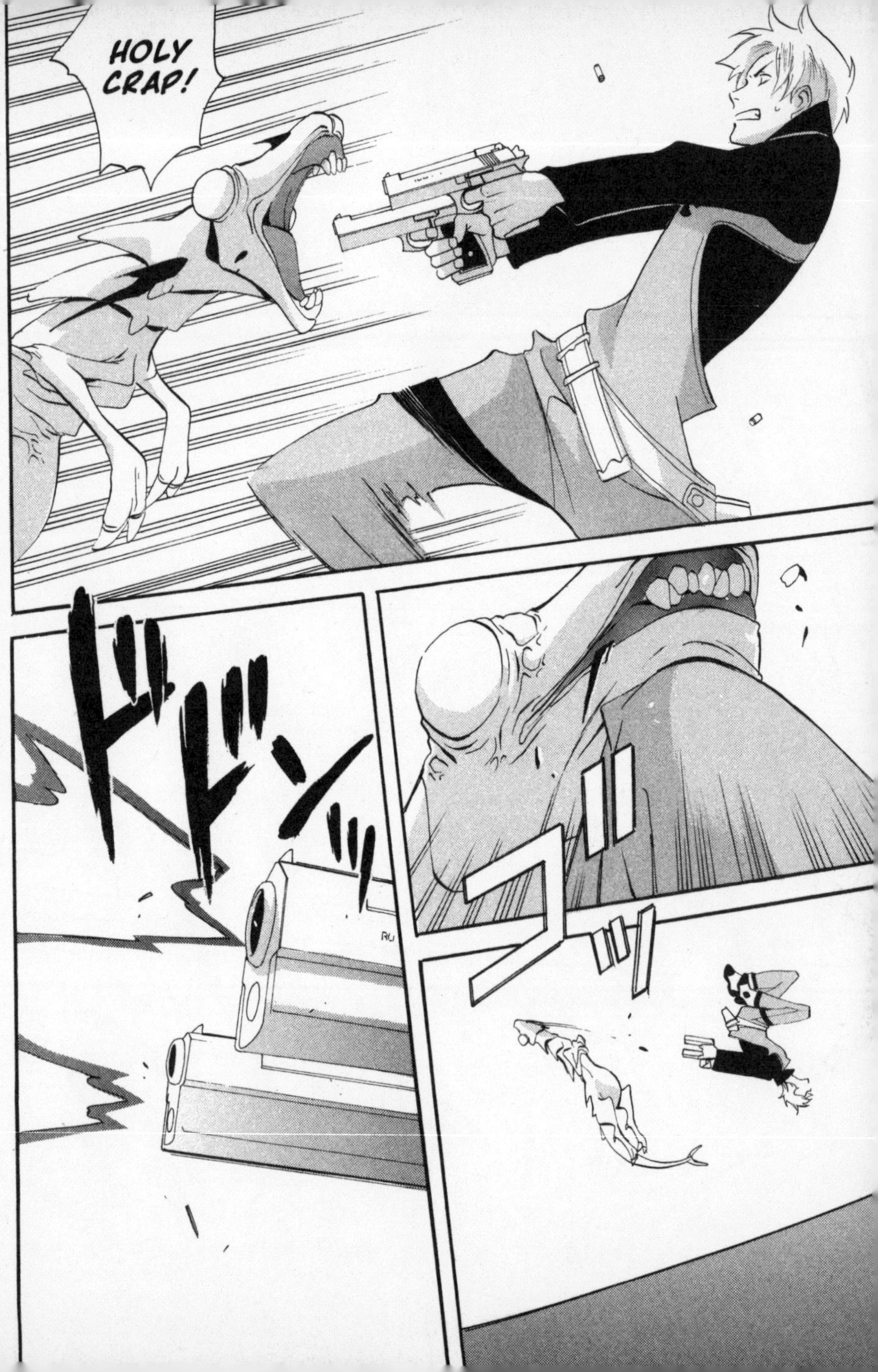
HOLY CRAP!

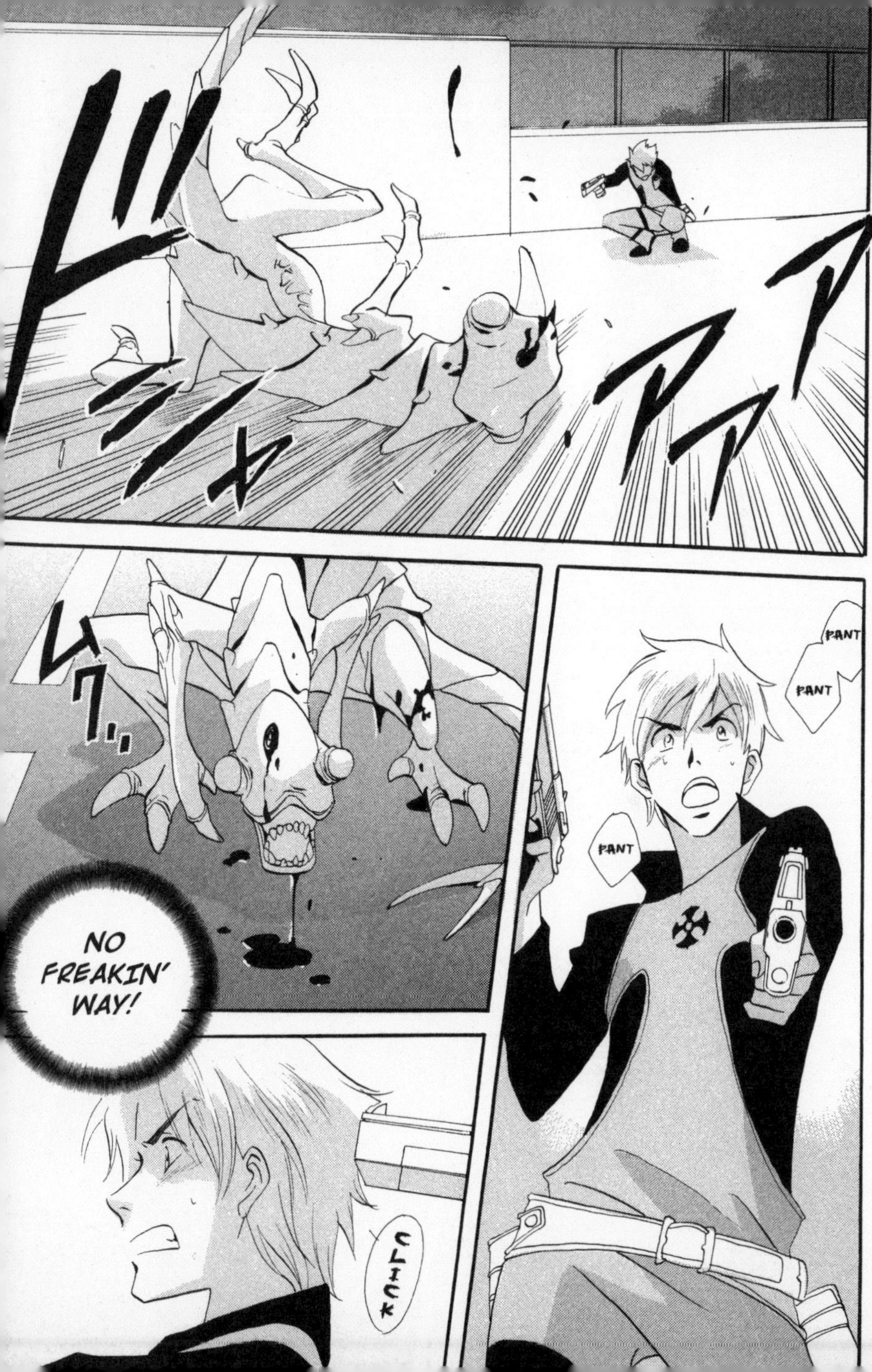
PANT
PANT
PANT
NO FREAKIN' WAY!
CLICK

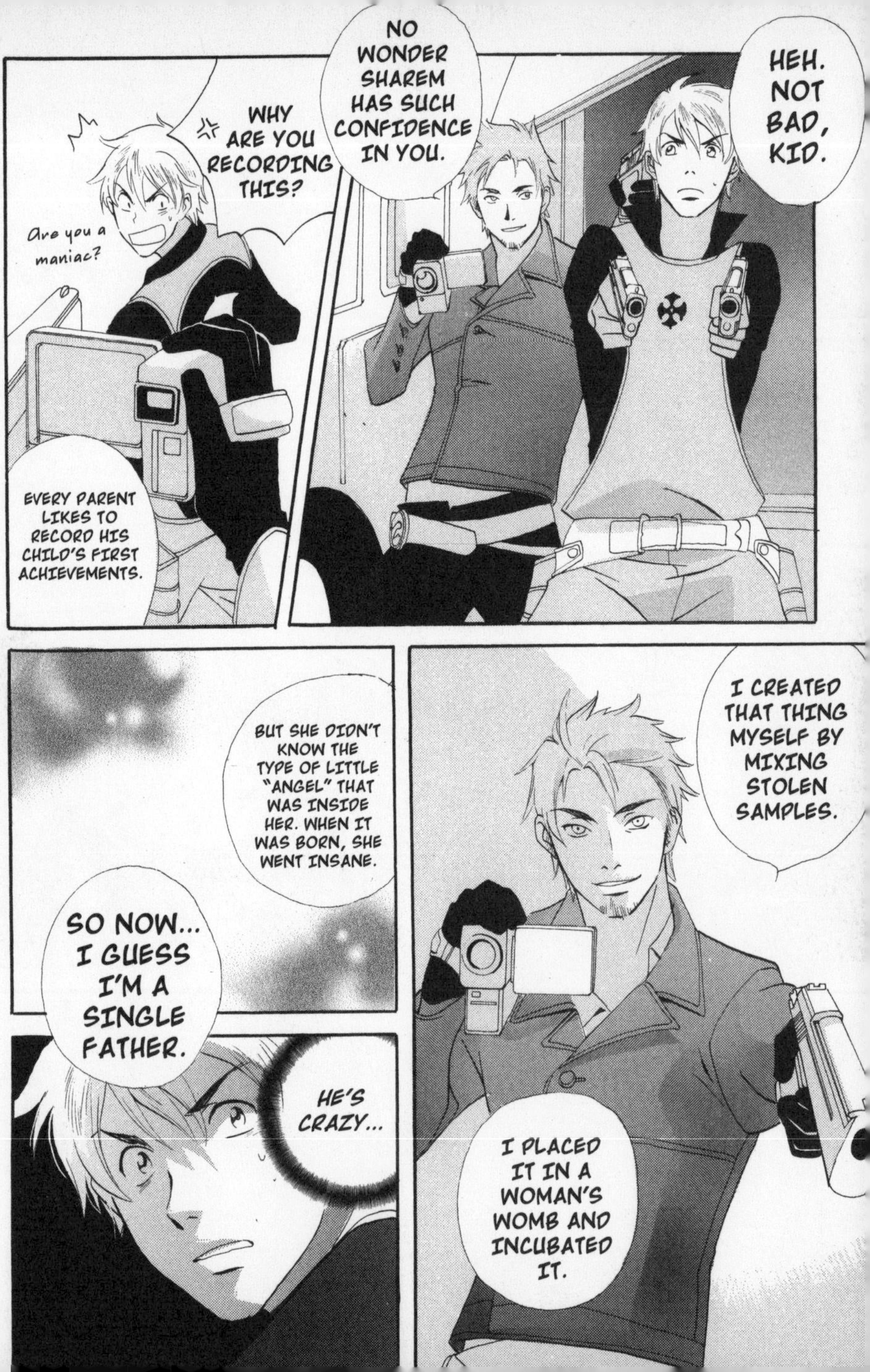
HEH. NOT BAD, KID.
NO WONDER SHAREM HAS SUCH CONFIDENCE IN YOU.
WHY ARE YOU RECORDING THIS?
Are you a maniac?
EVERY PARENT LIKES TO RECORD HIS CHILD'S FIRST ACHIEVEMENTS.
I CREATED THAT THING MYSELF BY MIXING STOLEN SAMPLES.
I PLACED IT IN A WOMAN'S WOMB AND INCUBATED IT.
BUT SHE DIDN'T KNOW THE TYPE OF LITTLE "ANGEL" THAT WAS INSIDE HER. WHEN IT WAS BORN, SHE WENT INSANE.
SO NOW... I GUESS I'M A SINGLE FATHER.
HE'S CRAZY...

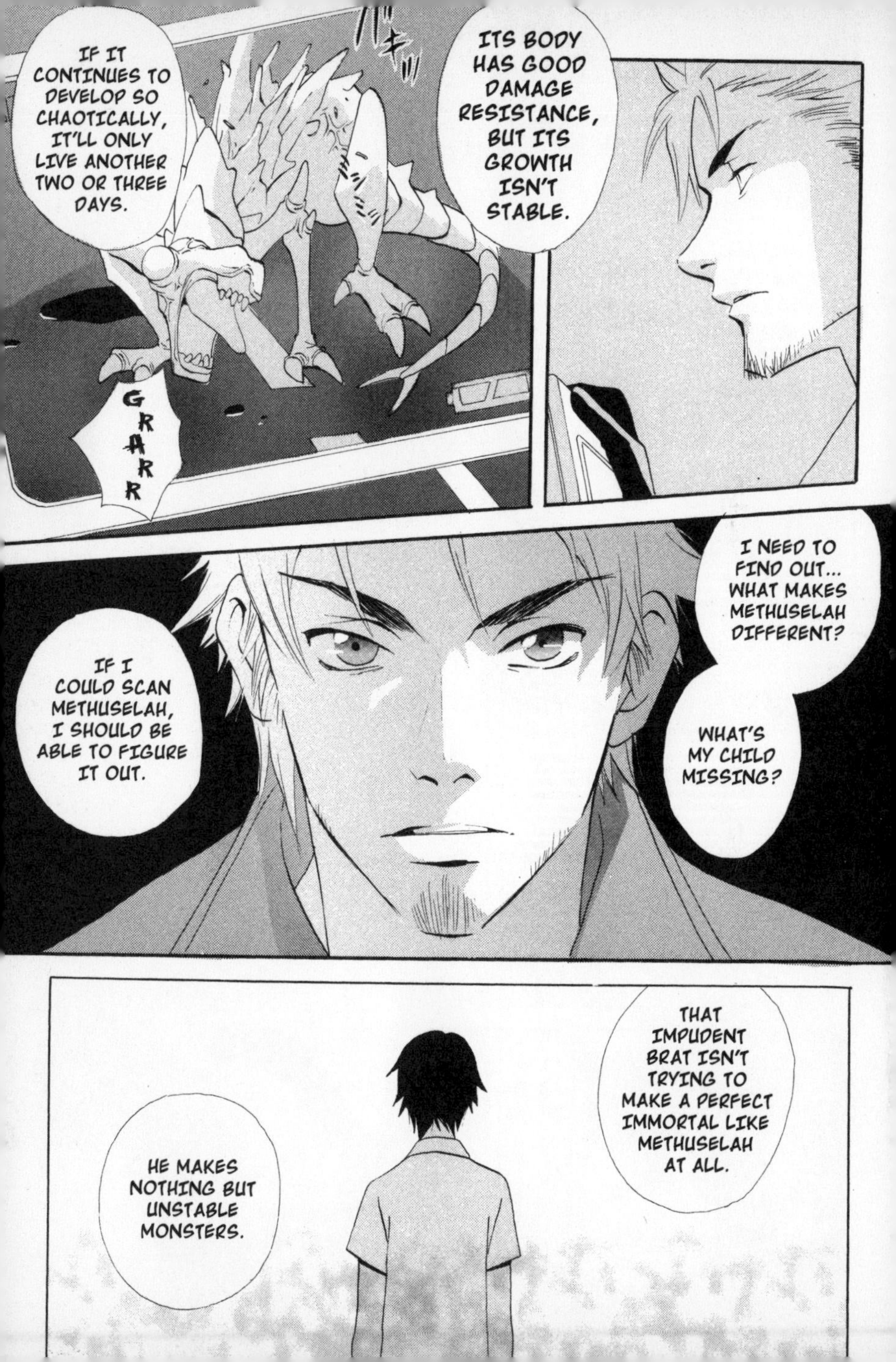
ITS BODY HAS GOOD DAMAGE RESISTANCE, BUT ITS GROWTH ISN'T STABLE.
IF IT CONTINUES TO DEVELOP SO CHAOTICALLY, IT'LL ONLY LIVE ANOTHER TWO OR THREE DAYS.
GRARR
I NEED TO FIND OUT... WHAT MAKES METHUSELAH DIFFERENT?
WHAT'S MY CHILD MISSING?
IF I COULD SCAN METHUSELAH, I SHOULD BE ABLE TO FIGURE IT OUT.
THAT IMPUDENT BRAT ISN'T TRYING TO MAKE A PERFECT IMMORTAL LIKE METHUSELAH AT ALL.
HE MAKES NOTHING BUT UNSTABLE MONSTERS.

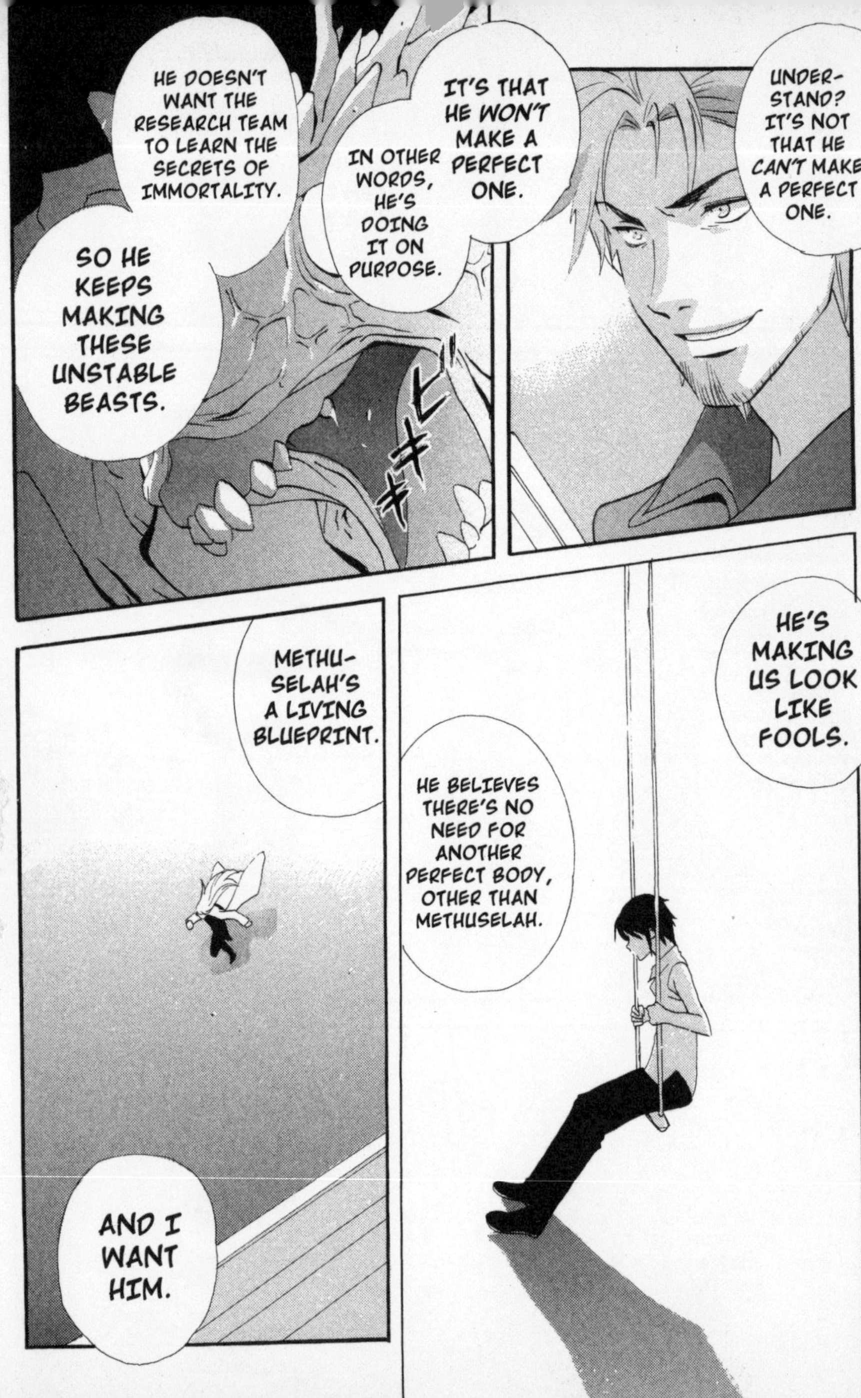
UNDER-STAND? IT'S NOT THAT HE CAN'T MAKE A PERFECT ONE.
IT'S THAT HE *WON'T* MAKE A PERFECT ONE.
IN OTHER WORDS, HE'S DOING IT ON PURPOSE.
HE DOESN'T WANT THE RESEARCH TEAM TO LEARN THE SECRETS OF IMMORTALITY.
SO HE KEEPS MAKING THESE UNSTABLE BEASTS.
HE'S MAKING US LOOK LIKE FOOLS.
HE BELIEVES THERE'S NO NEED FOR ANOTHER PERFECT BODY, OTHER THAN METHUSELAH.
METHU-SELAH'S A LIVING BLUEPRINT.
AND I WANT HIM.

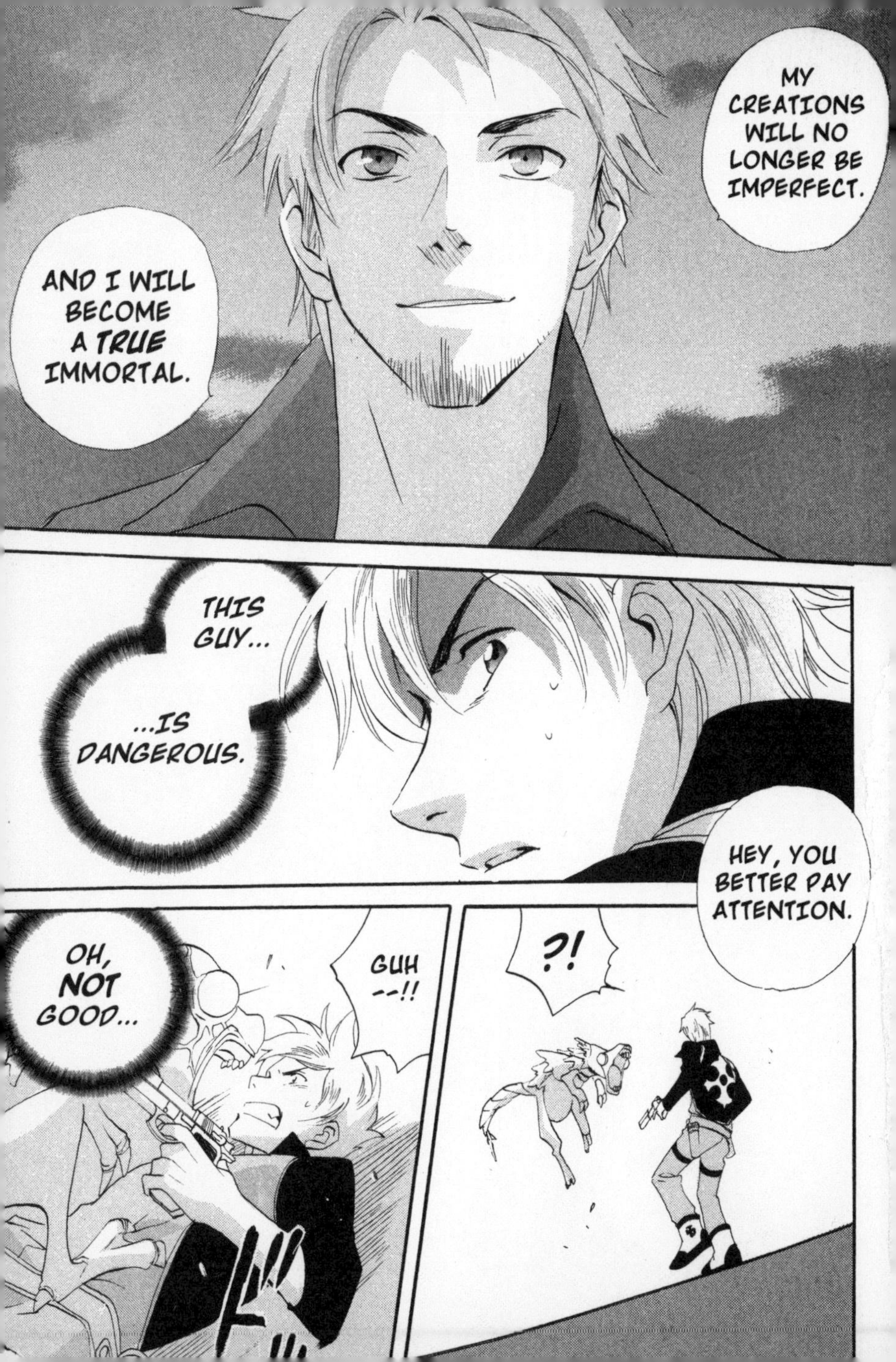
MY CREATIONS WILL NO LONGER BE IMPERFECT.
AND I WILL BECOME A TRUE IMMORTAL.
THIS GUY...
...IS DANGEROUS.
HEY, YOU BETTER PAY ATTENTION.
?!
GUH --!!
OH, NOT GOOD...

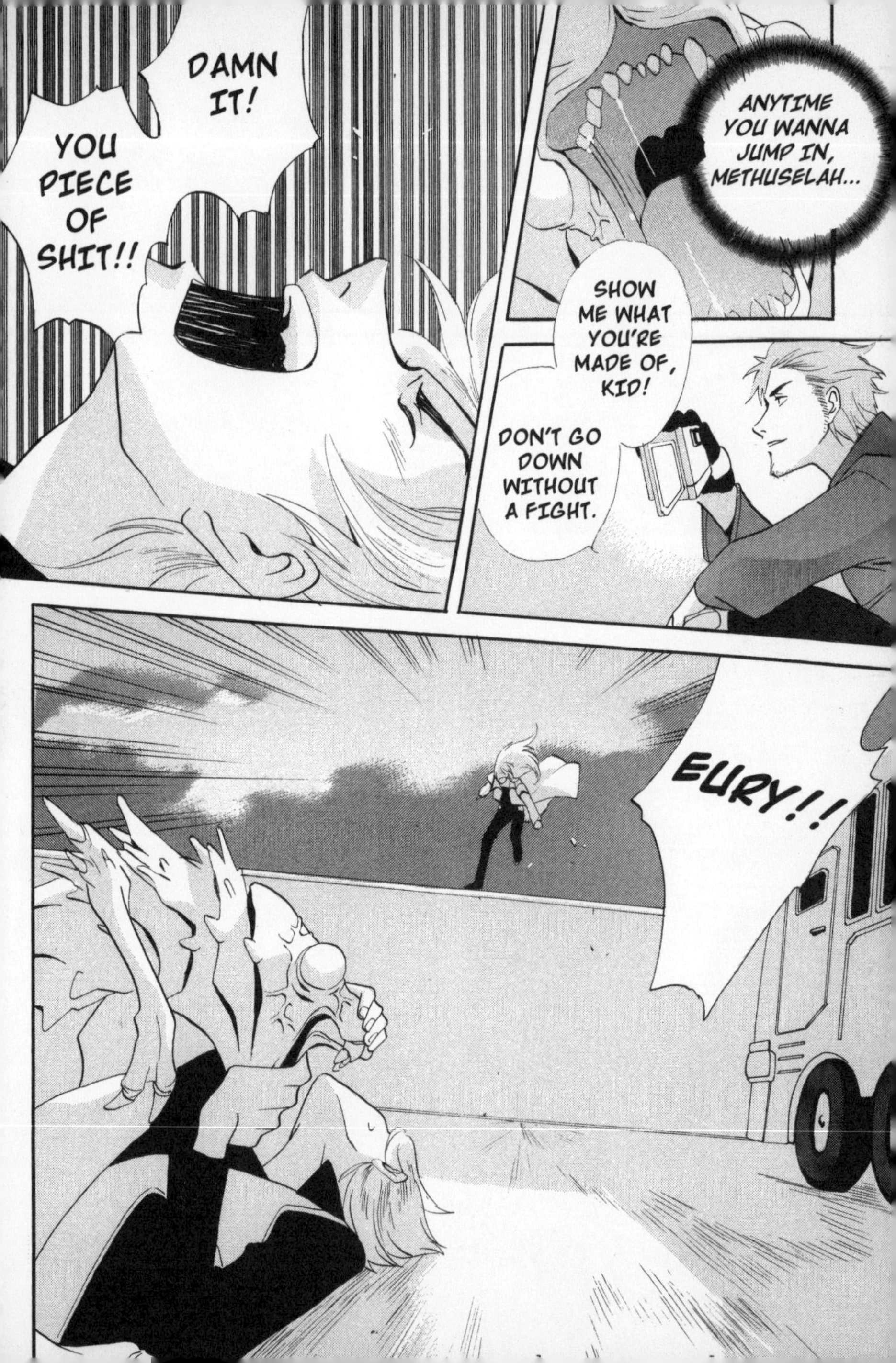
ANYTIME YOU WANNA JUMP IN, METHUSELAH...
SHOW ME WHAT YOU'RE MADE OF, KID!
DON'T GO DOWN WITHOUT A FIGHT.
DAMN IT!
YOU PIECE OF SHIT!!
EURY!!

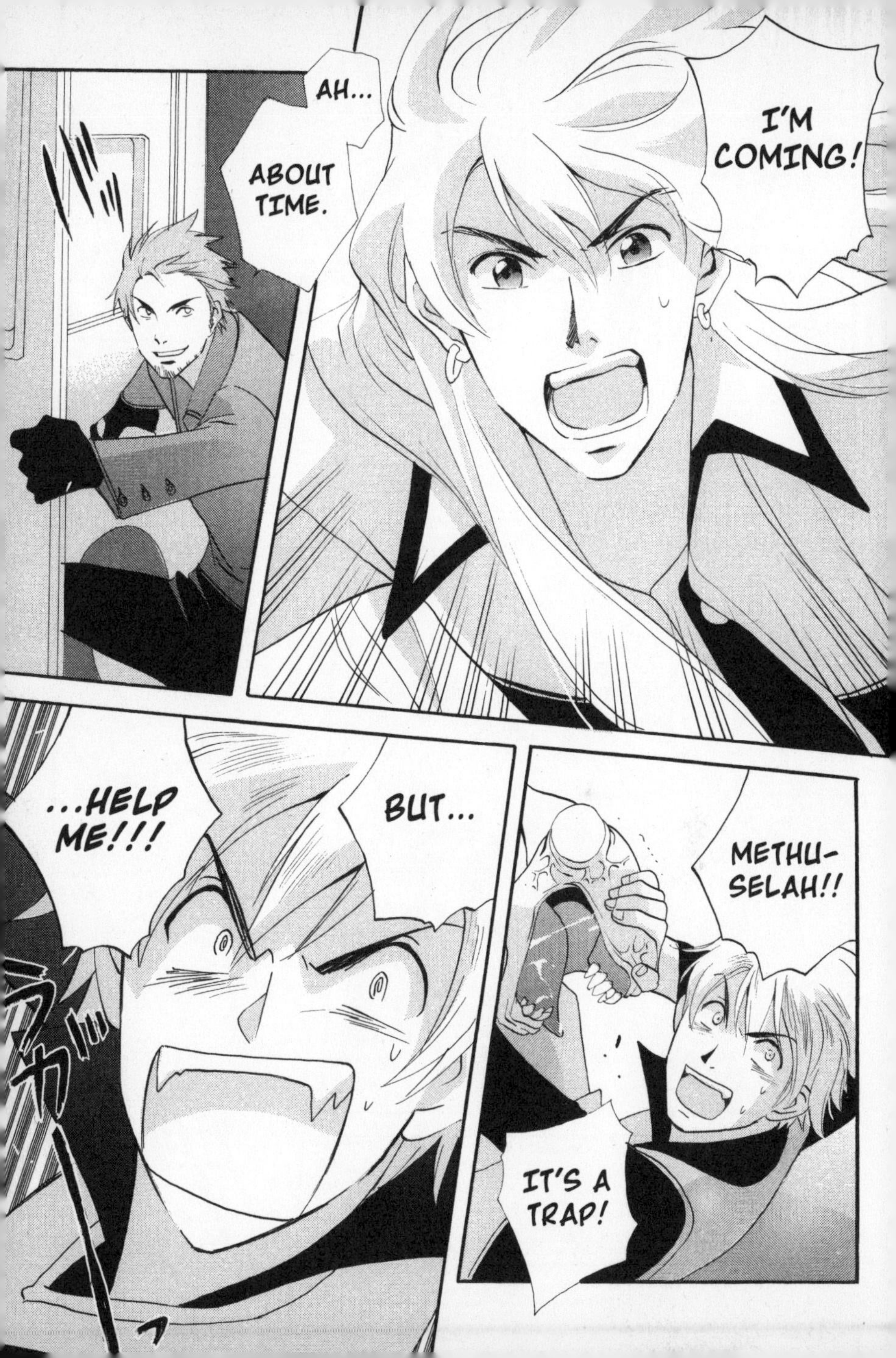
I'M COMING!
AH...
ABOUT TIME.
METHU-SELAH!!
IT'S A TRAP!
BUT...
...HELP ME!!!

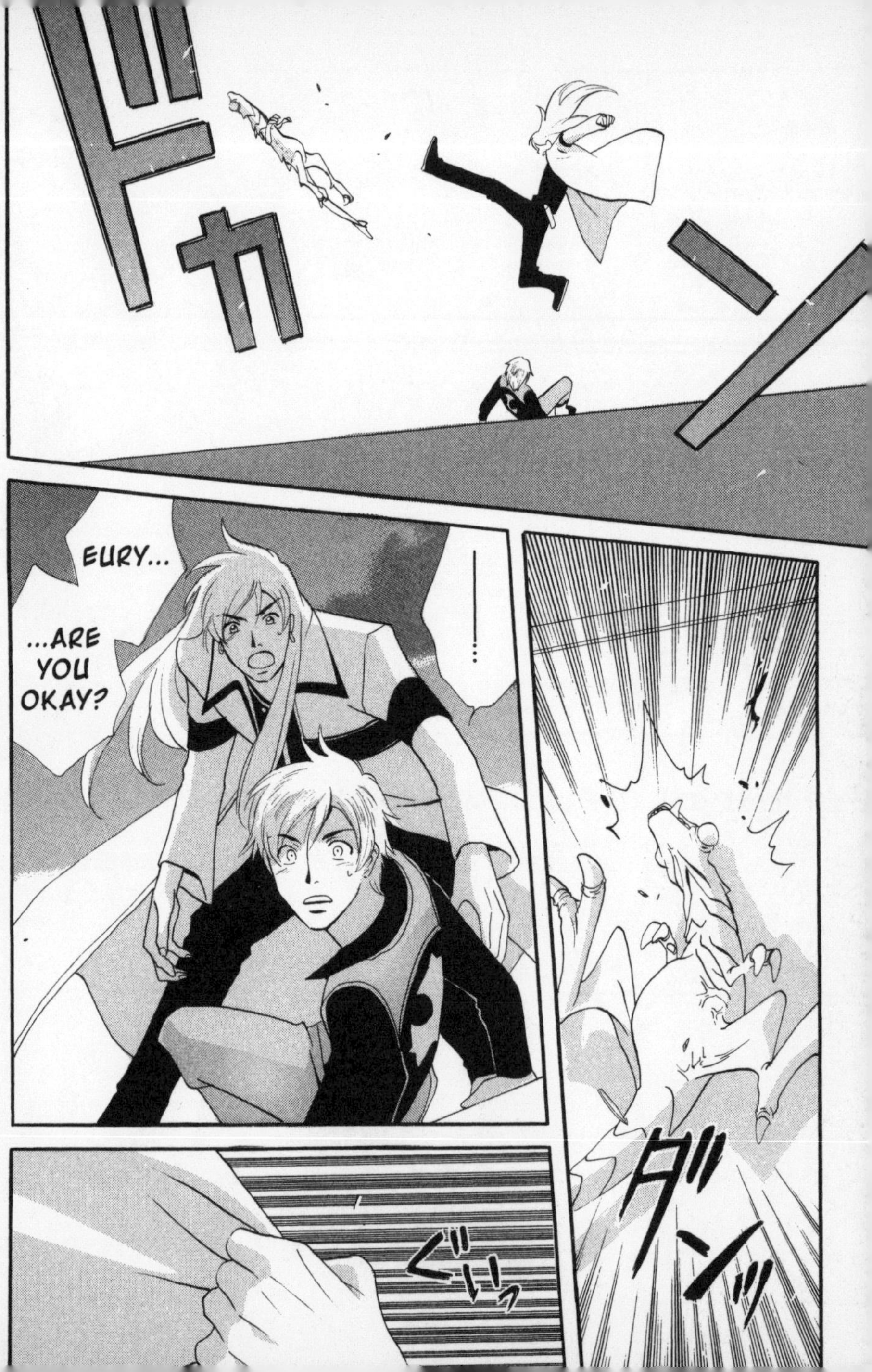
ドカーン
ダンッ
EURY...
...ARE YOU OKAY?
ぐいっ

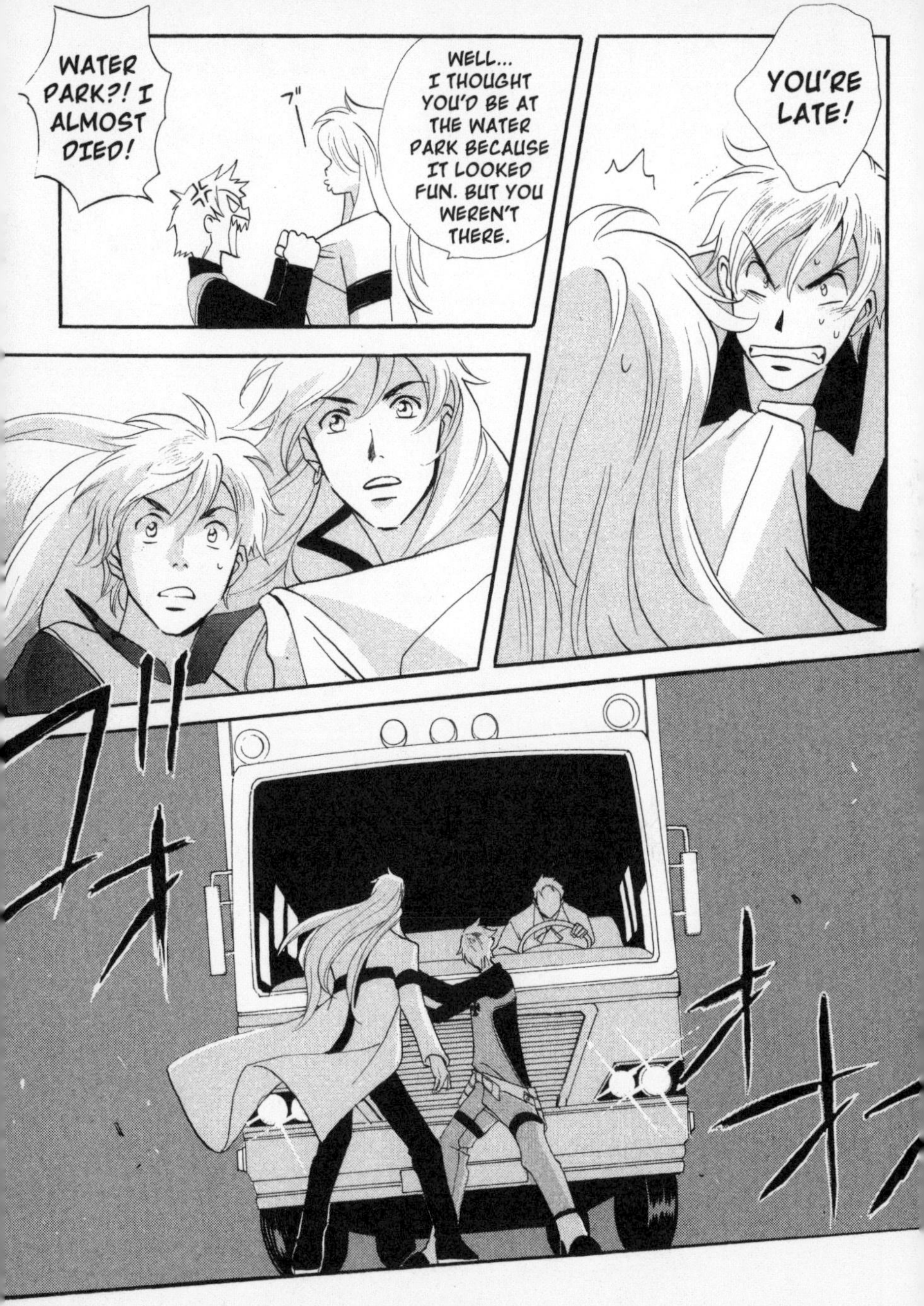
YOU'RE LATE!
WELL... I THOUGHT YOU'D BE AT THE WATER PARK BECAUSE IT LOOKED FUN. BUT YOU WEREN'T THERE.
WATER PARK?! I ALMOST DIED!

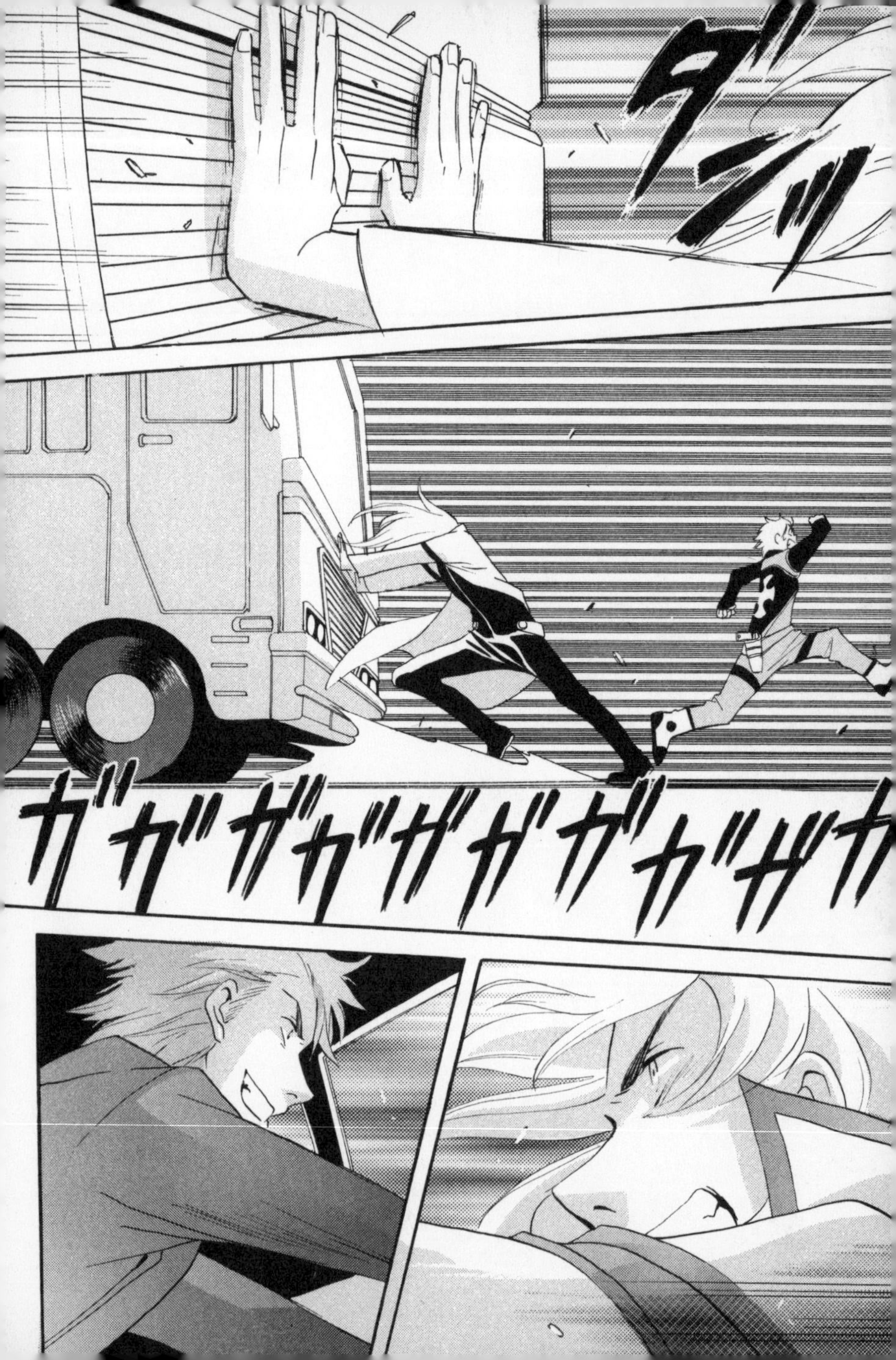
ダンッ
ガガガガガガガガガ

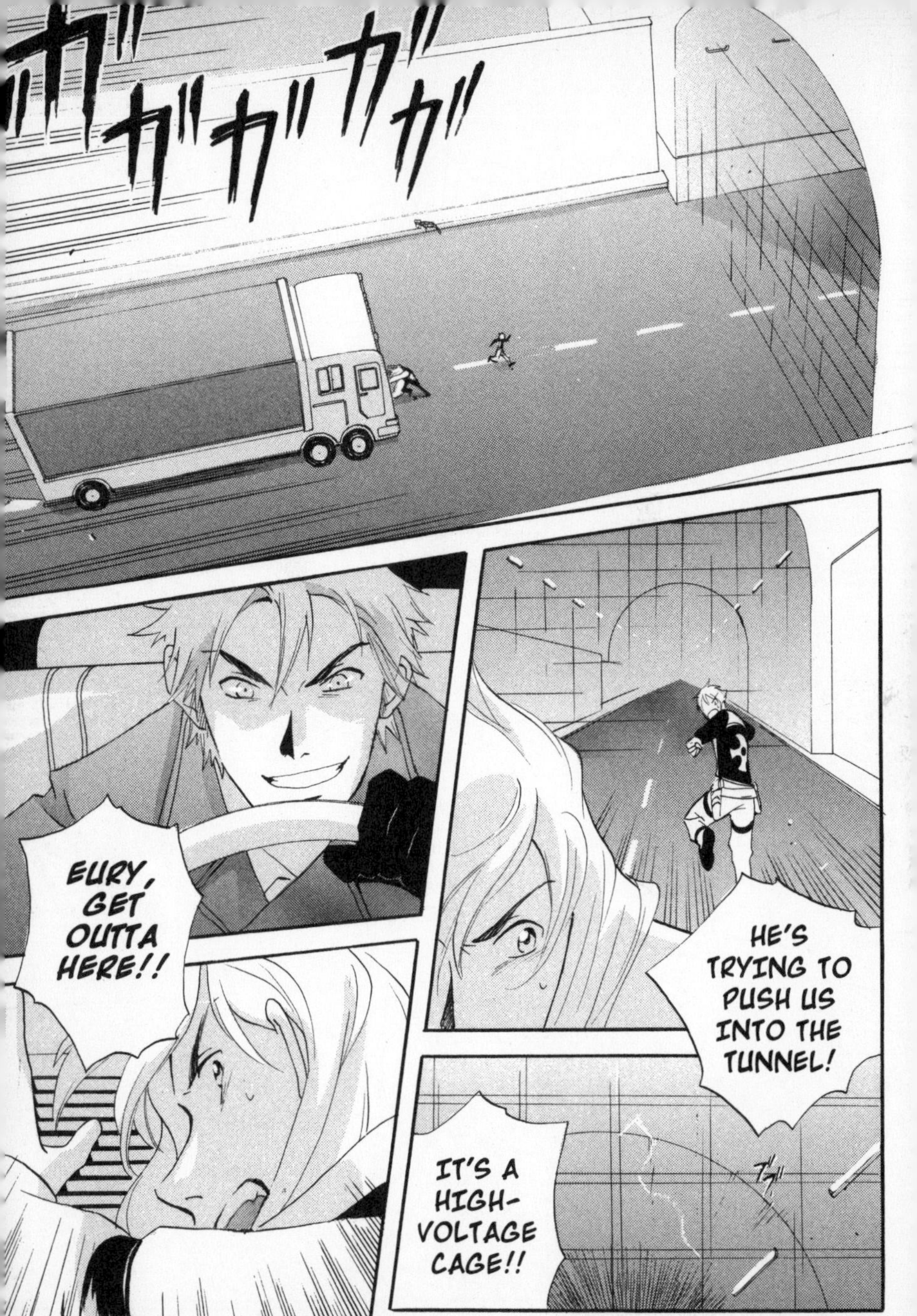
ガガガガガ
HE'S TRYING TO PUSH US INTO THE TUNNEL!
EURY, GET OUTTA HERE!!
IT'S A HIGH-VOLTAGE CAGE!!

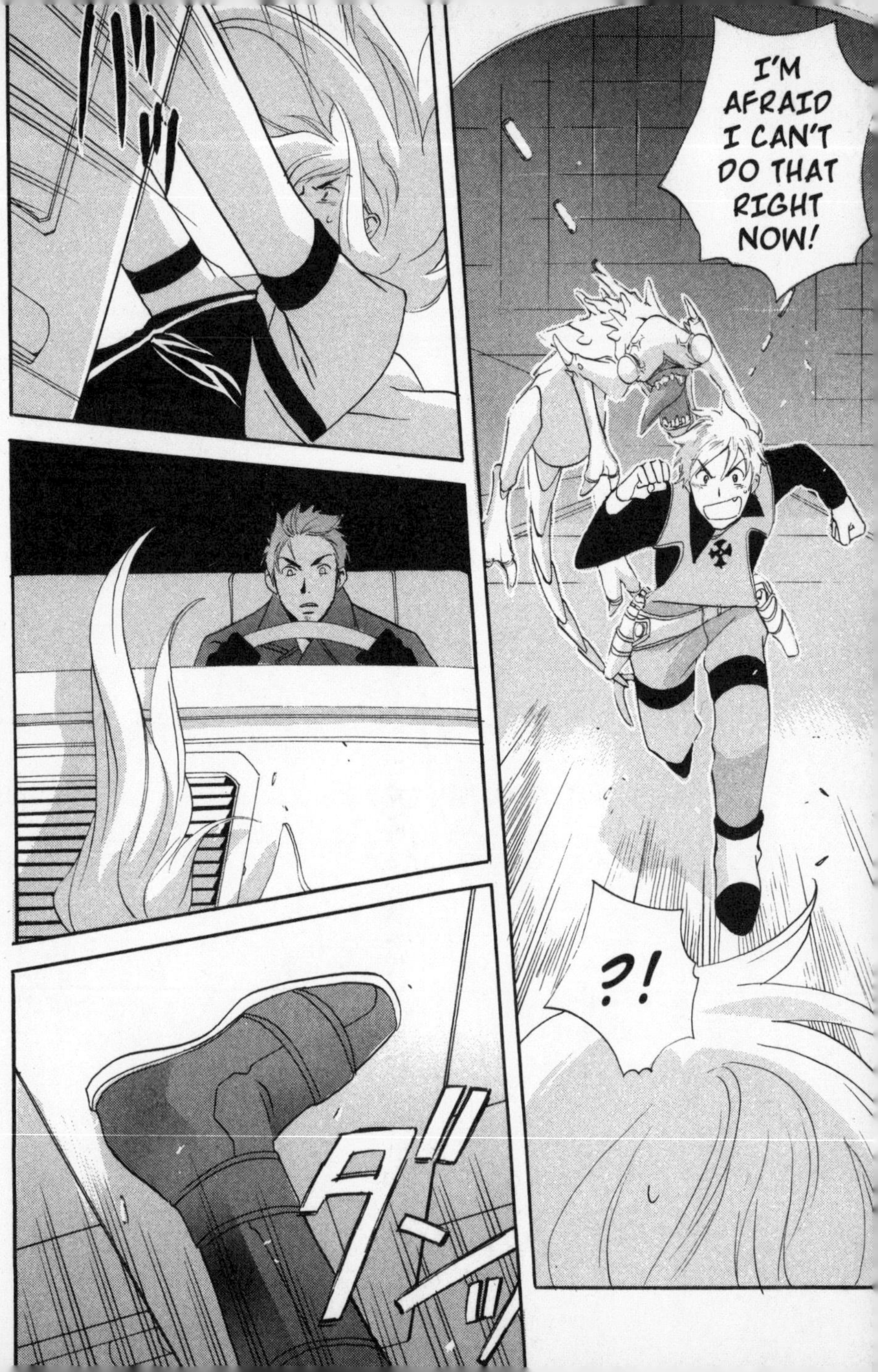

I'M AFRAID I CAN'T DO THAT RIGHT NOW!
?!

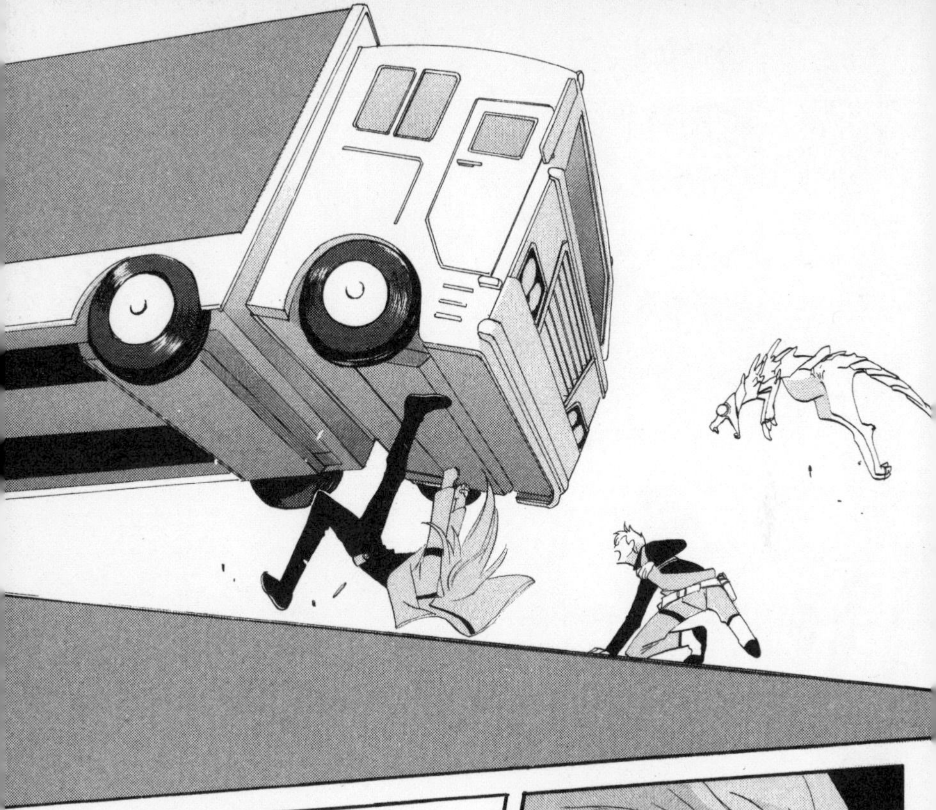

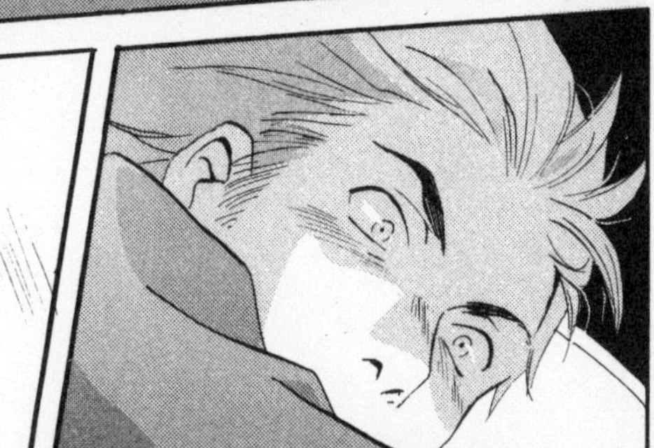

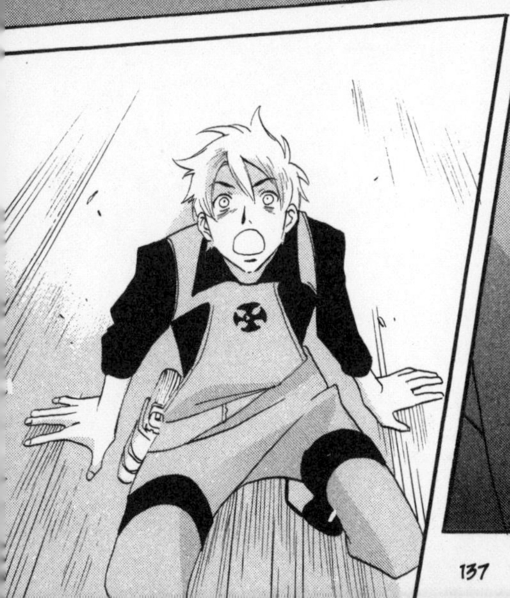

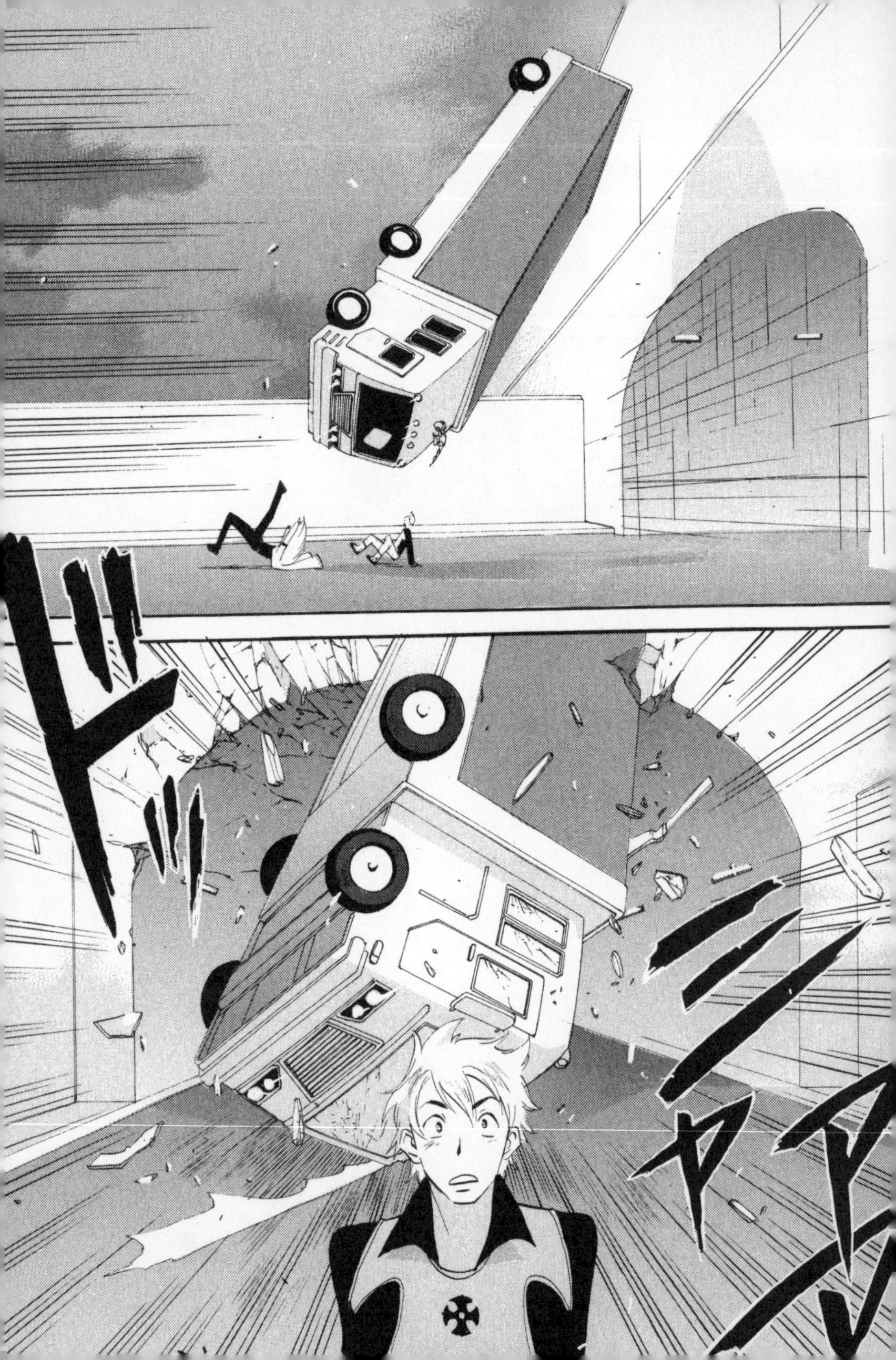
ドッ
シャアン

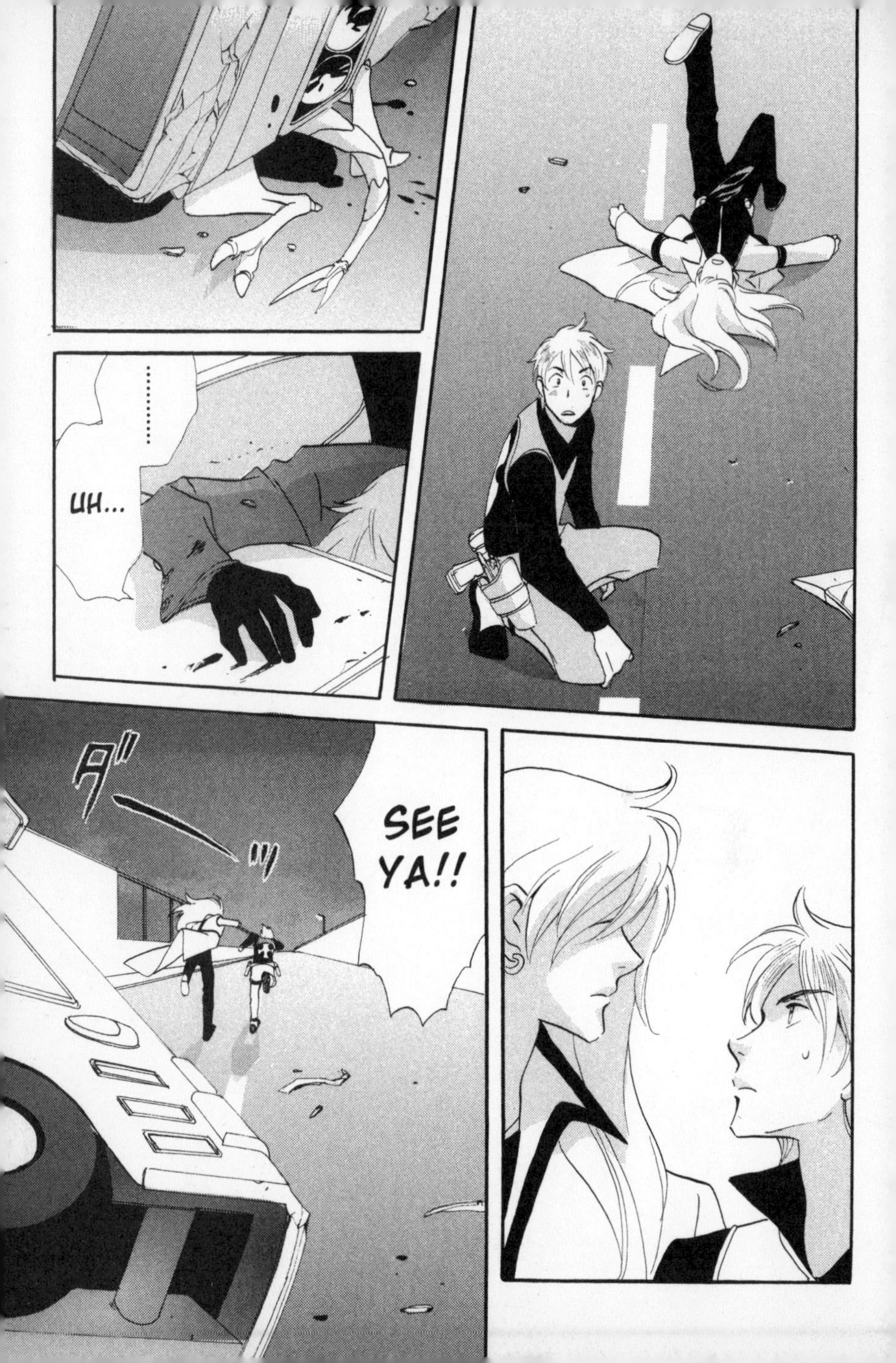
......
UH...
SEE YA!!

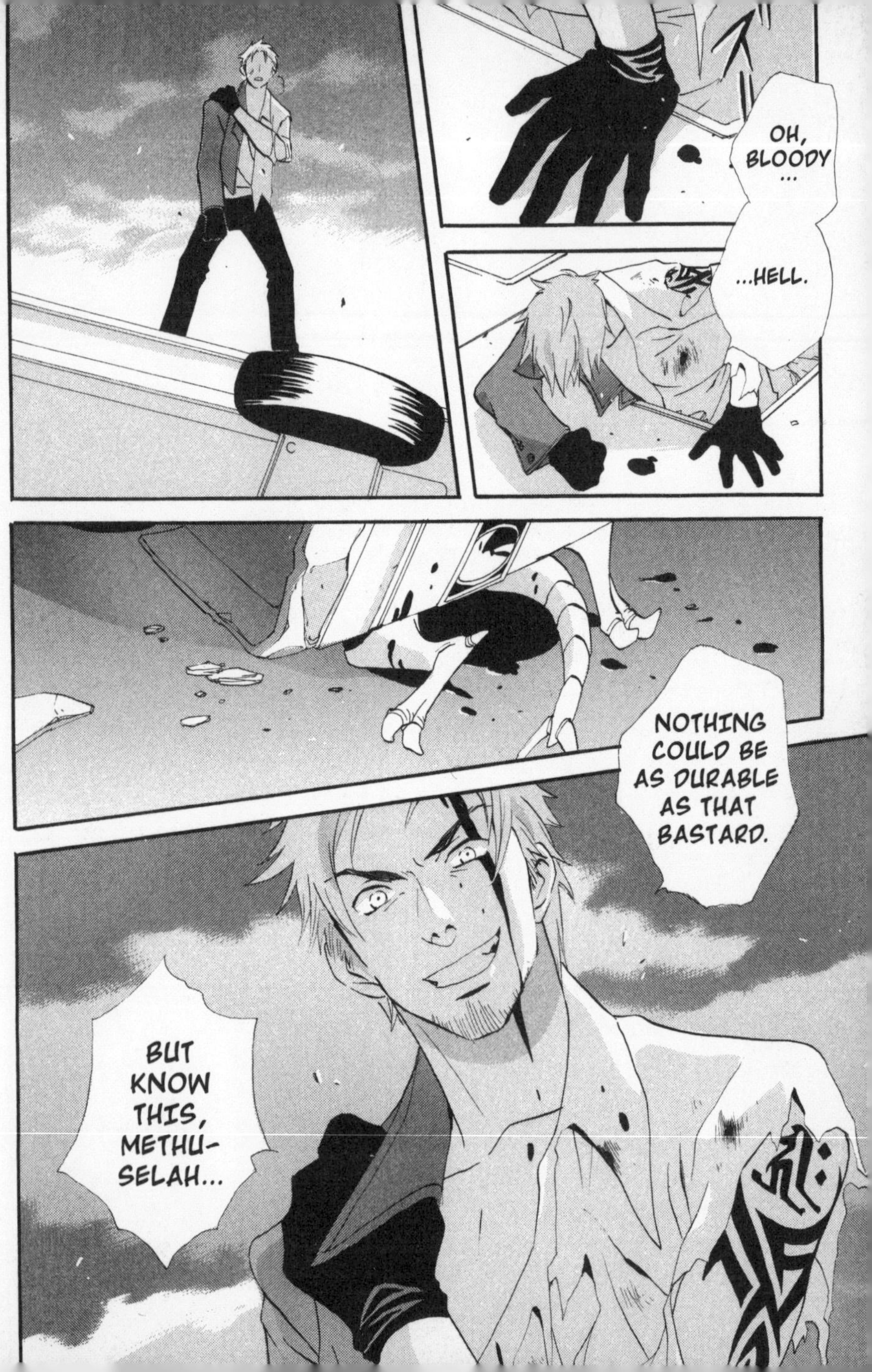
OH, BLOODY ...
...HELL.
NOTHING COULD BE AS DURABLE AS THAT BASTARD.
BUT KNOW THIS, METHU-SELAH...

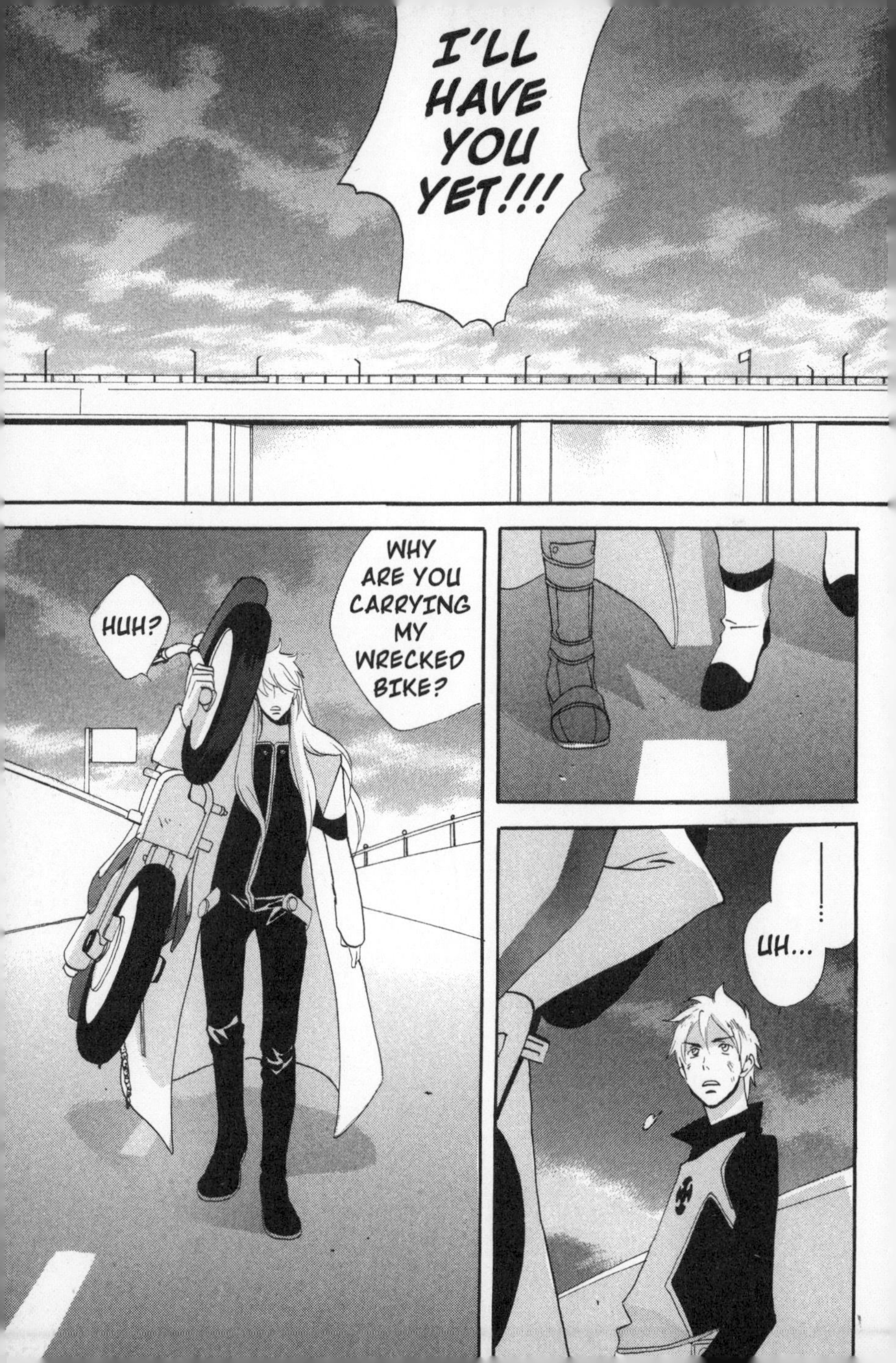
I'LL HAVE YOU YET!!!
WHY ARE YOU CARRYING MY WRECKED BIKE?
HUH?
UH...
......!

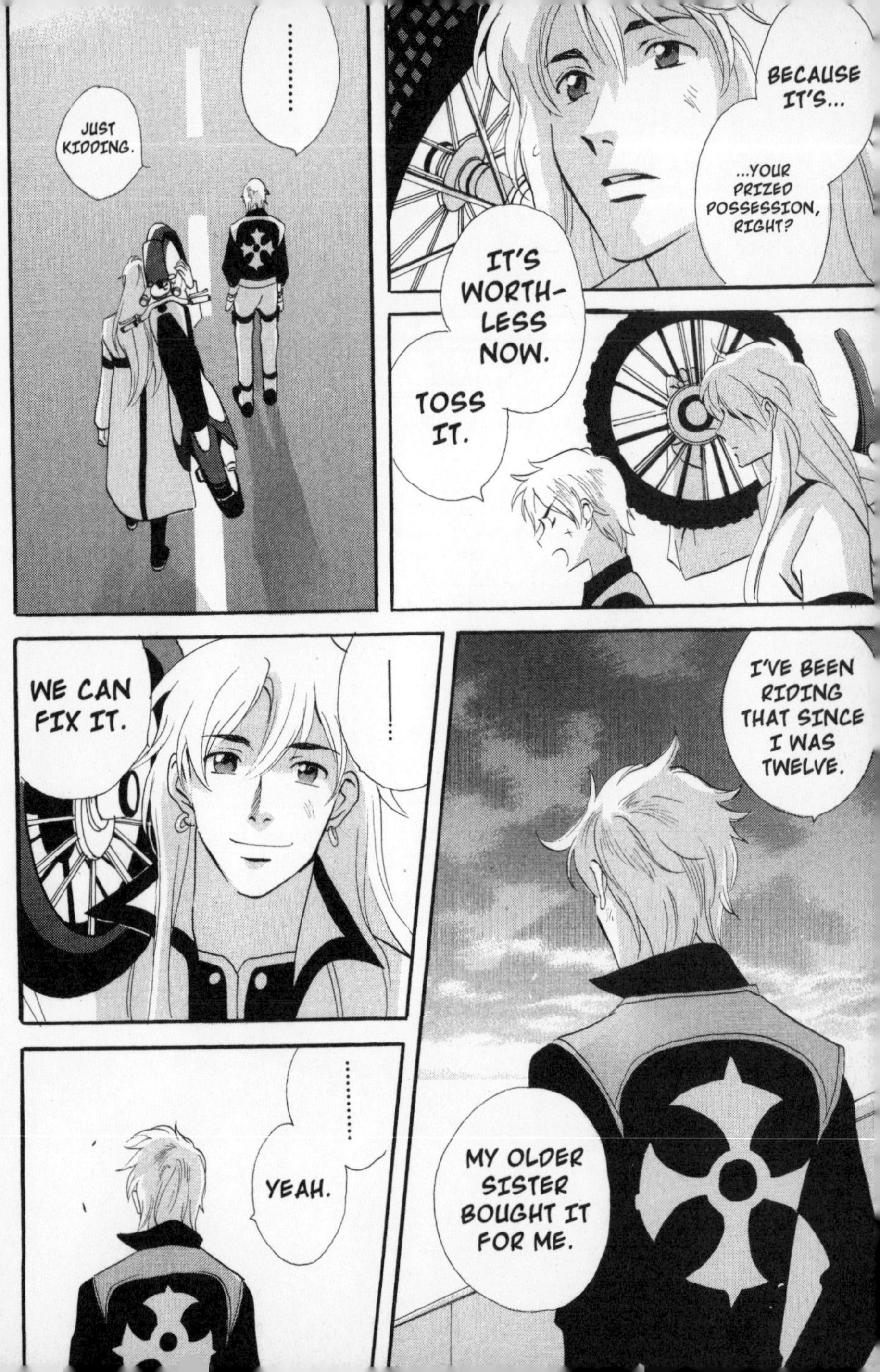
BECAUSE IT'S...
...YOUR PRIZED POSSESSION, RIGHT?
IT'S WORTH-LESS NOW.
TOSS IT.
......
JUST KIDDING.
I'VE BEEN RIDING THAT SINCE I WAS TWELVE.
MY OLDER SISTER BOUGHT IT FOR ME.
......
WE CAN FIX IT.
......
YEAH.

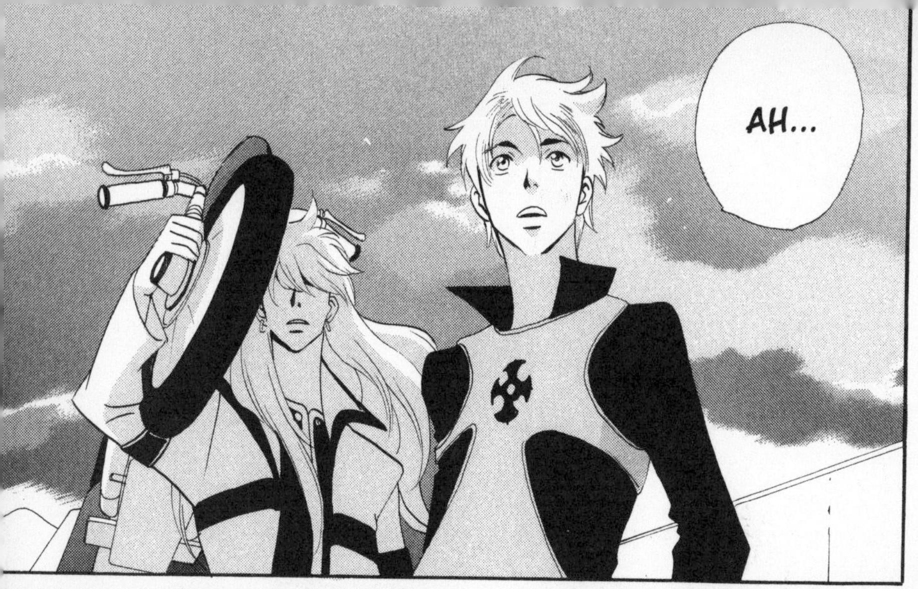
AH...

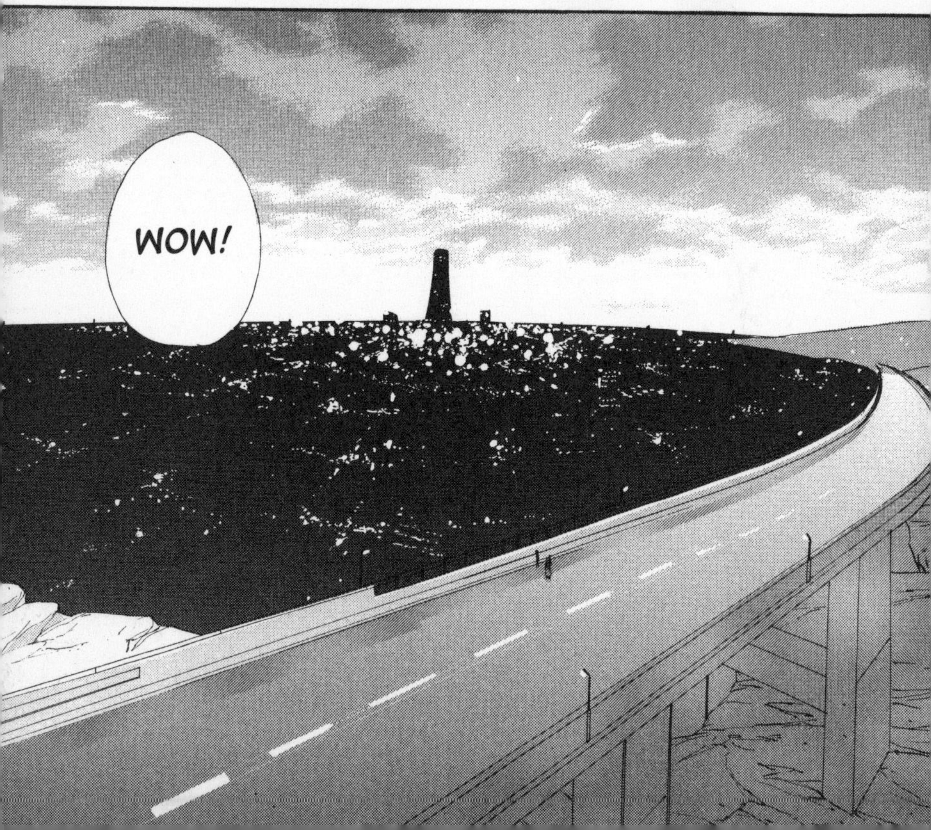
WOW!

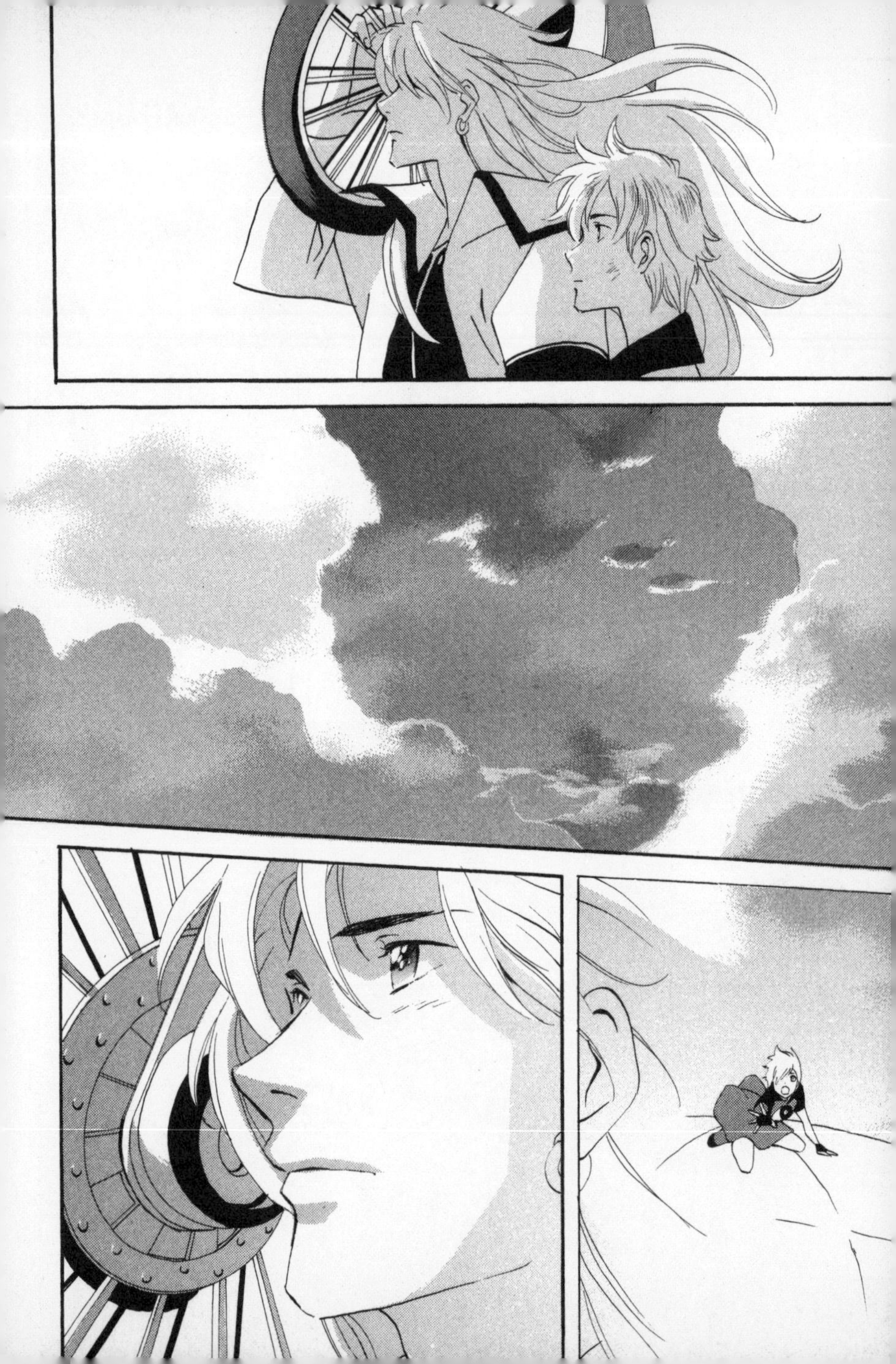

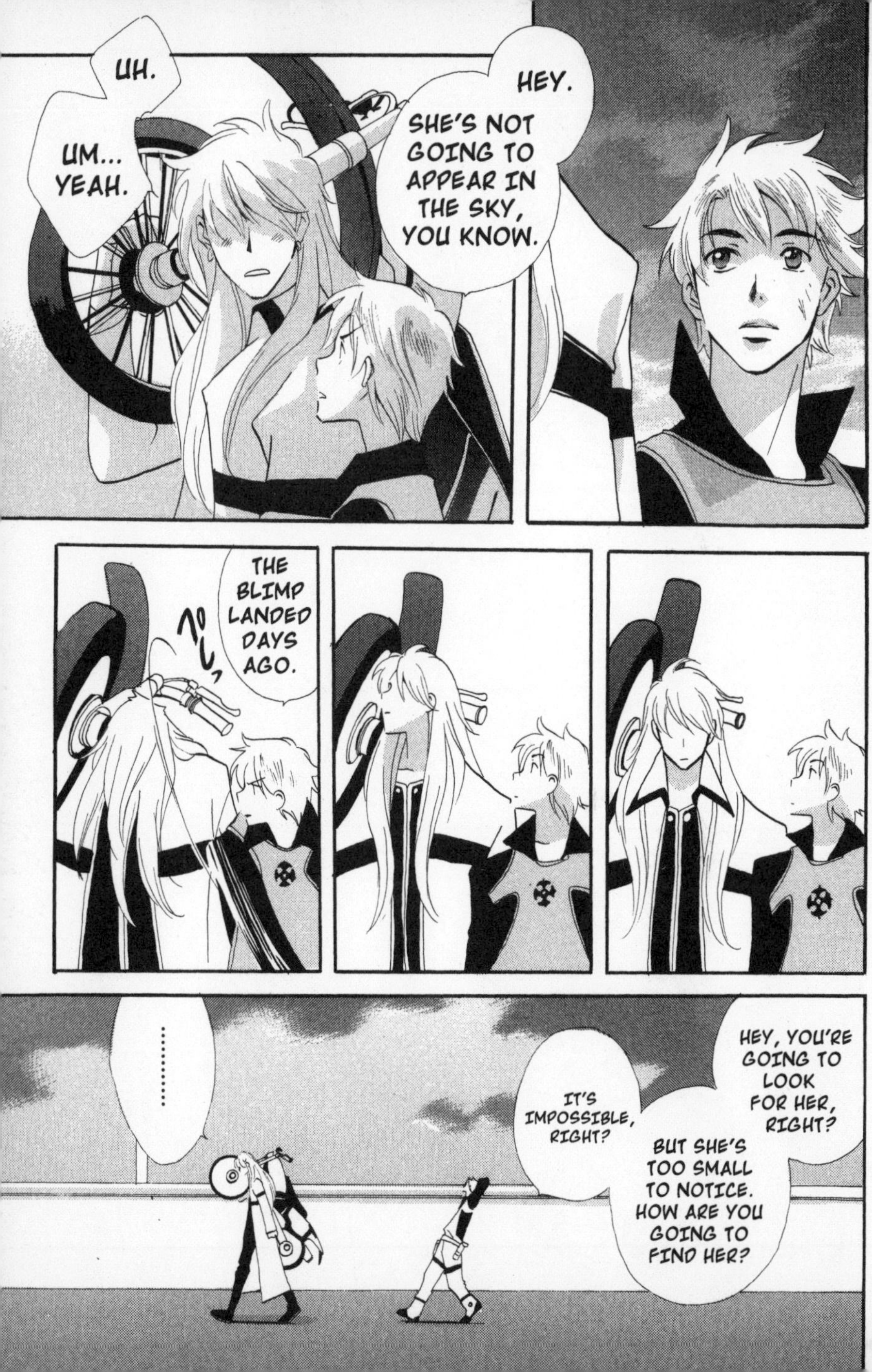
HEY.
SHE'S NOT GOING TO APPEAR IN THE SKY, YOU KNOW.
UH.
UM... YEAH.
THE BLIMP LANDED DAYS AGO.
HEY, YOU'RE GOING TO LOOK FOR HER, RIGHT?
BUT SHE'S TOO SMALL TO NOTICE. HOW ARE YOU GOING TO FIND HER?
IT'S IMPOSSIBLE, RIGHT?
....

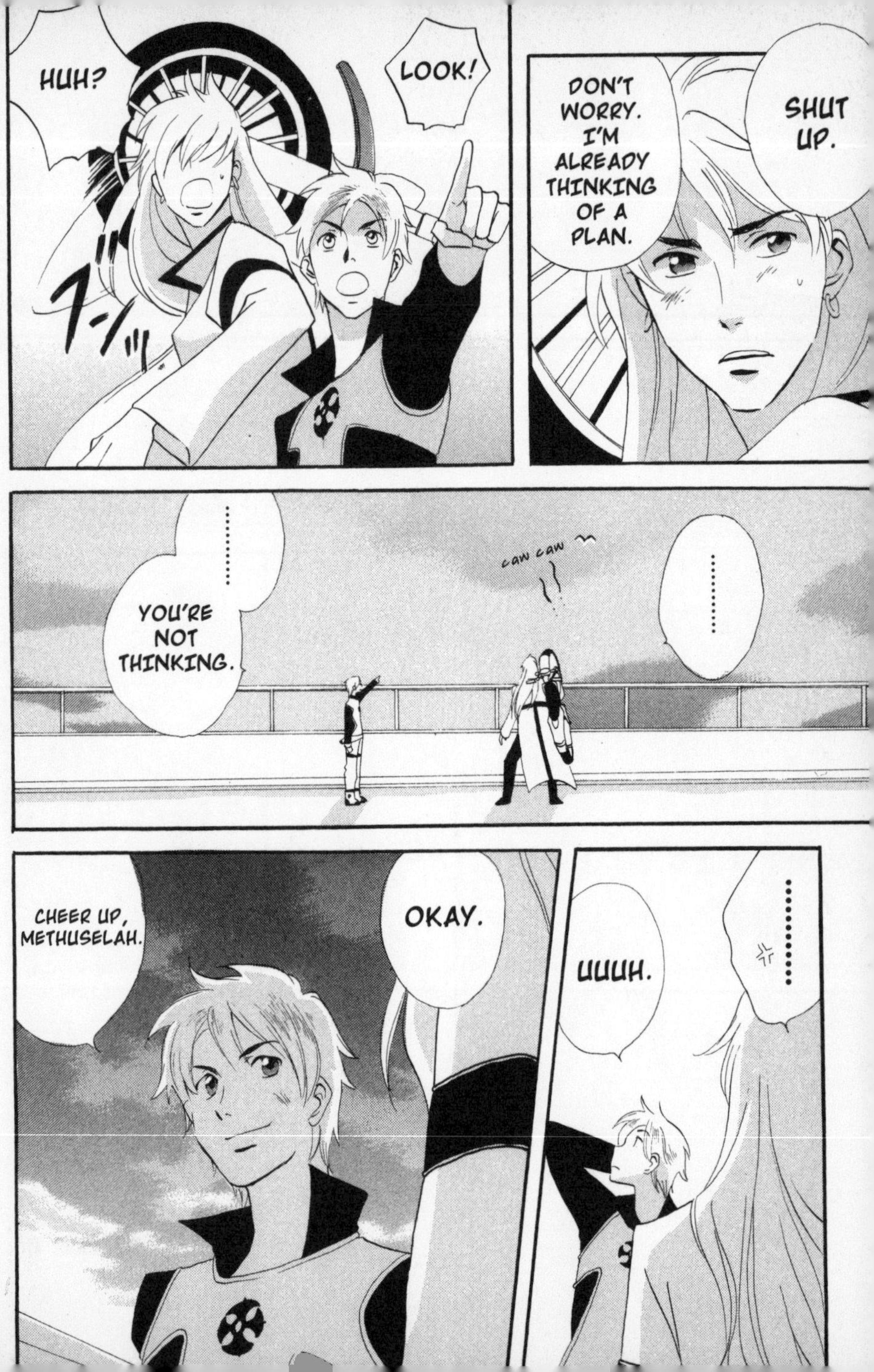
HUH?
LOOK!
DON'T WORRY. I'M ALREADY THINKING OF A PLAN.
SHUT UP.
......
YOU'RE NOT THINKING.
CAW CAW
......
CHEER UP, METHUSELAH.
OKAY.
UUUH.
....

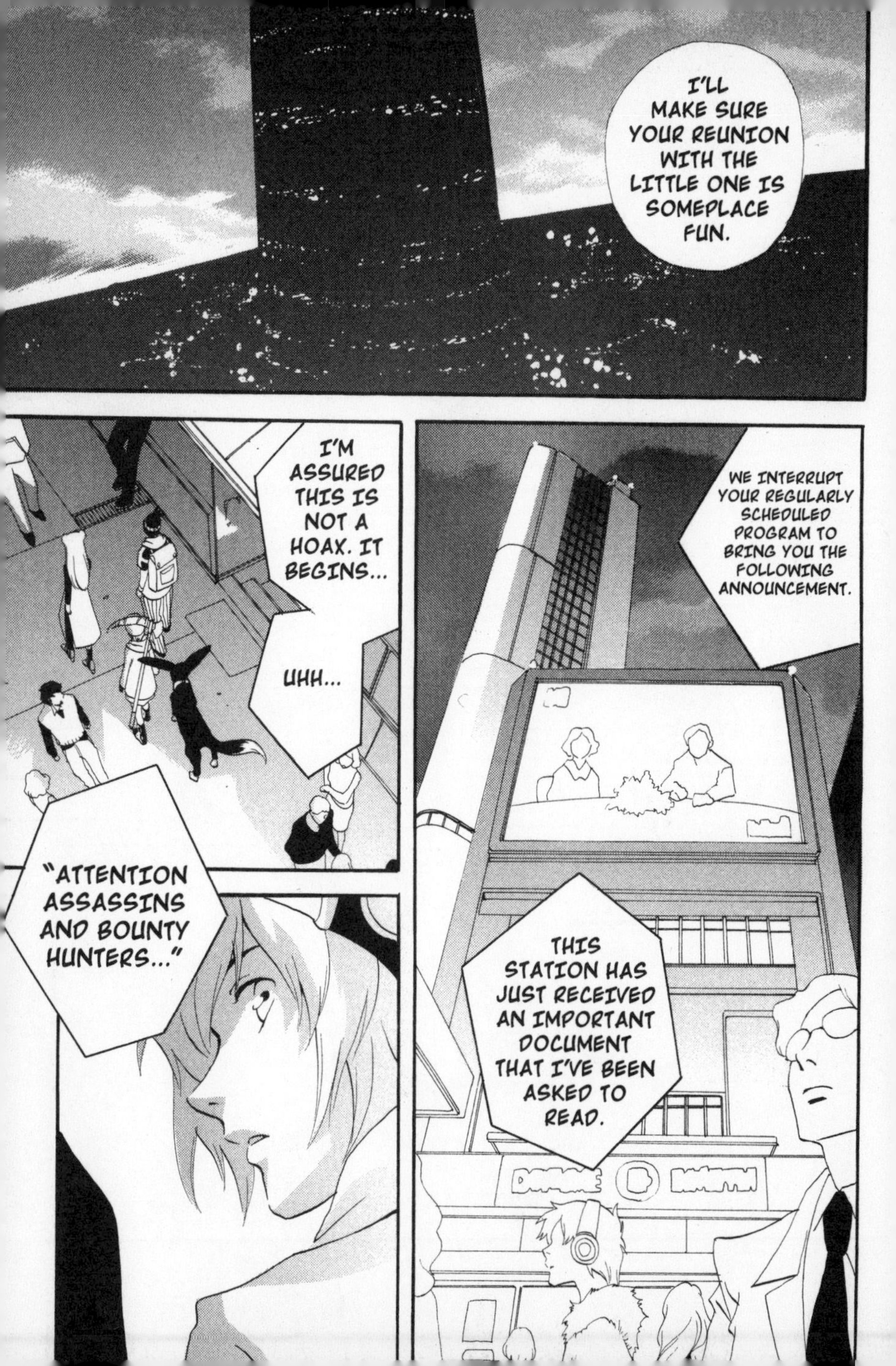
I'LL MAKE SURE YOUR REUNION WITH THE LITTLE ONE IS SOMEPLACE FUN.
WE INTERRUPT YOUR REGULARLY SCHEDULED PROGRAM TO BRING YOU THE FOLLOWING ANNOUNCEMENT.
THIS STATION HAS JUST RECEIVED AN IMPORTANT DOCUMENT THAT I'VE BEEN ASKED TO READ.
I'M ASSURED THIS IS NOT A HOAX. IT BEGINS...
UHH...
"ATTENTION ASSASSINS AND BOUNTY HUNTERS..."

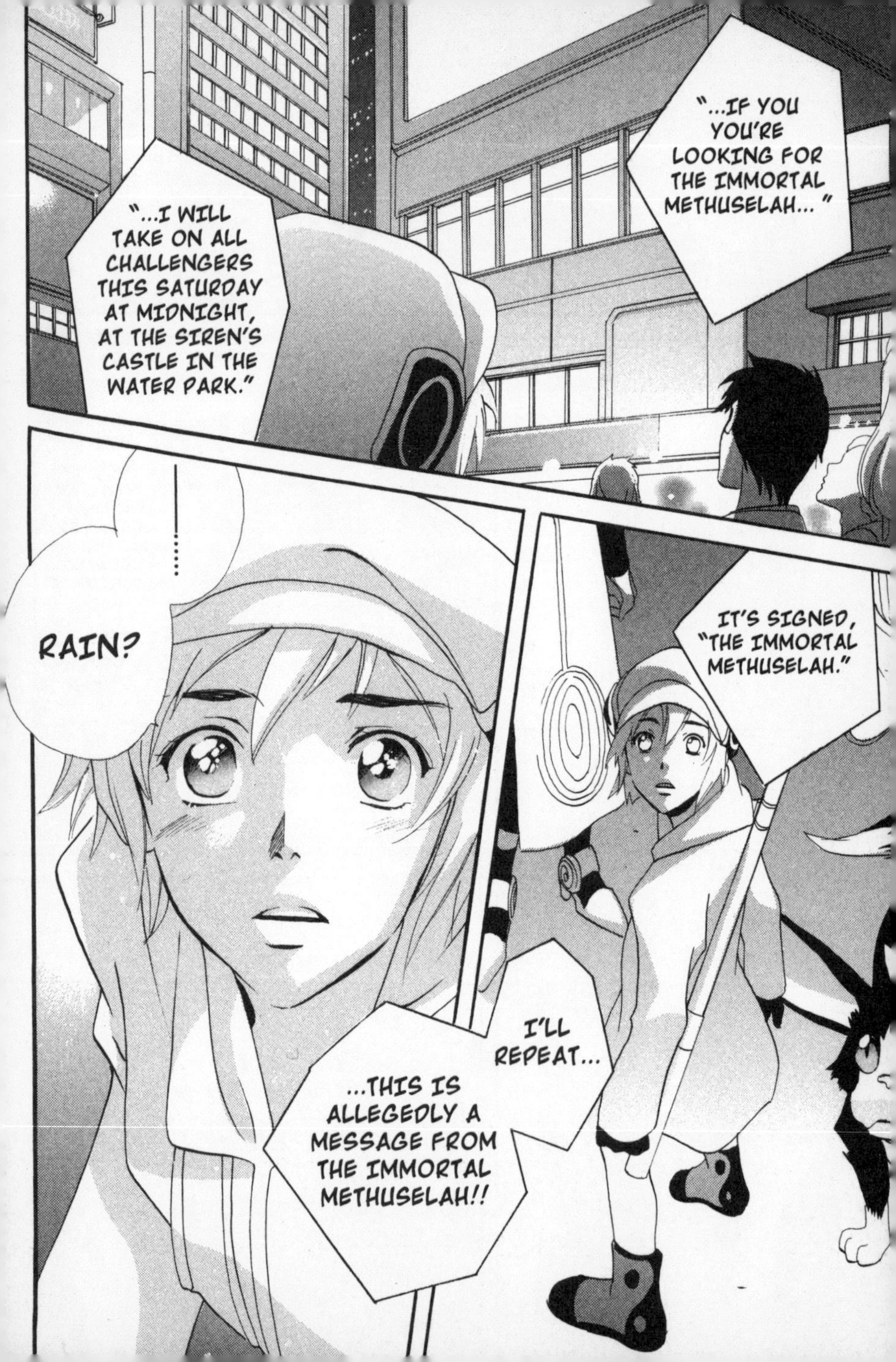
"...IF YOU YOU'RE LOOKING FOR THE IMMORTAL METHUSELAH... "
"...I WILL TAKE ON ALL CHALLENGERS THIS SATURDAY AT MIDNIGHT, AT THE SIREN'S CASTLE IN THE WATER PARK."
IT'S SIGNED, "THE IMMORTAL METHUSELAH."
I'LL REPEAT...
...THIS IS ALLEGEDLY A MESSAGE FROM THE IMMORTAL METHUSELAH!!
......
RAIN?

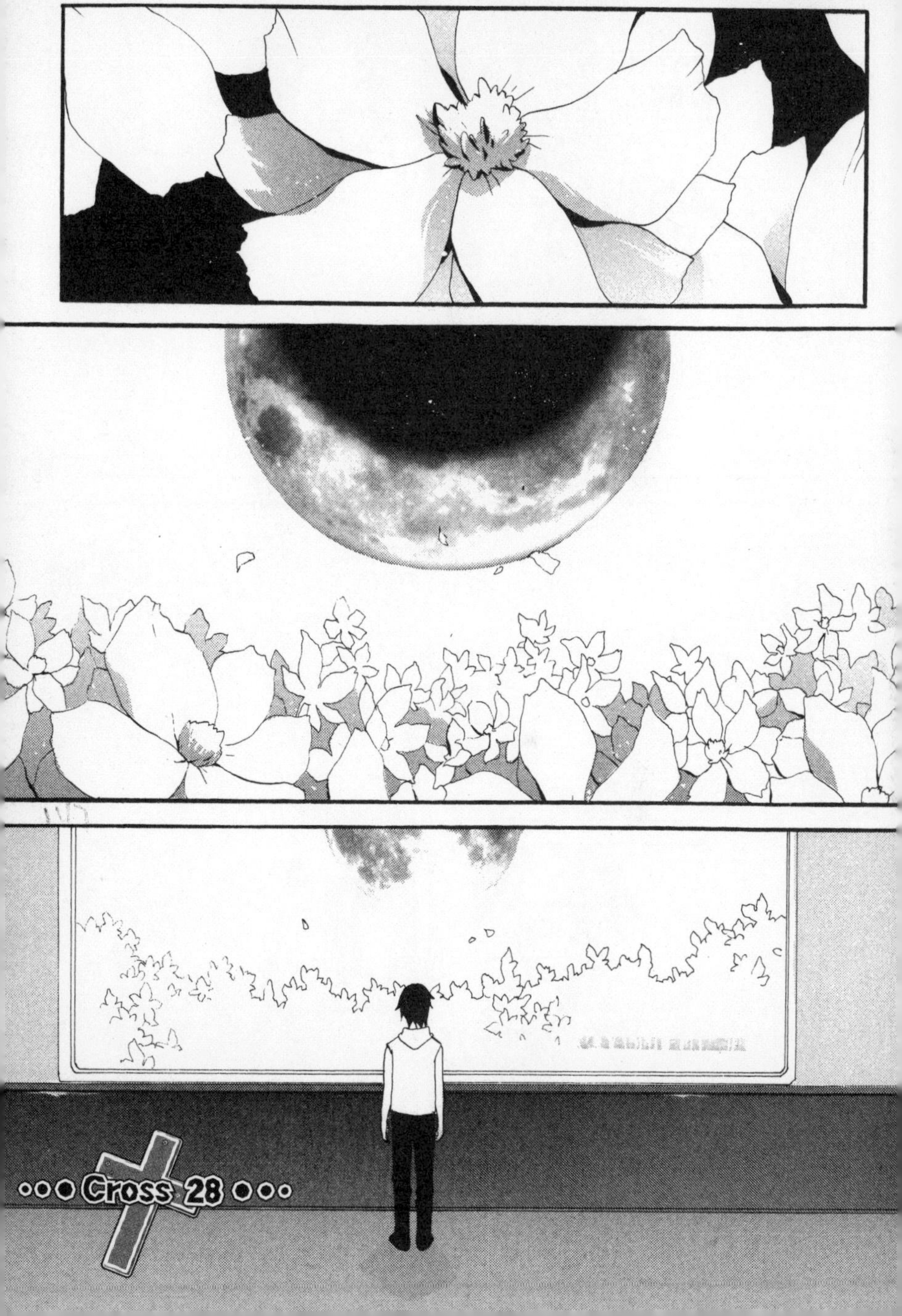
Cross 28

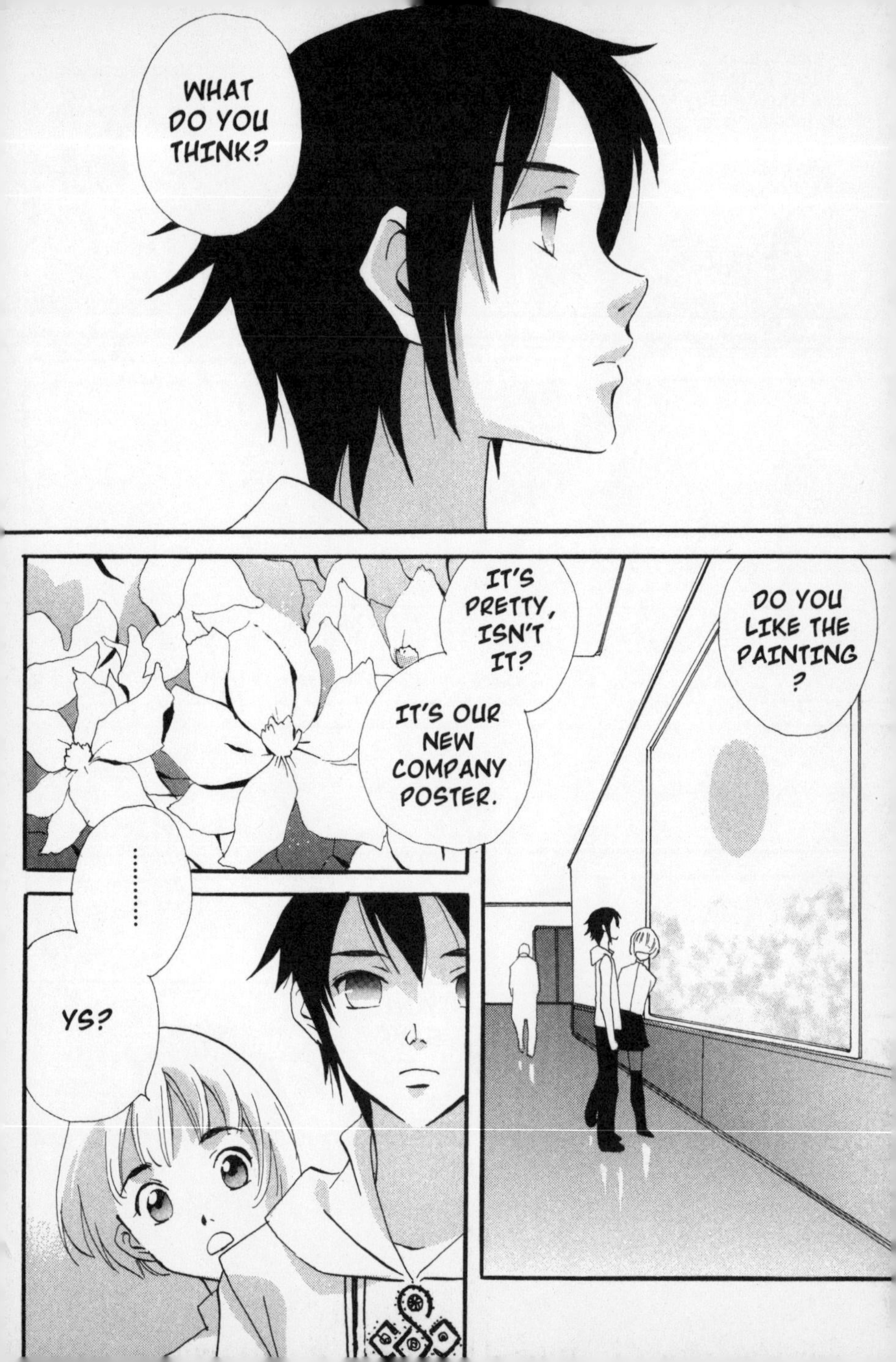
WHAT DO YOU THINK?
DO YOU LIKE THE PAINTING ?
IT'S PRETTY, ISN'T IT?
IT'S OUR NEW COMPANY POSTER.
......
YS?

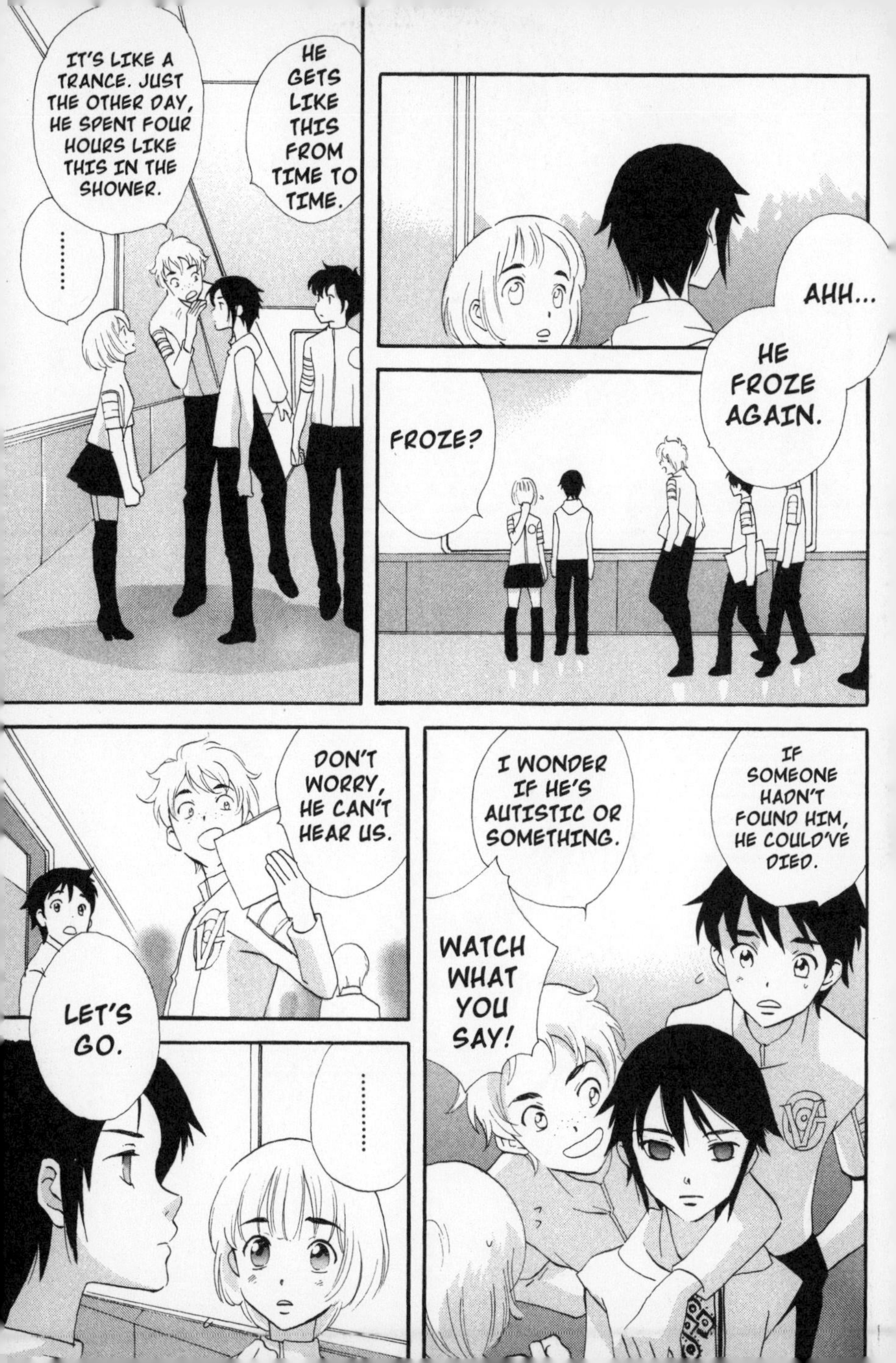
AHH...
HE FROZE AGAIN.
FROZE?
HE GETS LIKE THIS FROM TIME TO TIME.
IT'S LIKE A TRANCE. JUST THE OTHER DAY, HE SPENT FOUR HOURS LIKE THIS IN THE SHOWER.
......
IF SOMEONE HADN'T FOUND HIM, HE COULD'VE DIED.
I WONDER IF HE'S AUTISTIC OR SOMETHING.
WATCH WHAT YOU SAY!
DON'T WORRY, HE CAN'T HEAR US.
LET'S GO.
......

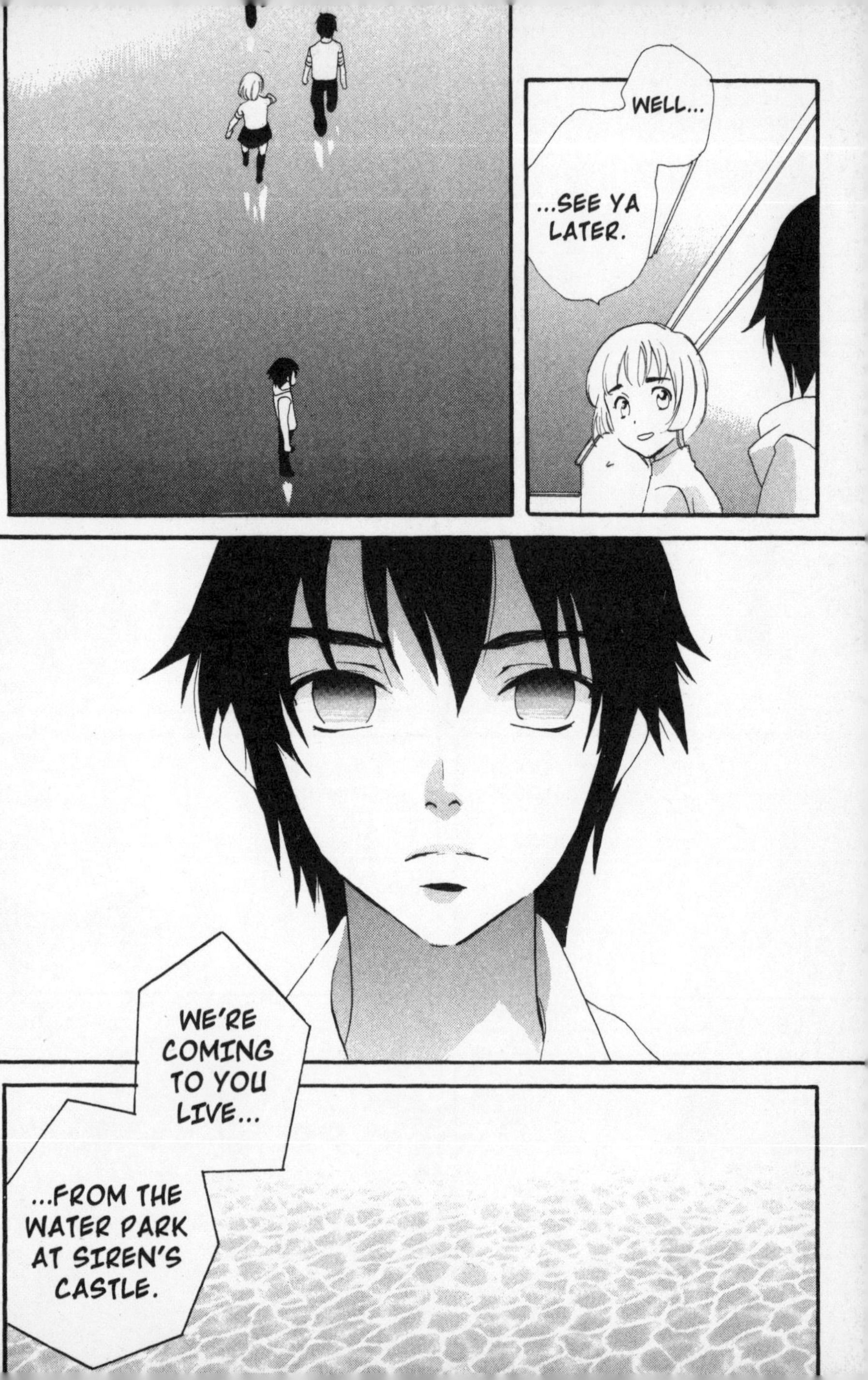
WELL...
...SEE YA LATER.
WE'RE COMING TO YOU LIVE...
...FROM THE WATER PARK AT SIREN'S CASTLE.

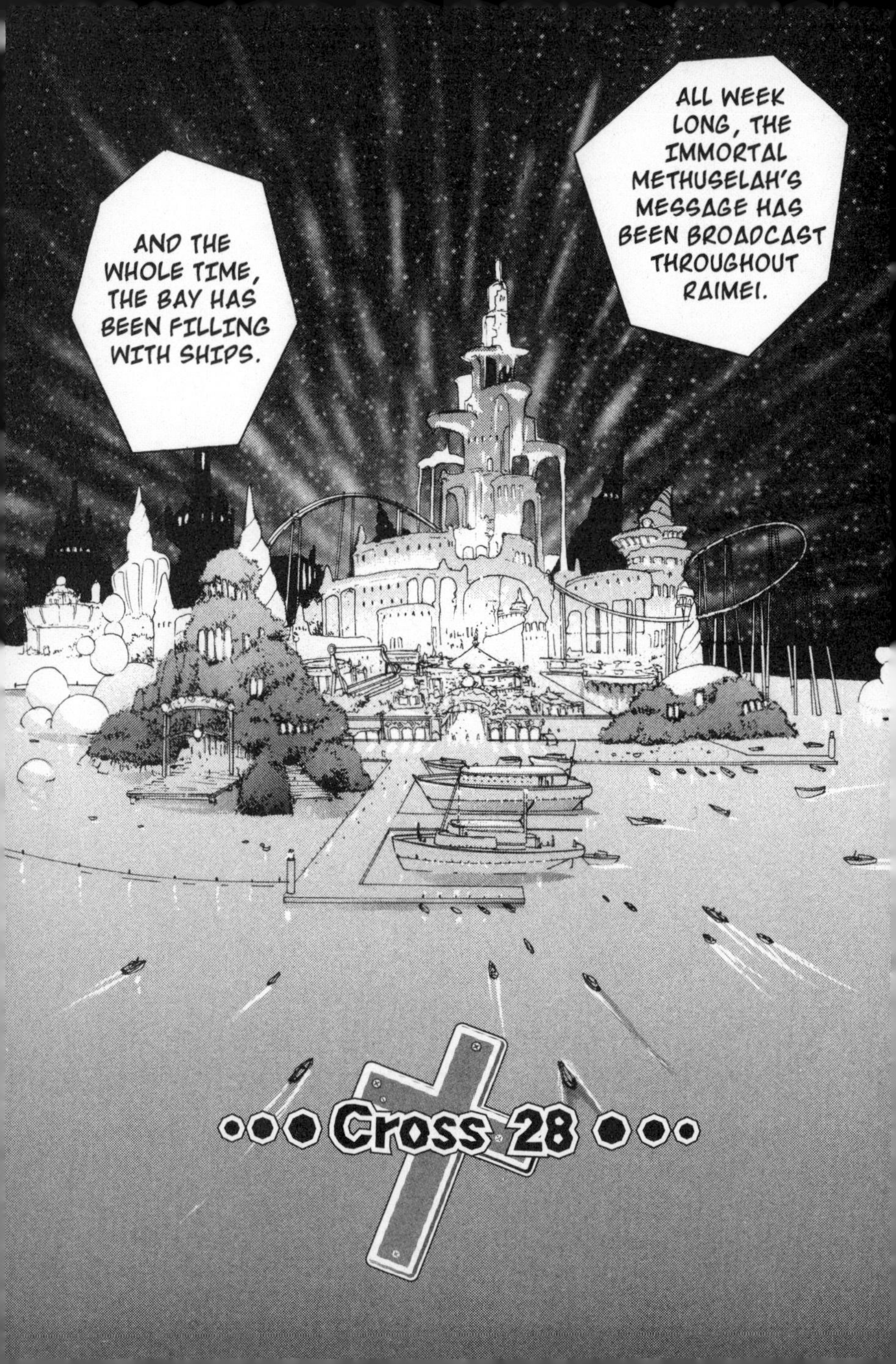
ALL WEEK LONG, THE IMMORTAL METHUSELAH'S MESSAGE HAS BEEN BROADCAST THROUGHOUT RAIMEI.
AND THE WHOLE TIME, THE BAY HAS BEEN FILLING WITH SHIPS.
Cross 28

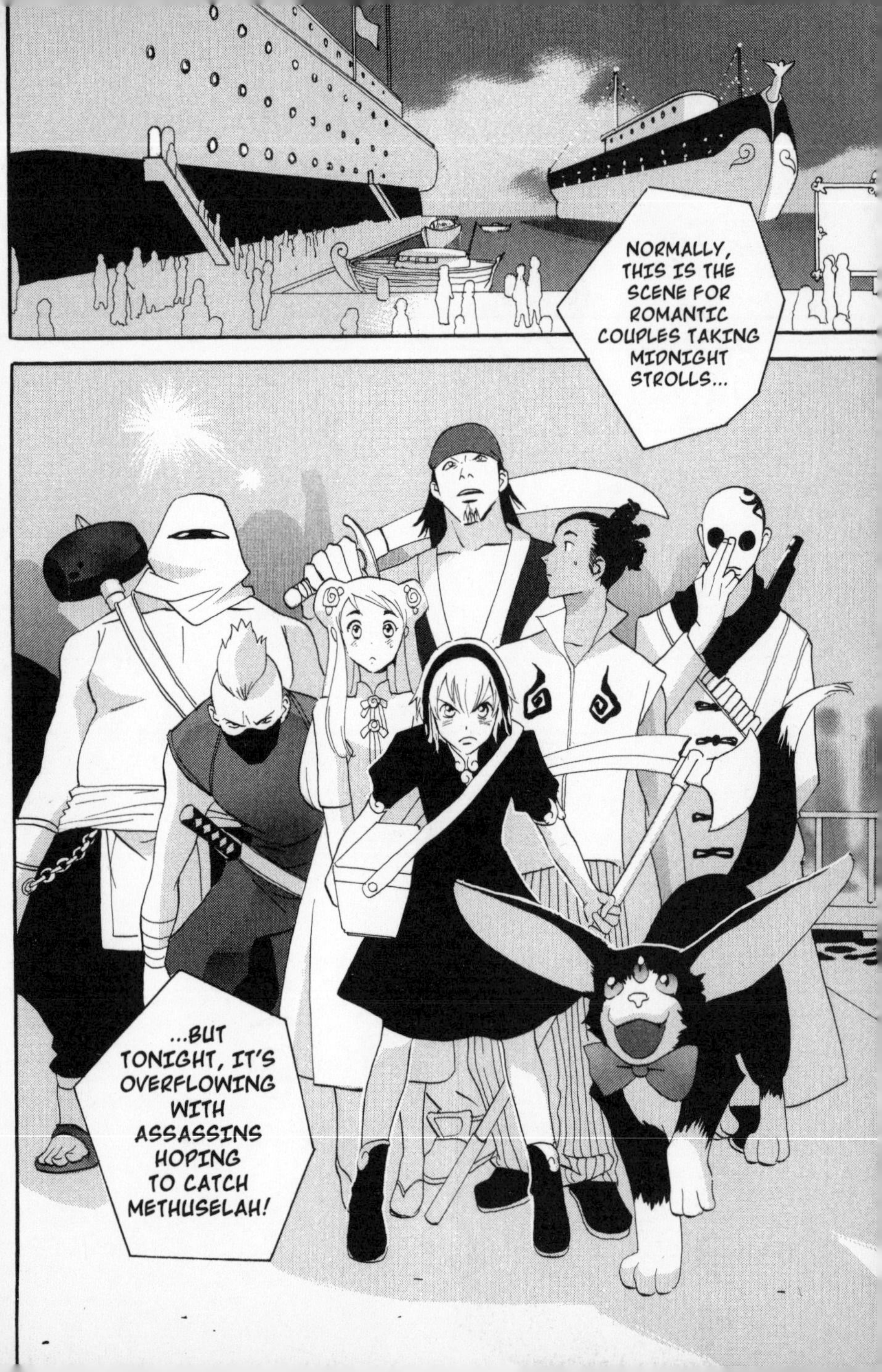
NORMALLY, THIS IS THE SCENE FOR ROMANTIC COUPLES TAKING MIDNIGHT STROLLS...
...BUT TONIGHT, IT'S OVERFLOWING WITH ASSASSINS HOPING TO CATCH METHUSELAH!

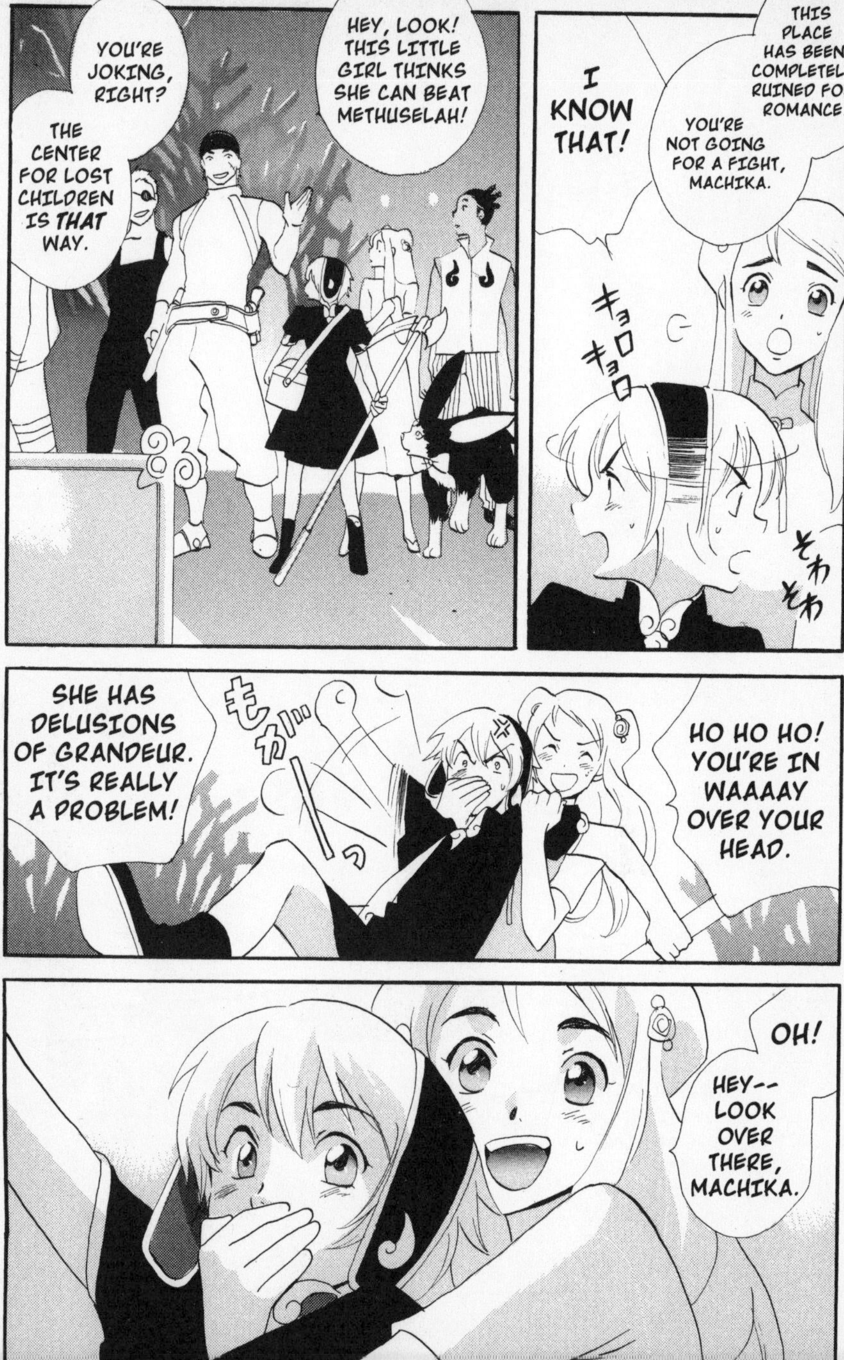
THIS PLACE HAS BEEN COMPLETELY RUINED FOR ROMANCE.
YOU'RE NOT GOING FOR A FIGHT, MACHIKA.
I KNOW THAT!
キョロキョロ
そわそわ
HEY, LOOK! THIS LITTLE GIRL THINKS SHE CAN BEAT METHUSELAH!
YOU'RE JOKING, RIGHT?
THE CENTER FOR LOST CHILDREN IS *THAT* WAY.
HO HO HO! YOU'RE IN WAAAAY OVER YOUR HEAD.
もがっ
SHE HAS DELUSIONS OF GRANDEUR. IT'S REALLY A PROBLEM!
OH!
HEY--LOOK OVER THERE, MACHIKA.

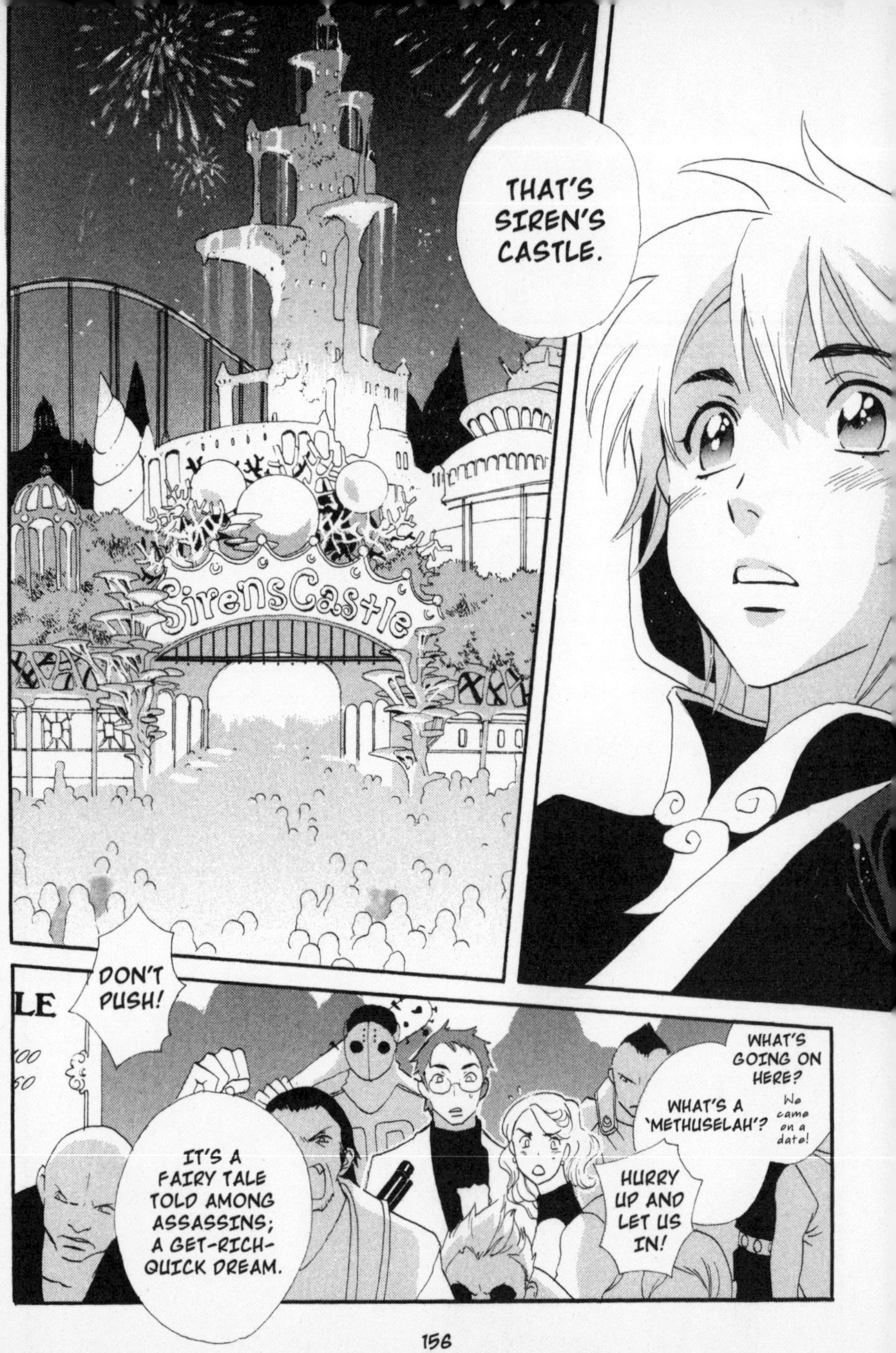
THAT'S SIREN'S CASTLE.
SirensCastle
WHAT'S GOING ON HERE?
WHAT'S A 'METHUSELAH'?
We came on a date!
HURRY UP AND LET US IN!
IT'S A FAIRY TALE TOLD AMONG ASSASSINS; A GET-RICH-QUICK DREAM.
DON'T PUSH!

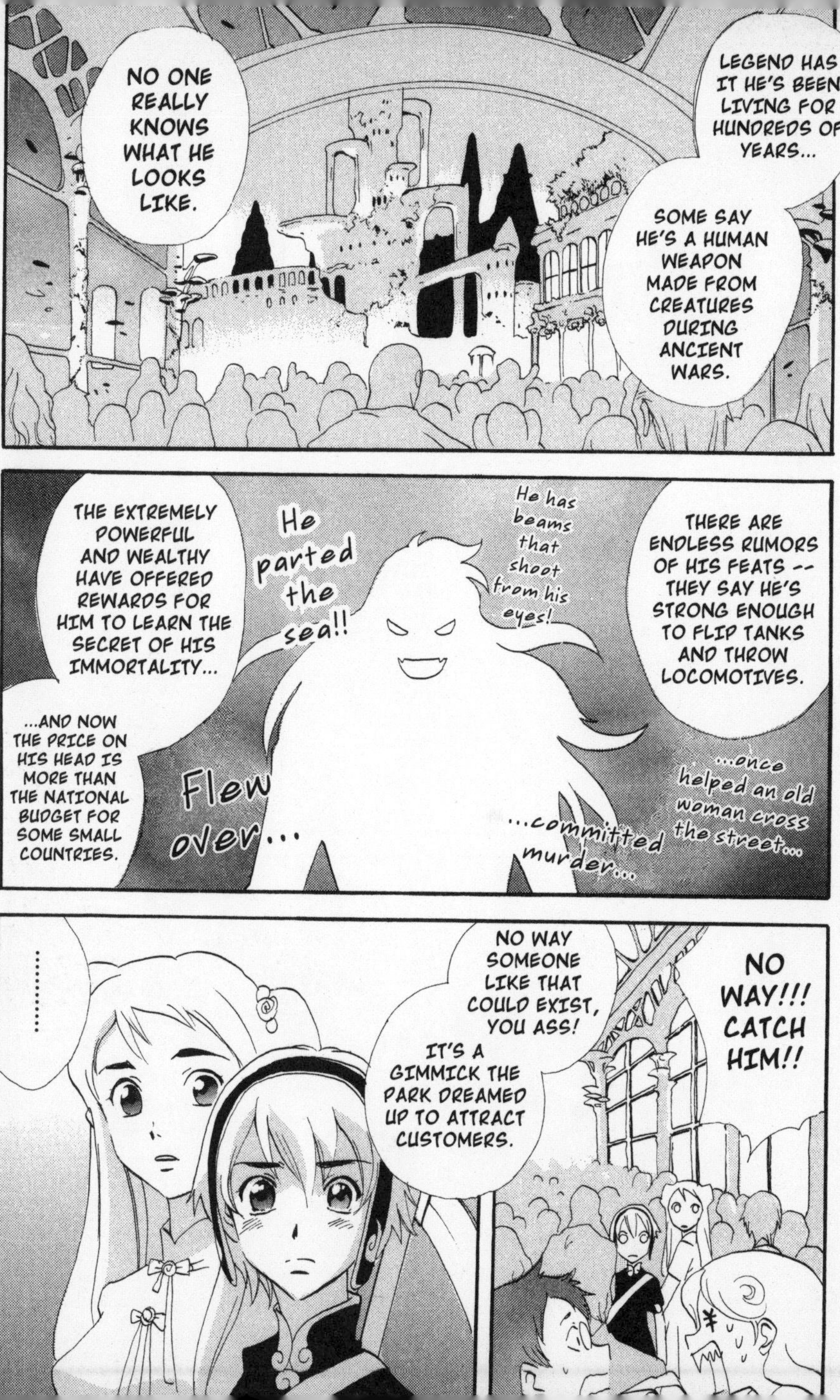
LEGEND HAS IT HE'S BEEN LIVING FOR HUNDREDS OF YEARS...
SOME SAY HE'S A HUMAN WEAPON MADE FROM CREATURES DURING ANCIENT WARS.
NO ONE REALLY KNOWS WHAT HE LOOKS LIKE.
THERE ARE ENDLESS RUMORS OF HIS FEATS -- THEY SAY HE'S STRONG ENOUGH TO FLIP TANKS AND THROW LOCOMOTIVES.
He has beams that shoot from his eyes!
He parted the sea!!
THE EXTREMELY POWERFUL AND WEALTHY HAVE OFFERED REWARDS FOR HIM TO LEARN THE SECRET OF HIS IMMORTALITY...
...AND NOW THE PRICE ON HIS HEAD IS MORE THAN THE NATIONAL BUDGET FOR SOME SMALL COUNTRIES.
...once helped an old woman cross the street...
...committed murder...
Flew over...
NO WAY!!! CATCH HIM!!
NO WAY SOMEONE LIKE THAT COULD EXIST, YOU ASS!
IT'S A GIMMICK THE PARK DREAMED UP TO ATTRACT CUSTOMERS.
....

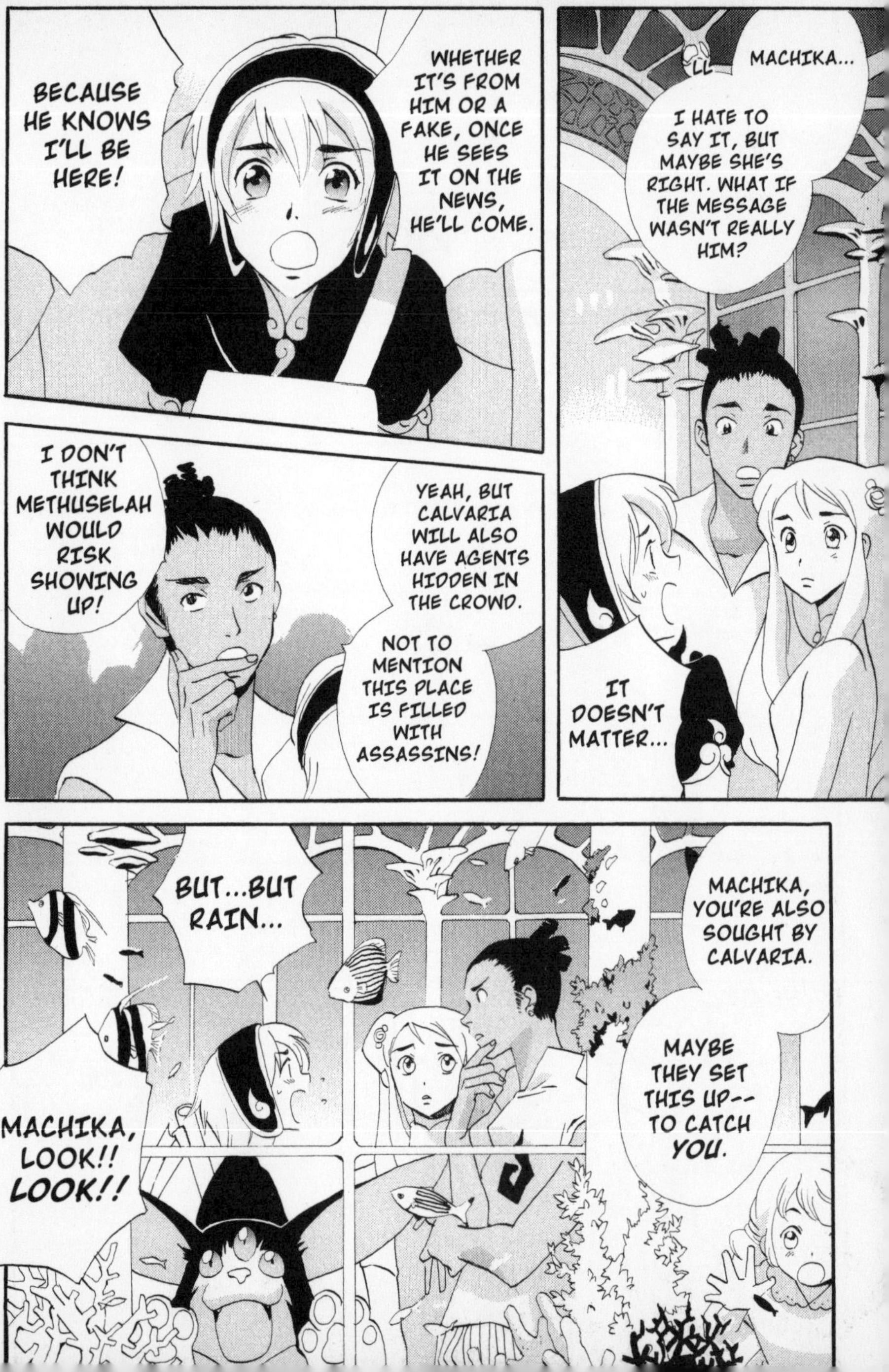
MACHIKA...
I HATE TO SAY IT, BUT MAYBE SHE'S RIGHT. WHAT IF THE MESSAGE WASN'T REALLY HIM?
IT DOESN'T MATTER...
WHETHER IT'S FROM HIM OR A FAKE, ONCE HE SEES IT ON THE NEWS, HE'LL COME.
BECAUSE HE KNOWS I'LL BE HERE!
YEAH, BUT CALVARIA WILL ALSO HAVE AGENTS HIDDEN IN THE CROWD.
NOT TO MENTION THIS PLACE IS FILLED WITH ASSASSINS!
I DON'T THINK METHUSELAH WOULD RISK SHOWING UP!
MACHIKA, YOU'RE ALSO SOUGHT BY CALVARIA.
MAYBE THEY SET THIS UP-- TO CATCH YOU.
BUT...BUT RAIN...
MACHIKA, LOOK!! LOOK!!

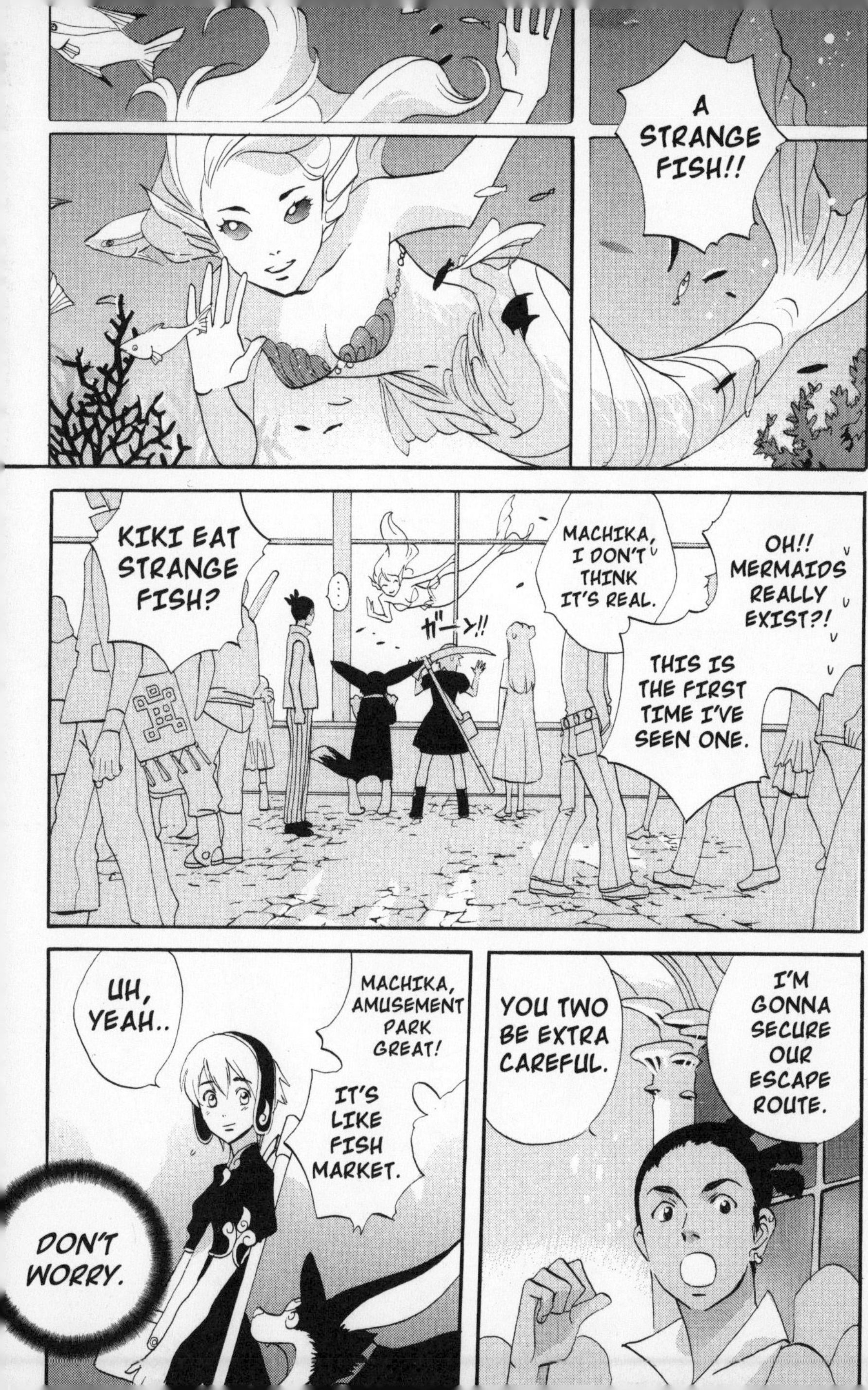
A STRANGE FISH!!
OH!! MERMAIDS REALLY EXIST?!
THIS IS THE FIRST TIME I'VE SEEN ONE.
MACHIKA, I DON'T THINK IT'S REAL.
ガーン!!
...
KIKI EAT STRANGE FISH?
I'M GONNA SECURE OUR ESCAPE ROUTE.
YOU TWO BE EXTRA CAREFUL.
MACHIKA, AMUSEMENT PARK GREAT!
UH, YEAH..
IT'S LIKE FISH MARKET.
DON'T WORRY.

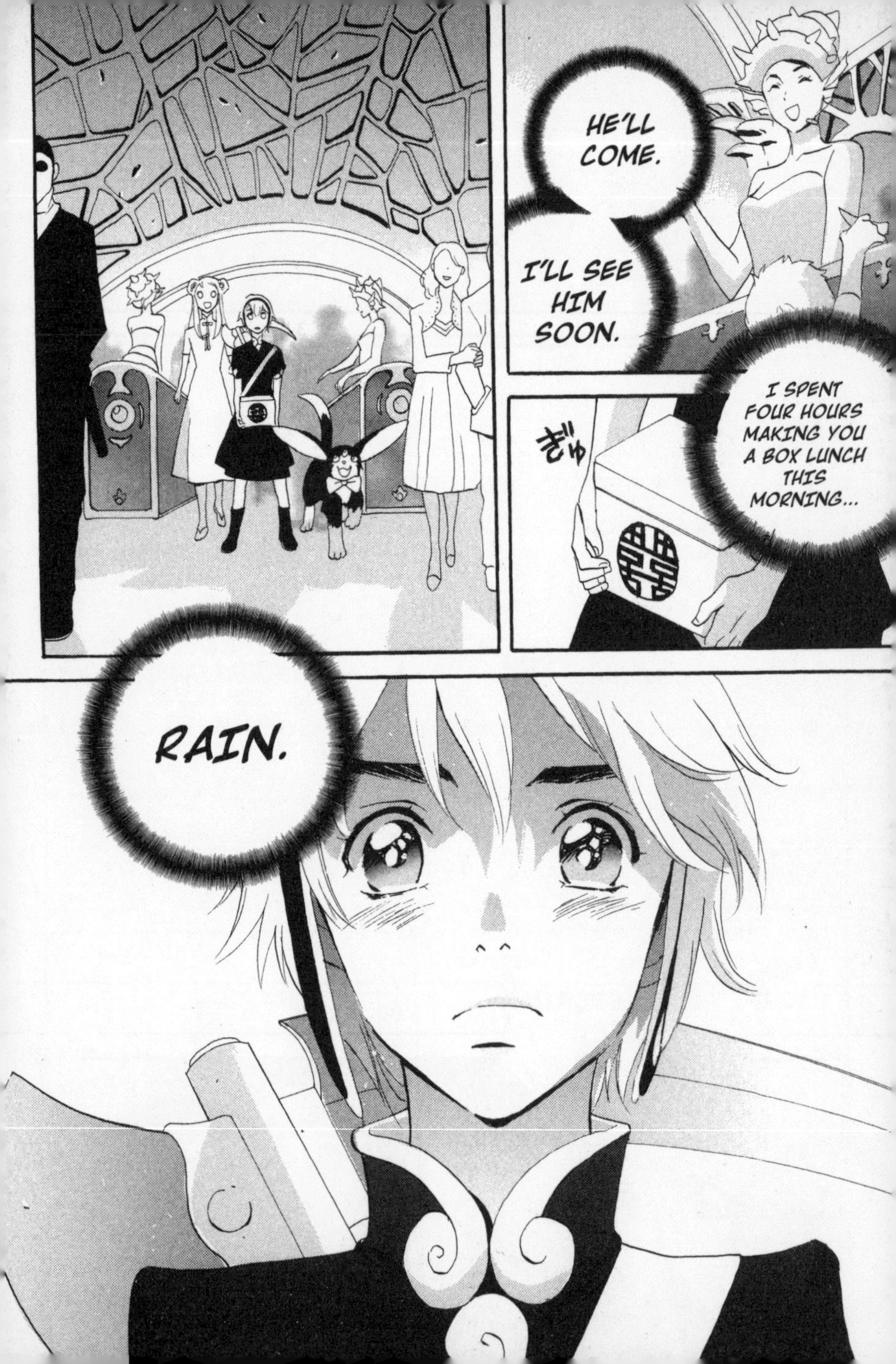
HE'LL COME.
I'LL SEE HIM SOON.
ぎゅ
I SPENT FOUR HOURS MAKING YOU A BOX LUNCH THIS MORNING...
RAIN.

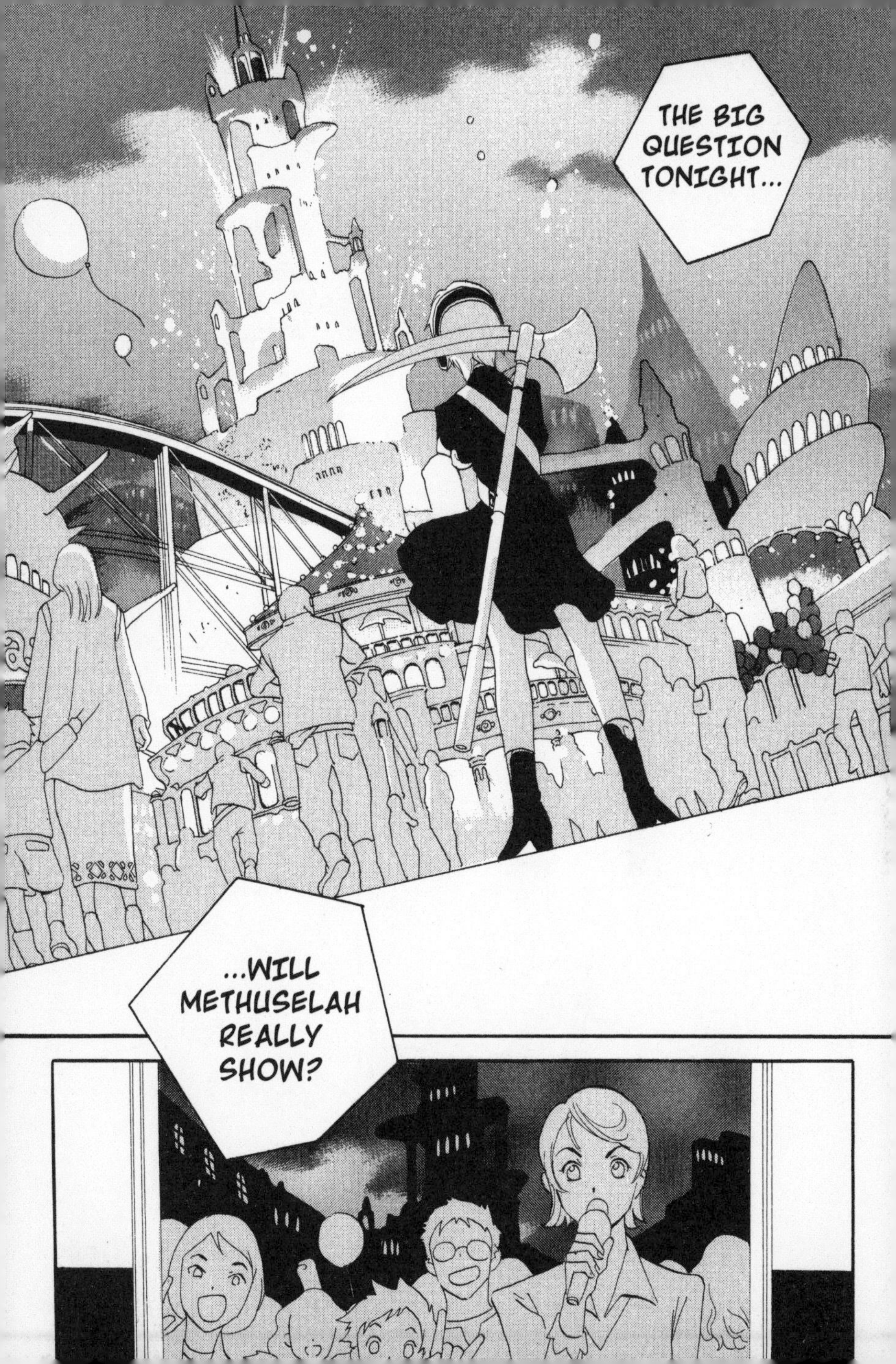
THE BIG QUESTION TONIGHT...
...WILL METHUSELAH REALLY SHOW?

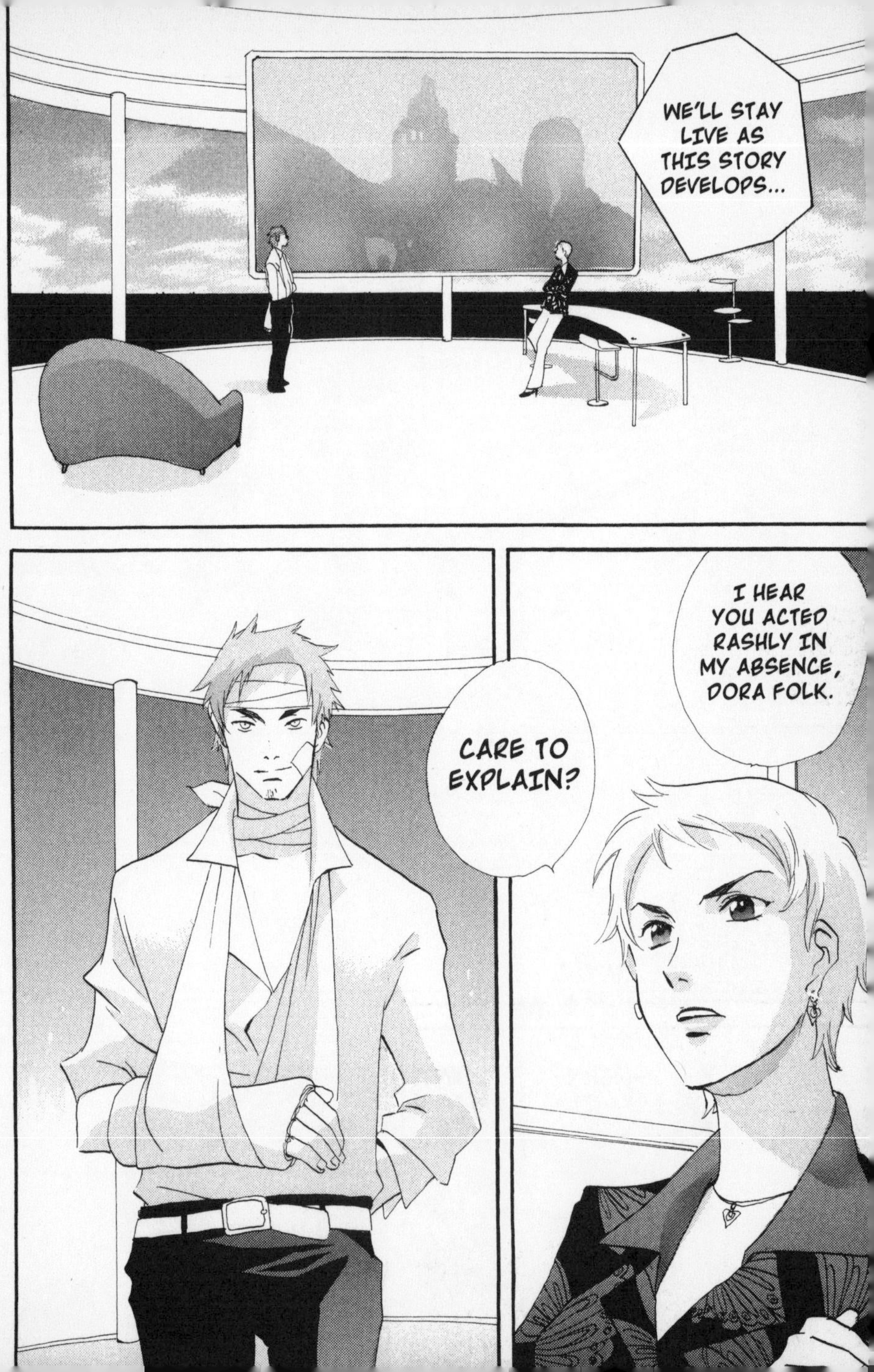
WE'LL STAY LIVE AS THIS STORY DEVELOPS...
I HEAR YOU ACTED RASHLY IN MY ABSENCE, DORA FOLK.
CARE TO EXPLAIN?

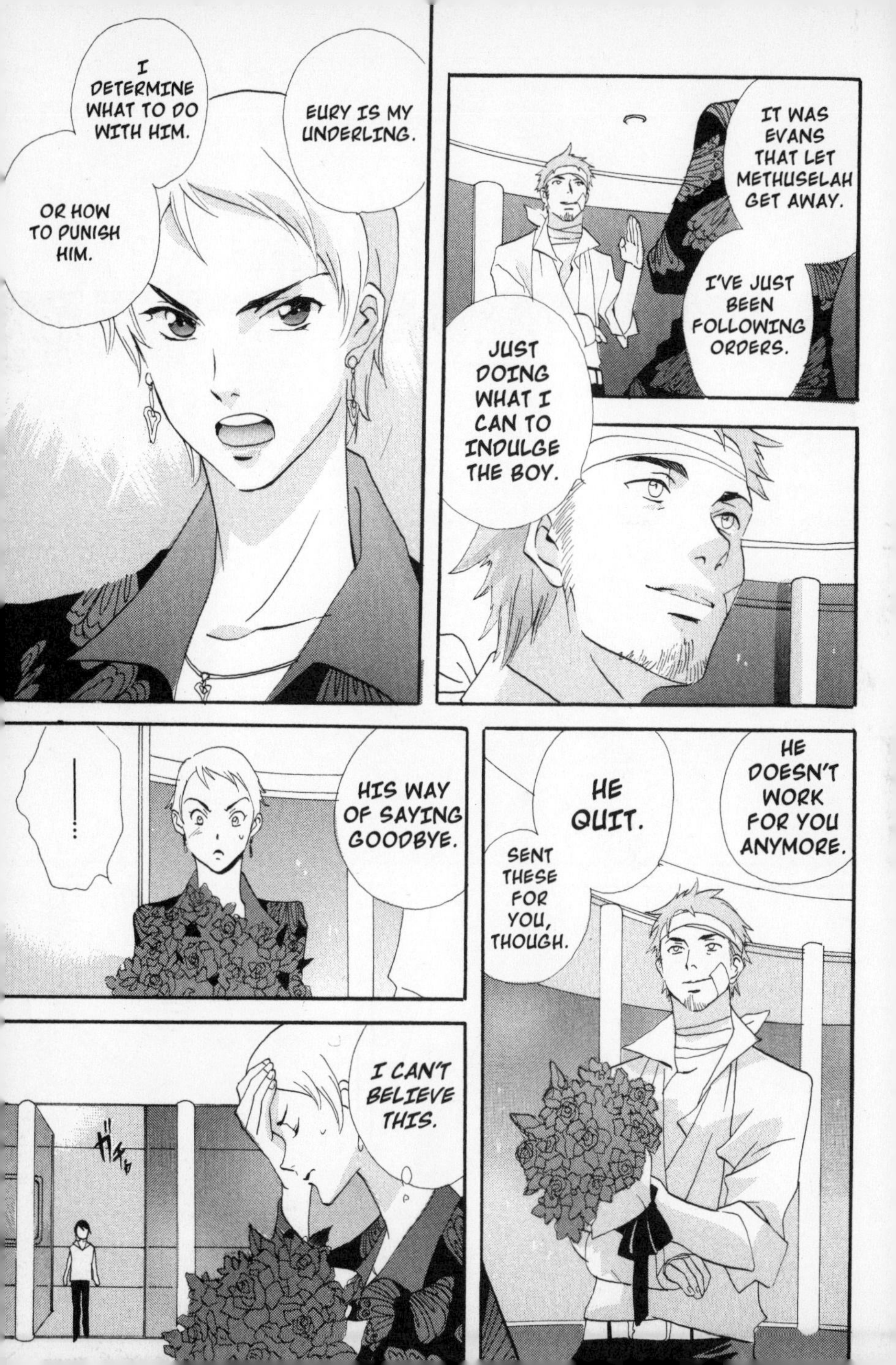
IT WAS EVANS THAT LET METHUSELAH GET AWAY.
I'VE JUST BEEN FOLLOWING ORDERS.
JUST DOING WHAT I CAN TO INDULGE THE BOY.
EURY IS MY UNDERLING.
I DETERMINE WHAT TO DO WITH HIM.
OR HOW TO PUNISH HIM.
HE DOESN'T WORK FOR YOU ANYMORE.
HE QUIT.
SENT THESE FOR YOU, THOUGH.
HIS WAY OF SAYING GOODBYE.
......
I CAN'T BELIEVE THIS.
ガチャ

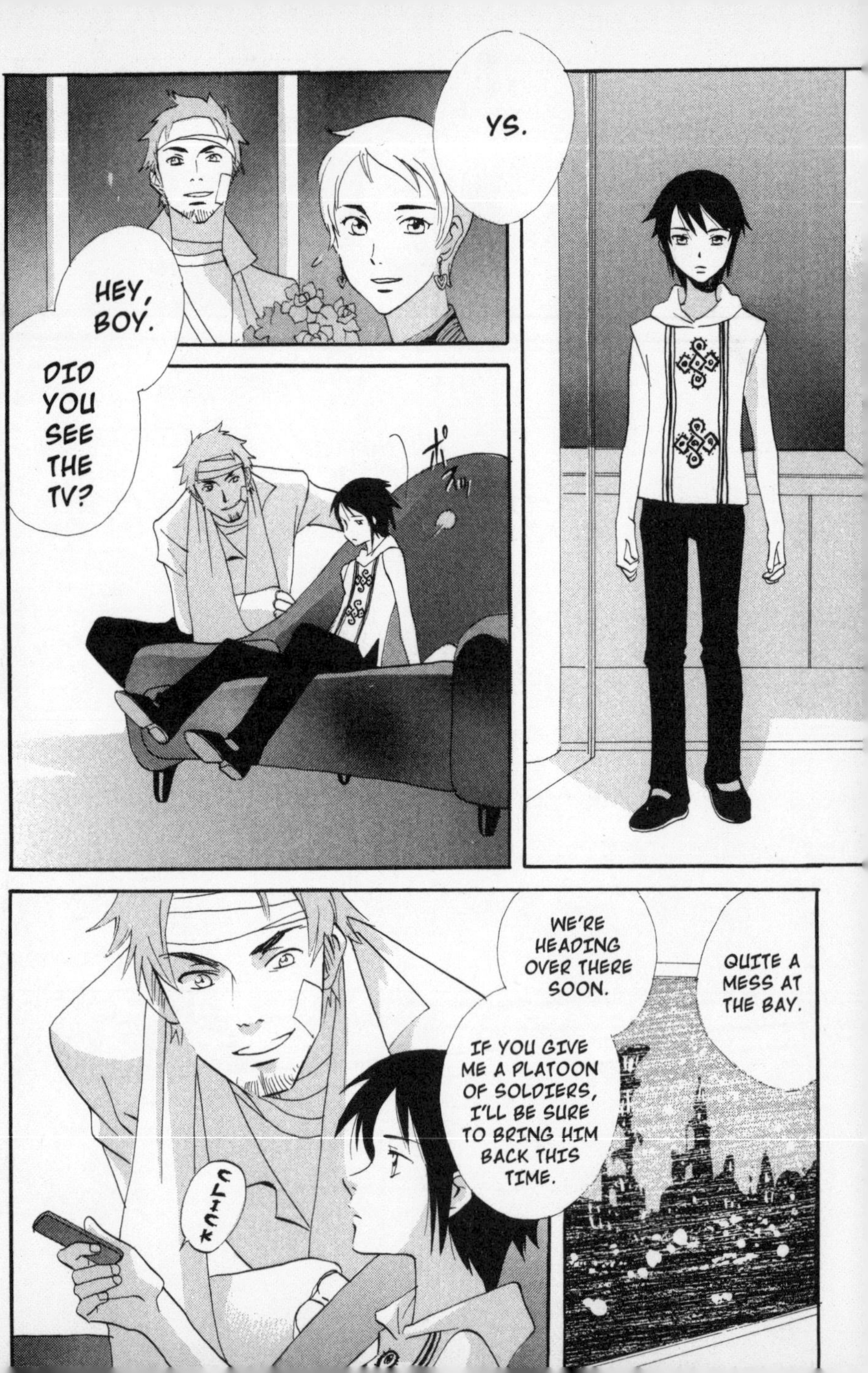
YS.
HEY, BOY.
DID YOU SEE THE TV?
ポスッ
QUITE A MESS AT THE BAY.
WE'RE HEADING OVER THERE SOON.
IF YOU GIVE ME A PLATOON OF SOLDIERS, I'LL BE SURE TO BRING HIM BACK THIS TIME.
CLICK

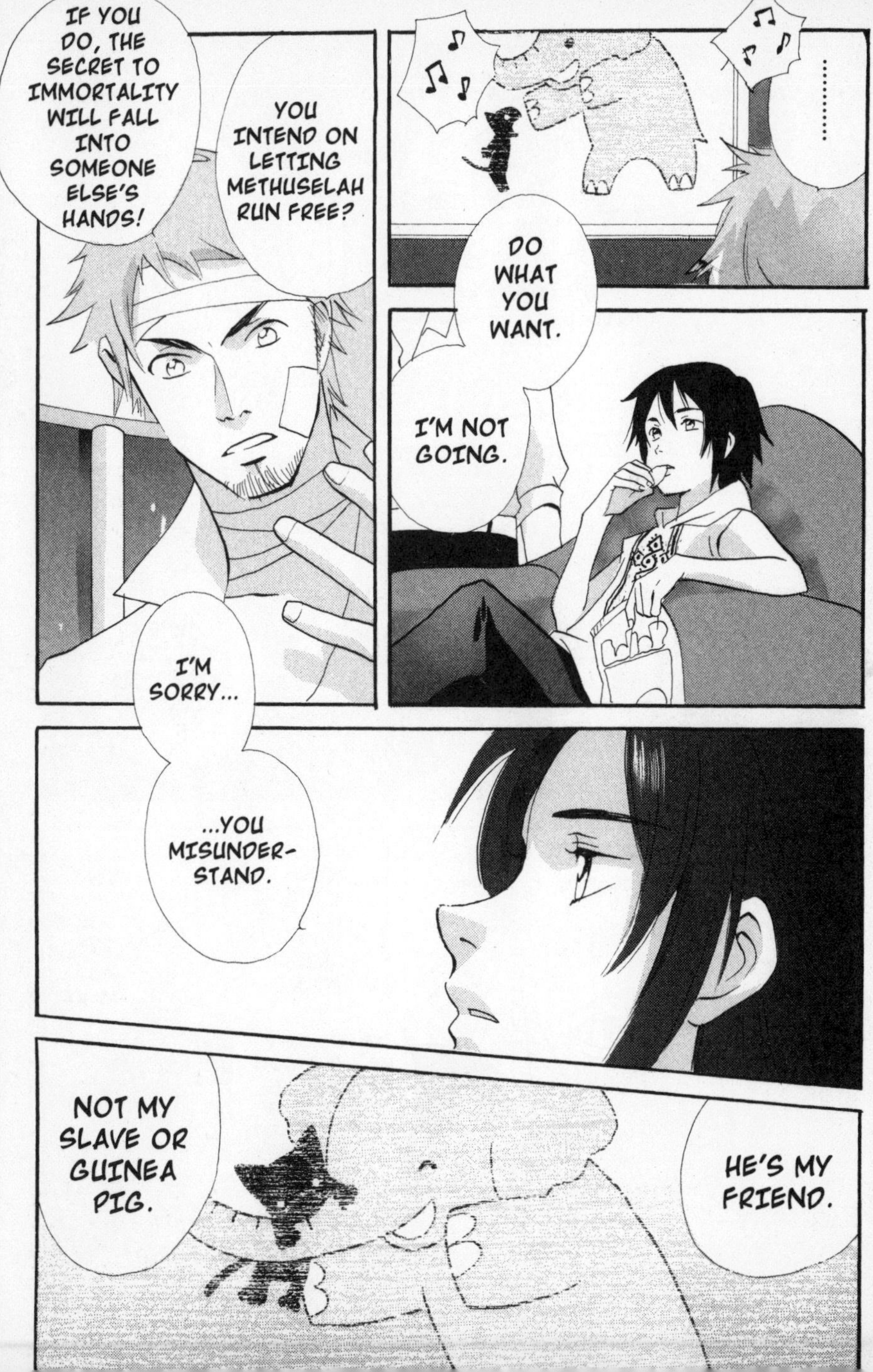
......
DO WHAT YOU WANT.
I'M NOT GOING.
YOU INTEND ON LETTING METHUSELAH RUN FREE?
IF YOU DO, THE SECRET TO IMMORTALITY WILL FALL INTO SOMEONE ELSE'S HANDS!
I'M SORRY...
...YOU MISUNDERSTAND.
HE'S MY FRIEND.
NOT MY SLAVE OR GUINEA PIG.

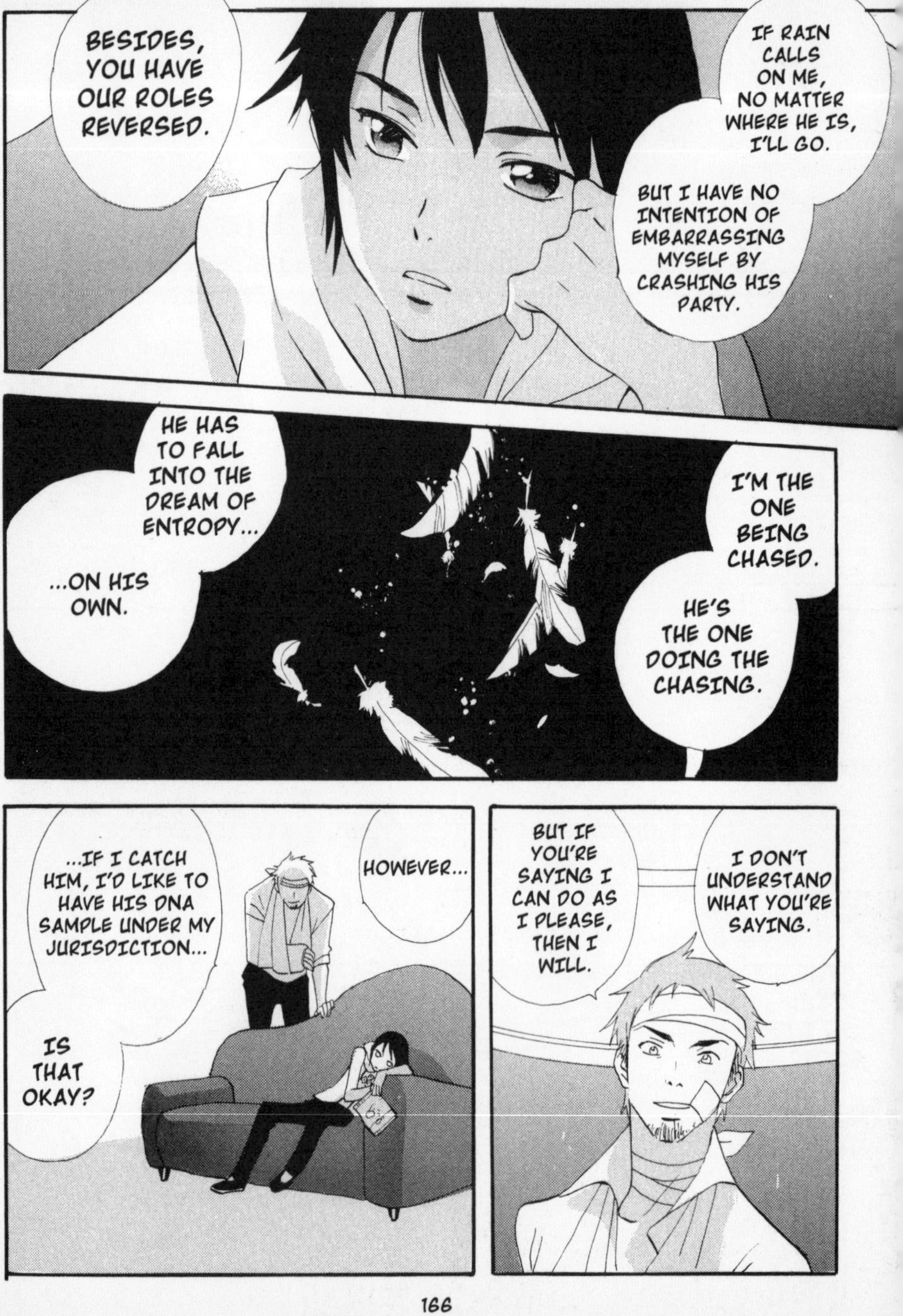
IF RAIN CALLS ON ME, NO MATTER WHERE HE IS, I'LL GO.
BUT I HAVE NO INTENTION OF EMBARRASSING MYSELF BY CRASHING HIS PARTY.
BESIDES, YOU HAVE OUR ROLES REVERSED.
I'M THE ONE BEING CHASED.
HE'S THE ONE DOING THE CHASING.
HE HAS TO FALL INTO THE DREAM OF ENTROPY...
...ON HIS OWN.
I DON'T UNDERSTAND WHAT YOU'RE SAYING.
BUT IF YOU'RE SAYING I CAN DO AS I PLEASE, THEN I WILL.
HOWEVER...
...IF I CATCH HIM, I'D LIKE TO HAVE HIS DNA SAMPLE UNDER MY JURISDICTION...
IS THAT OKAY?

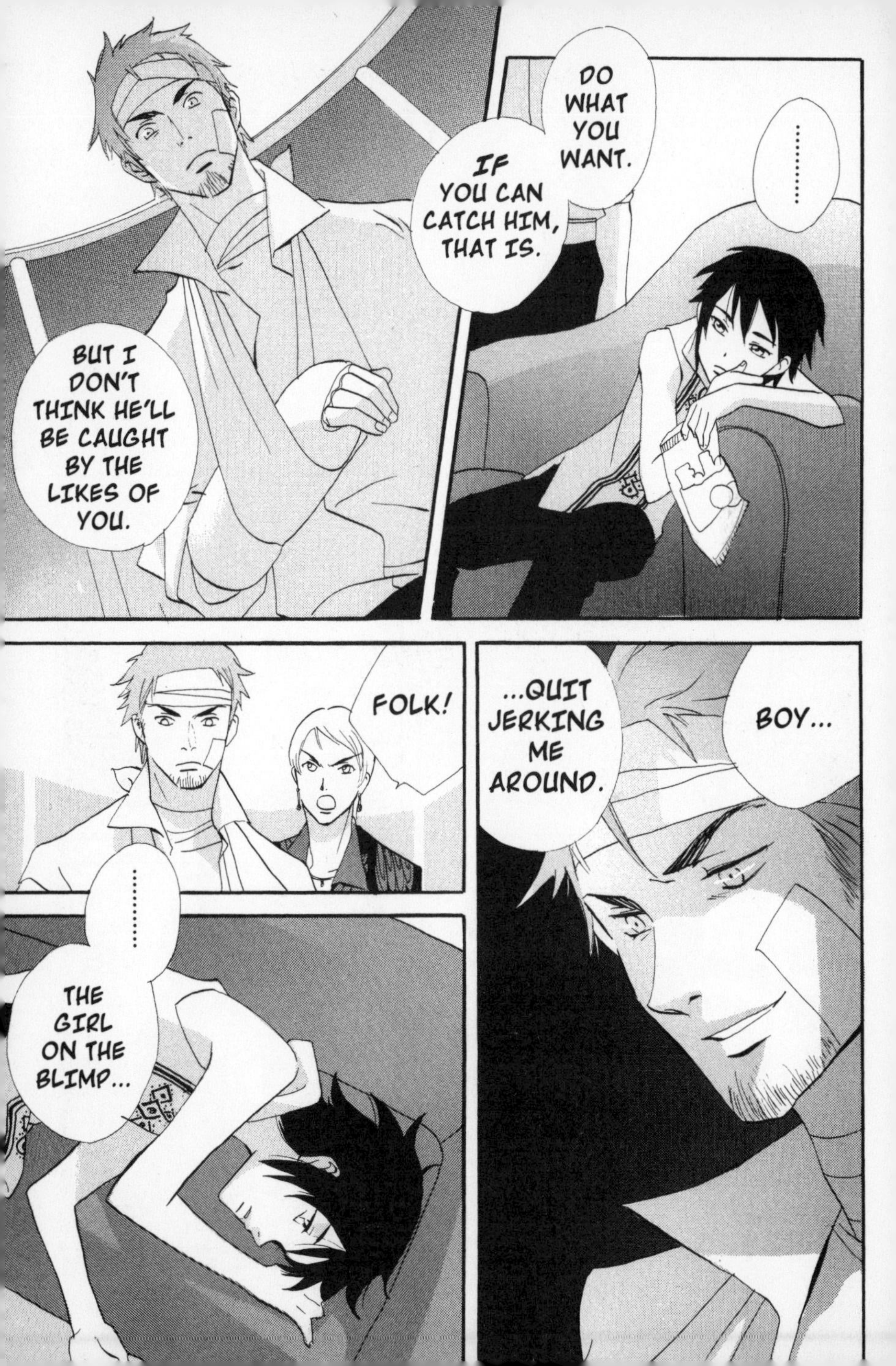
......
DO WHAT YOU WANT.
IF YOU CAN CATCH HIM, THAT IS.
BUT I DON'T THINK HE'LL BE CAUGHT BY THE LIKES OF YOU.
BOY...
...QUIT JERKING ME AROUND.
FOLK!
......
THE GIRL ON THE BLIMP...

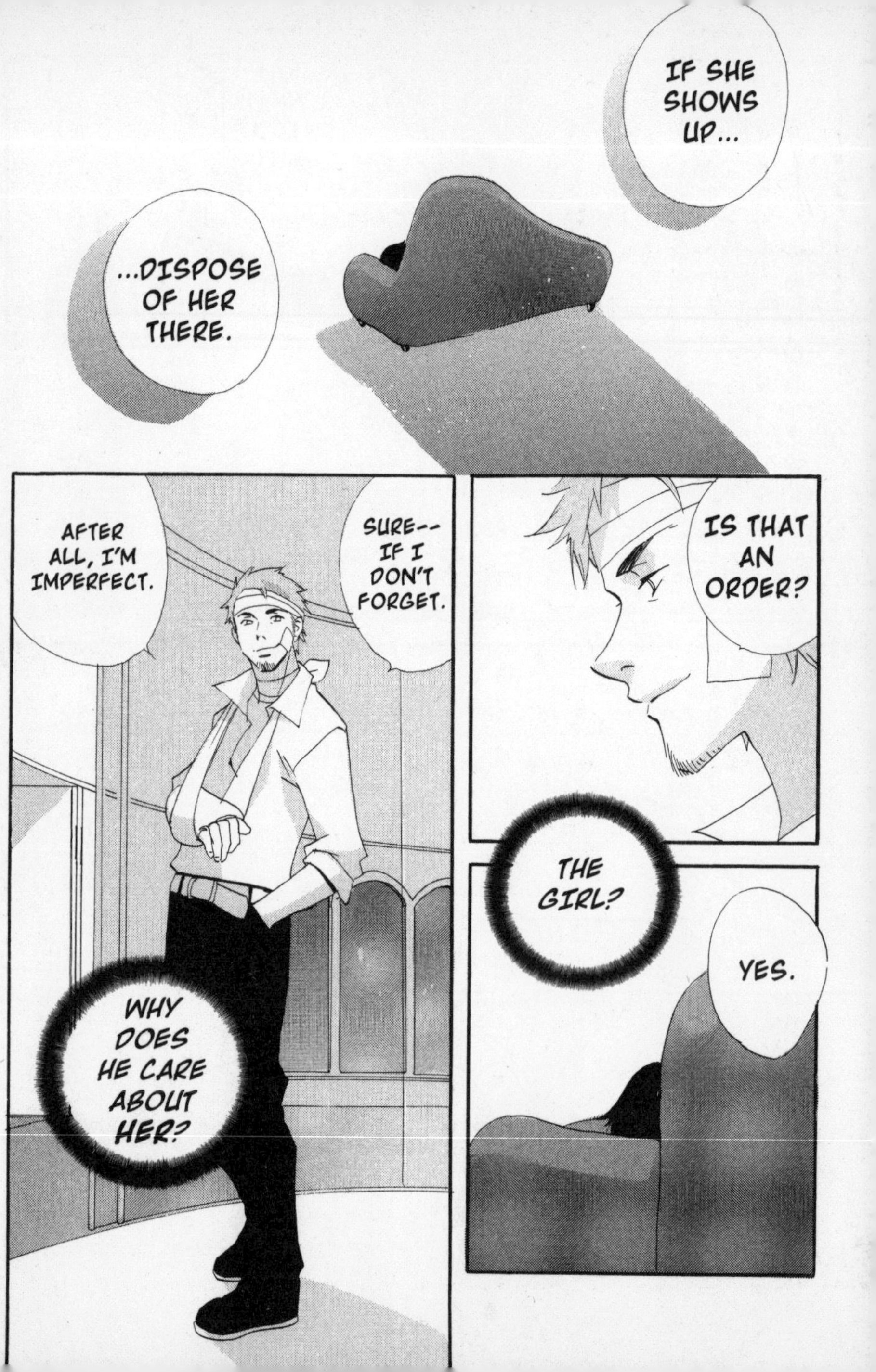
IF SHE SHOWS UP...
...DISPOSE OF HER THERE.
IS THAT AN ORDER?
THE GIRL?
YES.
SURE-- IF I DON'T FORGET.
AFTER ALL, I'M IMPERFECT.
WHY DOES HE CARE ABOUT HER?

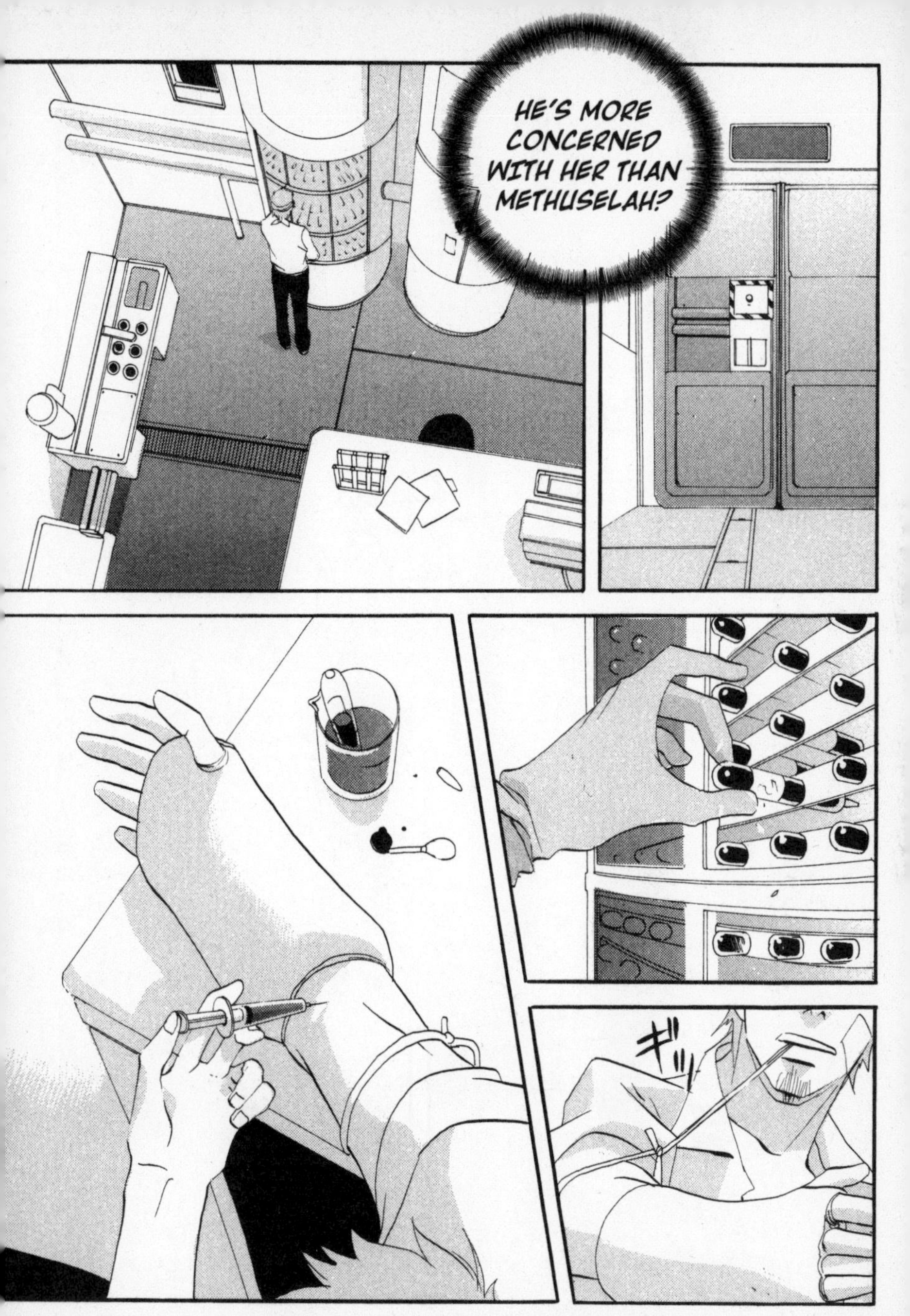
HE'S MORE CONCERNED WITH HER THAN METHUSELAH?
ギッ

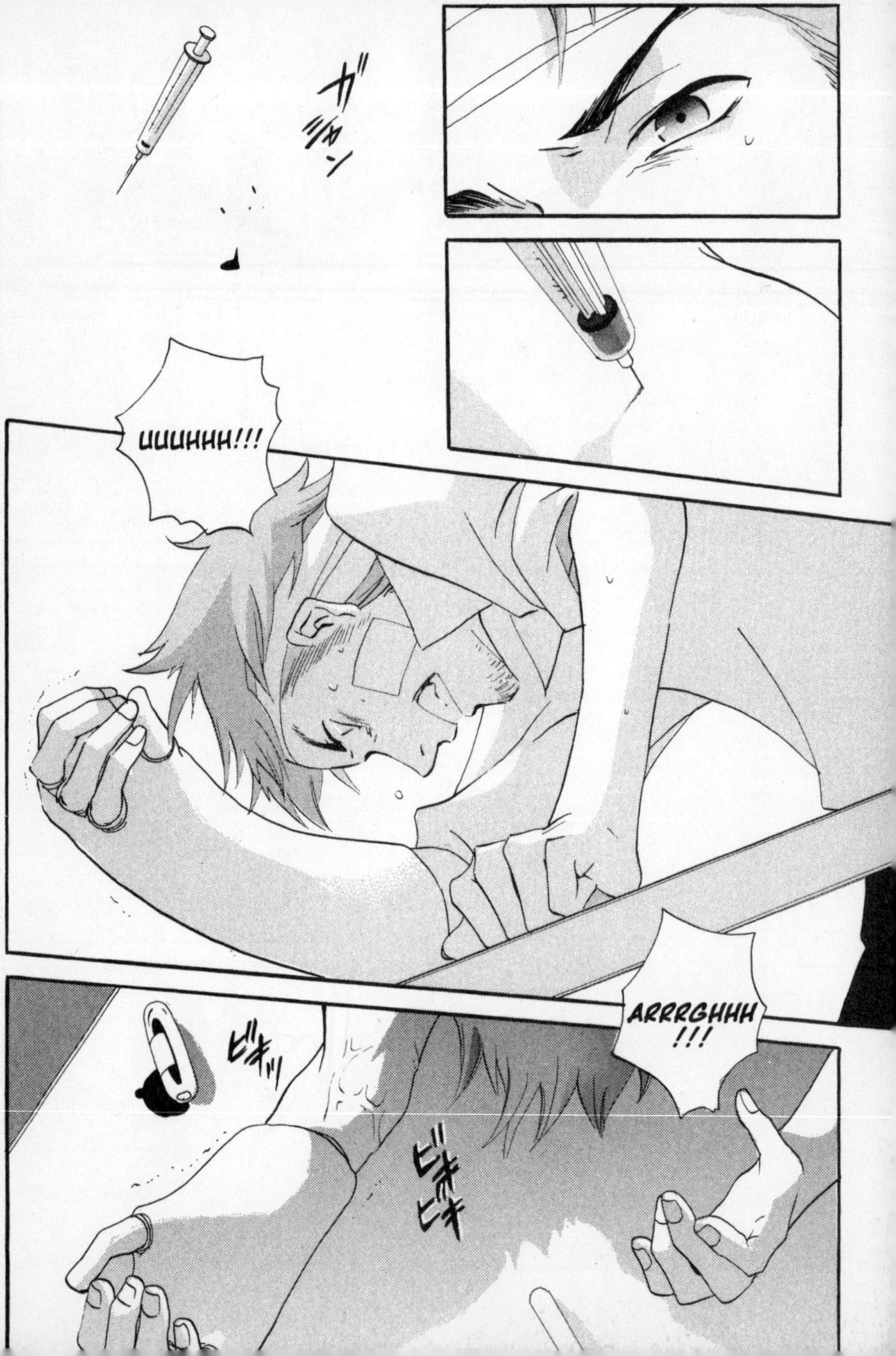
ガシャン
UUUHHH!!!
ARRRGHHH
!!!
ビキッ
ビキビキ

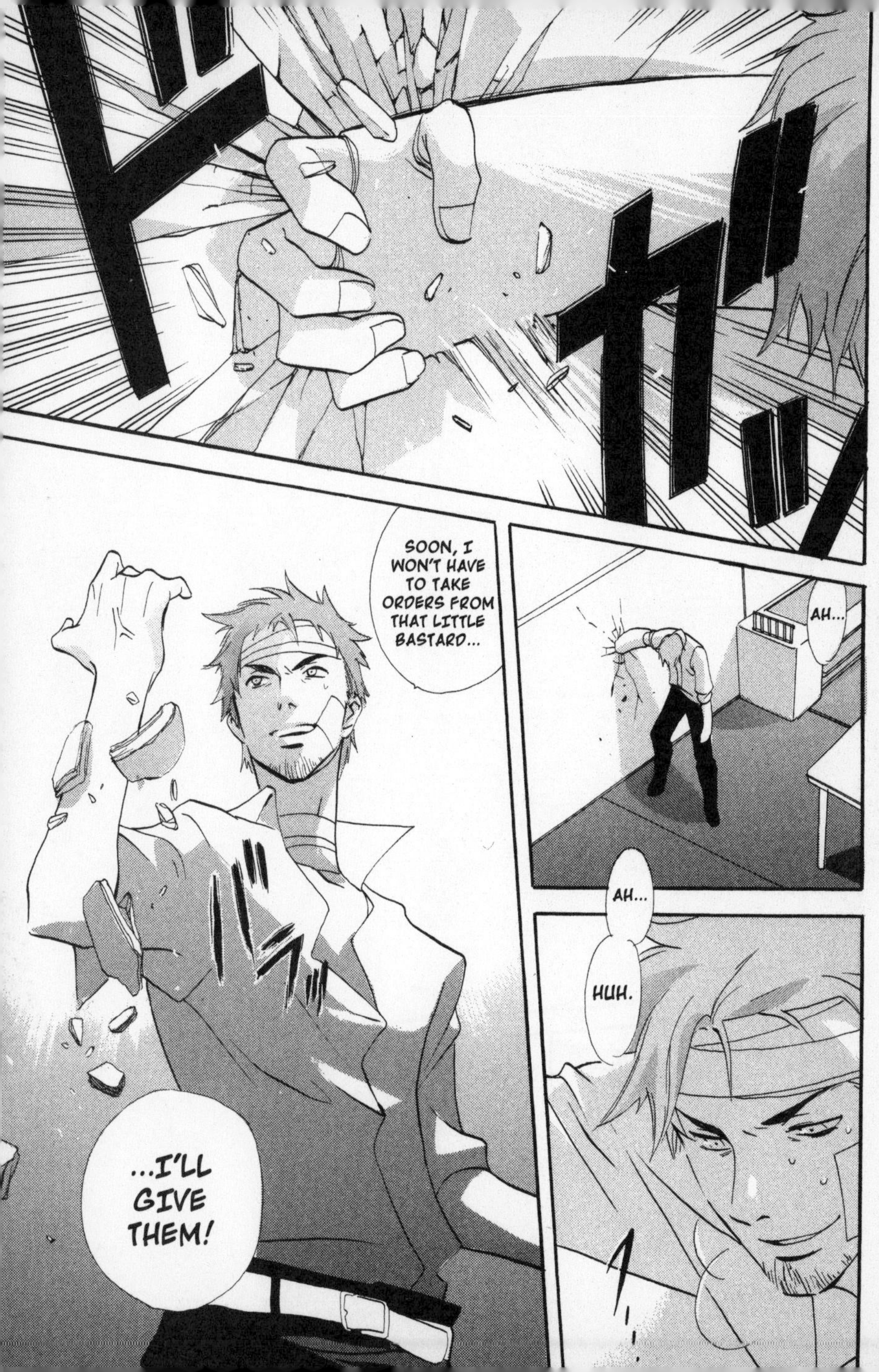
AH...
AH...
HUH.
SOON, I WON'T HAVE TO TAKE ORDERS FROM THAT LITTLE BASTARD...
...I'LL GIVE THEM!

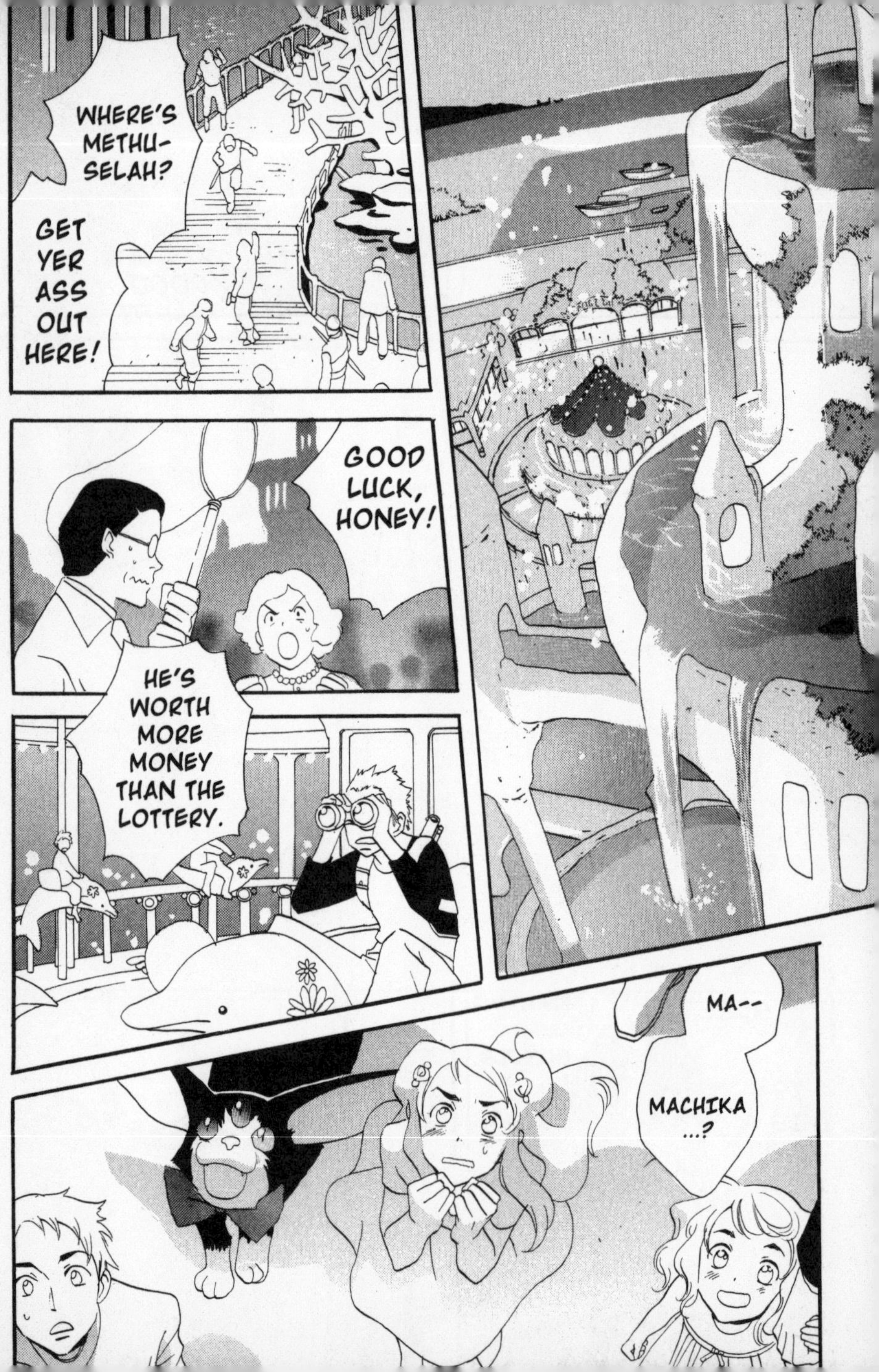
WHERE'S METHU-SELAH?
GET YER ASS OUT HERE!
GOOD LUCK, HONEY!
HE'S WORTH MORE MONEY THAN THE LOTTERY.
MA--
MACHIKA ...?

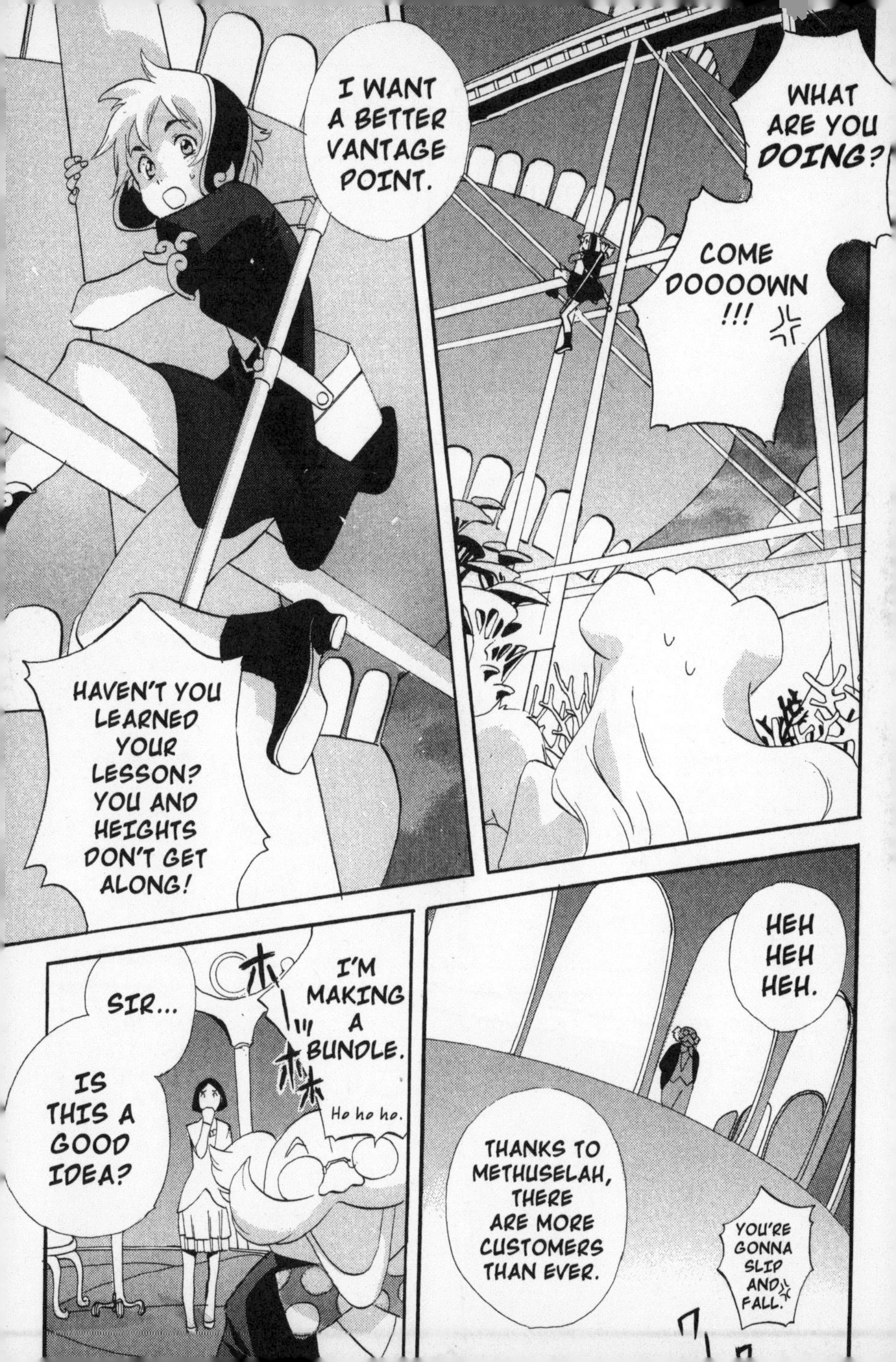
WHAT ARE YOU DOING?
COME DOOOOWN!!!
I WANT A BETTER VANTAGE POINT.
HAVEN'T YOU LEARNED YOUR LESSON? YOU AND HEIGHTS DON'T GET ALONG!
HEH HEH HEH.
THANKS TO METHUSELAH, THERE ARE MORE CUSTOMERS THAN EVER.
YOU'RE GONNA SLIP AND FALL.
I'M MAKING A BUNDLE.
Ho ho ho.
SIR...
IS THIS A GOOD IDEA?

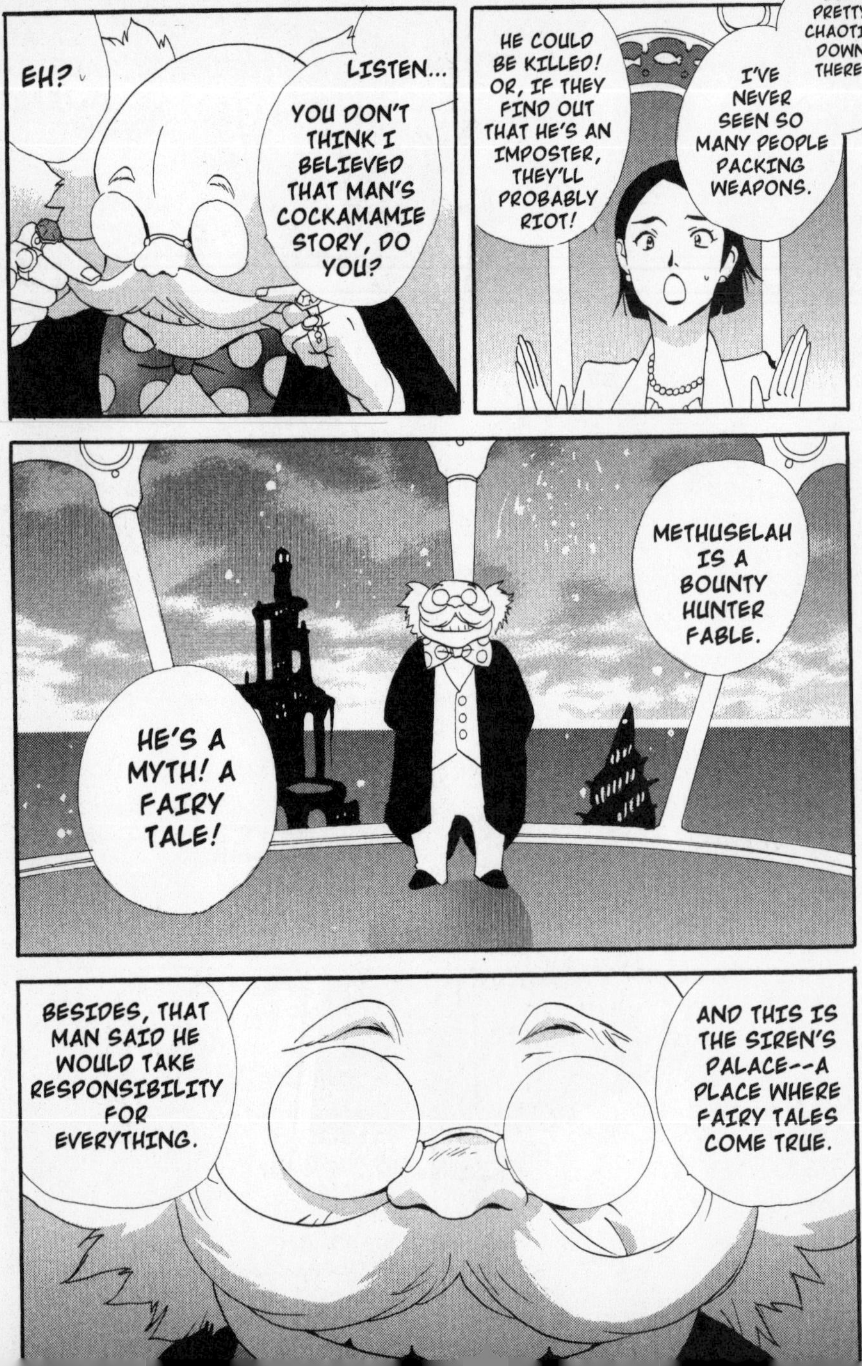
IT'S PRETTY CHAOTIC DOWN THERE.
I'VE NEVER SEEN SO MANY PEOPLE PACKING WEAPONS.
HE COULD BE KILLED! OR, IF THEY FIND OUT THAT HE'S AN IMPOSTER, THEY'LL PROBABLY RIOT!
LISTEN...
YOU DON'T THINK I BELIEVED THAT MAN'S COCKAMAMIE STORY, DO YOU?
EH?
METHUSELAH IS A BOUNTY HUNTER FABLE.
HE'S A MYTH! A FAIRY TALE!
AND THIS IS THE SIREN'S PALACE--A PLACE WHERE FAIRY TALES COME TRUE.
BESIDES, THAT MAN SAID HE WOULD TAKE RESPONSIBILITY FOR EVERYTHING.

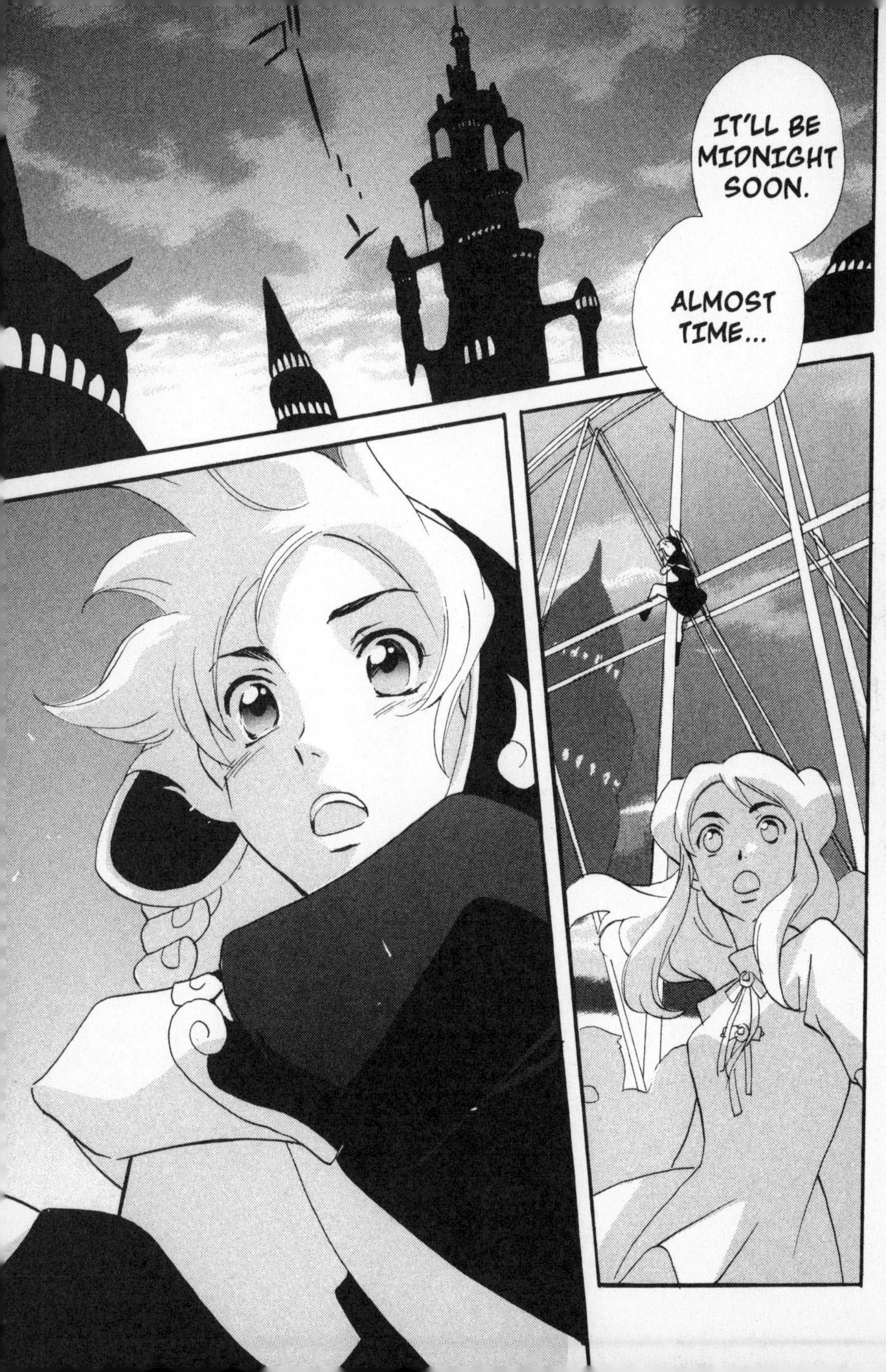
IT'LL BE MIDNIGHT SOON.
ALMOST TIME...

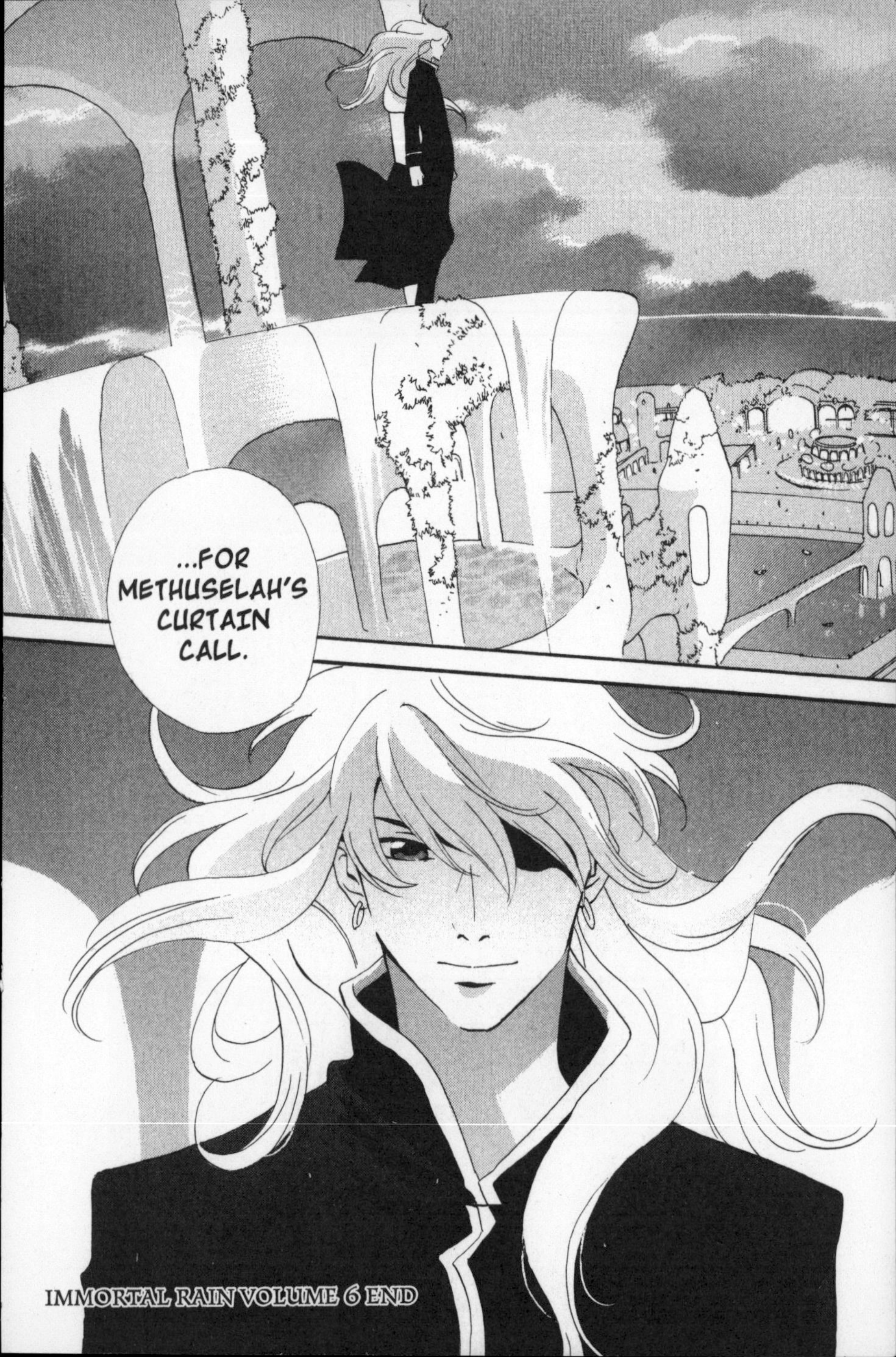
...FOR METHUSELAH'S CURTAIN CALL.
IMMORTAL RAIN VOLUME 6 END

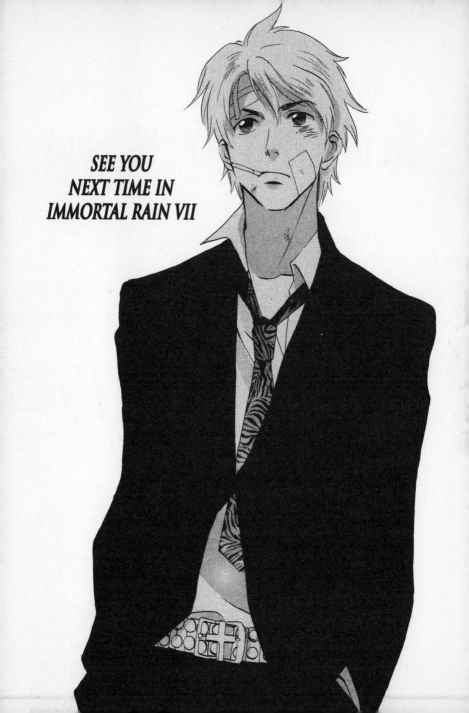

SEE YOU
NEXT TIME IN
IMMORTAL RAIN VII

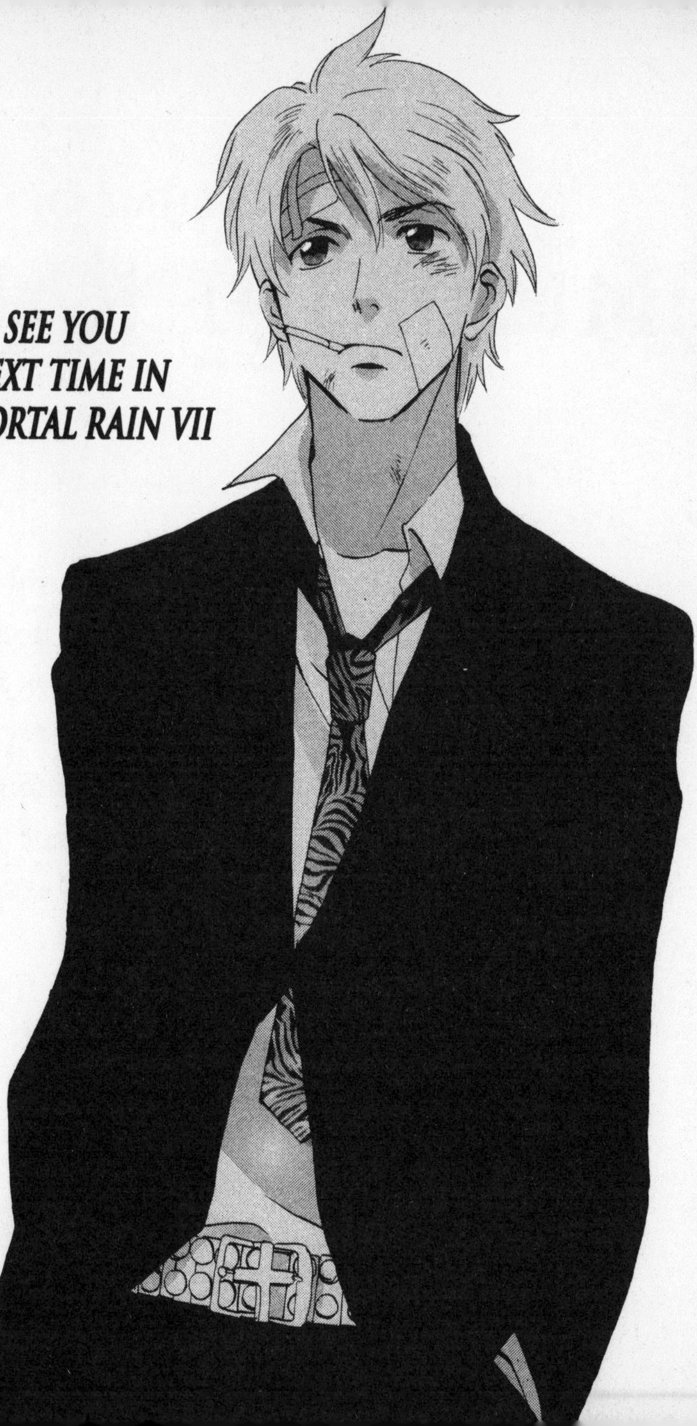

IN THE NEXT VOLUME OF

IMMORTAL RAIN

It's time for the big showdown
at the Siren's Castle!
Will Rain and Machika finally be reunited,
or will the bloodthirsty assassins and bounty
hunters strike it rich by bringing down the
Immortal Methuselah?
And what of Ys, whose behavior is becoming
increasingly erratic? Will he continue to
wait for Rain, or will he take matters
into his own hands?

Find out in the next installment of
Immortal Rain!

TOKYOPOP SHOP

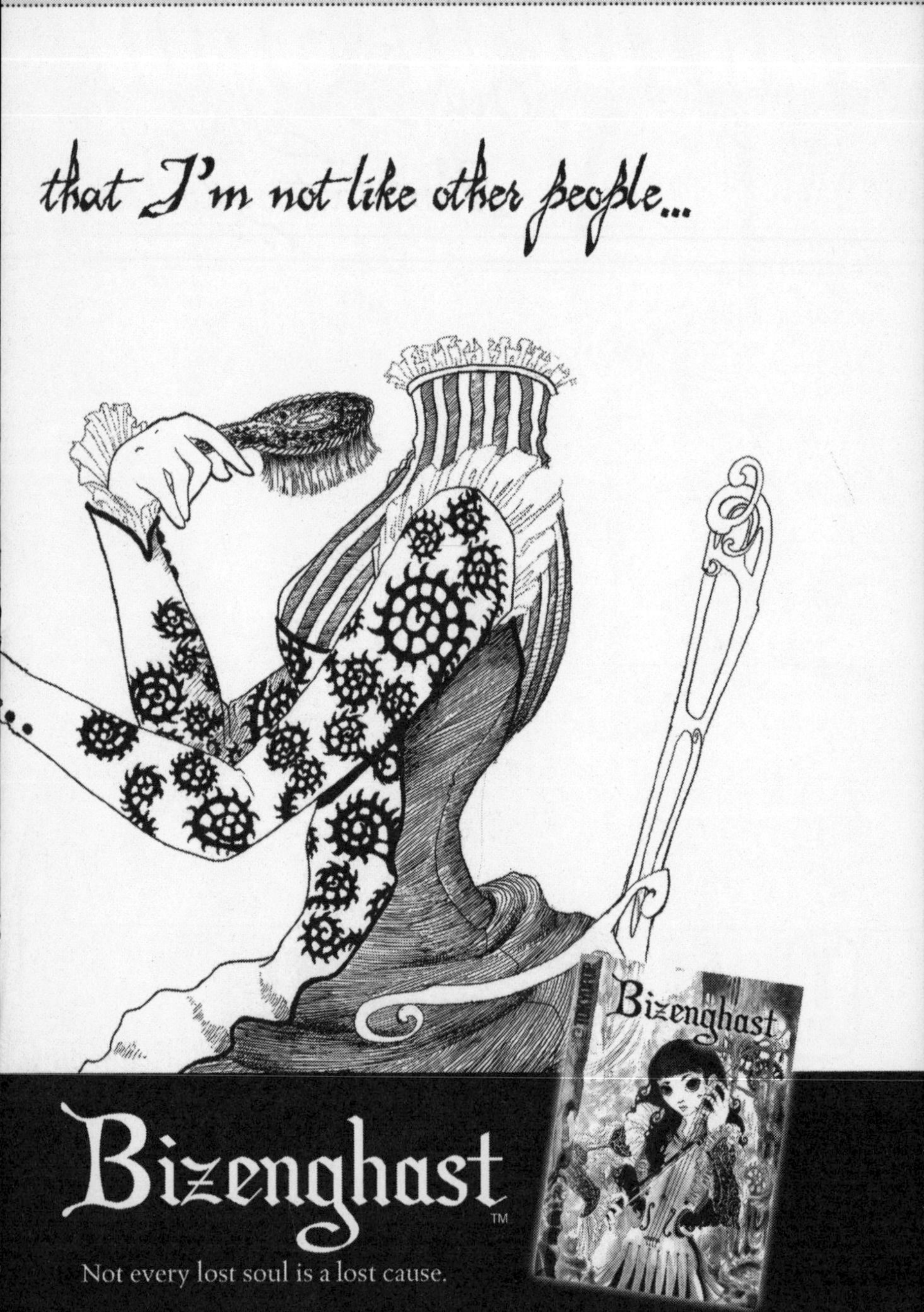
that I'm not like other people...
Bizenghast
Bizenghast™
Not every lost soul is a lost cause.

BIZENGHAST

Dear Diary,
I'm starting to feel

Preview the manga at:
www.TOKYOPOP.com/bizenghast

When a young girl moves to the forgotten town of Bizenghast, she uncovers a terrifying collection of lost souls that leads her to the brink of insanity. One thing becomes painfully clear: The residents of Bizenghast are just dying to come home.